S.sas.
THE POWER TO KNOW.

The Little SAS® Book

a primer

FIFTH EDITION

A Programming Approach

Lora D. Delwiche and *Susan J. Slaughter*

The correct bibliographic citation for this manual is as follows: Delwiche, Lora D., and Susan J. Slaughter. 2012. *The Little SAS® Book: A Primer, Fifth Edition*. Cary, NC: SAS Institute Inc.

The Little SAS® Book: A Primer, Fifth Edition

ISBN 978-1-61290-343-9 (Hard copy)
ISBN 978-1-61290-400-9 (EPUB)
ISBN 978-1-61290-945-5 (MOBI)
ISBN 978-1-62959-013-4 (PDF)

SAS Institute Inc., SAS Campus Drive, Cary, North Carolina 27513-2414

July 2015

Contents

Contents

Acknowledgments

As hard as we have worked on this book, we could never have done it alone. Many people at SAS helped make this book what it is. To our many hard-working reviewers: Amber Elam, Dan Heath, Chris Hemedinger, Anthony House, Sanjay Matange, Lelia McConnell, Sandy Owens, Peter Ruzsa, David Schlotzhauer, Jan Squillace, and Grace Whiteis, we say, "Thanks for hanging in there with us." To our copyeditor, Mary Beth Steinbach, and our designers, Patrice Cherry and Jennifer Dilley, "Thanks for making us look good." To our technical publishing specialist, Candy Farrell, "Thanks for straightening out our quotation marks, squeezing in those last few sentences, and finding those missing images." To our marketing specialists, Stacey Hamilton and Aimee Rodriguez, "Go, girls, go!" And last but not least we would like to thank—faster than a speeding deadline, stronger than Microsoft Word, able to leap tall drafts in a single bound—our editor-in-chief, Julie Platt; managing editor, Mary Beth Steinbach; and acquisitions editor, Stephenie Joyner.

Outside the walls of SAS many other people also contributed to this book. In particular we would like to thank our readers. We love meeting you at conferences even if we seem a little shy. Without you, of course, there would be no reason to keep writing. Most of all we would like to thank our families for their understanding and support.

Introducing SAS Software

SAS software is used by millions of people all over the world—in over 134 countries, at over 60,000 sites. SAS (pronounced sass) is both a company and software. When people say SAS, they sometimes mean the software running on their computers and sometimes mean the company.

People often ask what SAS stands for. Originally the letters S-A-S stood for Statistical Analysis System (not to be confused with Scandinavian Airlines System, San Antonio Shoemakers, or the Society for Applied Spectroscopy). SAS products have become so diverse that several years back SAS officially dropped the name Statistical Analysis System, now outgrown, and became simply SAS.

SAS products   The roots of SAS software reach back to the 1970s when it started out as a software package for statistical analysis, but SAS didn't stop there. By the mid-1980s SAS had already branched out into graphics, online data entry, and compilers for the C programming language. In the 1990s the SAS family tree grew to include tools for visualizing data, administering data warehouses, and building interfaces to the World Wide Web. In the new century, SAS has continued to grow with products designed for cleansing messy data, discovering and developing drugs, and detecting money laundering. Just as AT&T is now more than telephones and telegraphs, SAS is more than statistics.

While SAS has a diverse family of products, most of these products are integrated; that is, they can be put together like building blocks to construct a seamless system. For example, you might use SAS/ACCESS software to read data stored in an external database such as Oracle, analyze it using SAS/ETS software (business modeling and forecasting), use ODS Graphics to produce sophisticated plots, and then forward the results in an e-mail message to your colleagues, all in a single computer program. To find out more about products available from SAS, see the Web site

   www.sas.com

Operating environments   SAS software runs in a wide range of operating environments. You can take a program written on a personal computer and run it on a mainframe after changing only the file-handling statements specific to each operating environment. And because SAS programs are as portable as possible, SAS programmers are as portable as possible too. If you know SAS in one operating environment, you can switch to another operating environment without having to relearn SAS.

SASware Ballot   SAS puts a high percentage of its revenue into research and development, and each year SAS users help determine how that money will be spent by voting on the SASware Ballot. The ballot is a list of suggestions for new features and enhancements. All SAS users are eligible to vote and thereby influence the future development of SAS software. You can even make your own suggestions for the SASware Ballot by sending e-mail to

   suggest@sas.com

About This Book

Who needs this book This book is for all new SAS users in business, government, and academia, or for anyone who will be conducting data analysis using SAS software. You need no prior experience with SAS, but if you have some experience you may still find this book useful for learning techniques you missed or for reference.

What this book covers This book introduces you to the SAS language with lots of practical examples, clear and concise explanations, and as little technical jargon as possible. Most of the features covered here come from Base SAS, which contains the core of features used by all SAS programmers. One exception is chapter 9, which includes procedures from SAS/STAT. Other exceptions appear in chapters 2 and 10, which cover importing and exporting data from other types of software; some methods require SAS/ACCESS Interface to PC Files.

We have tried to include every feature of Base SAS that a beginner is likely to need. Some readers may be surprised that certain topics, such as macros, are included because they are normally considered advanced. But they appear here because sometimes new users need them. However, that doesn't mean that you need to know everything in this book. On the contrary, this book is designed so you can read just those sections you need to solve your problems. Even if you read this book from cover to cover, you may find yourself returning to refresh your memory as new programming challenges arise.

What this book does not cover To use this book you need no prior knowledge of SAS, but you must know something about your local computer and operating environment. The SAS language is virtually the same from one operating environment to another, but some differences are unavoidable. For example, every operating environment has a different way of storing and accessing files. Also, some operating environments have more of a capacity for interactive computing than others. Your employer may have rules limiting the size of files you can print. This book addresses operating environments as much as possible, but no book can answer every question about your local system. You must have either a working knowledge of your operating environment or someone you can turn to with questions.

This book is not a replacement for the SAS Help and Documentation, or the many SAS publications. Sooner or later you'll need to go to these and other sources to learn details not covered in this book.

We cover only a few of the many SAS statistical procedures. Fortunately, the statistical procedures share many of the same statements, options, and output, so these few can serve as an introduction to the others. Once you have read chapter 9, we think that other statistical procedures will feel familiar.

Unfortunately, a book of this type cannot provide a thorough introduction to statistical concepts such as degrees of freedom, or crossed and nested effects. There are underlying assumptions about your data that must be met for the tests to be valid. Experimental design and careful selection of the models are critical. Interpretation of the results can often be difficult and subjective. We assume that readers who are interested in statistical computing already know something about statistics. People who want to use statistical procedures but are unfamiliar with these concepts should consult a statistician, seek out an introductory statistics text, or, better yet, take a course in statistics.

Modular sections Our goal in writing this book is to make learning SAS as easy and enjoyable as possible. Let's face it—SAS is a big topic. You may have already spent some time scratching your head in front of a shelf full of SAS publications, or staring at a screen full of documentation until your eyes become blurry. We can't condense all of SAS into this little book, but we can condense topics into short, readable sections.

This entire book is composed of two-page sections, each section a complete topic. This way, you can easily skip over topics which do not apply to you. Of course, we think *every* section is important, or we would not have included it. You probably don't need to know everything in this book, however, to complete your job. By presenting topics in short digestible sections, we believe that learning SAS will be easier and more fun—like eating three meals a day instead of one giant meal a week.

Graphics Wherever possible, graphic illustrations either identify the contents of the section or help explain the topic. A box with rough edges indicates a raw data file, and a box with nice smooth edges indicates a SAS data set. The squiggles inside the box indicate data—any old data—and a period indicates a missing value. The arrow between boxes of these types means that the section explains how to get from data that look like the one box to data that look like the other. Some sections have graphics which depict printed output. These graphics look like a stack of papers with headers printed at the top of the page.

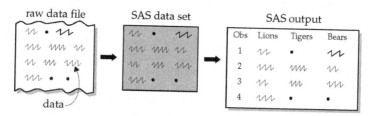

Typographical conventions SAS doesn't care whether your programs are written in uppercase or lowercase, so you can write your programs any way you want. In this book, we have used uppercase and lowercase to tell you something. The statements on the left below show the syntax, or general form, while the statements on the right show an example of actual statements as they might appear in a SAS program.

Syntax

```
PROC PRINT DATA = data-set-name;
   VAR variable-list;
```

Example

```
PROC PRINT DATA = bigcats;
   VAR Lions Tigers;
```

Notice that the keywords PROC PRINT, DATA, and VAR are the same on both sides and that the descriptive terms *data-set-name* and *variable-list* on the syntax side have been replaced with an actual data set name and variable names in the example.

In this book, all SAS keywords appear in uppercase letters. A keyword is an instruction to SAS and must be spelled correctly. Anything written in lowercase italics is a description of what goes in that spot in the statement, not what you actually type. Anything in lowercase or mixed case letters (and not in italics) is something that the programmer has made up such as a variable name, a name for a SAS data set, a comment, or a title. See section 1.2 for further discussion of the significance of case in SAS names.

Indention This book contains many SAS programs, each complete and executable. Programs are formatted in a way which makes them easy for you to read and understand. You do not have to format your programs this way, as SAS is very flexible, but attention to some of these details will make your programs easier to read. Easy-to-read programs are time-savers for you, or the consultant you hire at $100 per hour, when you need to go back and decipher the program months or years later.

The structure of programs is shown by indenting all statements after the first in a step. This is a simple way to make your programs more readable, and it's a good habit to form. SAS doesn't really care where statements start or even if they are all on one line. In the following program, the INFILE and INPUT statements are indented, indicating that they belong with the DATA statement:

```
* Read animals' weights from file. Print the results.;
DATA animals;
   INFILE 'c:\MyRawData\Zoo.dat';
   INPUT Lions Tigers;
RUN;

PROC PRINT DATA = animals;
RUN;
```

Data and programs used in this book You can access the example data and programs by linking to either of the author pages for this book at support.sas.com/delwiche or support.sas.com/slaughter. From that Web page, you can select **Example Code and Data** to display the data and programs that are included in the book.

Last, we have tried to make this book as readable as possible and, we hope, even enjoyable. Once you master the contents of this small book you will no longer be a beginning SAS programmer.

What's New

At first glance, this fifth edition of *The Little SAS Book: A Primer* looks a lot like the fourth, but, as they say, appearances can be deceiving. In fact, almost every one of the 150 sections in this edition has been revised in one way or another.

Many sections simply have output shown in the new default format (HTML), but other sections are completely new. ODS Graphics, which became production with SAS 9.2, has now matured to the point that we feel it deserves a complete chapter of its own. For the first time since the second edition, we have added a new section to our chapter on macro programming. And, of course, for people who prefer output in the former default format (text), we have added discussions of how to send results to the LISTING destination.

We are so pleased with this edition that we think it's the best one yet, and we hope you agree.

Here, listed by section, are the new topics:

Section	Feature
1.6, 1.9	**Results Viewer window** is now the default window for output
2.8	**$UPCASE., STIMER.,** and **COMMAX.** informats
2.17	**MIXED=YES** option in PROC IMPORT
3.4, 3.8, 3.9	**AGE** argument allows the YRDIF function to compute accurate ages
4.4	**SORTSEQ=LINGUISTIC** option in PROC SORT sorts character variables without regard to case
4.7	**$UPCASE., DTDATE., EUROX.,** and **PERCENT.** formats
4.10	**MAXDEC=** and **MISSING** options in PROC MEANS
4.12	**MISSPRINT** option in PROC FREQ
5.4	**LISTING destination** for text output
7.3	**Concatenating Macro Variables with Other Text**
8.2	**ALPHA=, DATALABEL=, DISCRETEOFFSET=, LIMITSTAT=, MISSING,** and **GROUPDISPLAY=** options for bar charts
8.3	**BINSTART=, BINWIDTH=, NBINS=,** and **TRANSPARENCY=** options for histograms
8.3	**TRANSPARENCY=** option for density curves
8.4	**EXTREME, GROUP=, MISSING,** and **TRANSPARENCY=** options for box plots

Section	Feature
8.5	**DATALABEL=, NOMISSINGGROUP,** and **TRANSPARENCY=** options for scatter plots
8.6	**CURVELABEL=, DATALABEL=, NOMISSINGGROUP,** and **TRANSPARENCY=** options for series plots
8.7	**ALPHA=, CLI, CURVELABEL=, NOLEGCLI,** and **CLMTRANSPARENCY=** options for fitted curves
8.8	**GRID** option for axes
8.9	**KEYLEGEND** and **INSET** statements
8.10	**FILLATTRS=, LABELATTRS=, LINEATTRS=, MARKERATTRS=,** and **VALUEATTRS=** options for controlling graph attributes
8.11	**PROC SGPANEL** for creating paneled graphs
8.12	**Options for specifying image properties and saving graphics output**
9.4, 9.5	**PROC TTEST for testing means**
9.7	**AGREEPLOT, RELRISKPLOT,** and **RISKDIFFPLOT** plots for PROC FREQ

SAS Studio, SAS University Edition, and SAS OnDemand for Academics

You can use SAS with several different interfaces. When this book was first printed, the SAS windowing environment (sometimes called Display Manager) and SAS Enterprise Guide were the two major interfaces for SAS. Now SAS Studio is an important new interface for SAS. For our readers who are using the SAS Studio interface, we wrote an online supplement to this book that addresses your needs.

SAS Studio is included in the license for Base SAS, is the interface for SAS University Edition, and is the default interface for SAS OnDemand for Academics. Both SAS University Edition and SAS OnDemand for Academics are available free of charge for noncommercial use.

SAS Studio is a browser-based interface to SAS. You write programs in the SAS Studio environment, submit the programs to a SAS server, and the results are returned to your SAS Studio session. The SAS server can be your local computer or a remote SAS server. SAS University Edition uses SAS Studio as the interface to a SAS server that runs on a virtual Linux server installed on your local computer. SAS OnDemand for Academics runs on Linux servers hosted by SAS Institute. Regardless of which operating system your computer runs (such as Windows, OS X for Macs, or Linux), SAS University Edition and SAS OnDemand for Academics still run Linux.

The SAS programming language is still the same, no matter which interface you use. Therefore the majority of this book is accurate and up-to-date. However, a few sections in this book (1.6 to 1.12) show you how to use the SAS windowing environment. If you are using SAS Studio as your interface, you can ignore these sections and read the online supplemental material instead.

The document "Using the SAS Studio Interface: Supplement to *The Little SAS Book, Fifth Edition*" can be downloaded from either of the authors' webpages at http://support.sas.com/publishing/authors.

1

"An honest tale speeds best being plainly told."

WILLIAM SHAKESPEARE, *KING RICHARD III*

CHAPTER 1

Getting Started Using SAS Software

1.1 The SAS Language

Many software applications are either menu driven, or command driven (enter a command—see the result). SAS is neither. With SAS, you use statements to write a series of instructions called a SAS program. The program communicates what you want to do and is written using the SAS language. There are some menu-driven front ends to SAS, for example SAS Enterprise Guide, which make SAS appear like a point-and-click program. However, these front ends still use the SAS language to write programs for you. You will have much more flexibility using SAS if you learn to write your own programs using the SAS language. Maybe learning a new language is the last thing you want to do, but be assured that although there are parallels between SAS and languages you know (be they English or JAVA), SAS is much easier to learn.

SAS programs   A SAS program is a sequence of statements executed in order. A statement gives information or instructions to SAS and must be appropriately placed in the program. An everyday analogy to a SAS program is a trip to the bank. You enter your bank, stand in line, and when you finally reach the teller's window, you say what you want to do. The statements you give can be written down in the form of a program:

```
I would like to make a withdrawal.
   My account number is 0937.
   I would like $200.
   Give me five 20s and two 50s.
```

Note that you first say what you want to do, then give all the information the teller needs to carry out your request. The order of the subsequent statements may not be important, but you must start with the general statement of what you want to do. You would not, for example, go up to a bank teller and say, "Give me five 20s and two 50s." This is not only bad form, but would probably make the teller's heart skip a beat or two. You must also make sure that all the subsequent statements belong with the first. You would not say, "I want the largest box you have" when making a withdrawal from your checking account. That statement belongs with "I would like to open a safe deposit box." A SAS program is an ordered set of SAS statements like the ordered set of instructions you use when you go to the bank.

SAS statements   As with any language, there are a few rules to follow when writing SAS programs. Fortunately for us, the rules for writing SAS programs are much fewer and simpler than those for English.

The most important rule is

Every SAS statement ends with a semicolon.

This sounds simple enough. But while children generally outgrow the habit of forgetting the period at the end of a sentence, SAS programmers never seem to outgrow forgetting the semicolon at the end of a SAS statement. Even the most experienced SAS programmer will at least occasionally forget the semicolon. You will be two steps ahead if you remember this simple rule.

Layout of SAS programs There really aren't any rules about how to format your SAS program. While it is helpful to have a neat looking program with each statement on a line by itself and indentions to show the various parts of the program, it isn't necessary.

- SAS statements can be in upper- or lowercase.

- Statements can continue on the next line (as long as you don't split words in two).

- Statements can be on the same line as other statements.

- Statements can start in any column.

So you see, SAS is so flexible that it is possible to write programs so disorganized that no one can read them, not even you. (Of course, we don't recommend this.)

Comments To make your programs more understandable, you can insert comments into your programs. It doesn't matter what you put in your comments—SAS doesn't look at it. You could put your favorite cookie recipe in there if you want. However, comments are usually used to annotate the program, making it easier for someone to read your program and understand what you have done and why.

There are two styles of comments you can use: one starts with an asterisk (*) and ends with a semicolon (;). The other style starts with a slash asterisk (/*) and ends with an asterisk slash (*/). The following SAS program shows the use of both of these style comments:

```
* Read animals' weights from file;
DATA animals;
   INFILE 'c:\MyRawData\Zoo.dat';
   INPUT Lions Tigers;
PROC PRINT DATA = animals;   /* Print the results */
RUN;
```

Since some operating environments interpret a slash asterisk (/*) in the first column as the end of a job, be careful when using this style of comment not to place it in the first column. For this reason, we chose the asterisk-semicolon style of comment for this book.

Programming tips People who are just starting to learn a programming language often get frustrated because their programs do not work correctly the first time they write them. Writing programs should be done in small steps. Don't try to tackle a long complicated program all at once. If you start small, build on what works, and always check your results along the way, you will increase your programming efficiency. Sometimes programs that do not produce errors are still incorrect. This is why it is vital to check your results as you go even when there are no errors. If you do get errors, don't worry. Most programs simply don't work the first time, if for no other reason than you are human. You forget a semicolon, misspell a word, have your fingers in the wrong place on the keyboard. It happens. Often one small mistake can generate a whole list of errors. If you build your programs piece by piece, programs are much easier to correct when something goes wrong.

1.2 SAS Data Sets

Before you run an analysis, before you write a report, before you do anything with your data, SAS must be able to read your data. Before SAS can analyze your data, the data must be in a special form called a SAS data set. (See section 2.1 for exceptions.) Getting your data into a SAS data set is usually quite simple as SAS is very flexible and can read almost any data. Once your data have been read into a SAS data set, SAS keeps track of what is where and in what form. All you have to do is specify the name and location of the data set you want, and SAS figures out what is in it.

Variables and observations Data, of course, are the primary constituent of any data set. In traditional SAS terminology the data consist of variables and observations. Adopting the terminology of relational databases, SAS data sets are also called tables, observations are also called rows, and variables are also called columns. Below you see a rectangular table containing a small data set. Each line represents one observation, while Id, Name, Height, and Weight are variables. The data point Charlie is one of the values of the variable Name and is also part of the second observation.

	Variables (Also Called Columns)			
	Id	Name	Height	Weight
1	53	Susie	42	41
2	54	Charlie	46	55
3	55	Calvin	40	35
4	56	Lucy	46	52
5	57	Dennis	44	.
6	58		43	50

Observations (Also Called Rows)

Data types Raw data come in many different forms, but SAS simplifies this. In SAS there are just two data types: numeric and character. Numeric fields are, well, numbers. They can be added and subtracted, can have any number of decimal places, and can be positive or negative. In addition to numerals, numeric fields can contain plus signs (+), minus signs (-), decimal points (.), or E for scientific notation. Character data are everything else. They may contain numerals, letters, or special characters (such as $ or !) and can be up to 32,767 characters long.

If a variable contains letters or special characters, it must be a character variable. However, if it contains only numbers, then it may be numeric or character. You should base your decision on how you will use the variable. (If disk space is a problem, you may also choose to base your decision on storage size. See section 11.14.) Sometimes data that consist solely of numerals make more sense as character data than as numeric. ZIP codes, for example, are made up of numerals, but it just doesn't make sense to add, subtract, multiply, or divide ZIP codes. Such numbers make more sense as character data. In the previous data set, Name is obviously a character variable, and Height and Weight are numeric. Id, however, could be either numeric or character. It's your choice.

Missing data Sometimes despite your best efforts, your data may be incomplete. The value of a particular variable may be missing for some observations. In those cases, missing character data are represented by blanks, and missing numeric data are represented by a single period (.). In the preceding data set, the value of Weight for observation 5 is missing, and its place is marked by a period. The value of Name for observation 6 is missing and is just left blank.

Size of SAS data sets Prior to SAS 9.1, SAS data sets could contain up to 32,767 variables. Beginning with SAS 9.1, the maximum number of variables in a SAS data set is limited by the resources available on your computer—but SAS data sets with more than 32,767 variables cannot be used with earlier versions of SAS. The number of observations, no matter which version of SAS you are using, is limited only by your computer's capacity to handle and store them.

Rules for names of variables and SAS data set members You make up names for the variables in your data and for the data sets themselves. It is helpful to make up names that identify what the data represent, especially for variables. While the variable names A, B, and C might seem like perfectly fine, easy-to-type names when you write your program, the names Sex, Height, and Weight will probably be more helpful when you go back to look at the program six months later. Follow these simple rules when making up names for variables and data set members:

♦ Names must be 32 characters or fewer in length.

♦ Names must start with a letter or an underscore (_).

♦ Names can contain only letters, numerals, or underscores (_). No %$!*&#@, please.[1]

♦ Names can contain upper- and lowercase letters.

This last point is an important one. SAS is insensitive to case so you can use uppercase, lowercase, or mixed case—whichever looks best to you. SAS doesn't care. The data set name heightweight is the same as HEIGHTWEIGHT or HeightWeight. Likewise, the variable name BirthDate is the same as BIRTHDATE and birThDaTe. However, there is one difference for variable names. SAS remembers the case of the first occurrence of each variable name and uses that case when printing results. That is why, in this book, we use mixed case for variable names but lowercase for other SAS names.

Documentation stored in SAS data sets In addition to your actual data, SAS data sets contain information about the data set such as its name, the date that you created it, and the version of SAS you used to create it. SAS also stores information about each variable, including its name, label (if any), type (numeric or character), length (or storage size), and position within the data set. This information is sometimes called the descriptor portion of the data set, and it makes SAS data sets self-documenting.

---

[1] It is possible to use special characters, including spaces, in variable names if you use the system option VALIDVARNAMES=ANY and a name literal of the form *'variable-name'*N. Starting with SAS 9.3, some special characters are allowed in SAS data set names when not running in the SAS windowing environment.

1.3 DATA and PROC Steps

SAS programs are constructed from two basic building blocks: DATA steps and PROC steps. A typical program starts with a DATA step to create a SAS data set and then passes the data to a PROC step for processing. Here is a simple program that converts miles to kilometers in a DATA step and prints the results with a PROC step:

| **DATA step** | ```
DATA distance;
    Miles = 26.22;
    Kilometers = 1.61 * Miles;
``` |
| **PROC step** | ```
PROC PRINT DATA = distance;
RUN;
``` |

DATA and PROC steps are made up of statements. A step may have as few as one or as many as hundreds of statements. Most statements work in only one type of step—in DATA steps but not PROC steps, or vice versa. A common mistake made by beginners is to try to use a statement in the wrong kind of step. You're not likely to make this mistake if you remember that DATA steps read and modify data while PROC steps analyze data, perform utility functions, or print reports.

DATA steps start with the DATA statement, which starts, not surprisingly, with the word DATA. This keyword is followed by a name that you make up for a SAS data set. The DATA step above produces a SAS data set named DISTANCE. In addition to reading data from external, raw data files, DATA steps can include DO loops, IF-THEN/ELSE logic, and a large assortment of numeric and character functions. DATA steps can also combine data sets in just about any way you want, including concatenation and match-merge.

Procedures, on the other hand, start with a PROC statement in which the keyword PROC is followed by the name of the procedure (PRINT, SORT, or MEANS, for example). Most SAS procedures have only a handful of possible statements. Like following a recipe, you use basically the same statements or ingredients each time. SAS procedures do everything from simple sorting and printing to analysis of variance and 3D graphics.

A step ends when SAS encounters a new step (marked by a DATA or PROC statement); a RUN, QUIT, STOP, or ABORT statement; or, if you are running in batch mode, the end of the program. RUN statements tell SAS to run all the preceding lines of the step and are among those rare, global statements that are not part of a DATA or PROC step. In the program above, SAS knows that the DATA step has ended when it reaches the PROC statement. The PROC step ends with a RUN statement, which coincides with the end of the program.

While a typical program starts with a DATA step to input or modify data and then passes the data to a PROC step, that is certainly not the only pattern for mixing DATA and PROC steps. Just as you can stack building blocks in any order, you can arrange DATA and PROC steps in any order. A program could even contain only DATA steps or only PROC steps.

To review, the table below outlines the basic differences between DATA and PROC steps:

DATA steps	PROC steps
▶ begin with DATA statements	▶ begin with PROC statements
▶ read and modify data	▶ perform specific analysis or function
▶ create a SAS data set	▶ produce results or report

As you read this table, keep in mind that it is a simplification. Because SAS is so flexible, the differences between DATA and PROC steps are, in reality, more blurry. The table above is not meant to imply that PROC steps never create SAS data sets (most do), or that DATA steps never produce reports (they can). Nonetheless, you will find it much easier to write SAS programs if you understand the basic functions of DATA and PROC steps.

The DATA Step's Built-in Loop

DATA steps read and modify data, and they do it in a way that is flexible, giving you lots of control over what happens to your data. However, DATA steps also have an underlying structure, an implicit, built-in loop. You don't tell SAS to execute this loop: SAS does it automatically. Memorize this:

DATA steps execute line by line and observation by observation.

This basic concept is rarely stated explicitly. Consequently, new users often grow into old users before they figure this out on their own.

The idea that DATA steps execute line by line is fairly straightforward and easy to understand. It means that, by default, SAS executes line one of your DATA step before it executes line two, and line two before line three, and so on. That seems common sense, and yet new users frequently run into problems because they try to use a variable before they create it. If a variable named Z is the product of X and Y, then you better make sure that the statements creating X and Y come before the statements creating Z.

What is not so obvious is that while DATA steps execute line by line, they also execute observation by observation. That means SAS takes the first observation and runs it all the way through the DATA step (line by line, of course) before looping back to pick up the second observation. In this way, SAS sees only one observation at a time.

Imagine a SAS program running in slow motion: SAS reads observation number one from your input data set. Then SAS executes your DATA step using that observation. If SAS reaches the end of the DATA step without encountering any serious errors, then SAS writes the current observation to a new, output data set and returns to the beginning of the DATA step to process the next observation. After the last observation has been written to the output data set, SAS terminates the DATA step and moves on to the next step, if there is one. End of slow motion; please return to normal gigahertz.

This diagram illustrates how an observation flows through a DATA step:

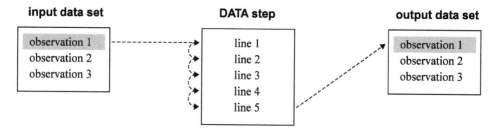

SAS reads observation number one and processes it using line one of the DATA step, then line two, and so on until SAS reaches the end of the DATA step. Then SAS writes the observation in the output data set. This diagram shows the first execution of the line-by-line loop. Once SAS finishes with the first observation, it loops back to the top of the DATA step and picks up observation two. When SAS reaches the last observation, it automatically stops.

Here is an analogy. DATA step processing is a bit like voting. When you arrive at your polling place, you stand in line behind other people who have come to vote. When you reach the front of the line you are asked standard questions: "What is your name? Where do you live?" Then you sign your name, and you cast your vote. In this analogy, the people are observations, and the voting process is the DATA step. People vote one at a time (or observation by observation). Each voter's choices are secret, and peeking at your neighbor's ballot is definitely frowned upon. In addition, each person completes each step of the process in the same order (line by line). You cannot cast your vote before you give your name and address. Everything must be done in the proper order.

If this seems a bit too structured, SAS offers a number of ways to override the line-by-line and observation-by-observation structure. These include the RETAIN statement (discussed in section 3.10) and the OUTPUT statement (discussed in sections 6.9 and 6.10).

1.5 ▶ Choosing a Mode for Submitting SAS Programs

So far we have talked about writing SAS programs, but simply writing a program does not give you any results. Just like writing a letter to your representative in Congress does no good unless you mail it, a SAS program does nothing until you submit or execute it. You can execute a SAS program several ways, but not all methods are available for all operating environments. Check the SAS Help and Documentation for your operating environment to find out which methods are available to you. The method you choose for executing a SAS program will depend on your preferences and on what is most appropriate for your application and your environment. If you are using SAS at a large site with many users, then ask around and find out which is the most accepted method of executing SAS. If you are using SAS on your own personal computer, then choose the method that suits you.

SAS windowing environment If you type SAS at your system prompt, or click the SAS icon, you will most likely get into the SAS windowing environment (also known as Display Manager). In this interactive environment, you can write and edit SAS programs, submit programs for processing, and view and print your results. In addition, there are many SAS windows for performing different tasks such as managing SAS files, customizing the interface, accessing SAS Help and Documentation, and importing or exporting data. Exactly what your windowing environment looks like depends on the type of computer you are using, the operating environment on the computer, and what options are in effect when you start up SAS. If you are using a personal computer, then the SAS windowing environment will look similar to other programs on your computer, and many of the features will be familiar to you. The following figure shows the SAS windowing environment in Microsoft Windows.

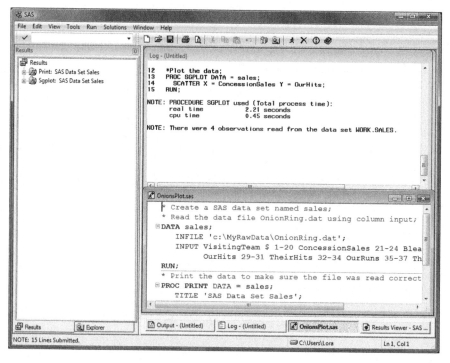

SAS Enterprise Guide If you have SAS Enterprise Guide software, which runs only under Windows, you may choose to submit your programs from within SAS Enterprise Guide. To do this, open a Program window where you can type in your SAS program or open an existing SAS program. The progam editor in SAS Enterprise Guide (starting with version 4.3) displays automatic syntax help as you type your program, and there is a program analyzer that will generate a diagram of your program to help you visualize the parts and how they fit together. You can choose to run your code on the local machine, or on a remote server where SAS is installed. To run your SAS program on a remote server, you may need to have additional SAS software installed. Also, SAS Enterprise Guide can write SAS code for you through its extensive menu system. SAS Enterprise Guide is project based, so all your programs, results, and references to data are stored in one project file. The following figure shows a project in SAS Enterprise Guide 4.3.

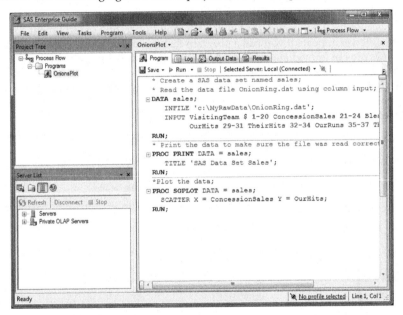

Batch or background mode With batch or background mode, your SAS program is in a file. You submit the file for processing with SAS. Your SAS program may start executing immediately, or it could be put in a queue behind other jobs. Batch processing is used a lot on mainframe computers. You can continue to work on your computer while your job is being processed, or better yet, you can go to the baseball game and let the computer work in your absence. Batch processing is usually less expensive than other methods and is especially good for large jobs which can be set up to execute during off-hours when the rates are at their lowest. When your job is complete, the results will be placed in a file or files, which you can display or print at any time.

To find out how to submit SAS programs for batch processing, check the SAS Help and Documentation for your operating environment, or check with other SAS users at your site. Even sites with the same operating environment may have different ways of submitting jobs in batch mode.

1.6 Windows and Commands in the SAS Windowing Environment

The SAS windowing environment (also known as Display Manager) adopts the look and feel of your operating environment. This is good for you because many aspects of the SAS windowing environment will be familiar. But there are many ways in which you can customize your SAS environment if you want. This makes writing about it challenging, because we can't tell you exactly what your SAS session will look like and how it will behave. However, there are common elements between the various operating environments, and you will probably already be familiar with those elements which are different.

The SAS Windows

There are five basic SAS windows: the Results and Explorer windows, and three programming windows: Editor, Log, and Output. In the Windows operating environment a sixth window, the Results Viewer appears if you run a program that generates printable results. Sometimes the windows are not immediately visible. For example, in the Windows operating environment, the Output window initially appears behind the Editor and Log windows. There are also many other SAS windows that you may use for tasks such as getting help, changing SAS system options, and customizing your SAS session. The following figure shows the windows for a Microsoft Windows SAS session, with pointers to the main SAS windows.

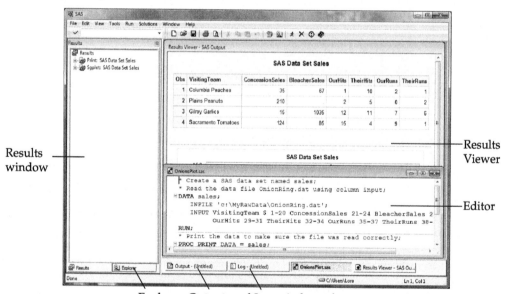

Explorer, Output, and Log window tabs

Editor This window is a text editor. You can use it to type in, edit, and submit SAS programs as well as edit other text files such as raw data files. In Windows operating environments, the default editor is the Enhanced Editor. The Enhanced Editor is syntax sensitive and color codes your programs making it easier to read them and find mistakes. The Enhanced Editor also allows you to collapse and expand the various steps in your program. For other operating environments, the default editor is the Program Editor whose features vary with the version of SAS and operating environment.

Log The Log window contains notes about your SAS session, and after you submit a SAS program, any notes, errors, or warnings associated with your program as well as the program statements themselves will appear in the Log window.

Output In the z/OS operating environment, all tabular results will appear in the Output window. By default, in the Windows and UNIX environments, nothing appears in the Output window. But if you turn on the LISTING destination (see section 5.4), then results will appear in the Output window.

Results Viewer In the Windows operating environment, if your program generates any printable results, then the Results Viewer window will open and display the results.

Results The Results window is like a table of contents for your Output and Results Viewer windows; the results tree lists each part of your results in an outline form.

Explorer The Explorer window gives you easy access to your SAS files and libraries.

The SAS Commands

There are SAS commands for performing a variety of tasks. Some tasks are probably familiar, such as opening and saving files, cutting and pasting text, and accessing Help. Other commands are specific to the SAS System, such as submitting a SAS program. You may have up to three ways to issue commands: menus, the toolbar, or the SAS command bar (or command line). The following figure shows the location of these three methods of issuing SAS commands in the Windows operating environment default view.

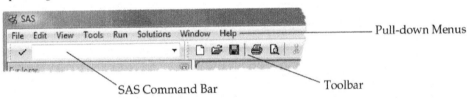

Menus Most operating environments will have pull-down menus located either at the top of each window, or at the top of your screen. If your menus are at the top of your screen, then the menus will change when you activate the different windows (usually by clicking on them). You may also have, for each window, context-sensitive pop-up menus that appear when you click the right or center button of your mouse.

Toolbar The toolbar, if you have one, gives you quick access to commands that are already accessible through the pull-down menus. Not all operating environments have a toolbar.

SAS command bar The command bar is a place that you can type in SAS commands. In some operating environments the command bar is located with the toolbar (as shown here); in other operating environments you may have a command line with each of the SAS windows (usually indicated by Command=>). Most of the commands that you can type in the command bar are also accessible through the pull-down menus or the toolbar.

Controlling your windows The Window pull-down menu gives you choices on how the windows are placed on your screen. You can also activate any of the programming windows by selecting it from the Window pull-down menu, or by simply clicking the window.

1.7 Submitting a Program in the SAS Windowing Environment

Naturally after going to the trouble of writing SAS programs, you want to see some results. As we have already discussed, there are several ways of submitting SAS programs. If you use the SAS windowing environment, then you can edit and submit programs, and see results all within the windowing environment.

Getting your program into the editor The first thing you need to do is get your program into the Editor window. You can either type your program into the editor, or you can bring the program into the Editor window from a file. The commands for editing in the editor and for opening files should be familiar. SAS tries to follow conventions that are common for your operating environment. For example, to open a file in the editor, you can select **File ▶ Open** from the menu bar. For some operating environments you may have an Open icon on the toolbar, and you may also have the option of pasting your file into the editor from the clipboard.

Submitting your program Once your program appears in the editor, you execute it (either the whole program or a part you have highlighted) using the SUBMIT command. Depending on your operating environment, you have a few choices on how to execute the SUBMIT command. First click the Editor window to make it active. Then do one of the following:

 Click the **Submit** button on the toolbar.

Enter SUBMIT in the command line area of your SAS session.

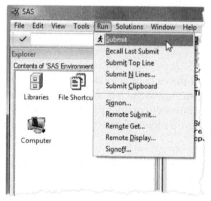

Select **Run ▶ Submit** from the menu bar.

Viewing the SAS Log and Results In the Windows operating environment, after you submit your program, the program remains in the Enhanced Editor window and the results of your program go into the Log and Results Viewer windows. In the UNIX environment, your results go into the Log window and a separate web browser window, while in z/OS your results go into the Log and Output windows. For both UNIX and z/OS, after submitting your program it disappears from the Program Editor window. At first it may be a shock for you to see your program disappear in front of your eyes.

Don't worry; the program you spent so long writing is not gone forever. If your program produced any output, then you will also get new entries in the Results window. The Results window is like a table of contents for your SAS output and is discussed in more detail in section 1.9. The following figure is an example of what your screen might look like after you submit a program from the Enhanced Editor in the Windows environment.

You may not see all the windows at the same time. In some operating environments, the windows are placed one on top of the other. In this figure the Explorer window is under the Results window and the Output and Log windows are beneath the Enhanced Editor and Results Viewer windows. You can bring a window to the top by clicking it

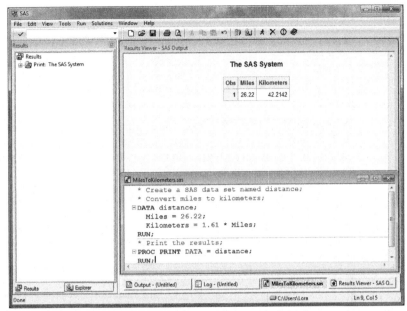

or its tab, typing its name in the command line area, or selecting it from the Window menu.

Getting your program back   Unfortunately for most of us, our programs do not run perfectly every time. If you have an error in your program, you will most likely want to edit the program and run it again. If you are using the Enhanced Editor, then your program will remain in the window after you submit it. However, if you are using the Program Editor window, you will need to get your program back in the Program Editor window using the RECALL command. You have two choices for executing the RECALL command.

Make the Program Editor the active window, then enter RECALL in the command line area of your SAS session.

Make the Program Editor the active window, then select **Run ▶ Recall Last Submit** from the menu bar.

The RECALL command will bring back the last block of statements you submitted. If you use the RECALL command again, it will insert the block of statements submitted before the last one, and so on and so on, until it retrieves all the statements you submitted.

1.8 Reading the SAS Log

Every time you submit a SAS program, SAS writes messages in your log. Many SAS programmers ignore the SAS log and go straight to the output. That's understandable, but dangerous. It is possible—and sooner or later it happens to all of us—to get bogus results that look fine in the output. The only way to know they are bad is to check the SAS log. Just because it runs doesn't mean it's right.

Where to find the SAS log The location of the SAS log varies depending on the operating environment you use, the mode you use (SAS windowing environment or batch), and local settings. If you submit a program in the windowing environment, you will, by default, see the SAS log in your Log window as in the following figure.

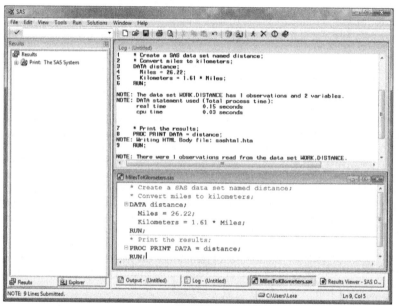

If you submit your program in batch mode, the log will be written to a file that you can view or print using your operating environment's commands for viewing and printing. The name given to the log file is generally some permutation of the name you gave the original program. For example, if you named your SAS program Marathon.sas, then it is a good bet that your log file will be Marathon.log.

What the log contains People tend to think of the SAS log as either a rehash of their program or as just a lot of gibberish. OK, we admit, there is some technical trivia in the SAS log, but there is also plenty of important information. Here is a simple program that converts miles to kilometers and prints the result:

```
* Create a SAS data set named distance;
* Convert miles to kilometers;
DATA distance;
   Miles = 26.22;
   Kilometers = 1.61 * Miles;
RUN;
* Print the results;
PROC PRINT DATA = distance;
RUN;
```

If you run this program, SAS will produce a log similar to this:

```
❶ NOTE: Copyright (c) 2002-2010 by SAS Institute Inc., Cary, NC, USA.
   NOTE: SAS (r) Proprietary Software Version 9.3 (TS1M0)
         Licensed to XYZ Inc., Site 0099999001.
   NOTE: This session is executing on the W32_VSPRO  platform.
   NOTE: SAS initialization used:
         real time           1.40 seconds
         cpu time            0.96 seconds
❷ 1    * Create a SAS data set named distance;
   2    * Convert miles to kilometers;
   3    DATA distance;
   4       Miles = 26.22;
   5       Kilometers = 1.61 * Miles;
   6    RUN;
❸ NOTE: The data set WORK.DISTANCE has 1 observations and 2 variables.
❹ NOTE: DATA statement used (Total process time):
         real time           0.03 seconds
         cpu time            0.03 seconds
❷ 7    * Print the results;
   8    PROC PRINT DATA = distance;
   9    RUN;
   NOTE: There were 1 observations read from the data set WORK.DISTANCE
❹ NOTE: PROCEDURE PRINT used (Total process time):
         real time           0.01 seconds
         cpu time            0.00 seconds
```

The SAS log above is a blow-by-blow account of how SAS executes the program.

❶   It starts with notes about the version of SAS and your SAS site number.

❷   It contains the original program statements with line numbers added on the left.

❸   The DATA step is followed by a note containing the name of the SAS data set created (WORK.DISTANCE), and the number of observations (1) and variables (2). A quick glance is enough to assure you that you did not lose any observations or accidentally create a lot of unwanted variables.

❹   Both DATA and PROC steps produce a note about the computer resources used. At first you probably won't care in the least. But if you run on a multi-user system or have long jobs with large data sets, these statistics may start to pique your interest. If you ever find yourself wondering why your job takes so long to run, a glance at the SAS log will tell you which steps are the culprits.

If there were error messages, they would appear in the log, indicating where SAS got confused and what action it took. You may also find warnings and other types of notes which sometimes indicate errors and other times just provide useful information. Chapter 11 discusses several of the more common errors SAS users encounter.

1.9 ▶ Viewing Your Results

How you view your output depends on what operating environment you are using and how you submit your program.

SAS windowing environment If you submit your program in the SAS windowing environment under Microsoft Windows, then your output will, by default, go to the Results Viewer window and be displayed in HTML. Under UNIX, your output will also be displayed in HTML by default, but it will be displayed in a separate web browser window. Under z/OS, output will display as text in the Output window.

Batch mode If you submit your program in batch mode, then your output will be in a file on your computer and you would use your operating environment's commands to view the output file (also called the listing). For example, if you execute your SAS program in batch mode on a UNIX system, then your output will be in a file with an extension .lst. To view the file, you can use either the `cat` or `more` commands.

Results Viewer window After submitting your program in the SAS windowing environment under Microsoft Windows, your results will go to the Results Viewer window. The Results Viewer window is automatically opened and appears on top of any of the other programming windows that are open. The following figure shows what your Results Viewer window might look like after submitting a program containing an ANOVA (Analysis of Variance) procedure. Notice that the Results Viewer window is automatically scrolled down so that you see the end of the procedure's output.

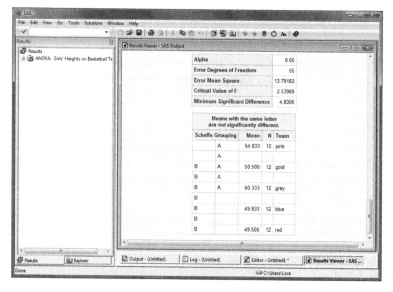

Results window   When you have a lot of output, the Results window can be very helpful. The Results window is like a table of contents for your output. It lists each procedure that produces output, and if you open or expand the procedure in the Results tree, you can see each part of the procedure output. Expand the results tree, by clicking the plus (+) signs, or by right-clicking the result and selecting **Expand All.**

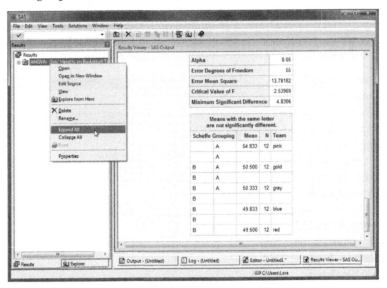

Double-click the output you want to see, and it will appear at the top of the Results Viewer window. The following figure shows what your Results Viewer window would look like after double-clicking the **Overall ANOVA** item in the Results Viewer window.

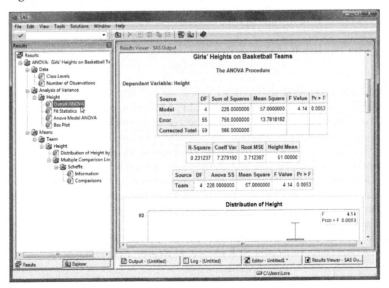

1.10 SAS Data Libraries

Before you can use a SAS data set, you have to tell SAS where to find it. You do that by setting up a SAS library. A SAS library is simply a location where SAS data sets (as well as other types of SAS files) are stored. Depending on your operating environment, a SAS library might be a folder or directory on your computer, or it might be a physical location like a hard drive, flash drive, or CD. To set up a library, all you have to do is make up a name for your library and tell SAS where it is. There are several ways to do this including using the LIBNAME statement (covered in sections 2.18 to 2.19) and using the New Library window in the SAS windowing environment.

When you start the SAS windowing environment, you see the basic SAS windows including the SAS Explorer window on the left. (If the Explorer window is under the Results window, click its tab to bring it forward.) If you double-click the Libraries icon, Explorer will open the Active Libraries window showing all the libraries that are currently defined. To go back to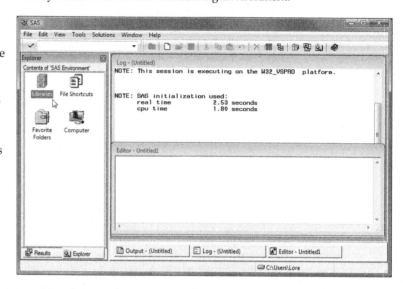
the previous window within Explorer, choose **View ▶ Up one level** from the menu bar, or click

the Explorer window to make it active, and then click the Up One Level button ⬆ on the toolbar.

Active Libraries window When you open the Active Libraries window, you will see at least three libraries: SASHELP, SASUSER, and WORK. You may have other libraries for specific SAS products (such as the MAPS library for SAS/GRAPH software), or libraries that have been set up by you or someone you work with. The SASHELP library contains information that controls your SAS session along with sample SAS data sets. The WORK library is a temporary storage location for SAS data sets. It is also the default library. If you create a SAS data set without specifying a library, SAS will put it in the WORK library, and then delete it when you end your session. If you make changes to the default settings for the SAS windowing environment, this information will be stored in the SASUSER library. You can also store SAS data sets, SAS programs, and other SAS files in the SASUSER library. However, many people prefer to create a new library for their SAS files.

Creating a new library You can create new SAS libraries using the New Library window. To open this window, either select **Tools ▶ New Library** from the menu bar, or right-click the Active Libraries window and choose **New** from the pop-up menu.

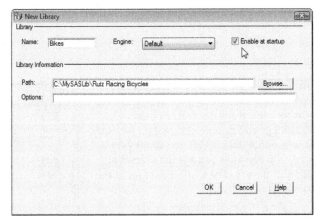

In the New Library window, type the name of the library you want to create. This name is called a libref, which is short for library reference. A libref must be 8 characters or fewer; start with a letter or underscore; and contain only letters, numerals, or underscores. In this window, the name BIKES has been typed in as the libref. In the Path field, enter the complete path to the folder or directory where you want your data sets to be stored, or click the **Browse...** button to navigate to the location. If you don't want to define your library reference every time you start up SAS, then check the **Enable at startup** box. Click **OK** and then your new library reference will appear in the Active Libraries window.

Here is the Active Libraries window showing the newly created BIKES library.

1.11 Viewing Data Sets in the Viewtable Window

In addition to listing your current libraries and creating new libraries, you can also use SAS Explorer to open SAS data sets for viewing in Viewtable. When you are writing programs, it is always a good idea to check the data sets you create to make sure they are correct. Viewtable is one way you can look at your SAS data sets.

Start by double-clicking the Libraries icon in the Explorer window as shown in the previous section. This will open the Active Libraries window showing all the libraries that are currently defined on your system. If you double-click a library icon, SAS will open a Contents window showing you all the SAS files in that particular library.

To go back to the previous window within Explorer, choose **View ▶ Up one level** from the menu bar, or click the Explorer window to make it active, and then click the Up One Level button on the toolbar.

Contents window This window shows the contents of a library. SAS data sets are represented by an icon showing a little table of data and a red ball. The library shown on the right contains three data sets named CUSTOMERS, MODELS, and ORDERS. If you double-click a data set, SAS will open a Viewtable window showing that data set. (If you don't yet have any SAS data sets of your own, you can view sample data sets that are provided with SAS in the SASHELP library. The CLASS data set in the SASHELP library is a good one to view.)

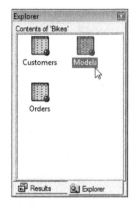

Viewtable window This window allows you to create, browse, and edit data sets. When you first open SAS data sets, the data are in browse mode so you cannot make any changes. To switch to edit mode, select **Edit ▶ Edit Mode** from the menu bar. Creating and editing data sets using Viewtable is discussed in more detail in section 2.2. This picture shows the data set named MODELS from the BIKES library.

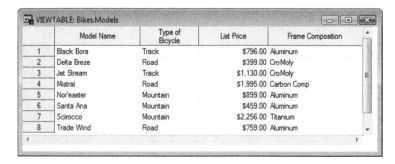

	Model Name	Type of Bicycle	List Price	Frame Composition
1	Black Bora	Track	$796.00	Aluminum
2	Delta Breze	Road	$399.00	CroMoly
3	Jet Stream	Track	$1,130.00	CroMoly
4	Mistral	Road	$1,995.00	Carbon Comp
5	Nor'easter	Mountain	$899.00	Aluminum
6	Santa Ana	Mountain	$459.00	Aluminum
7	Scirocco	Mountain	$2,256.00	Titanium
8	Trade Wind	Road	$759.00	Aluminum

Changing column headings By default, Viewtable uses variable labels for column headings, or, if a variable does not have a label, the variable name is displayed. Sometimes you may want to see the actual variable names instead of the labels. To do this, click the Viewtable window to make it active, then select **View ▶ Column Names** from the menu bar. Here is the MODELS SAS data set showing the column (also called variable) names instead of the labels.

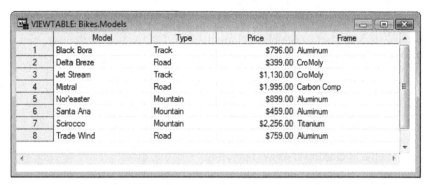

Column options If you right-click a column heading, several options will appear in the pop-up menu. You can control colors, fonts, and view the column attributes. You can choose to sort the data by the values in the column. If you are not in edit mode, then you are given the option of creating a new data set containing the sorted data. You can also hide or hold columns. If you choose to hide a column, the data will not be visible in the current Viewtable session. To unhide a column, select **Data ▶ Hide/Unhide** from the menu bar to open the Hide/Unhide window. In this window you can change the visibility of all columns. When you choose to hold a column, it and every column to the left of it will always be visible, even when you scroll to the right.

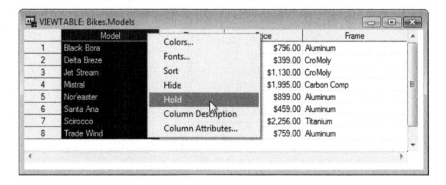

1.12 Viewing the Properties of Data Sets with SAS Explorer

The Properties window for a SAS data set contains some very useful information, such as the date and time the data set was created, the number of observations, all the variable names, and the attributes of the variables. The Properties window contains information similar to the output produced by the CONTENTS procedure described in section 2.21.

Opening the Properties window To open the Properties window, start by double-clicking the Libraries icon in the Explorer window and then double-clicking the library containing the SAS data set. SAS will display the contents of the library in the Explorer window. Right-click the icon for the data set, and select **Properties** from the pop-up menu. This opens the Properties window with the General tab on top. This figure shows what the Properties window looks like in the Microsoft Windows operating environment.

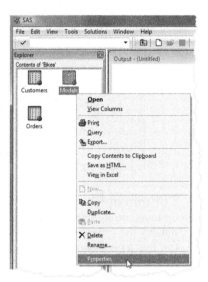

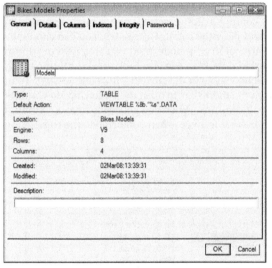

General tab This window displays information about the data set such as the date it was created and the number of rows (or observations) and columns (or variables).

Columns tab If you click the Columns tab, SAS displays information about the columns (or variables) in that data set. The variable name, type, and length are displayed along with any formats or informats assigned to the variable. The variable labels are also displayed in this window, but to see them you need to scroll to the right.

If you have lots of variables in your data set, using the sort and find features can make your work easier. You can sort any of these columns alphabetically by clicking the column heading. This window shows the variables sorted by name. You can find a colunm by typing its name in the box labeled **Find column name.**

1.13 Using SAS System Options

System options are parameters you can change that affect SAS—how it works, what the output looks like, how much memory is used, error handling, and a host of other things. SAS makes many assumptions about how you want it to work. This is good. You do not want to specify every little detail each time you use SAS. However, you may not always like the assumptions SAS makes. System options give you a way to change some of these assumptions.

Not all options are available for all operating environments. A list of options specific to your operating environment appears in the SAS Help and Documentation. You can see a list of system options and their current values by opening the SAS System Options window, or by using the OPTIONS procedure. To use the OPTIONS procedure, submit the following SAS program and view the results in the SAS log:

```
PROC OPTIONS;
RUN;
```

There are four ways to specify system options. Some options can be specified using only some of these methods. The SAS Help and Documentation for your operating environment tells you which methods are valid for each system option:

1. Create a SAS configuration file which contains settings for the system options. This file is accessed by SAS every time SAS is started. Configuration files are created by systems administrators. (This could be you if you are using a PC.)

2. Specify system options at the time you start up SAS from your system's prompt (called the invocation).

3. Change selected options in the SAS System Options window if you are using the SAS windowing environment.

4. Use the OPTIONS statement as a part of your SAS program.

The methods are listed here in order of increasing precedence; method 2 will override method 1, method 3 will override method 2, and so forth. If you are using the SAS windowing environment, methods 3 and 4, the SAS System Options window and OPTIONS statement, will override each other—so whichever was used last will be in effect. Only the last two methods are covered here. The first two methods are very system dependent; to find out more about these methods see the SAS Help and Documentation for your operating environment.

OPTIONS statement The OPTIONS statement is part of a SAS program and affects all steps that follow it. It starts with the keyword OPTIONS and follows with a list of options and their values. For example

```
OPTIONS LEFTMARGIN = 1IN NODATE;
```

The OPTIONS statement is one of the special SAS statements which do not belong to either a PROC or a DATA step. This global statement can appear anywhere in your SAS program, but it usually makes the most sense to let it be the first line in your program. This way you can easily see which options are in effect. If the OPTIONS statement is in a DATA or PROC step, then it affects that step and the following steps. Any subsequent OPTIONS statements in a program override previous ones.

SAS System Options window

You can view and change SAS system options through the SAS System Options window. Open it either by typing OPTIONS in the command line area on your screen, or by selecting **Tools ▶ Options ▶ System** from the menu bar. To change the value of an option, first locate the option by clicking the appropriate category on the left side of the screen. A list of options and their current values will appear on the right side of the screen. Right-click the option itself to modify the value or set it to the default.

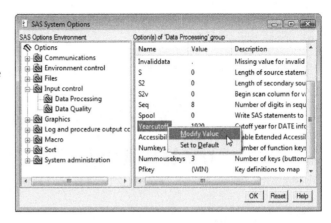

Options for printed results The following are some system options you might want to use that affect the appearance of results in formats meant for printing (in other words not HTML):

CENTER | NOCENTER   controls whether output is centered or left-justified. Default is CENTER.

DATE | NODATE   controls whether or not today's date will appear at the top of each page of output. Default is DATE.

NUMBER | NONUMBER   controls whether or not page numbers appear on each page of SAS output. Default is NUMBER.

ORIENTATION = *orientation*   specifies the orientation for printing output, either LANDSCAPE or PORTRAIT. Default is PORTRAIT.

PAGENO = *n*   starts numbering output pages with *n*. Default is 1.

RIGHTMARGIN = *n*
LEFTMARGIN = *n*
TOPMARGIN = *n*
BOTTOMMARGIN = *n*   specifies the size of the margin (such as 0.75in or 2cm) to be used for printing output. Default is 0.00in.

2

> " **Practice is the best of all instructors.** "

PUBLIUS SYRUS, CIRCA 42 B.C

> " **We all learned by doing, by experimenting (and often failing), and by asking questions.** "

JAY JACOB WIND

CHAPTER 2

Getting Your Data into SAS

2.1 Methods for Getting Your Data into SAS

Data come in many different forms. Your data may be handwritten on a piece of paper, or typed into a raw data file on your computer. Perhaps your data are in a database file on your personal computer, or in a database management system (DBMS) on the mainframe computer at your office. Wherever your data reside, there is a way for SAS to use them. You may need to convert your data from one form to another, or SAS may be able to use your data in their current form. This section outlines several methods for getting your data into SAS. Most of these methods are covered in this book, but a few of the more advanced methods are merely mentioned so that you know they exist. We do not attempt to cover all methods available for getting your data into SAS, as new methods are continually being developed, and creative SAS users can always come up with clever methods that work for their own situations. But there should be at least one method explained in this book that will work for you.

Methods for getting your data into SAS can be put into four general categories:

♦ entering data directly into SAS data sets

♦ creating SAS data sets from raw data files

♦ converting other software's data files into SAS data sets

♦ reading other software's data files directly

Naturally, the method you choose will depend on where your data are located, and what software tools are available to you.

Entering data directly into SAS data sets Sometimes the best method for getting your data into SAS is to enter the data directly into SAS data sets through your keyboard.

♦ The Viewtable window, discussed in section 2.2, is included with Base SAS software. Viewtable allows you to enter your data in a tabular format. You can define variables, or columns, and give them attributes such as name, length, and type (character or numeric).

♦ SAS Enterprise Guide software, which is included with Base SAS for Windows, has a data entry window that is very similar to the Viewtable window. As with Viewtable, you can define variables and give them attributes.

♦ SAS/FSP software allows you to design custom data entry screens. It also has the capability for detecting data entry errors as they happen. The SAS/FSP product is licensed separately from Base SAS software.

Creating SAS data sets from raw data files Much of this chapter is devoted to reading raw data files (also referred to as text, ASCII, sequential, or flat files). You can always read a raw data file since the DATA step is an integral part of Base SAS software. And, if your data are not already in a raw data file, chances are you can convert your data into a raw data file. There are two general methods for reading raw data files:

♦ The DATA step is so versatile that it can read almost any type of raw data file. This method is covered in this chapter starting with section 2.4.

♦ The Import Wizard, covered in section 2.3, and its cousin the IMPORT procedure, covered in section 2.16, are available for UNIX and Windows operating environments. These are simple methods for reading particular types of raw data files including comma-separated values (CSV) files, and other delimited files.

Converting other software's data files into SAS data sets Each software application has its own form for data files. While this is useful for software developers, it is troublesome for software users—especially when your data are in one application, but you need to analyze them with another. There are several options for converting data:

♦ The IMPORT procedure and the Import Wizard, available for UNIX and Windows operating environments, can be used to convert Microsoft Excel, Lotus, dBase, Stata, SPSS, JMP, Paradox, and Microsoft Access files into SAS data sets. All of these except JMP require that you have SAS/ACCESS Interface to PC Files installed on your computer. The IMPORT wizard is covered in section 2.3, and reading Excel files using the IMPORT procedure is covered in section 2.17.

♦ If you don't have SAS/ACCESS software, then you can always create a raw data file from your application and read the raw data file with either the DATA step or the IMPORT procedure. Many applications can create CSV files, which are easily read using the Import Wizard or IMPORT procedure (covered in sections 2.3 and 2.16) or the DATA step (covered in section 2.15).

♦ Dynamic Data Exchange (DDE), is available only for those working in the Windows operating environment. To use DDE, you must have the other Windows application (Microsoft Excel for example) running on your computer at the same time as SAS. Then using DDE and the DATA step, you can convert data into SAS data sets.

Reading other software's data files directly Under certain circumstances you may be able to read data without converting to a SAS data set. This method is particularly useful when you have many people updating data files, and you want to make sure that you are using the most current data.

♦ The SAS/ACCESS products allow you to read data without converting your data into SAS data sets. There are SAS/ACCESS products for most of the popular database management systems including ORACLE, DB2, INGRES, MYSQL, and SYBASE. This method of data access is not covered in this book.

♦ We already mentioned using SAS/ACCESS Interface to PC Files to convert several PC file types to SAS data sets, but you can also use the Excel, Access, and JMP engines to read these types of files directly without converting. See the SAS Help and Documentation for more information on these engines.

♦ There are also data engines that allow you to read data directly but are part of Base SAS software. There are engines for SPSS, OSIRIS, old versions of SAS data sets, and SAS data sets in transport format. Check the SAS Help and Documentation for your operating environment for a complete list of available engines.

Given all these methods for getting your data into SAS, you are sure to find at least one method that will work for you—probably more.

2.2 ▶ Entering Data with the Viewtable Window

The Viewtable window which is part of Base SAS software[1] is an easy way to create new data sets, or browse and edit existing data sets. True to its name, the Viewtable window displays tables (another name for data sets) in a tabular format. To open the Viewtable window, select **Tools ▶ Table Editor** from the menu bar. An empty Viewtable window will appear.

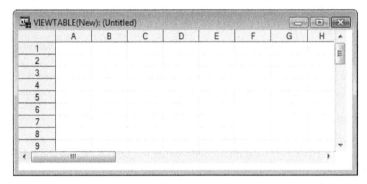

This table contains no data. Instead you see rows (or observations) labeled with numbers and columns (or variables) labeled with letters. You can start typing data into this default table, and SAS will automatically figure out if your columns are numeric or character. However, it's a good idea to tell SAS about your data so each column is set up the way you want. You do this with the Column Attributes window.

Column Attributes window   The letters at the tops of columns are default variable names. By right-clicking a letter, you can choose to open a Column Attributes window for that column. This window contains default values which you can replace with the values you desire. If you plan to enter date values, then you should choose a date informat so that dates entered will be automatically converted to SAS date values.[2] See sections 2.7 and 2.8 for more on informats. If you also choose a date format, then the dates will be displayed as readable dates. See sections 4.6 and 4.7 for more on formats. When you are satisfied with the values, click **Apply**. To switch to a new column, click that column in the Viewtable window. When you are finished changing column attributes, click **Close**.

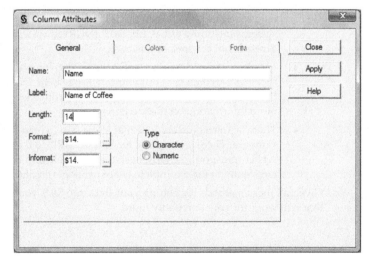

Entering data Once you have defined your columns, you are ready to type in your data. To move the cursor, click a field, or use tab and arrow keys. Here is a table with column attributes defined and data entered.

Saving your table To save a table, select **File ▶ Save As...** from the menu bar to open the Save As window (similar to the Open window shown below). The libraries displayed correspond to locations (such as directories) on your computer. If you want to save your table in a different location, you can add another library by clicking the New Library icon to open the New Library window (shown in sections 1.10 and 2.18). In the Save As window, specify a member name for your table, and click **Save**.

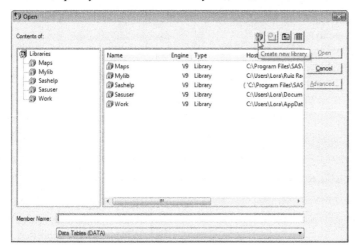

Opening an existing table To browse or edit an existing table, first select **Tools ▶ Table Editor** from the menu bar to open the Viewtable window. Then select **File ▶ Open** from the menu bar. In the Open window, click the library you want and then the table name, and click **Open**. If the table you want is not in any of the existing libraries, click the New Library icon and create a library. To switch from browse mode (the default) to edit mode, select **Edit ▶ Edit Mode** from the menu bar. You can also open an existing table by navigating to it in the SAS Explorer window, and double-clicking it.

Other features The Viewtable window has many other features including sorting, printing, adding and deleting rows, and viewing multiple rows (the default, called Table View), or viewing one row at a time (called Form View). You can control these features using either menus or icons.

Using your table in a SAS program Tables that you create in Viewtable can be used in programs just as tables created in programs can be used in Viewtable. For example, if you saved your table in the SASUSER library and named it COFFEE, you could print it with this program:

```
PROC PRINT DATA = Sasuser.coffee;
RUN;
```

---

[1] If you are using a non-graphical monitor, then SAS uses FSVIEW to display your tables, so you also need SAS/FSP software which is licensed separately.

[2] SAS date values are the number of days since January 1, 1960.

2.3 Reading Files with the Import Wizard

Using the Import Wizard, available in the Windows and UNIX operating environments, you can convert a variety of data file types into SAS data sets by simply answering a few questions. The Import Wizard will scan your file to determine variable types[3] and will, by default, use the first row of data for the variable names. The Import Wizard can read all types of delimited files including comma-separated values (CSV) files which are a common file type for moving data between applications. And, if you have SAS/ACCESS Interface to PC Files, then you can also read a number of popular PC file types.

Start the Import Wizard by choosing **File ▶ Import Data...** from the menu bar.

Select the type of file you are importing by choosing from the list of standard data sources. In this example the data file being imported is a comma-separated values (*.csv) file.

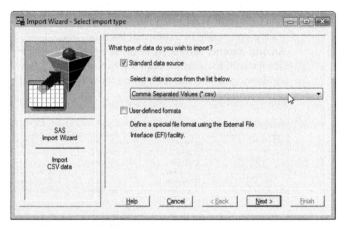

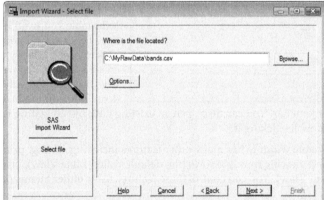

Next, specify the location of the file that you want to import. By default, SAS uses the first row in the file as the variable names for the SAS data set, and starts reading data in the second row. When reading delimited, CSV, or tab-delimited files, clicking the **Options**... button opens the Delimited File Options window.

For delimited files, specify the delimiter in the Delimiter box of the Delimited File Options window. For CSV or tab-delimited files, the delimiter is already determined so that section of the window is grayed out. Also in this window, you can choose to read variable names or not, specify the first row of data, and set the number of data rows used to guess variable types.

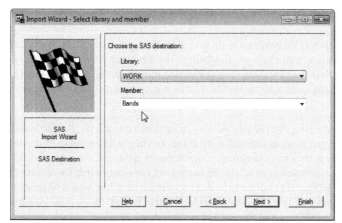

The next screen asks you to choose the SAS library and member name for the SAS data set that will be created. If you choose the WORK library, then the SAS data set will be deleted when you exit SAS. If you choose a different library, then the SAS data set will remain even after you exit SAS. There is no way to define a library from within the Import Wizard, so make sure your library is defined before entering the Import Wizard. You can define libraries using the New Library window discussed in section 1.10 (or using a LIBNAME statement as discussed in section 2.19). After choosing a library, enter a member name for the SAS data set.

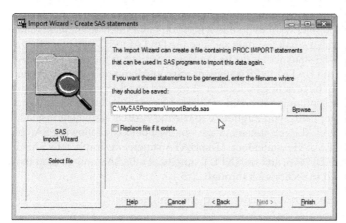

In the last window, the Import Wizard gives you the option of saving the PROC IMPORT statements used for importing the file.

For some types of files, the Import Wizard asks additional questions. For example, if you are importing Microsoft Access files, then you will be asked for the database name and the table you want to import.

Using imported data in a SAS program   Data that you import through the Import Wizard can be used in any SAS program. For example, if you saved your data in the WORK library and named it BANDS, you could print it with this program:

```
PROC PRINT DATA = WORK.bands;
RUN;
```

Or, since WORK is the default library, you could also use:

```
PROC PRINT DATA = bands;
RUN;
```

---

[3] By default the Import Wizard will scan the first 20 rows for delimited files, and the first 8 rows for Microsoft Excel files. If you have all missing data in these rows, or the data are not representative of the entire file, then the Import Wizard (and the IMPORT procedure) may not read the file correctly. See sections 2.16 and 2.17 for more information.

2.4 Telling SAS Where to Find Your Raw Data

If your data are in raw data files (also referred to as text, ASCII, sequential, or flat files), using the DATA step to read the data gives you the most flexibility. The first step toward reading raw data files is telling SAS where to find the raw data. Your raw data may be either internal (also called instream) to your SAS program, or in a separate file. Either way, you must tell SAS where to find your data.

A raw data file can be viewed using simple text editors or system commands. For PC users, raw data files will either have no program associated with them, or they will be associated with simple editors like Microsoft Notepad. In some operating environments, you can use commands to list the file, such as the `cat` or `more` commands in UNIX. Spreadsheet files are examples of data files that are not raw data. If you try using a text editor to look at a spreadsheet file, you will probably see lots of funny special characters you can't find on your keyboard. It may cause your computer to beep and chirp, making you wish you had that private office down the hall. It looks nothing like the nice neat rows and columns you see when you use your spreadsheet software to view the same file.

Internal raw data If you type raw data directly in your SAS program, then the data are internal to your program. You may want to do this when you have small amounts of data, or when you are testing a program with a small test data set. Use the DATALINES statement to indicate internal data. The DATALINES statement must be the last statement in the DATA step. All lines in the SAS program following the DATALINES statement are considered data until SAS encounters a semicolon. The semicolon can be on a line by itself or at the end of a SAS statement which follows the data lines. Any statements following the data are part of a new step. If you are old enough to remember punching computer cards, you might like to use the CARDS statement instead. The CARDS statement and the DATALINES statement are synonymous. The following SAS program illustrates the use of the DATALINES statement. (The DATA statement simply tells SAS to create a SAS data set named USPRESIDENTS, and the INPUT statement tells SAS how to read the data. The INPUT statement is discussed in sections 2.5 through 2.15.)

```
* Read internal data into SAS data set uspresidents;
DATA uspresidents;
   INPUT President $ Party $ Number;
   DATALINES;
Adams F 2
Lincoln R 16
Grant R 18
Kennedy D 35
   ;
RUN;
```

External raw data files Usually you will want to keep data in external files, separating the data from the program. This eliminates the chance that data will accidentally be altered when you are editing your SAS program. Use the INFILE statement to tell SAS the filename and path, if appropriate, of the external file containing the data. The INFILE statement follows the DATA statement and must precede the INPUT statement. After the INFILE keyword, the file path and name are enclosed in quotation marks. Examples from several operating environments follow:

Windows:	INFILE 'c:\MyDir\President.dat';
UNIX:	INFILE '/home/mydir/president.dat';
z/OS:	INFILE 'MYID.PRESIDEN.DAT';

Suppose the following data are in a file called President.dat in the directory MyRawData on the C drive (Windows):

```
Adams F 2
Lincoln R 16
Grant R 18
Kennedy D 35
```

The following program shows the use of the INFILE statement to read the external data file:

```
* Read data from external file into SAS data set;
DATA uspresidents;
   INFILE 'c:\MyRawData\President.dat';
   INPUT President $ Party $ Number;
RUN;
```

The SAS log Whenever you read data from an external file, SAS gives some very valuable information about the file in the SAS log. The following is an excerpt from the SAS log after running the previous program. Always check this information after you read a file as it could indicate problems. A simple comparison of the number of records read from the infile with the number of observations in the SAS data set can tell you a lot about whether SAS is reading your data correctly.

```
NOTE: The infile 'c:\MyRawData\President.dat' is:
      File Name=c:\MyRawData\President.dat,
      RECFM=V,LRECL=256
NOTE: 4 records were read from the infile 'c:\MyRawData\President.dat'.
      The minimum record length was 9.
      The maximum record length was 12.
NOTE: The data set WORK.USPRESIDENTS has 4 observations and 3 variables.
```

Long records In some operating environments, SAS assumes external files have a record length of 256 or less. (The record length is the number of characters, including spaces, in a data line.) If your data lines are long, and it looks like SAS is not reading all your data, then use the LRECL= option in the INFILE statement to specify a record length at least as long as the longest record in your data file.

```
INFILE 'c:\MyRawData\President.dat' LRECL=2000;
```

Check the SAS log to see that the maximum record length is as long as you think it should be.

2.5 ▶ Reading Raw Data Separated by Spaces

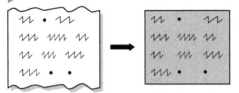 If the values in your raw data file are all separated by at least one space,[4] then using list input (also called free formatted input) to read the data may be appropriate. List input is an easy way to read raw data into SAS, but with ease come a few limitations. You must read all the data in a record—no skipping over unwanted values. Any missing data must be indicated with a period. Character data, if present, must be simple: no embedded spaces, and no values greater than 8 characters in length.[5] If the data file contains dates or other values which need special treatment, then list input may not be appropriate. This may sound like a lot of restrictions, but a surprising number of data files can be read using list input.

The INPUT statement, which is part of the DATA step, tells SAS how to read your raw data. To write an INPUT statement using list input, simply list the variable names after the INPUT keyword in the order they appear in the data file. Generally, variable names must be 32 characters or fewer, start with a letter or an underscore, and contain only letters, underscores, or numerals. If the values are character (not numeric), then place a dollar sign ($) after the variable name. Leave at least one space between names, and remember to place a semicolon at the end of the statement. The following is an example of a simple list style INPUT statement.

```
INPUT Name $ Age Height;
```

This statement tells SAS to read three data values. The $ after Name indicates that it is a character variable, whereas the Age and Height variables are both numeric.

Example   Your hometown has been overrun with toads this year. A local resident, having heard of frog jumping in California, had the idea of organizing a toad jump to cap off the annual town fair. For each contestant you have the toad's name, weight, and the jump distance from three separate attempts. If the toad is disqualified for any jump, then a period is used to indicate missing data. Here is what the data file ToadJump.dat looks like:

```
Lucky 2.3 1.9 . 3.0
Spot 4.6 2.5 3.1 .5
Tubs 7.1 . . 3.8
Hop 4.5 3.2 1.9 2.6
Noisy 3.8 1.3 1.8
1.5
Winner 5.7 . . .
```

This data file does not look very neat, but it does meet all the requirements for list input: the character data are 8 characters or fewer and have no embedded spaces, all values are separated by at least one space, and missing data are indicated by a period. Notice that the data for Noisy have spilled over to the next data line. This is not a problem since, by default SAS will go to the next data line to read more data if there are more variables in the INPUT statement than there are values in the data line.

Here is the SAS program that will read the data:

```
* Create a SAS data set named toads;
* Read the data file ToadJump.dat using list input;
DATA toads;
    INFILE 'c:\MyRawData\ToadJump.dat';
    INPUT ToadName $ Weight Jump1 Jump2 Jump3;
RUN;
* Print the data to make sure the file was read correctly;
PROC PRINT DATA = toads;
    TITLE 'SAS Data Set Toads';
RUN;
```

The variables ToadName, Weight, Jump1, Jump2, and Jump3 are listed after the keyword INPUT in the same order as they appear in the file. A dollar sign ($) after ToadName indicates that it is a character variable; all the other variables are numeric. A PROC PRINT statement is used to print the data values after reading them to make sure they are correct. The PRINT procedure, in its simplest form, prints the values for all variables and all observations in a SAS data set. The TITLE statement after the PROC PRINT tells SAS to put the text enclosed in quotation marks on the top of each page of output. If you had no TITLE statement in your program, SAS would put the words "The SAS System" at the top of each page.

Here are the results of the PRINT procedure. It is important to always check data sets you create to make sure they are correct. You can also use Viewtable (discussed in section 1.11) to view data.

SAS Data Set Toads

Obs	ToadName	Weight	Jump1	Jump2	Jump3
1	Lucky	2.3	1.9	.	3.0
2	Spot	4.6	2.5	3.1	0.5
3	Tubs	7.1	.	.	3.8
4	Hop	4.5	3.2	1.9	2.6
5	Noisy	3.8	1.3	1.8	1.5
6	Winner	5.7	.	.	.

Because SAS had to go to a second data line to get the data for Noisy's final jump, the following note appears in the SAS log:

```
NOTE: SAS went to a new line when INPUT statement reached past the end
       of a line.
```

If you find this note in your SAS log when you didn't expect it, then you may have a problem. If so, look in section 11.4 which discusses this note in more detail.

---

[4] SAS can read files with other delimiters such as commas or tabs using list input. See sections 2.15 and 2.16.

[5] It is possible to override this constraint using the LENGTH statement, discussed in section 11.12, which can change the length of character variables from the default of 8 to anything between 1 and 32,767.

2.6 Reading Raw Data Arranged in Columns

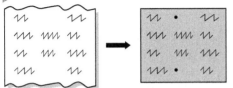

Some raw data files do not have spaces (or other delimiters) between all the values or periods for missing data—so the files can't be read using list input. But if each of the variable's values is always found in the same place in the data line, then you can use column input as long as all the values are character or standard numeric. Standard numeric data contain only numerals, decimal points, plus and minus signs, and E for scientific notation. Numbers with embedded commas or dates, for example, are not standard.

Column input has the following advantages over list input:

♦ spaces are not required between values

♦ missing values can be left blank

♦ character data can have embedded spaces

♦ you can skip unwanted variables

Survey data are good candidates for column input. Answers to survey questionnaires are often coded into single digits (0 through 9). If a space is entered between each value, then the file will be twice the size and require twice the typing of a file without spaces. Data files with street addresses, which often have embedded blanks, are also good candidates for column input. The street Martin Luther King Jr. Boulevard should be read as one variable not five, as it would be with list input. Data which can be read with column input can often also be read with formatted input or a combination of input styles (discussed in sections 2.7, 2.8, and 2.9).

With column input, the INPUT statement takes the following form. After the INPUT keyword, list the first variable's name. If the variable is character, leave a space; then place a $. After the $, or variable name if it is numeric, leave a space; then list the column or range of columns for that variable. The columns are positions of the characters or numbers in the data line and are not to be confused with columns like those you see in a spreadsheet. Repeat this for all the variables you want to read. The following shows a simple INPUT statement using column style:

```
INPUT Name $ 1-10 Age 11-13 Height 14-18;
```

The first variable, Name, is character and the data values are in columns 1 through 10. The Age and Height variables are both numeric, since they are not followed by a $, and data values for both of these variables are in the column ranges listed after their names.

Example The local minor league baseball team, the Walla Walla Sweets, is keeping records about concession sales. A ballpark favorite are the sweet onion rings which are sold at the concession stands and also by vendors in the bleachers. The ballpark owners have a feeling that in games with lots of hits and runs more onion rings are sold in the bleachers than at the concession stands. They think they should send more vendors out into the bleachers when the game heats up, but need more evidence to back up their feelings.

For each home game they have the following information: name of opposing team, number of onion ring sales at the concession stands and in the bleachers, the number of hits for each team, and the final score for each team. The following is a sample of the data file named OnionRing.dat. For your reference, a column ruler showing the column numbers has been placed above the data:

```
----+----1----+----2----+----3----+----4
Columbia Peaches     35  67  1 10  2  1
Plains Peanuts      210      2  5  0  2
Gilroy Garlics      151035 12 11  7  6
Sacramento Tomatoes 124  85 15  4  9  1
```

Notice that the data file has the following characteristics, all making it a prime candidate for column input. All the values line up in columns, the team names have embedded blanks, missing values are blank, and in one case there is not a space between data values. (Those Gilroy Garlics fans must really love onion rings.)

The following program shows how to read these data using column input:

```
* Create a SAS data set named sales;
* Read the data file OnionRing.dat using column input;
DATA sales;
   INFILE 'c:\MyRawData\OnionRing.dat';
   INPUT VisitingTeam $ 1-20 ConcessionSales 21-24 BleacherSales 25-28
         OurHits 29-31 TheirHits 32-34 OurRuns 35-37 TheirRuns 38-40;
RUN;
* Print the data to make sure the file was read correctly;
PROC PRINT DATA = sales;
   TITLE 'SAS Data Set Sales';
RUN;
```

The variable VisitingTeam is character (indicated by a $) and reads the visiting team's name in columns 1 through 20. The variables ConcessionSales and BleacherSales read the concession and bleacher sales in columns 21 through 24 and 25 through 28, respectively. The number of hits for the home team, OurHits, and the visiting team, TheirHits, are read in columns 29 through 31 and 32 through 34, respectively. The number of runs for the home team, OurRuns, is read in columns 35 through 37, while the number of runs for the visiting team, TheirRuns, is read in columns 38 through 40.

Here are the results of the PRINT procedure. You can also use Viewtable to view the data.

SAS Data Set Sales

Obs	VisitingTeam	ConcessionSales	BleacherSales	OurHits	TheirHits	OurRuns	TheirRuns
1	Columbia Peaches	35	67	1	10	2	1
2	Plains Peanuts	210	.	2	5	0	2
3	Gilroy Garlics	15	1035	12	11	7	6
4	Sacramento Tomatoes	124	85	15	4	9	1

2.7 Reading Raw Data Not in Standard Format

01/01/60	1,002
01/03/60	2,012
02/01/60	4,336

➡

0	1002
2	2012
31	4336

Sometimes raw data are not straightforward numeric or character. For example, we humans easily read the number 1,000,001 as one million and one, but your trusty computer sees it as a character string. While the embedded commas make the number easier for us to interpret, they make the number impossible for the computer to recognize without some instructions. In SAS, informats are used to tell the computer how to interpret these types of data.

Informats are useful anytime you have non-standard data. (Standard numeric data contain only numerals, decimal points, plus and minus signs, and E for scientific notation.) Numbers with embedded commas or dollar signs are examples of non-standard data. Other examples include data in hexadecimal or packed decimal formats. SAS has informats for reading these types of data as well.

Dates[6] are perhaps the most common non-standard data. Using date informats, SAS will convert conventional forms of dates like 10-31-2013 or 31OCT13 into a number, the number of days since January 1, 1960. This number is referred to as a SAS date value. (Why January 1, 1960? Who knows? Maybe 1960 was a good year for the SAS founders.) This turns out to be extremely useful when you want to do calculations with dates. For example, you can easily find the number of days between two dates by subtracting one from the other.

There are three general types of informats: character, numeric, and date. A table of selected SAS informats appears in the next section. The three types of informats have the following general forms:

Character	**Numeric**	**Date**
$informatw.	*informatw.d*	*informatw.*

The $ indicates character informats, *informat* is the name of the informat, *w* is the total width, and *d* is the number of decimal places (numeric informats only). The period is a very important part of the informat name. Without a period, SAS may try to interpret the informat as a variable name, which by default, cannot contain any special characters except the underscore. Two informats do not have names: $*w*., which reads standard character data, and *w.d*, which reads standard numeric data.

Use informats by placing the informat after the variable name in the INPUT statement; this is called formatted input. The following INPUT statement is an example of formatted input:

```
INPUT Name $10. Age 3. Height 5.1 BirthDate MMDDYY10.;
```

The columns read for each variable are determined by the starting point and the width of the informat. SAS always starts with the first column; so the data values for the first variable, Name, which has an informat of $10., are in columns 1 through 10. Now the starting point for the second variable is column 11, and SAS reads values for Age in columns 11 through 13. The values for the third variable, Height, are in columns 14 through 18. The five columns include the decimal place and the decimal point itself (150.3 for example). The values for the last variable, BirthDate, start in column 19 and are in a date form.

Example This example illustrates the use of informats for reading data. The following data file, Pumpkin.dat, represents the results from a local pumpkin-carving contest. Each line includes the contestant's name, age, type (carved or decorated), the date the pumpkin was entered, and the scores from each of five judges.

```
Alicia Grossman   13 c 10-28-2012 7.8 6.5 7.2 8.0 7.9
Matthew Lee        9 D 10-30-2012 6.5 5.9 6.8 6.0 8.1
Elizabeth Garcia  10 C 10-29-2012 8.9 7.9 8.5 9.0 8.8
Lori Newcombe      6 D 10-30-2012 6.7 5.6 4.9 5.2 6.1
Jose Martinez      7 d 10-31-2012 8.9 9.510.0 9.7 9.0
Brian Williams    11 C 10-29-2012 7.8 8.4 8.5 7.9 8.0
```

The following program reads these data. Please note there are many ways to input these data, so if you imagined something else, that's OK.

```
* Create a SAS data set named contest;
* Read the file Pumpkin.dat using formatted input;
DATA contest;
   INFILE 'c:\MyRawData\Pumpkin.dat';
   INPUT Name $16. Age 3. +1 Type $1. +1 Date MMDDYY10.
      (Score1 Score2 Score3 Score4 Score5) (4.1);
RUN;
* Print the data set to make sure the file was read correctly;
PROC PRINT DATA = contest;
   TITLE 'Pumpkin Carving Contest';
RUN;
```

The variable Name has an informat of $16., meaning that it is a character variable 16 columns wide. Variable Age has an informat of 3, is numeric, three columns wide, and has no decimal places. The +1 skips over one column. Variable Type is character, and it is one column wide. Variable Date has an informat MMDDYY10. and reads dates in the form 10-31-2013 or 10/31/2013, each 10 columns wide. The remaining variables, Score1 through Score5, all require the same informat, 4.1. By putting the variables and the informat in separate sets of parentheses, you only have to list the informat once.

Here are the results of the PRINT procedure. You can also use Viewtable to view the data.

Pumpkin Carving Contest

Obs	Name	Age	Type	Date[7]	Score1	Score2	Score3	Score4	Score5
1	Alicia Grossman	13	c	19294	7.8	6.5	7.2	8.0	7.9
2	Matthew Lee	9	D	19296	6.5	5.9	6.8	6.0	8.1
3	Elizabeth Garcia	10	C	19295	8.9	7.9	8.5	9.0	8.8
4	Lori Newcombe	6	D	19296	6.7	5.6	4.9	5.2	6.1
5	Jose Martinez	7	d	19297	8.9	9.5	10.0	9.7	9.0
6	Brian Williams	11	C	19295	7.8	8.4	8.5	7.9	8.0

---

[6] Using dates in SAS is discussed in more detail in section 3.8.

[7] Notice that these dates are printed as the number of days since January 1, 1960. Section 4.6 discusses how to format these values into readable dates.

2.8 Selected Informats

Informat	Definition	Width range	Default width
Character			
$CHAR*w*.	Reads character data—does not trim leading or trailing blanks	1-32,767	8 or length of variable
$UPCASE*w*.	Converts character data to uppercase	1-32,767	8
$*w*.	Reads character data—trims leading blanks	1-32,767	none
Date, Time, and Datetime[8]			
ANYDTDTE*w*.	Reads dates in various date forms	5-32	9
DATE*w*.	Reads dates in form: *ddmmmyy* or *ddmmmyyyy*	7-32	7
DATETIME*w*.	Reads datetime values in the form: *ddmmmyy hh:mm:ss.ss*	13-40	18
DDMMYY*w*.	Reads dates in form: *ddmmyy* or *ddmmyyyy*	6-32	6
JULIAN*w*.	Reads Julian dates in form: *yyddd* or *yyyyddd*	5-32	5
MMDDYY*w*.	Reads dates in form: *mmddyy* or *mmddyyyy*	6-32	6
STIMER*w*.	Reads time in form: *hh:mm:ss.ss* (or *mm:ss.ss,* or *ss.ss*)	1-32	10
TIME*w*.	Reads time in form: *hh:mm:ss.ss* (or *hh:mm*)	5-32	8
Numeric			
COMMA*w.d*	Removes embedded commas and $, converts left parentheses to minus sign	1-32	1
COMMAX*w.d*	Like COMMA*w.d* but reverses role of comma and period	1-32	1
PERCENT*w*.	Converts percentages to numbers	1-32	6
w.d	Reads standard numeric data	1-32	none

Informat	Input data	INPUT statement	Results
Character			

$CHAR*w*.	my cat
	    my cat
		INPUT Animal $CHAR10.;	my cat
			    my cat

$UPCASE*w*.	my cat	INPUT Name $UPCASE10.;	MY CAT
$*w*.	my cat my cat	INPUT Animal $10.;	my cat my cat
Date, Time, and Datetime			
ANYDTDTE*w*.	1jan1961 01/01/61	INPUT Day ANYDTDTE10.;	366 366
DATE*w*.	1jan1961 1 jan 61	INPUT Day DATE10.;	366 366
DATETIME*w*.	1jan1960 10:30:15 1jan1961,10:30:15	INPUT Dt DATETIME18.;	37815 31660215
DDMMYY*w*.	01.01.61 02/01/61	INPUT Day DDMMYY8.;	366 367
JULIAN*w*.	61001 1961001	INPUT Day JULIAN7.;	366 366
MMDDYY*w*.	01-01-61 01/01/61	INPUT Day MMDDYY8.;	366 366
STIMER*w*.	10:30 10:30:15	INPUT Time STIMER8.;	630 37815
TIME*w*.	10:30 10:30:15	INPUT Time TIME8.;	37800 37815
Numeric			
COMMA*w.d*	$1,000,001 (1,234)	INPUT Income COMMA10.;	1000001 -1234
COMMAX*w.d*	$1.000.001 (1.234,25)	INPUT Value COMMAX10.;	1000001 -1234.25
PERCENT*w*.	5% (20%)	INPUT Value PERCENT5.;	0.05 -0.2
w.d	1234 -12.3	INPUT Value 5.1;	123.4 -12.3

---

[8] SAS date values are the number of days since January 1, 1960. Time values are the number of seconds past midnight, and datetime values are the number of seconds past midnight January 1, 1960.

2.9 Mixing Input Styles

Each of the three major input styles has its own advantages. List style is the easiest; column style is a bit more work; and formatted style is the hardest of the three. However, column and formatted styles do not require spaces (or other delimiters) between variables and can read embedded blanks. Formatted style can read special data such as dates. Sometimes you use one style, sometimes another, and sometimes the easiest way is to use a combination of styles. SAS is so flexible that you can mix and match any of the input styles for your own convenience.

Example   The following raw data contain information about U.S. national parks: name, state (or states as the case may be), year established, and size in acres:

```
Yellowstone             ID/MT/WY 1872      4,065,493
Everglades              FL 1934            1,398,800
Yosemite                CA 1864              760,917
Great Smoky Mountains NC/TN 1926            520,269
Wolf Trap Farm          VA 1966                  130
```

You could write the INPUT statement for these data in many ways—that is the point of this section. The following program shows one way to do it:

```
* Create a SAS data set named nationalparks;
* Read a data file NatPark.dat mixing input styles;
DATA nationalparks;
   INFILE 'c:\MyRawData\NatPark.dat';
   INPUT ParkName $ 1-22 State $ Year @40 Acreage COMMA9.;
RUN;
PROC PRINT DATA = nationalparks;
   TITLE 'Selected National Parks';
RUN;
```

Notice that the variable ParkName is read with column style input, State and Year are read with list style input, and Acreage is read with formatted style input. Here is the result of the PRINT procedure. You can also use Viewtable to view the data.

Selected National Parks

Obs	ParkName	State	Year	Acreage
1	Yellowstone	ID/MT/WY	1872	4065493
2	Everglades	FL	1934	1398800
3	Yosemite	CA	1864	760917
4	Great Smoky Mountains	NC/TN	1926	520269
5	Wolf Trap Farm	VA	1966	130

Sometimes programmers run into problems when they mix input styles. When SAS reads a line of raw data it uses a pointer to mark its place, but each style of input uses the pointer a little differently. With list style input, SAS automatically scans to the next non-blank field and starts reading. With column style input, SAS starts reading in the exact column you specify. But with formatted input, SAS just starts reading—wherever the pointer is, that is where SAS reads.

Sometimes you need to move the pointer explicitly, and you can do that by using the column pointer, @*n*, where *n* is the number of the column SAS should move to.

In the preceding program, the column pointer @40 tells SAS to move to column 40 before reading the value for Acreage. If you removed the column pointer from the INPUT statement, as shown in the following statement, then SAS would start reading Acreage right after Year:

```
INPUT ParkName $ 1-22 State $ Year Acreage COMMA9.;
```

The resulting output would look like this:

Selected National Parks

Obs	ParkName	State	Year	Acreage
1	Yellowstone	ID/MT/WY	1872	4065
2	Everglades	FL	1934	.
3	Yosemite	CA	1864	.
4	Great Smoky Mountains	NC/TN	1926	5
5	Wolf Trap Farm	VA	1966	.

Because Acreage was read with formatted input, SAS started reading right where the pointer was. Here is the data file with a column ruler for counting columns at the top and asterisks marking the place where SAS started reading the values of Acreage:

```
----+----1----+----2----+----3----+----4----+----5
Yellowstone          ID/MT/WY 1872 *   4,065,493
Everglades           FL 1934 *         1,398,800
Yosemite             CA 1864 *           760,917
Great Smoky Mountains NC/TN 1926 *       520,269
Wolf Trap Farm       VA 1966 *               130
```

The COMMA9. informat told SAS to read nine columns, and SAS did that even when those columns were completely blank.

The column pointer, @*n*, has other uses, too, and can be used anytime you want SAS to skip backwards or forwards within a data line. You could use it, for example, to skip over unneeded data, or to read a variable twice using different informats.

2.10 Reading Messy Raw Data

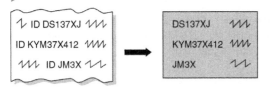

Sometimes you need to read data that just don't line up in nice columns or have predictable lengths. When you have these types of messy files, ordinary list, column, or formatted input simply aren't enough. You need more tools in your bag: tools like the @'*character*' column pointer and the colon modifier.

The @'*character*' column pointer In section 2.9 we showed you how you can use the @ column pointer to move to a particular column before reading data. However, sometimes you don't know the starting column of the data, but you do know that it always comes after a particular character or word. For these types of situations, you can use the @'*character*' column pointer. For example, suppose you have a data file that has information about dog ownership. Nothing in the file lines up, but you know that the breed of the dog always follows the word Breed:. You could read the dog's breed using the following INPUT statement:

```
INPUT @'Breed:' DogBreed $;
```

The colon modifier The above INPUT statement will work just fine as long as the dog's breed name is 8 characters or less (the default length for a character variable). So if the dog is a Shepherd you're fine, but if the dog is a Rottweiler, all you will get is Rottweil. If you assign the variable an informat in the INPUT statement such as $20. to tell SAS that the variable's field is 20 characters, then SAS will read for 20 columns whether or not there is a space in those columns.[9] So the DogBreed variable may include unwanted characters which appear after the dog's breed on the data line. If you only want SAS to read until it encounters a space or the end of the data line,[10] then you can use a colon modifier on the informat. To use a colon modifier, simply put a colon (:) before the informat (such as :$20. instead of $20.).

For example, given this line of raw data,

```
My dog Sam  Breed: Rottweiler  Vet Bills: $478
```

the following table shows the results you would get using different INPUT statements:

Statements	Value of variable DogBreed
`INPUT @'Breed: ' DogBreed $;`	Rottweil
`INPUT @'Breed: ' DogBreed $20.;`	Rottweiler Vet Bill
`INPUT @'Breed: ' DogBreed :$20.;`	Rottweiler

Example Each year engineering students from around the USA and Canada build concrete canoes and hold regional and national competitions. Part of the competition involves racing the canoes. The following data contain the final results of a men's sprint competition. The data lines start with the name of the canoe, followed by the school, and the time.

```
Bellatorum   School: CSULA Time: 1:40.5
The Kraken   School: ASU Time: 1:45.35
Black Widow  School: UoA Time: 1:33.7
Koicrete  School: CSUF Time: 1:40.25
Khaos  School: UNLV  Time: 2:03.45
Max  School: UCSD Time: 1:26.47
Hakuna Matata  School: UCLA Time: 1:20.64
Prospector  School: CPSLO Time: 1:12.08
Andromeda  School: CPP  Time: 1:25.1
Kekoapohaku  School: UHM Time: 1:24.49
```

You can see that because the canoe names are not always the same number of characters, the school names do not line up in the same column. Also, the time values are sometimes six characters and sometimes seven. This SAS program reads just the school name, and the time:

```
DATA canoeresults;
   INFILE 'c:\MyRawData\Canoes.dat';
   INPUT @'School:' School $ @'Time:' RaceTime :STIMER8.;
RUN;
PROC PRINT DATA = canoeresults;
   TITLE "Concrete Canoe Men's Sprint Results";
RUN;
```

This INPUT statement uses @'School:' and @'Time:' to position the column pointer to read the school name and time. Because the time is not always the same number of characters, an informat with a colon modifier, :STIMER8., is used to read the time. Without the colon modifier, SAS would go to a new data line to try to read the time values when it ran out of characters on the data line.

Here are the results of the PRINT procedure. You can also use Viewtable to view the data.

Concrete Canoe Men's Sprint Results

Obs	School	RaceTime[11]
1	CSULA	100.50
2	ASU	105.35
3	UoA	93.70
4	CSUF	100.25
5	UNLV	123.45
6	UCSD	86.47
7	UCLA	80.64
8	CPSLO	72.08
9	CPP	85.10
10	UHM	84.49

---

[9] It is also possible to define a variable's length in a LENGTH or INFORMAT statement instead of in an INPUT statement. When a variable's length is defined before the INPUT statement, then SAS will read until it encounters a space or reaches the length of the variable—the same behavior as using the colon modifier. The INFORMAT statement is covered in section 2.21 and the LENGTH statement is covered in section 11.12.

[10] A space is the default delimiter. This method works for files with other delimiters as well. See sections 2.15 and 2.16 for more information on reading delimited data.

[11] Notice that the times are printed in seconds. Section 4.6 discusses how to format these values into minutes and seconds.

2.11 Reading Multiple Lines of Raw Data per Observation

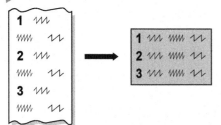

In a typical raw data file each line of data represents one observation, but sometimes the data for each observation are spread over more than one line. Since SAS will automatically go to the next line if it runs out of data before it has read all the variables in an INPUT statement, you could just let SAS take care of figuring out when to go to a new line. But if you know that your data file has multiple lines of raw data per observation, it is better for you to explicitly tell SAS when to go to the next line than to make SAS figure it out. That way you won't get that suspicious SAS-went-to-a-new-line note in your log. To tell SAS when to skip to a new line, you simply add line pointers to your INPUT statement.

The line pointers, slash (/) and pound-*n* (#*n*), are like road signs telling SAS, "Go this way." To read more than one line of raw data for a single observation, you simply insert a slash into your INPUT statement when you want to skip to the next line of raw data. The #*n* line pointer performs the same action except that you specify the line number. The *n* in #*n* stands for the number of the line of raw data for that observation; so #2 means to go to the second line for that observation, and #4 means go to the fourth line. You can even go backwards using the #*n* line pointer, reading from line 4 and then from line 3, for example. The slash is simpler, but #*n* is more flexible.

Example A colleague is trying to plan his next summer vacation, but he wants to go someplace where the weather is just right. He obtains data from a meteorology database. Unfortunately, he has not quite figured out how to export from this database and makes a rather odd file.

The file contains information about temperatures for the month of July for Alaska, Florida, and North Carolina. (If your colleague chooses the last state, maybe he can visit SAS headquarters.) The first line contains the city and state, the second line lists the normal high temperature and normal low (in degrees Fahrenheit), and the third line contains the record high and low:

```
Nome AK
55 44
88 29
Miami FL
90 75
97 65
Raleigh NC
88 68
105 50
```

The following program reads the weather data from a file named Temperature.dat:

```
* Create a SAS data set named highlow;
* Read the data file using line pointers;
DATA highlow;
    INFILE 'c:\MyRawData\Temperature.dat';
    INPUT City $ State $
          / NormalHigh NormalLow
          #3 RecordHigh RecordLow;
RUN;
PROC PRINT DATA = highlow;
    TITLE 'High and Low Temperatures for July';
RUN;
```

The INPUT statement reads the values for City and State from the first line of data. Then the slash tells SAS to move to column 1 of the next line of data before reading NormalHigh and NormalLow. Likewise, the #3 tells SAS to move to column 1 of the third line of data for that observation before reading RecordHigh and RecordLow. As usual, there is more than one way to write this INPUT statement. You could replace the slash with #2 or replace #3 with a slash.

These notes appear in the log:

```
NOTE: 9 records were read from the infile 'c:\MyRawData\Temperature.dat'.
      The minimum record length was 5.
      The maximum record length was 10.

NOTE: The data set WORK.HIGHLOW has 3 observations and 6 variables.
```

Notice that while nine records were read from the infile, the SAS data set contains just three observations. Usually this would set off alarms in your mind, but here it confirms that indeed three data lines were read for every observation just as planned. You should always check your log, particularly when using line pointers.

Here are the results of the PRINT procedure. You can also view the data using Viewtable.

High and Low Temperatures for July

Obs	City	State	NormalHigh	NormalLow	RecordHigh	RecordLow
1	Nome	AK	55	44	88	29
2	Miami	FL	90	75	97	65
3	Raleigh	NC	88	68	105	50

2.12 Reading Multiple Observations per Line of Raw Data

  There ought to be a Murphy's law of data: whatever form data can take, it will. Normally SAS assumes that each line of raw data represents no more than one observation. When you have multiple observations per line of raw data, you can use double trailing at signs (@@) at the end of your INPUT statement. This line-hold specifier is like a stop sign telling SAS, "Stop, hold that line of raw data." SAS will hold that line of data, continuing to read observations until it either runs out of data or reaches an INPUT statement that does not end with a double trailing @.

Example Suppose you have a colleague who is planning a vacation and has obtained a file containing data about rainfall (in inches) for the three cities he is considering. The file contains the name of each city, the state, average rainfall for the month of July, and average number of days with measurable precipitation in July. The raw data look like this:

```
Nome AK 2.5 15 Miami FL 6.75
18 Raleigh NC . 12
```

Notice that in this data file the first line stops in the middle of the second observation. The following program reads these data from a file named Precipitation.dat and uses an @@ so SAS does not automatically go to a new line of raw data for each observation:

```
* Input more than one observation from each record;
DATA rainfall;
   INFILE 'c:\MyRawData\Precipitation.dat';
   INPUT City $ State $ NormalRain MeanDaysRain @@;
RUN;
PROC PRINT DATA = rainfall;
   TITLE 'Normal Total Precipitation and';
   TITLE2 'Mean Days with Precipitation for July';
RUN;
```

These notes will appear in the log:

```
NOTE: 2 records were read from the infile 'c:\MyRawData\Precipitation.dat'
      The minimum record length was 18.
      The maximum record length was 28.
NOTE: SAS went to a new line when INPUT statement reached past the
      end of a line.
NOTE: The data set WORK.RAINFALL has 3 observations and
      4 variables.
```

While only two records were read from the raw data file, the RAINFALL data set contains three observations. The log also includes a note saying SAS went to a new line when the INPUT statement reached past the end of a line. This means that SAS came to the end of a line in the middle of an observation and continued reading with the next line of raw data. Normally these messages would indicate a problem, but in this case they are exactly what you want.

Here are the results of the PRINT procedure. You can also use Viewtable to view the data.

Normal Total Precipitation and
Mean Days with Precipitation for July

Obs	City	State	NormalRain	MeanDaysRain
1	Nome	AK	2.50	15
2	Miami	FL	6.75	18
3	Raleigh	NC	.	12

2.13 Reading Part of a Raw Data File

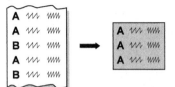

At some time you may find that you need to read a small fraction of the records in a large data file. For example, you might be reading U.S. census data and want only female heads-of-household who have incomes above $225,000 and live in Walla Walla, Washington. You could read all the records in the data file and then throw out the unneeded ones, but that would waste time.

Luckily, you don't have to read all the data before you tell SAS whether to keep an observation. Instead, you can read just enough variables to decide whether to keep the current observation, then end the INPUT statement with an at sign (@), called a trailing at. This tells SAS to hold that line of raw data. While the trailing @ holds that line, you can test the observation with an IF statement to see if it's one you want to keep. If it is, then you can read data for the remaining variables with a second INPUT statement. Without the trailing @, SAS would automatically start reading the next line of raw data with each INPUT statement.

The trailing @ is similar to the column pointer, @*n*, introduced in section 2.9. By specifying a number after the @ sign, you tell SAS to move to a particular column. By using an @ without specifying a column, it is as if you are telling SAS, "Stay tuned for more information. Don't touch that dial!" SAS will hold that line of data until it reaches either the end of the DATA step, or an INPUT statement that does not end with a trailing @.

Example You want to read part of a raw data file containing local traffic data for freeways and surface streets. The data include information about the type of street, name of street, the average number of vehicles per hour traveling that street during the morning, and the average number of vehicles per hour for the evening. Here are the raw data:

```
freeway 408                           3684 3459
surface Martin Luther King Jr. Blvd.  1590 1234
surface Broadway                      1259 1290
surface Rodeo Dr.                     1890 2067
freeway 608                           4583 3860
freeway 808                           2386 2518
surface Lake Shore Dr.                1590 1234
surface Pennsylvania Ave.             1259 1290
```

Suppose you want to see only the freeway data at this point so you read the raw data file, Traffic.dat, with this program:

```
* Use a trailing @, then delete surface streets;
DATA freeways;
   INFILE 'c:\MyRawData\Traffic.dat';
   INPUT Type $ @;
   IF Type = 'surface' THEN DELETE;
   INPUT Name $ 9-38 AMTraffic PMTraffic;
RUN;
PROC PRINT DATA = freeways;
   TITLE 'Traffic for Freeways';
RUN;
```

Notice that there are two INPUT statements. The first reads the character variable Type and then ends with an @. The trailing @ holds each line of data while the IF statement tests it. The second INPUT statement reads Name (in columns 9 through 38), AMTraffic, and PMTraffic. If an observation has a value of surface for the variable Type, then the second INPUT statement never executes. Instead SAS returns to the beginning of the DATA step to process the next observation and does not add the unwanted observation to the FREEWAYS data set. (Do not pass go, do not collect $200.)

When you run this program, the log will contain the following two notes, one saying that eight records were read from the input file and another saying that the new data set contains only three observations:

```
NOTE: 8 records were read from the infile 'c:\MyRawData\Traffic.dat'.
      The minimum record length was 47.
      The maximum record length was 47.
NOTE: The data set WORK.FREEWAYS has 3 observations and 4 variables.
```

The other five observations had a value of surface for the variable Type and were deleted by the IF statement. Here is the result of the PRINT procedure. You can also view the data in Viewtable.

Traffic for Freeways

Obs	Type	Name	AMTraffic	PMTraffic
1	freeway	408	3684	3459
2	freeway	608	4583	3860
3	freeway	808	2386	2518

Trailing @ versus double trailing @ The double trailing @, discussed in the previous section, is similar to the trailing @. Both are line-hold specifiers; the difference is how long they hold a line of data for input. The trailing @ holds a line of data for subsequent INPUT statements, but releases that line of data when SAS returns to the top of the DATA step to begin building the next observation. The double trailing @ holds a line of data for subsequent INPUT statements even when SAS starts building a new observation. In both cases, the line of data is released if SAS reaches a subsequent INPUT statement that does not contain a line-hold specifier.

2.14   Controlling Input with Options in the INFILE Statement

So far in this chapter, we have seen ways to use the INPUT statement to read many different types of raw data. When reading raw data files, SAS makes certain assumptions. For example, SAS starts reading with the first data line and, if SAS runs out of data on a line, it automatically goes to the next line to read values for the rest of the variables. Most of the time this is OK, but some data files can't be read using the default assumptions. The options in the INFILE statement change the way SAS reads raw data files. The following options are useful for reading particular types of data files. Place these options after the filename in the INFILE statement.

FIRSTOBS=   The FIRSTOBS= option tells SAS at what line to begin reading data. This is useful if you have a data file that contains descriptive text or header information at the beginning, and you want to skip over these lines to begin reading the data. The following data file, for example, has a description of the data in the first two lines:

```
Ice-cream sales data for the summer
Flavor      Location    Boxes sold
Chocolate   213         123
Vanilla     213         512
Chocolate   415         242
```

The following program uses the FIRSTOBS= option to tell SAS to start reading data on the third line of the file:

```
DATA icecream;
   INFILE 'c:\MyRawData\IceCreamSales.dat' FIRSTOBS = 3;
   INPUT Flavor $ 1-9 Location BoxesSold;
RUN;
```

OBS=   The OBS= option can be used anytime you want to read only a part of your data file. It tells SAS to stop reading when it gets to that line in the raw data file. Note that it does not necessarily correspond to the number of observations. If, for example, you are reading two raw data lines for each observation, then an OBS=100 would read 100 data lines, and the resulting SAS data set would have 50 observations. The OBS= option can be used with the FIRSTOBS= option to read lines from the middle of the file. For example, suppose the ice-cream sales data had a remark at the end of the file that was not part of the data.

```
Ice-cream sales data for the summer
Flavor      Location    Boxes sold
Chocolate   213         123
Vanilla     213         512
Chocolate   415         242
Data verified by Blake White
```

With FIRSTOBS=3 and OBS=5, SAS will start reading this file on the third data line and stop reading after the fifth data line.

```
DATA icecream;
   INFILE 'c:\MyRawData\IceCreamSales2.dat' FIRSTOBS = 3 OBS=5;
   INPUT Flavor $ 1-9 Location BoxesSold;
RUN;
```

MISSOVER By default, SAS will go to the next data line to read more data if SAS has reached the end of the data line and there are still more variables in the INPUT statement that have not been assigned values. The MISSOVER option tells SAS that if it runs out of data, don't go to the next data line. Instead, assign missing values to any remaining variables. The following data file illustrates where this option may be useful. This file contains test scores for a self-paced course. Since not all students complete all the tests, some have more scores than others.

```
Nguyen    89 76 91 82
Ramos     67 72 80 76 86
Robbins   76 65 79
```

The following program reads the data for the five test scores, assigning missing values to tests not completed:

```
DATA class102;
   INFILE 'c:\MyRawData\AllScores.dat' MISSOVER;
   INPUT Name $ Test1 Test2 Test3 Test4 Test5;
RUN;
```

TRUNCOVER You need the TRUNCOVER option when you are reading data using column or formatted input and some data lines are shorter than others. If a variable's field extends past the end of the data line, then, by default, SAS will go to the next line to start reading the variable's value. This option tells SAS to read data for the variable until it reaches the end of the data line, or the last column specified in the format or column range, whichever comes first. The next file contains addresses and must be read using column or formatted input because the street names have embedded blanks. Note that the data lines are all different lengths:

```
John Garcia      114  Maple Ave.
Sylvia Chung    1302  Washington Drive
Martha Newton     45  S.E. 14th St.
```

This program uses column input to read the address file. Because some of the addresses stop before the end of the variable Street's field (columns 22 through 37), you need the TRUNCOVER option. Without the TRUNCOVER option, SAS would try to go to the next line to read the data for Street on the first and third records.

```
DATA homeaddress;
   INFILE 'c:\MyRawData\Address.dat' TRUNCOVER;
   INPUT Name $ 1-15 Number 16-19 Street $ 22-37;
RUN;
```

TRUNCOVER is similar to MISSOVER. Both will assign missing values to variables if the data line ends before the variable's field starts. But when the data line ends in the middle of a variable field, TRUNCOVER will take as much as is there, whereas MISSOVER will assign the variable a missing value.

2.15   Reading Delimited Files with the DATA Step

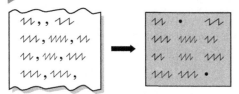

Delimited files are raw data files that have a special character separating data values. Many programs can save data as delimited files, often with commas or tab characters for delimiters. SAS gives you two options for the INFILE statement that make it easy to read delimited data files: the DLM= option and the DSD option.

The DLM= option   If you read your data using list input, the DATA step expects your file to have spaces between your data values. The DELIMITER=, or DLM=, option in the INFILE statement allows you to read data files with other delimiters. The comma and tab characters are common delimiters found in data files, but you could read data files with any delimiter character by just enclosing the delimiter character in quotation marks after the DLM= option (for example, DLM='&'). If your delimiter is a string of characters, then use the DLMSTR= option.

Example   The following file is comma-delimited where students' names are followed by the number of books they read for each week in a summer reading program:

```
Grace,3,1,5,2,6
Martin,1,2,4,1,3
Scott,9,10,4,8,6
```

This program uses list input to read the books data file specifying the comma as the delimiter:

```
DATA reading;
   INFILE 'c:\MyRawData\Books.dat' DLM = ',';
   INPUT Name $ Week1 Week2 Week3 Week4 Week5;
RUN;
```

If the same data had tab characters between values instead of commas, then you could use the following program to read the file. This program uses the DLM='09'X option. In ASCII, 09 is the hexadecimal equivalent of a tab character, and the notation '09'X means a hexadecimal 09. If your computer uses EBCDIC (IBM mainframes) instead of ASCII, then use DLM='05'X.

```
DATA reading;
   INFILE 'c:\MyRawData\Books.txt' DLM = '09'X;
   INPUT Name $ Week1 Week2 Week3 Week4 Week5;
RUN;
```

By default, SAS interprets two or more delimiters in a row as a single delimiter. If your file has missing values, and two delimiters in a row indicate a missing value, then you will also need the DSD option in the INFILE statement.

The DSD option   The DSD (Delimiter-Sensitive Data) option for the INFILE statement does three things for you. First, it ignores delimiters in data values enclosed in quotation marks. Second, it does not read quotation marks as part of the data value. Third, it treats two delimiters in a row as a missing value. The DSD option assumes that the delimiter is a comma. If your delimiter is not a comma, then you can use the DLM= option with the DSD option to specify the delimiter. For example, to read a tab-delimited ASCII file with missing values indicated by two consecutive tab characters use

```
INFILE 'file-specification' DLM = '09'X DSD;
```

CSV files Comma-separated values files, or CSV files, are a common type of file that can be read with the DSD option. Many programs, such as Microsoft Excel, can save data in CSV format. These files have commas for delimiters and consecutive commas for missing values; if there are commas in any of the data values, then those values are enclosed in quotation marks.

Example The following example illustrates how to read a CSV file using the DSD option. Jerry's Coffee Shop employs local bands to attract customers. Jerry keeps records of the number of customers for each band, for each night they play in his shop. The band's name is followed by the date and the number of customers present at 8 p.m., 9 p.m., 10 p.m., and 11 p.m.

```
Lupine Lights,12/3/2012,45,63,70,
Awesome Octaves,12/15/2012,17,28,44,12
"Stop, Drop, and Rock-N-Roll",1/5/2013,34,62,77,91
The Silveyville Jazz Quartet,1/18/2013,38,30,42,43
Catalina Converts,1/31/2013,56,,65,34
```

Notice that one group's name has embedded commas, and is enclosed in quotation marks. Also, the last group has a missing data point for the 9 p.m. hour as indicated by two consecutive commas. Use the DSD option in the INFILE statement to read this data file. It is also prudent, when using the DSD option, to add the MISSOVER option if there is any chance that you have missing data at the end of your data lines (as in the first line of this data file). The MISSOVER option tells SAS that if it runs out of data, don't go to the next data line to continue reading. Here is the program that will read this data file:

```
DATA music;
   INFILE 'c:\MyRawData\Bands.csv' DLM = ',' DSD MISSOVER;
   INPUT BandName :$30. GigDate :MMDDYY10. EightPM NinePM TenPM ElevenPM;
RUN;
PROC PRINT DATA = music;
   TITLE 'Customers at Each Gig';
RUN;
```

Notice that for BandName and GigDate we use colon modified informats. The colon modifier tells SAS to read for the length of the informat (30 for BandName and 10 for GigDate), or until it encounters a delimiter, whichever comes first. Because the names of the bands are longer than the default length of 8 characters, we use the :$30. informat for BandName to read up to 30 characters.

Here are the results of the PROC PRINT. You can also view the data in the Viewtable window.

Customers at Each Gig

Obs	BandName	GigDate[12]	EightPM	NinePM	TenPM	ElevenPM
1	Lupine Lights	19330	45	63	70	.
2	Awesome Octaves	19342	17	28	44	12
3	Stop, Drop, and Rock-N-Roll	19363	34	62	77	91
4	The Silveyville Jazz Quartet	19376	38	30	42	43
5	Catalina Converts	19389	56	.	65	34

---

[12] Notice that these dates are printed as the number of days since January 1, 1960. Section 4.6 discusses how to format these values into readable dates.

2.16 Reading Delimited Files with the IMPORT Procedure

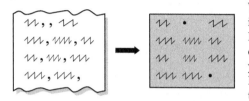

We suspect that by now you have realized that with SAS there is usually more than one way to accomplish the same result. In the previous section we showed you how to read delimited data files using the DATA step; now we are going to show you how to read delimited files a different way: using the IMPORT procedure. The IMPORT procedure is available in the UNIX and Windows operating environments.

There are a few things that PROC IMPORT does for you that make it easy to read certain types of data files. PROC IMPORT will scan your data file (the first 20 rows by default) and automatically determine the variable types (character or numeric), will assign lengths to the character variables, and can recognize some date formats. PROC IMPORT will treat two consecutive delimiters in your data file as a missing value, will read values enclosed by quotation marks, and assign missing values to variables when it runs out of data on a line. Also, if you want, you can use the first line in your data file for the variable names.

The general form of the IMPORT procedure is

```
PROC IMPORT DATAFILE = 'filename' OUT = data-set;
```

where *filename* is the file you want to read and *data-set* is the name of the SAS data set you want to create. SAS will determine the file type by the extension of the file as shown in the following table.

Type of File	Extension	DBMS Identifier
Comma-delimited	.csv	CSV
Tab-delimited	.txt	TAB
Delimiters other than commas or tabs		DLM

If your file does not have the proper extension, or your file is of type DLM, then you must use the DBMS= option in the PROC IMPORT statement. Use the REPLACE option if you already have a SAS data set with the name you specified in the OUT= option, and you want to overwrite it. Here is the general form of PROC IMPORT with both the REPLACE and the DBMS options:

```
PROC IMPORT DATAFILE = 'filename' OUT = data-set
    DBMS = identifier REPLACE;
```

Optional statements Some types of files need a few more instructions to be read correctly. If the data do not start in the first line of the file, use the DATAROWS statement. If the delimiter is not a comma, tab, or space, use the DELIMITER statement. If your file contains only data and no headings, use the GETNAMES=NO statement to assign default variable names. Lastly, if your data file has all missing values or non-representative data in the first 20 data rows, you may need the GUESSINGROWS statement to make sure variables are assigned the correct data type and length.

`DATAROWS = n;`	start reading data in row *n*. Default is 1.
`DELIMITER = 'delimiter-character';`	delimiter for DLM files. Default is space.
`GETNAMES = NO;`	do not get variable names from the first line of input file. Default is YES. If NO, then variables are named VAR1, VAR2, VAR3, and so on.
`GUESSINGROWS = n;`	use *n* rows to determine variable types. Default is 20.

The following shows the general form of PROC IMPORT with the GETNAMES=NO statement:

```
PROC IMPORT DATAFILE = 'filename' OUT = data-set;
   GETNAMES = NO;
```

Example The following example uses data about Jerry's Coffee Shop where Jerry employs local bands to attract customers. Jerry keeps records of the number of customers present throughout the evening for each band. The data are the band name, followed by the gig date, and the number of customers present at 8 p.m., 9 p.m., 10 p.m., and 11 p.m. Notice that one of the bands, "Stop, Drop, and Rock-N-Roll," has commas in the name of the band. When a data value contains the delimiter, then the value must be enclosed in quotation marks.

```
Band Name,Gig Date,Eight PM,Nine PM,Ten PM,Eleven PM
Lupine Lights,12/3/2012,45,63,70,
Awesome Octaves,12/15/2012,17,28,44,12
"Stop, Drop, and Rock-N-Roll",1/5/2013,34,62,77,91
The Silveyville Jazz Quartet,1/18/2013,38,30,42,43
Catalina Converts,1/31/2013,56,,65,34
```

Here is the program that will read this data file and print out the SAS data set after importing:

```
PROC IMPORT DATAFILE ='c:\MyRawData\Bands2.csv' OUT = music REPLACE;
RUN;
PROC PRINT DATA = music;
   TITLE 'Customers at Each Gig';
RUN;
```

Here are the results of the PROC PRINT. Notice that GigDate is a readable date. This is because IMPORT automatically assigns informats and formats to some forms of dates. (See section 4.6 for a discussion of formats.) Also note that PROC IMPORT used the first data row for variable names and that spaces in names were replaced with underscores to conform to standard SAS naming rules for variables. You can also use Viewtable to view the data.

Customers at Each Gig

Obs	Band_Name	Gig_Date	Eight_PM	Nine_PM	Ten_PM	Eleven_PM
1	Lupine Lights	12/03/2012	45	63	70	.
2	Awesome Octaves	12/15/2012	17	28	44	12
3	Stop, Drop, and Rock-N-Roll	01/05/2013	34	62	77	91
4	The Silveyville Jazz Quartet	01/18/2013	38	30	42	43
5	Catalina Converts	01/31/2013	56	.	65	34

2.17 Reading Excel Files with the IMPORT Procedure

If you have SAS/ACCESS Interface to PC Files, then you can use the IMPORT procedure to import Microsoft Excel files in the Windows and UNIX operating environments. Here is the general form of the IMPORT procedure for reading Excel files:

```
PROC IMPORT DATAFILE = 'filename' OUT = data-set
    DBMS = identifier  REPLACE;
```

where *filename* is the file you want to read and *data-set* is the name of the SAS data set you want to create. The REPLACE option tells SAS to replace the SAS data set named in the OUT= option if it already exists. The DBMS= option tells SAS the type of Excel file to read and may not be necessary.

DBMS identifiers There are several DBMS identifiers you can use to read Excel files. Three commonly used identifiers are: EXCEL, XLS, and XLSX. In the UNIX operating environment, use the XLS identifier for older style files (.xls extension), and the XLSX identifier for newer style files (.xlsx extension). In the Windows operating environment, in addition to the XLS and XLSX identifiers, you can use the EXCEL identifier to read all types of Excel files. The EXCEL identifier uses different technology to read files than do the XLS and XLSX identifiers, so the results may be different. By default, the XLS and XLSX identifiers look at more data rows to determine the column type than does the EXCEL identifier. Not all of these identifiers may work for you if your Windows computer has a mixture of 64-bit and 32-bit applications. In addition, some computer configurations may require that a PC Files Server be installed. The PC Files Server uses the EXCELCS identifier. See the SAS Help and Documentation for more information.

Optional statements If you have more than one sheet in your file, then you can specify which sheet to read using the following statement:

```
SHEET = "sheet-name";
```

If you want to read only specific cells in the sheet, you can specify a range. The range can be a named range (if defined), or you can specify the upper-left and lower-right cells for the range as follows:

```
RANGE = "sheet-name$UL:LR";
```

By default, the IMPORT procedure will take the variable names from the first row of the spreadsheet. If you do not want this, then you can add the following statement (EXCEL identifier only) to the procedure and SAS will name the variables F1, F2, and so on.

```
GETNAMES = NO;
```

When using the EXCEL identifier, if you have a column that contains both numeric and character values, then by default, the numbers will be converted to missing values. To read the numbers as character values instead of converting them to missing values, use the following statement:

```
MIXED = YES;
```

Example Suppose you have the following Microsoft Excel spreadsheet which contains data about onion ring sales for the local minor league baseball team games. The visiting team name is followed by the sales in the concession stands and in the bleachers, then the number of hits and runs for each team.

	A	B	C	D	E	F	G
			fx	'VisitingTeam			
1	VisitingTeam	C Sales	B Sales	Our Hits	Their Hits	Our Runs	Their Runs
2	Columbia Peaches	35	67	1	10	2	1
3	Plains Peanuts	210		2	5	0	2
4	Gilroy Garlics	15	1035	12	11	7	6
5	Sacramento Tomatoes	124	85	15	4	9	1
6							
7							

Sheet1

The following program reads the Microsoft Excel file using the IMPORT procedure and the XLS DBMS identifier.

```
* Read an Excel spreadsheet using PROC IMPORT;
PROC IMPORT DATAFILE = 'c:\MyExcel\OnionRing.xls' DBMS=XLS OUT = sales;
RUN;
PROC PRINT DATA = sales;
   TITLE 'SAS Data Set Read From Excel File';
RUN;
```

Here are the results of the PROC PRINT. Notice how the variable names were taken from the first row in the spreadsheet, and that spaces were converted to underscores so that the variable names would conform to standard SAS naming conventions (32 characters or fewer, start with a letter or an underscore, and contain only letters, underscores, or numerals). You can also use Viewtable to view the data.

SAS Data Set Read From Excel File

Obs	Visiting_Team	C_Sales	B_Sales	Our_Hits	Their_hits	Our_Runs	Their_Runs
1	Columbia Peaches	35	67	1	10	2	1
2	Plains Peanuts	210	.	2	5	0	2
3	Gilroy Garlics	15	1035	12	11	7	6
4	Sacramento Tomatoes	124	85	15	4	9	1

2.18   Temporary versus Permanent SAS Data Sets

SAS data sets are available in two varieties: temporary and permanent. A temporary SAS data set is one that exists only during the current job or session and is automatically erased by SAS when you finish. If a SAS data set is permanent, that doesn't mean that it lasts for eternity, just that it remains when the job or session is finished.

Each type of data set has its own advantages. Sometimes you want to keep a data set for later use, and sometimes you don't. In this book, most of our examples use temporary data sets because we don't want to clutter up your disks. But, in general, if you use a data set more than once, it is more efficient to save it as a permanent SAS data set than to create a new temporary SAS data set every time you want to use the data.

SAS data set names   All SAS data sets have a two-level name such as WORK.BIKESALES, with the two levels separated by a period. The first level of a SAS data set name, WORK in this case, is called its libref (short for SAS data library reference). A libref is like an arrow pointing to a particular location. Sometimes a libref refers to a physical location, such as a flash drive or CD, while other times it refers to a logical location such as a directory or folder. The second level, BIKESALES, is the member name that uniquely identifies the data set within the library.

Both the libref and member name follow the standard rules for valid SAS names. They must start with a letter or underscore and contain only letters, numerals, or underscores. However, librefs cannot be longer than 8 characters while member names can be up to 32 characters long.

You never explicitly tell SAS to make a data set temporary or permanent, it is just implied by the name you give the data set when you create it. Most data sets are created in DATA steps, but PROC steps can also create data sets. If you specify a two-level name (and the libref is something other than WORK), then your data set will be permanent. If you specify just one level of the data set name (as we have in most of the examples in this book), then your data set will be temporary. SAS will use your one-level name as the member name and automatically append the libref WORK. By definition, any SAS data set with a libref of WORK is a temporary data set and will be erased by SAS at the end of your job or session. Here are some sample DATA statements and the characteristics of the data sets they create:

DATA statement	Libref	Member name	Type
DATA ironman;	WORK	ironman	temporary
DATA WORK.tourdefrance;	WORK	tourdefrance	temporary
DATA Bikes.doublecentury;	Bikes	doublecentury	permanent

Temporary SAS data sets   The following program creates and then prints a temporary SAS data set named DISTANCE:

```
DATA distance;
    Miles = 26.22;
    Kilometers = 1.61 * Miles;
RUN;
PROC PRINT DATA = distance;
RUN;
```

Notice that the libref WORK does not appear in the DATA statement. Because the data set has just a one-level name, SAS assigns the default library, WORK, and uses DISTANCE as the member name within that library. The log contains this note with the complete, two-level name:

```
NOTE: The data set WORK.DISTANCE has 1 observations and 2 variables.
```

Permanent SAS data sets   Before you can use a libref, you need to define it. You can define libraries using the New Library window. You can also use the LIBNAME statement (covered in the next section) or you can let SAS define the libref for you using direct referencing (covered in section 2.20).[13]

To open the New Library window, select **Tools ► New Library** from the menu bar. The BIKES library, defined in the New Library window shown on the right, points to the 'Ruiz Racing Bicycles' folder under the 'MySASLib' folder, on the C drive (Windows).

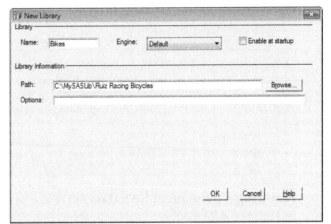

Librefs defined using the New Library window will appear in the Active Libraries window of the SAS Explorer as shown in the figure on the left. If you double-click the library icon, all the SAS data sets in the library will be listed in the Contents window for the library.

The following program is the same as the preceding one except that it creates a permanent SAS data set. Notice that a two-level name appears in the DATA statement and DATA= option.

```
DATA Bikes.distance;
   Miles = 26.22;
   Kilometers = 1.61 * Miles;
RUN;
PROC PRINT DATA = Bikes.distance;
RUN;
```

This time the log contains this note:

```
NOTE: The data set BIKES.DISTANCE has 1 observations and 2 variables.
```

This is a permanent SAS data set because the libref is not WORK.

---

[13] With batch processing under z/OS, you may also use Job Control Language (JCL). The DDname is your libref.

2.19 Using Permanent SAS Data Sets with LIBNAME Statements

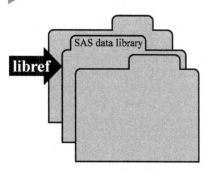

A libref is a nickname that corresponds to the location of a SAS data library. When you use a libref as the first level in the name of a SAS data set, SAS knows to look for that data set in that location. This section shows you how to define a libref using the LIBNAME statement which is the most universal (and therefore most portable) method of creating a libref. You can also define a libref using the New Library window (covered in the previous section) or for some computers, operating environment control language.[14] The basic form of the LIBNAME statement is

```
LIBNAME libref 'your-SAS-data-library';
```

After the keyword LIBNAME, you specify the libref and then the location of your permanent SAS data set in quotation marks. Librefs must be 8 characters or shorter; start with a letter or underscore; and contain only letters, numerals, or underscores. Here is the general form of LIBNAME statements for individual operating environments:

Windows:	`LIBNAME libref 'drive:\directory';`
UNIX:	`LIBNAME libref '/home/path';`
z/OS:	`LIBNAME libref 'data-set-name';`

Creating a permanent SAS data set The following example creates a permanent SAS data set containing information about magnolia trees. For each type of tree the raw data file includes the scientific name, common name, maximum height, age at first blooming when planted from seed, whether evergreen or deciduous, and color of flowers.

```
M. grandiflora Southern Magnolia 80 15 E white
M. campbellii                     80 20 D rose
M. liliiflora  Lily Magnolia      12  4 D purple
M. soulangiana Saucer Magnolia    25  3 D pink
M. stellata    Star Magnolia      10  3 D white
```

This program sets up a libref named PLANTS pointing to the MySASLib directory on the C drive (Windows). Then it reads the raw data from a file called Mag.dat, creating a permanent SAS data set named MAGNOLIA which is stored in the PLANTS library.

```
LIBNAME plants 'c:\MySASLib';
DATA plants.magnolia;
   INFILE 'c:\MyRawData\Mag.dat';
   INPUT ScientificName $ 1-14 CommonName $ 16-32 MaximumHeight
      AgeBloom Type $ Color $;
RUN;
```

The log contains this note showing the two-level data set name:

```
NOTE: The data set PLANTS.MAGNOLIA has 5 observations and 6 variables.
```

Librefs defined using LIBNAME statements will appear in the Active Libraries window of the SAS Explorer. If you double-click the library icon, all the SAS data sets in the library will be listed in the Contents window for the library.

If you print a directory of files on your computer, you will not see a file named PLANTS.MAGNOLIA. That is because operating environments have their own systems for naming files. When run under Windows or UNIX, this data set will be called magnolia.sas7bdat. Under z/OS, the filename would be the *data-set-name* specified in the LIBNAME statement.

Reading a permanent SAS data set To use a permanent SAS data set, you can include a LIBNAME statement in your program and refer to the data set by its two-level name. For instance, if you wanted to go back later and print the permanent data set created in the last example, you could use the following statements:

```
LIBNAME example 'c:\MySASLib';
PROC PRINT DATA = example.magnolia;
    TITLE 'Magnolias';
RUN;
```

This time the libref in the LIBNAME statement is EXAMPLE instead of PLANTS, but it points to the same location as before, the MySASLib directory on the C drive. The libref can change, but the member name, MAGNOLIA, stays the same.

The output looks like this:

Magnolias

Obs	ScientificName	CommonName	MaximumHeight	AgeBloom	Type	Color
1	M. grandiflora	Southern Magnolia	80	15	E	white
2	M. campbellii		80	20	D	rose
3	M. liliiflora	Lily Magnolia	12	4	D	purple
4	M. soulangiana	Saucer Magnolia	25	3	D	pink
5	M. stellata	Star Magnolia	10	3	D	white

---

[14] With batch processing under z/OS, you may use Job Control Language (JCL). The DDname is your libref.

2.20 Using Permanent SAS Data Sets by Direct Referencing

If you don't want to be bothered with setting up librefs and defining SAS libraries, but you still want to use permanent SAS data sets, then you can use direct referencing. Direct referencing still uses SAS libraries, but instead of defining the library yourself, you let SAS do it for you.

Using direct referencing is easy. Just take your operating environment's name for a file, enclose it in quotation marks, and put it in your program. The quotation marks tell SAS that this is a permanent SAS data set. Here is the general form of the DATA statement for creating permanent SAS data sets under different operating environments:

Windows:	DATA '*drive*:*directory**filename*';
UNIX:	DATA '*/home/path/filename*';
z/OS:	DATA '*data-set-name*';

For directory-based operating environments, if you leave out the directory or path, then SAS uses the current working directory. For example, this statement would create a permanent SAS data set named TREES in your current working directory.

```
DATA 'trees';
```

For the UNIX operating environment, by default, your current directory is the directory where you started SAS. You can change the current directory for the SAS session by selecting **Tools ▶ Options ▶ Change Directory** from the menu bar. Under Windows the name of the current working directory is displayed at the bottom of the SAS window. You can change the directory for the current SAS session by double-clicking the directory name which will open the Change Folder window.

Example The following example creates a permanent SAS data set containing information about magnolia trees. For each type of tree the raw data file includes the scientific name, common name, maximum height, age at first blooming when planted from seed, whether evergreen or deciduous, and color of flowers.

```
M. grandiflora Southern Magnolia 80 15 E white
M. campbellii                     80 20 D rose
M. liliiflora  Lily Magnolia      12  4 D purple
M. soulangiana Saucer Magnolia    25  3 D pink
M. stellata    Star Magnolia      10  3 D white
```

This program reads the raw data from a file called Mag.dat, creating a permanent SAS data set named MAGNOLIA. The MAGNOLIA data set is stored in the MySASLib directory on the C drive (Windows).

```
DATA 'c:\MySASLib\magnolia';
   INFILE 'c:\MyRawData\Mag.dat';
   INPUT ScientificName $ 1-14 CommonName $ 16-32 MaximumHeight
      AgeBloom Type $ Color $;
RUN;
```

If you look in your SAS log you will see this note:

```
NOTE: The data set c:\MySASLib\magnolia has 5 observations and 6 variables.
```

This is a permanent SAS data set, so SAS will not erase it. If you list the files in the MySASLib directory, you will see a file named magnolia.sas7bdat. Notice that SAS automatically appended a file extension, even though no extension appeared in the SAS program.

When you put quotation marks around your data set name, you are using direct referencing, and SAS creates a permanent SAS data set. Since you haven't specified a libref, SAS makes up a libref for you. You don't need to know the name of the libref that SAS makes up, but it is there and you can see it in the Active Libraries window. This is what the Active Libraries window looks like after running the previous program. SAS has created a library named WC000001 which contains the MAGNOLIA data set.

Reading SAS data sets using direct referencing To read a permanent SAS data set using direct referencing, simply enclose the path and name for the data set in quotation marks wherever you would use a SAS data set name. For example, to print the MAGNOLIA data set, you could use the following statements:

```
PROC PRINT DATA = 'c:\MySASLib\magnolia';
   TITLE 'Magnolias';
RUN;
```

The output looks like this:

Magnolias

Obs	ScientificName	CommonName	MaximumHeight	AgeBloom	Type	Color
1	M. grandiflora	Southern Magnolia	80	15	E	white
2	M. campbellii		80	20	D	rose
3	M. liliiflora	Lily Magnolia	12	4	D	purple
4	M. soulangiana	Saucer Magnolia	25	3	D	pink
5	M. stellata	Star Magnolia	10	3	D	white

2.21 Listing the Contents of a SAS Data Set

To use a SAS data set, all you need to do is tell SAS the name and location of the data set you want, and SAS will figure out what is in it. SAS can do this because SAS data sets are self-documenting, which is another way of saying that SAS automatically stores information about the data set (also called the descriptor portion) along with the data. You can't display a SAS data set on your computer screen using a word processor. However, there is an easy way to get a description of a SAS data set; you simply run the CONTENTS procedure.

PROC CONTENTS is a simple procedure. You just type the keywords PROC CONTENTS and specify the data set you want with the DATA= option:

```
PROC CONTENTS DATA = data-set;
```

Example The following DATA step creates a data set so we can run PROC CONTENTS:

```
DATA funnies (LABEL = 'Comics Character Data');
   INPUT Id Name $ Height Weight DoB MMDDYY8. @@;
   LABEL Id = 'Identification no. '
      Height = 'Height in inches'
      Weight = 'Weight in pounds'
      DoB    = 'Date of birth';
   INFORMAT DoB MMDDYY8.;
   FORMAT DoB WORDDATE18.;
   DATALINES;
53 Susie    42   41   07-11-81 54 Charlie  46   55   10-26-54
55 Calvin   40   35   01-10-81 56 Lucy     46   52   01-13-55
   ;
* Use PROC CONTENTS to describe data set funnies;
PROC CONTENTS DATA = funnies;
RUN;
```

Note that the DATA step above includes a LABEL= data set option[15] on the DATA statement and a LABEL statement. The LABEL= data set option gives a label for the entire data set while the LABEL statement assigns labels to individual variables. These optional labels, which can be up to 256 characters long, allow you to document your data in more detail than is possible with just variable or data set names. For variables, if you specify a LABEL statement in a DATA step, then the descriptions will be stored in the data set and will be printed by PROC CONTENTS. You can also use LABEL statements in PROC steps to customize your reports, but then the labels apply only for the duration of the PROC step and are not stored in the data set.

INFORMAT and FORMAT statements also appear in this program. You can use these optional statements to associate informats or formats with variables. Just as informats give SAS special instructions for reading a variable, formats give SAS special instructions for writing a variable. If you specify an INFORMAT or FORMAT statement in a DATA step, then the name of that informat or format will be saved in the data set and printed by PROC CONTENTS. FORMAT statements, like LABEL statements, can be used in PROC steps to customize your reports, but then the name of the format is not stored in the data set.[16]

The output from PROC CONTENTS is like a table of contents for your data set:

The CONTENTS Procedure

❶ Data Set Name	WORK.FUNNIES	❷ Observations	4
Member Type	DATA	❸ Variables	5
Engine	V9	Indexes	0
❹ Created	Monday, March 19, 2012 09:23:43 PM	Observation Length	40
Last Modified	Monday, March 19, 2012 09:23:43 PM	Deleted Observations	0
Protection		Compressed	NO
Data Set Type		Sorted	NO
❺ Label	Comics Character Data		
Data Representation	WINDOWS_32		
Encoding	wlatin1 Western (Windows)		

Engine/Host Dependent Information	
Data Set Page Size	4096
Number of Data Set Pages	1
First Data Page	1
Max Obs per Page	101
Obs in First Data Page	4
Number of Data Set Repairs	0
Filename	C:\Users\Lora\AppData\Local\Temp\SAS Temporary Files\funnies.sas7bdat
Release Created	9.0301M0
Host Created	W32_VSPRO

Alphabetic List of Variables and Attributes						
#	Variable	❻ Type	❼ Len	❽ Format	❾ Informat	❿ Label
5	DoB	Num	8	WORDDATE18.	MMDDYY8.	Date of birth
3	Height	Num	8			Height in inches
1	Id	Num	8			Identification no.
2	Name	Char	8			
4	Weight	Num	8			Weight in pounds

The output starts with information about your data set and then describes each variable.

For the data set
❶ Data set name
❷ Number of observations
❸ Number of variables
❹ Date created
❺ Data set label (if any)

For each variable
❻ Type (numeric or character)
❼ Length (storage size in bytes)
❽ Format for printing (if any)
❾ Informat for input (if any)
❿ Variable label (if any)

---

[15] See section 6.11 for more information on data set options.

[16] Sections 4.6 and 4.7 discuss standard SAS formats more thoroughly.

3

"Contrariwise," continued Tweedledee," if it was so, it might be; and if it were so, it would be; but as it isn't, it ain't. That's logic.

Lewis Carroll

From *Alice Through the Looking Glass* by Lewis Carroll. Public domain.

CHAPTER 3

Working with Your Data

3.1 Creating and Redefining Variables

If someone were to compile a list of the most popular things to do with SAS software, creating and redefining variables would surely be near the top. Fortunately, SAS is flexible and uses a common sense approach to these tasks. You create and redefine variables with assignment statements using this basic form:

```
variable = expression;
```

On the left side of the equal sign is a variable name, either new or old. On the right side of the equal sign may appear a constant, another variable, or a mathematical expression. Here are examples of these basic types of assignment statements:

Type of expression	Assignment statement
numeric constant	Qwerty = 10;
character constant	Qwerty = 'ten';
a variable	Qwerty = OldVar;
addition	Qwerty = OldVar + 10;
subtraction	Qwerty = OldVar - 10;
multiplication	Qwerty = OldVar * 10;
division	Qwerty = OldVar / 10;
exponentiation	Qwerty = OldVar ** 10;

Whether the variable Qwerty is numeric or character depends on the expression that defines it. When the expression is numeric, Qwerty will be numeric; when it is character, Qwerty will be character.

When deciding how to interpret your expression, SAS follows the standard mathematical rules of precedence: SAS performs exponentiation first, then multiplication and division, followed by addition and subtraction. You can use parentheses to override that order. Here are two similar SAS statements showing that a couple of parentheses can make a big difference:

Assignment statement	Result
x = 10 * 4 + 3 ** 2;	x = 49
x = 10 * (4 + 3 ** 2);	x = 130

While SAS can read expressions with or without parentheses, people often can't. If you use parentheses, your programs will be a lot easier to read.

Example The following raw data are from a survey of home gardeners. Gardeners were asked to estimate the number of pounds they harvested for four crops: tomatoes, zucchini, peas, and grapes.

```
Gregor   10  2  40     0
Molly    15  5  10  1000
Luther   50 10  15    50
Susan    20  0   .    20
```

This program reads the data from a file called Garden.dat, and then modifies the data:

```
* Modify homegarden data set with assignment statements;
DATA homegarden;
    INFILE 'c:\MyRawData\Garden.dat';
    INPUT Name $ 1-7 Tomato Zucchini Peas Grapes;
    Zone = 14;
    Type = 'home';
    Zucchini = Zucchini * 10;
    Total = Tomato + Zucchini + Peas + Grapes;
    PerTom = (Tomato / Total) * 100;
RUN;
PROC PRINT DATA = homegarden;
    TITLE 'Home Gardening Survey';
RUN;
```

This program contains five assignment statements. The first creates a new variable, Zone, equal to a numeric constant, 14. The variable Type is set equal to a character constant, home. The variable Zucchini is multiplied by 10 because that just seems natural for zucchini. Total is the sum for all the types of plants. PerTom is not a genetically engineered tomato but the percentage of harvest which were tomatoes. The report from PROC PRINT contains all the variables, old and new:

Home Gardening Survey

Obs	Name	Tomato	Zucchini	Peas	Grapes	Zone	Type	Total	PerTom
1	Gregor	10	20	40	0	14	home	70	14.2857
2	Molly	15	50	10	1000	14	home	1075	1.3953
3	Luther	50	100	15	50	14	home	215	23.2558
4	Susan	20	0	.	20	14	home	.	.

Notice that the variable Zucchini appears only once because the new value replaced the old value. The other four assignment statements each created a new variable. When a variable is new, SAS adds it to the data set you are creating. When a variable already exists, SAS replaces the original value with the new one. Using an existing name has the advantage of not cluttering your data set with a lot of similar variables. However, you don't want to overwrite a variable unless you are really sure you won't need the original value later.

The variable Peas had a missing value for the last observation. Because of this, the variables Total and PerTom, which are calculated from Peas, were also set to missing and this message appeared in the log:

```
NOTE: Missing values were generated as a result of performing an operation
      on missing values.
```

This message is a flag that often indicates an error. However, in this case it is not an error but simply the result of incomplete data collection.[1]

---

[1] If you want to add only non-missing values, you can use the SUM function discussed in section 11.7.

3.2 ▸ Using SAS Functions

Sometimes a simple expression, using only arithmetic operators, does not give you the new value you are looking for. This is where functions are handy, simplifying your task because SAS has already done the programming for you. All you need to do is plug the right values into the function and out comes the result—like putting a dollar in a change machine and getting back four quarters.

SAS has hundreds of functions in general areas including:

Character	Macro
Character String Matching	Mathematical
Date and Time	Probability
Descriptive Statistics	Random Number
Distance	State and ZIP Code
Financial	Variable Information

The next two sections give a sample of the most common SAS functions.

Functions perform a calculation on, or a transformation of, the arguments given in parentheses following the function name. SAS functions have the following general form:

```
function-name(argument, argument, ...)
```

All functions must have parentheses even if they don't require any arguments. Arguments are separated by commas and can be variable names, constant values such as numbers or characters enclosed in quotation marks, or expressions. The following statement computes Birthday as a SAS date value using the function MDY and the variables MonthBorn, DayBorn, and YearBorn. The MDY function takes three arguments, one each for the month, day, and year:

```
Birthday = MDY(MonthBorn, DayBorn, YearBorn);
```

Functions can be nested, where one function is the argument of another function. For example, the following statement calculates NewValue using two nested functions, INT and LOG:

```
NewValue = INT(LOG(10));
```

The result for this example is 2, the integer portion of the natural log of the numeric constant 10 (2.3026). Just be careful when nesting functions that each parenthesis has a mate.

Example Data from a pumpkin carving contest illustrate the use of several functions. The contestants' names are followed by their age, type of pumpkin (carved or decorated), date of entry, and the scores from five judges:

```
Alicia Grossman   13 c 10-28-2012 7.8 6.5 7.2 8.0 7.9
Matthew Lee        9 D 10-30-2012 6.5 5.9 6.8 6.0 8.1
Elizabeth Garcia  10 C 10-29-2012 8.9 7.9 8.5 9.0 8.8
Lori Newcombe      6 D 10-30-2012 6.7 5.6 4.9 5.2 6.1
Jose Martinez      7 d 10-31-2012 8.9 9.510.0 9.7 9.0
Brian Williams    11 C 10-29-2012 7.8 8.4 8.5 7.9 8.0
```

The following program reads the data, creates two new variables (AvgScore and DayEntered) and transforms another (Type):

```
DATA contest;
    INFILE 'c:\MyRawData\Pumpkin.dat';

    INPUT Name $16. Age 3. +1 Type $1. +1 Date MMDDYY10.
          (Scr1 Scr2 Scr3 Scr4 Scr5) (4.1);
    AvgScore = MEAN(Scr1, Scr2, Scr3, Scr4, Scr5);
    DayEntered = DAY(Date);
    Type = UPCASE(Type);
RUN;
PROC PRINT DATA = contest;
    TITLE 'Pumpkin Carving Contest';
RUN;
```

The variable AvgScore is created using the MEAN function, which returns the mean of the non-missing arguments. This differs from simply adding the arguments together and dividing by their number, which would return a missing value if any of the arguments were missing.

The variable DayEntered is created using the DAY function, which returns the day of the month. SAS has all sorts of functions for manipulating dates, and what's great about them is that you don't have to worry about things like leap year—SAS takes care of that for you.

The variable Type is transformed using the UPCASE function. SAS is case sensitive when it comes to variable values; a 'd' is not the same as 'D'. The data file has both lowercase and uppercase letters for the variable Type, so the function UPCASE is used to make all the values uppercase.

Here are the results:

Pumpkin Carving Contest

Obs	Name	Age	Type	Date[2]	Scr1	Scr2	Scr3	Scr4	Scr5	AvgScore	DayEntered
1	Alicia Grossman	13	C	19294	7.8	6.5	7.2	8.0	7.9	7.48	28
2	Matthew Lee	9	D	19296	6.5	5.9	6.8	6.0	8.1	6.66	30
3	Elizabeth Garcia	10	C	19295	8.9	7.9	8.5	9.0	8.8	8.62	29
4	Lori Newcombe	6	D	19296	6.7	5.6	4.9	5.2	6.1	5.70	30
5	Jose Martinez	7	D	19297	8.9	9.5	10.0	9.7	9.0	9.42	31
6	Brian Williams	11	C	19295	7.8	8.4	8.5	7.9	8.0	8.12	29

---

[2] Notice that these dates are printed as the number of days since January 1, 1960. Section 4.6 discusses how to format these values into readable dates.

3.3 Selected SAS Character Functions

Function name	Syntax[3]	Definition
Character		
ANYALNUM	ANYALNUM(*arg,start*)	Returns position of first occurrence of any alphabetic character or numeral at or after optional start position
ANYALPHA	ANYALPHA(*arg,start*)	Returns position of first occurrence of any alphabetic character at or after optional start position
ANYDIGIT	ANYDIGIT(*arg,start*)	Returns position of first occurrence of any numeral at or after optional start position
ANYSPACE	ANYSPACE(*arg,start*)	Returns position of first occurrence of a white space character at or after optional start position
CAT	CAT(*arg-1,arg-2,…arg-n*)	Concatenates two or more character strings together leaving leading and trailing blanks
CATS	CATS(*arg-1,arg-2,…arg-n*)	Concatenates two or more character strings together stripping leading and trailing blanks
CATX	CATX('*separator-string*', *arg-1,arg-2,…arg-n*)	Concatenates two or more character strings together stripping leading and trailing blanks and inserting a separator string between arguments
COMPRESS	COMPRESS(*arg*, '*char*')	Removes spaces or optional characters from character string
INDEX	INDEX(*arg*, '*string*')	Returns starting position for string of characters
LEFT	LEFT(*arg*)	Left aligns a SAS character expression
LENGTH	LENGTH(*arg*)	Returns the length of an argument not counting trailing blanks (missing values have a length of 1)
PROPCASE	PROPCASE(*arg*)	Converts first character in word to uppercase and remaining characters to lowercase
SUBSTR	SUBSTR(*arg,position,n*)	Extracts a substring from an argument starting at *position* for *n* characters or until end if no *n*[4]
TRANSLATE	TRANSLATE(*source,to-1, from-1,...to-n,from-n*)	Replaces *from* characters in *source* with *to* characters (one to one replacement only—you can't replace one character with two, for example)
TRANWRD	TRANWRD(*source,from,to*)	Replaces *from* character string in *source* with *to* character string
TRIM	TRIM(*arg*)	Removes trailing blanks from character expression
UPCASE	UPCASE(*arg*)	Converts all letters in argument to uppercase

Function name	Example	Result	Example	Result
Character				
ANYALNUM	a='123 E St, #2 '; x=ANYALNUM(a);	x=1	a='123 E St, #2 '; y=ANYALNUM(a,10);	y=12
ANYALPHA	a='123 E St, #2 '; x=ANYALPHA(a);	x=5	a='123 E St, #2 '; y=ANYALPHA(a,10);	y=0
ANYDIGIT	a='123 E St, #2 '; x=ANYDIGIT(a);	x=1	a='123 E St, #2 '; y=ANYDIGIT(a,10);	y=12
ANYSPACE	a='123 E St, #2 '; x=ANYSPACE(a);	x=4	a='123 E St, #2 '; y=ANYSPACE(a,10);	y=10
CAT	a=' cat';b='dog '; x=CAT(a,b);	x=' catdog '	a='cat ';b=' dog'; y=CAT(a,b);	y='cat dog'
CATS	a=' cat';b='dog '; x=CATS(a,b);	x='catdog'	a='cat ';b=' dog'; y=CATS(a,b);	y='catdog'
CATX	a=' cat';b='dog '; x=CATX(' ',a,b);	x='cat dog'	a=' cat';b='dog '; y=CATX('&',a,b);	y='cat&dog'
COMPRESS	a=' cat & dog'; x=COMPRESS(a);	x='cat&dog'	a=' cat & dog'; y=COMPRESS(a,'&');	y=' cat dog'
INDEX	a='123 E St, #2'; x=INDEX(a,'#');	x=11	a='123 E St, #2'; y=INDEX(a,'St');	y=7
LEFT	a=' cat'; x=LEFT(a);	x='cat '	a=' my cat'; y=LEFT(a);	y='my cat '
LENGTH	a='my cat'; x=LENGTH(a);	x=6	a=' my cat '; y=LENGTH(a);	y=7
PROPCASE	a='MyCat'; x=PROPCASE(a);	x='Mycat'	a='TIGER'; y=PROPCASE(a);	y='Tiger'
SUBSTR[4]	a='(916)734-6281'; x=SUBSTR(a,2,3);	x='916'	y=SUBSTR('1cat',2);	y='cat'
TRANSLATE	a='6/16/99'; x=TRANSLATE (a,'-','/');	x='6-16-99'	a='my cat can'; y=TRANSLATE (a, 'r','c');	y='my rat ran'
TRANWRD	a='Main Street'; x=TRANWRD (a,'Street','St');	x='Main St'	a='my cat can'; y=TRANWRD (a,'cat','rat');	y='my rat can'
TRIM	a='my '; b='cat'; x=TRIM(a)||b;[5]	x='mycat '	a='my cat '; b='s'; y=TRIM(a)||b;	y='my cats '
UPCASE	a='MyCat'; x=UPCASE(a);	x='MYCAT'	y=UPCASE('Tiger');	y='TIGER'

---

[3] arg is short for argument, which means a literal value, variable name, or expression.

[4] SUBSTR has a different function when on the left side of an equal sign.

[5] The concatenation operator | | concatenates character strings.

3.4   Selected SAS Numeric Functions

Function name	Syntax[6]	Definition
Numeric		
INT	INT(*arg*)	Returns the integer portion of argument
LOG	LOG(*arg*)	Natural logarithm
LOG10	LOG10(*arg*)	Logarithm to the base 10
MAX	MAX(*arg-1,arg-2,...arg-n*)	Largest non-missing value
MEAN	MEAN(*arg-1,arg-2,...arg-n*)	Arithmetic mean of non-missing values
MIN	MIN(*arg-1,arg-2,...arg-n*)	Smallest non-missing value
N	N(*arg-1,arg-2,...arg-n*)	Number of non-missing values
NMISS	NMISS(*arg-1,arg-2,...arg-n*)	Number of missing values
ROUND	ROUND(*arg, round-off-unit*)	Rounds to nearest round-off unit
SUM	SUM(*arg-1,arg-2,...arg-n*)	Sum of non-missing values
Date		
DATEJUL	DATEJUL(*julian-date*)	Converts a Julian date to a SAS date value[7]
DAY	DAY(*date*)	Returns the day of the month from a SAS date value
MDY	MDY(*month,day,year*)	Returns a SAS date value from month, day, and year values
MONTH	MONTH(*date*)	Returns the month (1–12) from a SAS date value
QTR	QTR(*date*)	Returns the yearly quarter (1–4) from a SAS date value
TODAY	TODAY()	Returns the current date as a SAS date value
WEEKDAY	WEEKDAY(*date*)	Returns day of week (1=Sunday) from SAS date value
YEAR	YEAR(*date*)	Returns year from a SAS date value
YRDIF	YRDIF(*start-date,end-date,*'AGE')	Computes difference in years between two SAS date values taking leap years into account

Function name	Example	Result	Example	Result
Numeric				
INT	x=INT(4.32);	x=4	y=INT(5.789);	y=5
LOG	x=LOG(1);	x=0.0	y=LOG(10);	y=2.30259
LOG10	x=LOG10(1);	x=0.0	y=LOG10(10);	y=1.0
MAX	x=MAX(9.3,8,7.5);	x=9.3	y=MAX(-3,.,5);	y=5
MEAN	x=MEAN(1,4,7,2);	x=3.5	y=MEAN(2,.,3);	y=2.5
MIN	x=MIN(9.3,8,7.5);	x=7.5	y=MIN(-3,.,5);	y=-3
N	x=N(1,.,7,2);	x=3	y=N(.,4,.,.);	y=1
NMISS	x=NMISS(1,.,7,2);	x=1	y=NMISS(.,4,.,.);	y=3
ROUND	x=ROUND(12.65);	x=13	y=ROUND(12.65,.1);	y=12.7
SUM	x=SUM(3,5,1);	x=9.0	y=SUM(4,7,.);	y=11
Date				
DATEJUL	a=60001; x=DATEJUL(a);	x=0	a=60365; y=DATEJUL(a);	y=364
DAY	a=MDY(4,18,2012); x=DAY(a);	x=18	a=MDY(9,3,60); y=DAY(a);	y=3
MDY	x=MDY(1,1,1960);	x=0	m=2; d=1; y=60; Date=MDY(m,d,y);	Date=31
MONTH	a=MDY(4,18,2012); x=MONTH(a);	x=4	a=MDY(9,3,60); y=MONTH(a);	y=9
QTR	a=MDY(4,18,2012); x=QTR(a);	x=2	a=MDY(9,3,60); y=QTR(a);	y=3
TODAY	x=TODAY();	x=*today's date*	y=TODAY()-1;	y=*yesterday's date*
WEEKDAY	a=MDY(4,13,2012); x=WEEKDAY(a);	x=6	a=MDY(4,18,2012); y=WEEKDAY(a);	y=4
YEAR	a=MDY(4,13,2012); x=YEAR(a);	x=2012	a=MDY(1,1,1960); y=YEAR(a);	y=1960

YRDIF	a=MDY(4,13,2000);
	b=MDY(4,13,2012);
	x=YRDIF(a,b,'AGE');
		x=12.0	a=MDY(4,13,2000);
			b=MDY(8,13,2012);
			y=YRDIF(a,b,'AGE');
				y=12.3342

[6] *arg* is short for argument, which means a literal value, variable name, or expression.

[7] A SAS date value is the number of days since January 1, 1960.

Using IF-THEN Statements

Frequently, you want an assignment statement to apply to some observations, but not all—under some conditions, but not others. This is called conditional logic, and you do it with IF-THEN statements:

```
IF condition THEN action;
```

The *condition* is an expression comparing one thing to another, and the *action* is what SAS should do when the expression is true, often an assignment statement. For example

```
IF Model = 'Berlinetta' THEN Make = 'Ferrari';
```

This statement tells SAS to set the variable Make equal to Ferrari whenever the variable Model equals Berlinetta. The terms on either side of the comparison may be constants, variables, or expressions. Those terms are separated by a comparison operator, which may be either symbolic or mnemonic. The decision of whether to use symbolic or mnemonic operators depends on your personal preference and the symbols available on your keyboard. Here are the basic comparison operators:

Symbolic	Mnemonic	Meaning
=	EQ	equals
¬ =, ^ =, or ~ =	NE	not equal
>	GT	greater than
<	LT	less than
> =	GE	greater than or equal
< =	LE	less than or equal

The IN operator also makes comparisons, but it works a bit differently. IN compares the value of a variable to a list of values. Here is an example:

```
IF Model IN ('Model T', 'Model A') THEN Make = 'Ford';
```

This statement tells SAS to set the variable Make equal to Ford whenever the value of Model is Model T or Model A.

A single IF-THEN statement can only have one action. If you add the keywords DO and END, then you can execute more than one action. For example

```
IF condition THEN DO;        IF Model = 'DMC-12' THEN DO;
   action;                      Make = 'DeLorean';
   action;                      BodyStyle = 'coupe';
END;                         END;
```

The DO statement causes all SAS statements coming after it to be treated as a unit until a matching END statement appears. Together, the DO statement, the END statement, and all the statements in between are called a DO group.

You can also specify multiple conditions with the keywords AND and OR:

```
IF condition AND condition THEN action;
```

For example

```
IF Make = 'Alfa Romeo' AND Model = 'Tipo B' THEN Seats = 1;
```

Like the comparison operators, AND and OR may be symbolic or mnemonic:

Symbolic	Mnemonic	Meaning
&	AND	all comparisons must be true
|, ¦, or !	OR	only one comparison must be true

Be careful with long strings of comparisons; they can be a logical maze.

Example The following data show information about rare antique cars sold at auction. The data values are the make, model, the year the car was made, the number of seats , and the selling price in millions of dollars:

```
DeDion          LaMarquise       1884 4   4.6
Rolls-Royce     Silver Ghost     1912 4   1.7
Mercedes-Benz SSK                1929 2   7.4
                F-88             1954 .   3.2
Ferrari         250 Testa Rossa 1957 2  16.3
```

This program reads the data from a file called Auction.dat, and uses IF-THEN statements.

```
DATA oldcars;
   INFILE 'c:\MyRawData\Auction.dat';
   INPUT Make $ 1-13 Model $ 15-29 YearMade Seats MillionsPaid;
   IF YearMade < 1890 THEN Veteran = 'Yes';
   IF Model = 'F-88' THEN DO;
      Make = 'Oldsmobile';
      Seats = 2;
   END;
RUN;
PROC PRINT DATA = oldcars;
   TITLE 'Cars Sold at Auction';
RUN;
```

This program contains two IF-THEN statements. Cars built before 1890 are classified as Veteran. The first IF-THEN creates a new variable named Veteran and gives it a value of Yes for any car made before 1890. The second IF-THEN uses DO and END to fill in missing data for the model F-88. The output looks like this:

Cars Sold at Auction

Obs	Make	Model	YearMade	Seats	MillionsPaid	Veteran
1	DeDion	LaMarquise	1884	4	4.6	Yes
2	Rolls-Royce	Silver Ghost	1912	4	1.7	
3	Mercedes-Benz	SSK	1929	2	7.4	
4	Oldsmobile	F-88	1954	2	3.2	
5	Ferrari	250 Testa Rossa	1957	2	16.3	

3.6 Grouping Observations with IF-THEN/ELSE Statements

red	warm
orange	warm
yellow	warm
green	cool
blue	cool
purple	cool

One common use of IF-THEN statements is for grouping observations. For example, you might have data for each day but need a report by season, or perhaps you have data for each census tract but want to analyze it by state. There are many possible reasons for grouping data, so sooner or later you'll probably need to do it.

The simplest and most common way to create a grouping variable is with a series of IF-THEN statements.[8] By adding the keyword ELSE to your IF statements, you can tell SAS that these statements are related.

IF-THEN/ELSE logic takes this basic form:

```
IF condition THEN action;
   ELSE IF condition THEN action;
   ELSE IF condition THEN action;
```

Notice that the ELSE statement is simply an IF-THEN statement with an ELSE tacked onto the front. You can have any number of these statements.

IF-THEN/ELSE logic has two advantages when compared to a simple series of IF-THEN statements without any ELSE statements. First, it is more efficient, using less computer time; once an observation satisfies a condition, SAS skips the rest of the series. Second, ELSE logic ensures that your groups are mutually exclusive so you don't accidentally have an observation fitting into more than one group.

Sometimes the last ELSE statement in a series is a little different, containing just an action, with no IF or THEN. Note the final ELSE statement in this series:

```
IF condition THEN action;
   ELSE IF condition THEN action;
   ELSE action;
```

An ELSE of this kind becomes a default which is automatically executed for all observations failing to satisfy any of the previous IF statements. You can only have one of these statements, and it must be the last in the IF-THEN/ELSE series.

Example Here are data from a survey of home improvements. Each record contains three data values: owner's name, description of the work done, and cost of the improvements in dollars:

```
Bob      kitchen cabinet face-lift  1253.00
Shirley  bathroom addition         11350.70
Silvia   paint exterior                   .
Al       backyard gazebo            3098.63
Norm     paint interior              647.77
Kathy    second floor addition     75362.93
```

This program reads the raw data from a file called Home.dat, and then assigns a grouping variable called CostGroup. This variable has a value of high, medium, low, or missing, depending on the value of Cost:

```
* Group observations by cost;
DATA homeimprovements;
    INFILE 'c:\MyRawData\Home.dat';
    INPUT Owner $ 1-7 Description $ 9-33 Cost;
    IF Cost = . THEN CostGroup = 'missing';
        ELSE IF Cost < 2000 THEN CostGroup = 'low';
        ELSE IF Cost < 10000 THEN CostGroup = 'medium';
        ELSE CostGroup = 'high';
RUN;
PROC PRINT DATA = homeimprovements;
    TITLE 'Home Improvement Cost Groups';
RUN;
```

Notice that there are four statements in this IF-THEN/ELSE series, one for each possible value of the variable CostGroup. The first statement deals with observations that have missing data for the variable Cost. Without this first statement, observations with a missing value for Cost would be incorrectly assigned a CostGroup of low. SAS considers missing values to be smaller than non-missing values, smaller than any printable character for character variables, and smaller than negative numbers for numeric variables. Unless you are sure that your data contain no missing values, you should allow for missing values when you write IF-THEN/ELSE statements.

The results look like this:

Home Improvement Cost Groups

Obs	Owner	Description	Cost	CostGroup
1	Bob	kitchen cabinet face-lift	1253.00	low
2	Shirley	bathroom addition	11350.70	high
3	Silvia	paint exterior	.	missing
4	Al	backyard gazebo	3098.63	medium
5	Norm	paint interior	647.77	low
6	Kathy	second floor addition	75362.93	high

---

[8] Other ways to create grouping variables include using a SELECT statement, or using a PUT function with a user-defined format from PROC FORMAT.

3.7 ▶ Subsetting Your Data

Often programmers find that they want to use some of the observations in a data set and exclude the rest. The most common way to do this is with a subsetting IF statement in a DATA step.[9] The basic form of a subsetting IF is

```
IF expression;
```

Consider this example:

```
IF Sex = 'f';
```

At first subsetting IF statements may seem odd. People naturally ask, "IF Sex = 'f', then what?" The subsetting IF looks incomplete, as if a careless typist pressed the delete key too long. But it is really a special case of the standard IF-THEN statement. In this case the action is merely implied. If the expression is true, then SAS continues with the DATA step. If the expression is false, then no further statements are processed for that observation; that observation is not added to the data set being created; and SAS moves on to the next observation. You can think of the subsetting IF as a kind of on-off switch. If the condition is true, then the switch is on and the observation is processed. If the condition is false, then that observation is turned off.

If you don't like subsetting IFs, there is another alternative, the DELETE statement. DELETE statements do the opposite of subsetting IFs. While the subsetting IF statement tells SAS which observations to include, the DELETE statement tells SAS which observations to exclude:

```
IF expression THEN DELETE;
```

The following two statements are equivalent (assuming there are only two values for the variable Sex, and no missing data):

```
IF Sex = 'f';        IF Sex = 'm' THEN DELETE;
```

Example   The members of a local amateur playhouse want to choose a Shakespearean comedy for this spring's play. You volunteer to compile a list of titles using an online encyclopedia. For each play your data file contains title, approximate year of first performance, and type of play:

```
A Midsummer Night's Dream 1595 comedy
Comedy of Errors         1590 comedy
Hamlet                   1600 tragedy
Macbeth                  1606 tragedy
Richard III              1594 history
Romeo and Juliet         1596 tragedy
Taming of the Shrew      1593 comedy
Tempest                  1611 romance
```

This program reads the data from a raw data file called Shakespeare.dat, and then uses a subsetting IF statement to select only comedies:

```
* Choose only comedies;
DATA comedy;
    INFILE 'c:\MyRawData\Shakespeare.dat';
    INPUT Title $ 1-26 Year Type $;
    IF Type = 'comedy';
RUN;
PROC PRINT DATA = comedy;
    TITLE 'Shakespearean Comedies';
RUN;
```

The output looks like this:

Shakespearean Comedies

Obs	Title	Year	Type
1	A Midsummer Night's Dream	1595	comedy
2	Comedy of Errors	1590	comedy
3	Taming of the Shrew	1593	comedy

These notes appear in the log stating that although eight records were read from the input file, the data set WORK.COMEDY contains only three observations:

```
NOTE: 8 records were read from the infile 'c:\MyRawData\Shakespeare.dat'
NOTE: The data set WORK.COMEDY has 3 observations and 3 variables.
```

It is always a good idea to check the SAS log when you subset observations to make sure that you ended up with what you expected.

In the program above, you could substitute the statement

```
IF Type = 'tragedy' OR Type = 'romance' OR Type = 'history' THEN DELETE;
```

for the statement

```
IF Type = 'comedy';
```

But you would have to do a lot more typing. Generally, you use the subsetting IF when it is easier to specify a condition for including observations, and use the DELETE statement when it is easier to specify a condition for excluding observations.

---

[9] For more on subsetting IF statements, see sections 2.13 and 6.9. Other ways to subset data include the WHERE statement (section 4.2 and the appendix), and WHERE= option (section 6.13).

3.8 Working with SAS Dates

Dates can be tricky to work with. Some months have 30 days, some 31, some 28, and don't forget leap year. SAS dates simplify all this. A SAS date is a numeric value equal to the number of days since January 1, 1960. The table below lists four dates and their values as SAS dates:

Date	SAS date value	Date	SAS date value
January 1, 1959	-365	January 1, 1961	366
January 1, 1960	0	January 1, 2020	21915

SAS has special tools for working with dates: informats for reading dates, functions for manipulating dates, and formats for printing dates.[10] A table of selected date informats, formats, and functions appears in the next section.

Informats To read variables that are dates, you use formatted style input. SAS has a variety of date informats for reading dates in many different forms. All of these informats convert your data to a number equal to the number of days since January 1, 1960. The INPUT statement below tells SAS to read a variable named BirthDate using the ANYDTDTE9. informat:[11]

```
INPUT BirthDate ANYDTDTE9.;
```

Setting the default century for input When SAS sees a date with a two-digit year like 07/04/76, SAS has to decide in which century the year belongs. Is the year 1976, 2076, or perhaps 1776? The system option YEARCUTOFF= specifies the first year of a hundred-year span for SAS to use. At the time this book was written, the default value for this option was 1920. You can change this value with an OPTIONS statement. To avoid problems, you may want to specify the YEARCUTOFF= option whenever you input data containing two-digit years. This statement tells SAS to interpret two-digit dates as occurring between 1950 and 2049:

```
OPTIONS YEARCUTOFF = 1950;
```

Dates in SAS expressions Once a variable has been read with a SAS date informat, it can be used in arithmetic expressions like other numeric variables. For example, if a library book is due in three weeks, you could find the due date by adding 21 days to the date it was checked out:

```
DueDate = CheckDate + 21;
```

You can use a date as a constant in a SAS expression. Put the date in DATE*w.* format (such as 01JAN60). Then add quotation marks followed by the letter D. The assignment statement below creates a variable named EarthDay14, which is equal to the SAS date value for April 22, 2014:

```
EarthDay14 = '22APR2014'D;
```

Functions SAS date functions perform a number of handy operations. The statement below uses three functions to compute age from a variable named BirthDate.

```
CurrentAge = INT (YRDIF (BirthDate, TODAY(), 'AGE') );
```

The YRDIF function, with the 'AGE' argument, computes the number of years between the variable BirthDate and the current date (from the TODAY function). Then the INT function returns the integer portion of the value.

Formats If you print a SAS date value, SAS will by default print the actual value—the number of days since January 1, 1960. Since this is not very meaningful to most people, SAS has a variety of formats for printing dates in different forms.[12] The FORMAT statement below tells SAS to print the variable BirthDate using the WORDDATE18. format:

```
FORMAT BirthDate WORDDATE18.;
```

Example A local library has a data file containing details about library cards. Each record contains the card holder's name, birthdate, the date that the card was issued, and the due date for the last book borrowed.

```
A. Jones     1-1-60      9-15-96     18JUN12
R. Grandage 03/18/1988 31 10 2007 5jul2012
K. Kaminaka 052903       2012024    12-MAR-12
```

The program below reads the raw data, and then computes the variable DaysOverDue by subtracting DueDate from the current date. The card holder's current age is computed. Then an IF statement uses a date constant to identify cards issued after January 1, 2012.

```
DATA librarycards;
   INFILE 'c:\MyRawData\Library.dat' TRUNCOVER;
   INPUT Name $11. + 1 BirthDate MMDDYY10. +1 IssueDate ANYDTDTE10.
      DueDate DATE11.;
   DaysOverDue = TODAY() - DueDate;
   CurrentAge = INT(YRDIF(BirthDate, TODAY(), 'AGE'));
   IF IssueDate > '01JAN2012'D THEN NewCard = 'yes';
RUN;
PROC PRINT DATA = librarycards;
   FORMAT Issuedate MMDDYY8. DueDate WEEKDATE17.;
   TITLE 'SAS Dates without and with Formats';
RUN;
```

Here is the output from PROC PRINT. Notice that the variable BirthDate is printed without a date format, while IssueDate and DueDate use formats. Because DaysOverDue and CurrentAge are computed using the TODAY() function, their values will change depending on the day the program is run. The value of DaysOverDue is negative for books due in the future.

SAS Dates without and with Formats

Obs	Name	BirthDate	IssueDate	DueDate	DaysOverDue	CurrentAge	NewCard
1	A. Jones	0	09/15/96	Mon, Jun 18, 2012	0	52	
2	R. Grandage	10304	10/31/07	Thu, Jul 5, 2012	-17	24	
3	K. Kaminaka	15854	01/24/12	Mon, Mar 12, 2012	98	9	yes

---

[10] SAS also has informats, functions, and formats for working with time values (the number of seconds since midnight), and datetime values (the number of seconds since midnight, you guessed it, January 1, 1960).

[11] ANYDTDTE*w*. is a special informat that can read dates in almost any form. If a date is ambiguous such as 01-02-03, then SAS uses the value of the DATESTYLE= system option to determine the order of month, day and year. The default value of DATESTYLE= is MDY (month, then day, then year).

[12] For more information on formats, see section 4.6.

3.9 ► Selected Date Informats, Functions, and Formats

Informats	Definition	Width range	Default width
ANYDTDTE*w*.	Reads dates in various date forms	5–32	9
DATE*w*.	Reads dates in form: *ddmmmyy* or *ddmmmyyyy*	7–32	7
DDMMYY*w*.	Reads dates in form: *ddmmyy* or *ddmmyyyy*	6–32	6
JULIAN*w*.	Reads Julian dates in form: *yyddd* or *yyyyddd*	5–32	5
MMDDYY*w*.	Reads dates in form: *mmddyy* or *mmddyyyy*	6–32	6

Functions	Syntax	Definition
DATEJUL	DATEJUL(*julian-date*)	Converts a Julian date to a SAS date value[13]
DAY	DAY(*date*)	Returns the day of the month from a SAS date value
MDY	MDY(*month,day,year*)	Returns a SAS date value from month, day, and year values
MONTH	MONTH(*date*)	Returns the month (1–12) from a SAS date value
QTR	QTR(*date*)	Returns the yearly quarter (1–4) from a SAS date value
TODAY	TODAY()	Returns the current date as a SAS date value
WEEKDAY	WEEKDAY(*date*)	Returns day of week (1=Sunday) from SAS date value
YEAR	YEAR(*date*)	Returns year from a SAS date value
YRDIF	YRDIF(*start-date,end-date,* 'AGE')	Computes difference in years between two SAS date values taking leap years into account

Formats	Definition	Width range	Default width
DATE*w*.	Writes SAS date values in form: *ddmmmyy*	5–11	7
EURDFDD*w*.	Writes SAS date values in form: *dd.mm.yy*	2–10	8
JULIAN*w*.	Writes a Julian date from a SAS date value	5–7	5
MMDDYY*w*.	Writes SAS date values in form: *mmddyy* or *mmddyyyy*	2–10	8
WEEKDATE*w*.	Writes SAS date values in form: *day-of-week, month-name dd, yy* or *yyyy*	3–37	29
WORDDATE*w*.	Writes SAS date values in form: *month-name dd, yyyy*	3–32	18

Informats	Input data	INPUT statement	Results
ANYDTDTE*w*.	1jan1961 01/01/61	INPUT Day ANYDTDTE10.;	366 366
DATE*w*.	1jan1961	INPUT Day DATE10.;	366
DDMMYY*w*.	01.01.61 02/01/61	INPUT Day DDMMYY8.;	366 367
JULIAN*w*.	61001	INPUT Day JULIAN7.;	366
MMDDYY*w*.	01-01-61	INPUT Day MMDDYY8.;	366

Functions	Example	Result	Example	Results
DATEJUL	a=60001; x=DATEJUL(a);	x=0	a=60365; y=DATEJUL(a);	y=364
DAY	a=MDY(4,18,2012); x=DAY(a);	x=18	a=MDY(9,3,60); y=DAY(a);	y=3
MDY	x=MDY(1,1,1960);	x=0	m=2; d=1; y=60; Date=MDY(m,d,y);	Date=31
MONTH	a=MDY(4,18,2012); x=MONTH(a);	x=4	a=MDY(9,3,60); y=MONTH(a);	y=9
QTR	a=MDY(4,18,2012); x=QTR(a);	x=2	a=MDY(9,3,60); y=QTR(a);	y=3
TODAY	x=TODAY();	x=*today's date*	y=TODAY()-1;	y=*yesterday's date*
WEEKDAY	a=MDY(4,13,2012); x=WEEKDAY(a);	x=6	a=MDY(4,18,2012); y=WEEKDAY(a);	y=4
YEAR	a=MDY(4,13,2000); x=YEAR(a);	x=2000	a=MDY(1,1,1960); y=YEAR(a);	y=1960

YRDIF	a=MDY(4,13,2000);
	b=MDY(4,13,2012);
	x=YRDIF(a,b,'AGE');
		x=12	a=MDY(4,13,2000);
			b=MDY(8,13,2012);
			y=YRDIF(a,b,'AGE');
				y=12.3342

Formats	Input data	PUT statement[14]	Results
DATE*w*.	366	PUT Birth DATE7.; PUT Birth DATE9.;	01JAN61 01JAN1961
EURDFDD*w*.	366	PUT Birth EURDFDD8. PUT Birth EURDFDD10.;	01.01.61 01.01.1961
JULIAN*w*.	366	PUT Birth JULIAN5.; PUT Birth JULIAN7.;	61001 1961001
MMDDYY*w*.	366	PUT Birth MMDDYY6.; PUT Birth MMDDYY10.;	010161 01/01/1961
WEEKDATE*w*.	366	PUT Birth WEEKDATE9.; PUT Birth WEEKDATE29.;	Sunday Sunday, January 1, 1961
WORDDATE*w*.	366	PUT Birth WORDDATE12.; PUT Birth WORDDATE18.;	Jan 1, 1961 January 1, 1961

---

[13] A SAS date value is the number of days since January 1, 1960.

[14] Formats can be used in PUT statements and PUT functions in DATA steps, and in FORMAT statements in either DATA or PROC steps.

3.10 Using the RETAIN and Sum Statements

When reading raw data, SAS sets the values of all variables equal to missing at the start of each iteration of the DATA step. These values may be changed by INPUT or assignment statements, but they are set back to missing again when SAS returns to the top of the DATA step to process the next observation. RETAIN and sum statements change this. If a variable appears in a RETAIN statement, then its value will be retained from one iteration of the DATA step to the next. A sum statement also retains a value from the previous iteration, but then it adds the value to an expression.

RETAIN statement Use the RETAIN statement when you want SAS to preserve a variable's value from the previous iteration of the DATA step. The RETAIN statement can appear anywhere in the DATA step and has the following form, where all variables to be retained are listed after the RETAIN keyword:

```
RETAIN variable-list;
```

You can also specify an initial value, instead of missing, for the variables. All variables listed before an initial value will start the first iteration of the DATA step with that value:

```
RETAIN variable-list initial-value;
```

Sum statement A sum statement also retains values from the previous iteration of the DATA step, but you use it for the special cases where you simply want to cumulatively add the value of an expression to a variable. A sum statement, like an assignment statement, contains no keywords. It has the following form:

```
variable + expression;
```

No, there is no typo here and no equal sign either. This statement adds the value of the expression to the variable while retaining the variable's value from one iteration of the DATA step to the next. The variable must be numeric and has the initial value of zero. This statement can be re-written using the RETAIN statement and SUM function as follows:

```
RETAIN variable 0;
variable = SUM(variable, expression);
```

As you can see, a sum statement is really a special case of using RETAIN.

Example This example illustrates the use of both the RETAIN and sum statements. The minor league baseball team, the Walla Walla Sweets, has the following data about their games. The date the game was played and the team played are followed by the number of hits and runs for the game:

```
6-19 Columbia Peaches       8    3
6-20 Columbia Peaches      10    5
6-23 Plains Peanuts         3    4
6-24 Plains Peanuts         7    2
6-25 Plains Peanuts        12    8
6-30 Gilroy Garlics         4    4
7-1  Gilroy Garlics         9    4
7-4  Sacramento Tomatoes   15    9
7-4  Sacramento Tomatoes   10   10
7-5  Sacramento Tomatoes    2    3
```

The team wants two additional variables in their data set. One shows the cumulative number of runs for the season, and the other shows the maximum number of runs in a game to date. The following program uses a sum statement to compute the cumulative number of runs, and the RETAIN statement and MAX function to determine the maximum number of runs in a game to date:

```
* Using RETAIN and sum statements to find most runs and total runs;
DATA gamestats;
   INFILE 'c:\MyRawData\Games.dat';
   INPUT Month 1 Day 3-4 Team $ 6-25 Hits 27-28 Runs 30-31;
   RETAIN MaxRuns;
   MaxRuns = MAX(MaxRuns, Runs);
   RunsToDate + Runs;
RUN;
PROC PRINT DATA = gamestats;
   TITLE "Season's Record to Date";
RUN;
```

The variable MaxRuns is set equal to the maximum of its value from the previous iteration of the DATA step (since it appears in the RETAIN statement) or the value of the variable Runs. The variable RunsToDate adds the number of runs per game, Runs, to itself while retaining its value from one iteration of the DATA step to the next. This produces a cumulative record of the number of runs.

Here are the results:

Season's Record to Date

Obs	Month	Day	Team	Hits	Runs	MaxRuns	RunsToDate
1	6	19	Columbia Peaches	8	3	3	3
2	6	20	Columbia Peaches	10	5	5	8
3	6	23	Plains Peanuts	3	4	5	12
4	6	24	Plains Peanuts	7	2	5	14
5	6	25	Plains Peanuts	12	8	8	22
6	6	30	Gilroy Garlics	4	4	8	26
7	7	1	Gilroy Garlics	9	4	8	30
8	7	4	Sacramento Tomatoes	15	9	9	39
9	7	4	Sacramento Tomatoes	10	10	10	49
10	7	5	Sacramento Tomatoes	2	3	10	52

3.11 Simplifying Programs with Arrays

Sometimes you want to do the same thing to many variables. You may want to take the log of every numeric variable or change every occurrence of zero to a missing value. You could write a series of assignment statements or IF statements, but if you have a lot of variables to transform, using arrays will simplify and shorten your program.

An array is an ordered group of similar items. You might think your local mall has a nice array of stores to choose from. In SAS, an array is a group of variables. You can define an array to be any group of variables you like, as long as they are either all numeric or all character. The variables can be ones that already exist in your data set, or they can be new variables that you want to create.

Arrays are defined using the ARRAY statement in the DATA step. The ARRAY statement has the following general form:

```
ARRAY name (n) $ variable-list;
```

In this statement, *name* is a name you give to the array, and *n* is the number of variables in the array. Following the (*n*) is a list of variable names. The number of variables in the list must equal the number given in parentheses. (You may use { } or [ ] instead of parentheses if you like.) This is called an explicit array, where you explicitly state the number of variables in the array. The $ is needed if the variables are character, and is only necessary if the variables have not previously been defined.

The array itself is not stored with the data set; it is defined only for the duration of the DATA step. You can give the array any name, as long as it does not match any of the variable names in your data set or any SAS keywords. The rules for naming arrays are the same as those for naming variables (must be 32 characters or fewer and start with a letter or underscore followed by letters, numerals, or underscores).

To reference a variable using the array name, give the array name and the subscript for that variable. The first variable in the variable list has subscript 1, the second has subscript 2, and so forth. So if you have an array defined as

```
ARRAY store (4) Macys Penneys Sears Target;
```

STORE(1) is the variable Macys, STORE(2) is the variable Penneys, STORE(3) is the variable Sears, and STORE(4) is the variable Target. This is all just fine, but simply defining an array doesn't do anything for you. You want to be able to use the array to make things easier for you.

Example The radio station KBRK is conducting a survey asking people to rate five different songs. Songs are rated on a scale of 1 to 5, where 1 equals change the station when it comes on, and 5 equals turn up the volume when it comes on. If listeners had not heard the song or didn't care to comment on it, a 9 was entered for that song. The following are the data collected:

```
Albany       54 3 9 4 4 9
Richmond     33 2 9 3 3 3
Oakland      27 3 9 4 2 3
Richmond     41 3 5 4 5 5
Berkeley     18 4 4 9 3 2
```

The listener's city of residence, age, and their responses to all five songs are listed. The following program changes all the 9s to missing values. (The variables are named using the first letters of the words in the song's title.)

```
* Change all 9s to missing values;
DATA songs;
   INFILE 'c:\MyRawData\KBRK.dat';
   INPUT City $ 1-15 Age wj kt tr filp ttr;
   ARRAY song (5) wj kt tr filp ttr;
   DO i = 1 TO 5;
      IF song(i) = 9 THEN song(i) = .;
   END;
RUN;
PROC PRINT DATA = songs;
   TITLE 'KBRK Song Survey';
RUN;
```

An array, SONG, is defined as having five variables, the same five variables that appear in the INPUT statement representing the five songs. Next comes an iterative DO statement. All statements between the DO statement and the END statement are executed, in this case, five times, once for each variable in the array.

The variable I is used as an index variable and is incremented by 1 each time through the DO loop. The first time through the DO loop, the variable I has a value of 1 and the IF statement would read `IF song(1)=9 THEN song(1)=.;`, which is the same as `IF wj=9 THEN wj=.;`. The second time through, I has a value of 2 and the IF statement would read `IF song(2)=9 THEN song(2)=.;`, which is the same as `IF kt=9 THEN kt=.;`. This continues through all five variables in the array.

Here are the results:

KBRK Song Survey

Obs	City	Age	wj	kt	tr	filp	ttr	i
1	Albany	54	3	.	4	4	.	6
2	Richmond	33	2	.	3	3	3	6
3	Oakland	27	3	.	4	2	3	6
4	Richmond	41	3	5	4	5	5	6
5	Berkeley	18	4	4	.	3	2	6

Notice that the array members SONG(1) to SONG(5) did not become part of the data set, but the variable I did. You could have written five IF statements instead of using arrays and accomplished the same result. In this program it would not have made a big difference, but if you had 100 songs in your survey instead of five, then using arrays would clearly be a better solution.

3.12 Using Shortcuts for Lists of Variable Names

While writing SAS programs, you will often need to write a list of variable names. If you only have a handful of variables, you might not feel a need for a shortcut. But if, for example, you need to define an array with 100 elements, you might be a little grumpy after typing in the 49th variable name knowing you still have 51 more to go. You might even think, "There must be an easier way." Well, there is.

You can use an abbreviated list of variable names almost anywhere you can use a regular variable list. In functions, abbreviated lists must be preceded by the keyword OF (for example, SUM(OF Cat8 - Cat12)). Otherwise, you simply replace the regular list with the abbreviated one.

Numbered range lists Variables which start with the same characters and end with consecutive numbers can be part of a numbered range list. The numbers can start and end anywhere as long as the number sequence between is complete. For example, the following INPUT statement shows a variable list and its abbreviated form:

Variable list	Abbreviated list
`INPUT Cat8 Cat9 Cat10 Cat11 Cat12;`	`INPUT Cat8 - Cat12;`

Name range lists Name range lists depend on the internal order, or position, of the variables in the SAS data set. This is determined by the order of appearance of the variables in the DATA step. For example, given the following DATA step, the internal variable order would be Y A C H R B:

```
DATA example;
   INPUT y a c h r;
   b = c + r;
RUN;
```

To specify a name range list, put the first variable, then two hyphens, then the last variable. The following PUT statements show the variable list and its abbreviated form using a named range:

Variable list	Abbreviated list
`PUT y a c h r b;`	`PUT y -- b;`

If you are not sure of the internal order, you can find out using PROC CONTENTS with the POSITION option. The following program will list the variables in the permanent SAS data set DISTANCE sorted by position:

```
LIBNAME mydir 'c:\MySASLib';
PROC CONTENTS DATA = mydir.distance POSITION;
RUN;
```

Use caution when including name range lists in your programs. Although they can save on typing, they may also make your programs more difficult to understand and debug.

Name prefix lists Variables which start with the same characters can be part of a name prefix list, and can be used in some SAS statements and functions. For example:

Variable list	Abbreviated list
`DogBills = SUM(DogVet,DogFood,Dog_Care);`	`DogBills = SUM(OF Dog:);`

Special SAS name lists The special name lists, _ALL_, _CHARACTER_, and _NUMERIC_ can also be used any place you want either all the variables, all the character variables, or all the numeric variables in a SAS data set. These name lists are useful when you want to do something like compute the mean of all the numeric variables for an observation (MEAN(OF _NUMERIC_)), or list the values of all variables in an observation (PUT _ALL_;).

Example The radio station KBRK wants to modify the program from the previous section, which changes all 9s to missing values. Now, instead of changing the original variables, they create new variables (Song1 through Song5) which will have the new missing values. This program also computes the average score using the MEAN function. Here are the data:

```
Albany        54 3 9 4 4 9
Richmond      33 2 9 3 3 3
Oakland       27 3 9 4 2 3
Richmond      41 3 5 4 5 5
Berkeley      18 4 4 9 3 2
```

Here is the new program:

```
DATA songs;
   INFILE 'c:\MyRawData\KBRK.dat';
   INPUT City $ 1-15 Age wj kt  tr filp ttr;
   ARRAY new (5) Song1 - Song5;
   ARRAY old (5) wj -- ttr;
   DO i = 1 TO 5;
      IF old(i) = 9 THEN new(i) = .;
         ELSE new(i) = old(i);
   END;
   AvgScore = MEAN(OF Song1 - Song5);
PROC PRINT DATA = songs;
   TITLE 'KBRK Song Survey';
RUN;
```

Note that both ARRAY statements use abbreviated variable lists; array NEW uses a numbered range list and array OLD uses a name range list. Inside the iterative DO loop, the Song variables (array NEW) are set equal to missing if the original variable (array OLD) had a value of 9. Otherwise, they are set equal to the original values. After the DO loop, a new variable, AvgScore, is created using an abbreviated variable list in the function MEAN. The output includes variables from both the OLD array (wj -- ttr) and NEW array (Song1 – Song5):

KBRK Song Survey

Obs	City	Age	wj	kt	tr	filp	ttr	Song1	Song2	Song3	Song4	Song5	i	AvgScore
1	Albany	54	3	9	4	4	9	3	.	4	4	.	6	3.66667
2	Richmond	33	2	9	3	3	3	2	.	3	3	3	6	2.75000
3	Oakland	27	3	9	4	2	3	3	.	4	2	3	6	3.00000
4	Richmond	41	3	5	4	5	5	3	5	4	5	5	6	4.40000
5	Berkeley	18	4	4	9	3	2	4	4	.	3	2	6	3.25000

4

"**O**nce in a while the simple things work right off."

PHIL GALLAGHER

From the SAS-L Listserv, 1994. Reprinted by permission of the author.

CHAPTER 4

Sorting, Printing, and Summarizing Your Data

4.1 ▸ Using SAS Procedures

```
PROC whatever
DATA= _____
BY      _____
TITLE   _____
FOOTNOTE _____
LABEL   _____
```

Using a procedure, or PROC, is like filling out a form. Someone else designed the form, and all you have to do is fill in the blanks and choose from a list of options. Each PROC has its own unique form with its own list of options. But while each procedure is unique, there are similarities too. This section discusses some of those similarities.

All procedures have required statements, and most have optional statements. PROC PRINT, for example, requires only two words:

```
PROC PRINT;
```

However, by adding optional statements you could make this procedure a dozen lines or even longer.

PROC statement All procedures start with the keyword PROC followed by the name of the procedure, such as PRINT or CONTENTS. Options, if there are any, follow the procedure name. The DATA= option tells SAS which data set to use as input for that procedure. In this case, SAS will use a temporary SAS data set named BANANA:

```
PROC CONTENTS DATA = banana;
```

The DATA= option is, of course, optional. If you skip it, then SAS will use the most recently created data set, which is not necessarily the same as the most recently used. Sometimes it is easier to specify the data set you want than to figure out which data set SAS will use by default. To use a permanent SAS data set, issue a LIBNAME statement to set up a libref pointing to the location of your data set, and put the data set's two-level name in the DATA= option, as discussed in section 2.19,

```
LIBNAME tropical 'c:\MySASLib';
PROC CONTENTS DATA = tropical.banana;
```

or refer to it directly by placing your operating environment's name for the permanent SAS data set between quotation marks, as discussed in section 2.20.

```
PROC CONTENTS DATA = 'c:\MySASLib\banana';
```

BY statement The BY statement is required for only one procedure, PROC SORT. In PROC SORT the BY statement tells SAS how to arrange the observations. In all other procedures, the BY statement is optional, and tells SAS to perform a separate analysis for each combination of values of the BY variables rather than treating all observations as one group. For example, this statement tells SAS to run a separate analysis for each state:

```
BY State;
```

All procedures, except PROC SORT, assume that your data are already sorted by the variables in your BY statement. If your observations are not already sorted, then use PROC SORT to do the job.

TITLE and FOOTNOTE statements You have seen TITLE statements many times in this book. FOOTNOTE works the same way, but prints at the bottom of the page. These global statements are not technically part of any step. You can put them anywhere in your program, but since they apply to the procedure output it generally makes sense to put them with the procedure. The most basic TITLE statement consists of the keyword TITLE followed by your title enclosed in quotation marks. SAS doesn't care if the two quotation marks are single or double as long as they are the same:

```
TITLE 'This is a title';
```

If you find that your title contains an apostrophe, use double quotation marks around the title, or replace the single apostrophe with two:

```
TITLE "Here's another title";
TITLE 'Here''s another title';
```

You can specify up to ten titles or footnotes by adding numbers to the keywords TITLE and FOOTNOTE:

```
FOOTNOTE3 'This is the third footnote';
```

Titles and footnotes stay in effect until you replace them with new ones or cancel them with a null statement. The following null statement would cancel all current titles:

```
TITLE;
```

When you specify a new title or footnote, it replaces the old title or footnote with the same number and cancels those with a higher number. For example, a new TITLE2 cancels an existing TITLE3, if there is one.

LABEL statement By default, SAS uses variable names to label your output, but with the LABEL statement you can create more descriptive labels, up to 256 characters long, for each variable. This statement creates labels for the variables ReceiveDate and ShipDate:

```
LABEL ReceiveDate  = 'Date order was received'
      ShipDate = 'Date merchandise was shipped';
```

When a LABEL statement is used in a DATA step, the labels become part of the data set; but when used in a PROC, the labels stay in effect only for the duration of that particular step.

Customizing output You have a lot of control over the output produced by procedures. Using system options, you can set many features such as centering, dates, and paper orientation (see section 1.13). With the Output Delivery System, you can also change the overall style of your output, produce output in different formats (such as PDF or RTF), or change almost any detail of your output (chapter 5).

Output data sets Most procedures produce some kind of report, but sometimes you would like the results of the procedure saved as a SAS data set so you can perform further analysis. You can create SAS data sets from any procedure output using the ODS OUTPUT statement (section 5.3). Some procedures can also write a SAS data set using an OUTPUT statement or OUT= option.

4.2 ▶ Subsetting in Procedures with the WHERE Statement

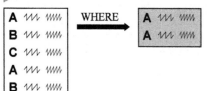

One optional statement for any PROC that reads a SAS data set is the WHERE statement. The WHERE statement tells a procedure to use a subset of the data. There are other ways to subset data, as you probably remember, so you could get by without ever using the WHERE statement.[1] However, the WHERE statement is a shortcut. While subsetting IFs work only in DATA steps, the WHERE statement works in PROC steps too.

Unlike subsetting in a DATA step, using a WHERE statement in a procedure does not create a new data set. That is one of the reasons why WHERE statements are sometimes more efficient than other ways of subsetting.

The basic form of a WHERE statement is

```
WHERE condition;
```

Only observations satisfying the condition will be used by the PROC. This may look familiar since it is similar to a subsetting IF. The left side of the condition is a variable name, and the right side is a variable name, a constant, or a mathematical expression. Mathematical expressions can contain the standard arithmetic symbols for addition (+), subtraction (-), multiplication (*), division (/), and exponentiation (**). Between the two sides of the expression, you can use comparison and logical operators; those operators may be symbolic or mnemonic. Here are the most frequently used operators:

Symbolic	Mnemonic	Example
=	EQ	WHERE Region = 'Spain';
¬=, ~=, ^=	NE	WHERE Region ~= 'Spain';
>	GT	WHERE Rainfall > 20;
<	LT	WHERE Rainfall < AvgRain;
>=	GE	WHERE Rainfall >= AvgRain + 5;
<=	LE	WHERE Rainfall <= AvgRain / 1.25;
&	AND	WHERE Rainfall > 20 AND Temp < 90;
|,¦,!	OR	WHERE Rainfall > 20 OR Temp < 90;
	IS NOT MISSING	WHERE Region IS NOT MISSING;
	BETWEEN AND	WHERE Region BETWEEN 'Plain' AND 'Spain';
	CONTAINS	WHERE Region CONTAINS 'ain';
	IN (*LIST*)	WHERE Region IN ('Rain', 'Spain', 'Plain');

Example You have a database containing information about well-known painters. A subset of the data appears below. For each artist, the data include the painter's name, primary style, and nation of origin:

```
Mary Cassatt            Impressionism        U
Paul Cezanne            Post-impressionism   F
Edgar Degas             Impressionism        F
Paul Gauguin            Post-impressionism   F
Claude Monet            Impressionism        F
Pierre Auguste Renoir   Impressionism        F
Vincent van Gogh        Post-impressionism   N
```

To make this example more realistic, it has two parts: one to create a permanent SAS data set, the other to subset the data. First a DATA step reads the data from a file named Artists.dat, and uses direct referencing (you could use a LIBNAME statement instead) to create a permanent SAS data set named STYLE in a directory named MySASLib (Windows).

```
DATA 'c:\MySASLib\style';
   INFILE 'c:\MyRawData\Artists.dat';
   INPUT Name $ 1-21 Genre $ 23-40 Origin $ 42;
RUN;
```

Suppose a day later you wanted to print a list of just the impressionist painters. The quick-and-easy way to do this is with a WHERE statement and PROC PRINT. The quotation marks around the data set name tell SAS that this is a permanent SAS data set.

```
PROC PRINT DATA = 'c:\MySASLib\style';
   WHERE Genre = 'Impressionism';
   TITLE 'Major Impressionist Painters';
   FOOTNOTE 'F = France N = Netherlands U = US';
RUN;
```

The output looks like this:

Major Impressionist Painters

Obs	Name	Genre	Origin
1	Mary Cassatt	Impressionism	U
3	Edgar Degas	Impressionism	F
5	Claude Monet	Impressionism	F
6	Pierre Auguste Renoir	Impressionism	F

F = France N = Netherlands U = US

---

[1] For more on the WHERE statement, see the appendix. Other ways to subset data include subsetting IF statements (sections 2.13, 3.7, and 6.9), and the WHERE= option (section 6.13).

4.3 ▸ Sorting Your Data with PROC SORT

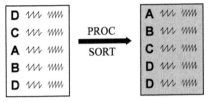

There are many reasons for sorting your data: to organize data for a report, before combining data sets, or before using a BY statement in another PROC or DATA step. Fortunately, PROC SORT is quite simple. The basic form of this procedure is

```
PROC SORT;
   BY variable-list;
```

The variables named in the BY statement are called BY variables. You can specify as many BY variables as you wish. With one BY variable, SAS sorts the data based on the values of that variable. With more than one variable, SAS sorts observations by the first variable, then by the second variable within categories of the first, and so on. A BY group is all the observations that have the same values of BY variables. If, for example, your BY variable is State then all the observations for North Dakota form one BY group.

Controlling the output data set The DATA= and OUT= options specify the input and output data sets. If you don't specify the DATA= option, then SAS will use the most recently created data set. If you don't specify the OUT= option, then SAS will replace the original data set with the newly sorted version. This sample statement tells SAS to sort the data set named MESSY, and then put the sorted data into a data set named NEAT:

```
PROC SORT DATA = messy OUT = neat;
```

The NODUPKEY option tells SAS to eliminate any duplicate observations that have the same values for the BY variables. If you specify the DUPOUT= option, then SAS will put the deleted observations in that data set. To use these options, just add them to the PROC SORT statement:

```
PROC SORT DATA = messy OUT = neat  NODUPKEY  DUPOUT = extraobs;
```

Ascending versus descending sorts By default SAS sorts data in ascending order, from lowest to highest. To have your data sorted in the opposite order, add the keyword DESCENDING to the BY statement before each variable that should be sorted in reverse order. This statement tells SAS to sort first by State (from A to Z) and then by City (from Z to A) within State:

```
BY State DESCENDING City;
```

Example The following data show the typical length in feet of selected whales and sharks. Notice that each line includes data for more than one species.

```
beluga    whale   15   dwarf      shark   .5    sperm    whale   60
basking   shark   30   humpback   .       50    whale    shark   40
gray      whale   50   blue       whale   100   killer   whale   30
mako      shark   12   whale      shark   40
```

This program reads and sorts the data:

```
DATA marine;
   INFILE 'c:\MyRawData\Lengths.dat';
   INPUT Name $ Family $ Length @@;
RUN;
* Sort the data;
PROC SORT DATA = marine OUT = seasort NODUPKEY;
   BY Family DESCENDING Length;
PROC PRINT DATA = seasort;
   TITLE 'Whales and Sharks';
RUN;
```

The DATA step reads the raw data from a file called Lengths.dat and creates a SAS data set named MARINE. Then PROC SORT rearranges the observations by Family in ascending order, and by Length in descending order. The NODUPKEY option of PROC SORT eliminates any duplicates, while the OUT= option writes the sorted data into a new data set named SEASORT. The output from PROC PRINT looks like this:

Whales and Sharks

Obs	Name	Family	Length
1	humpback		50.0
2	whale	shark	40.0
3	basking	shark	30.0
4	mako	shark	12.0
5	dwarf	shark	0.5
6	blue	whale	100.0
7	sperm	whale	60.0
8	gray	whale	50.0
9	killer	whale	30.0
10	beluga	whale	15.0

Notice that the humpback, with a missing value for Family, became observation 1. That is because missing values are always low for both numeric and character variables. Also, the NODUPKEY option eliminated a duplicate observation for the whale shark. The log contains these notes showing that the sorted data set has one fewer observation than the original data set.

```
NOTE: The data set WORK.MARINE has 11 observations and 3 variables.
NOTE: 1 observations with duplicate key values were deleted.
NOTE: The data set WORK.SEASORT has 10 observations and 3 variables.
```

4.4 ▶ Changing the Sort Order for Character Data

At first glance, sorting character data appears straightforward. After all, everyone knows that "A" comes before "B." However, it is less obvious whether "A" comes before "a." SAS offers dozens of options for controlling the sort order of character data (also called the collating sequence). This section describes a few of them.

ASCII versus EBCDIC The default collating sequence for the z/OS operating environment is EBCDIC. The default collating sequence for most other operating environments is ASCII. From lowest to highest, the basic sort orders for character data are

| **ASCII** | blank | numerals | uppercase letters | lowercase letters |
| **EBCDIC** | blank | lowercase letters | uppercase letters | numerals |

If you work in only one operating environment, this may not matter to you. However, if you need to create a data set on Windows that will be used on z/OS or vice versa, then you might want your data to be sorted in the order expected by that environment. You can use the options SORTSEQ=EBCDIC and SORTSEQ=ASCII to change the sort order:[2]

```
PROC SORT SORTSEQ = EBCDIC;
```

Linguistic sorting By default, upper- and lowercase letters will be sorted separately, but this is not the way that people generally sort them. You can use linguistic sorting to produce a more intuitive order. The SORTSEQ=LINGUISTIC option with the STRENGTH=PRIMARY suboption tells SAS to ignore case. To use these options, add them to the PROC SORT statement like this

```
PROC SORT SORTSEQ = LINGUISTIC (STRENGTH = PRIMARY);
```

Here are data that are unsorted, sorted in the default ASCII order and then sorted ignoring case:

Unsorted order	Default Sort	Linguistic Sort (STRENGTH=PRIMARY)
eva	ANNA	amanda
amanda	Zenobia	ANNA
Zenobia	amanda	eva
ANNA	eva	Zenobia

When numerals are sorted as character data, the value "10" comes before "2." The NUMERIC_COLLATION=ON suboption tells SAS to treat numerals as their numeric equivalent.

```
PROC SORT SORTSEQ = LINGUISTIC (NUMERIC_COLLATION = ON);
```

Here are data that are unsorted, sorted in the default order and sorted with numeric collation:

Unsorted order	Default Sort	Linguistic Sort (NUMERIC_COLLATION=ON)
1500m freestyle	100m backstroke	50m freestyle
200m breaststroke	1500m freestyle	100m backstroke
100m backstroke	200m breaststroke	200m breaststroke
50m freestyle	50m freestyle	1500m freestyle

Example The following data contain names and addresses.

```
Seiki   100 A St.           juneau    alaska
Wong    2 A St.             Honolulu  Hawaii
Shaw    10 A St. Apt. 10 Juneau    Alaska
Smith   10 A St. Apt. 2  honolulu  hawaii
```

This program reads the raw data, and then sorts the data twice. First the data are sorted by Street using numeric collation, and then by State ignoring case.

```
DATA addresses;
   INFILE 'c:\MyRawData\Mail.dat';
   INPUT Name $6. Street $18. City $9. State $6.;
RUN;
PROC SORT DATA = addresses OUT = sortone
     SORTSEQ = LINGUISTIC (NUMERIC_COLLATION = ON);
   BY Street;
PROC PRINT DATA = sortone;
   TITLE 'addresses Sorted by Street';
RUN;
PROC SORT DATA = addresses OUT = sorttwo
     SORTSEQ = LINGUISTIC (STRENGTH = PRIMARY);
   BY State;
PROC PRINT DATA = sorttwo;
   TITLE 'Addresses Sorted by State';
RUN;
```

Here are the results:

Addresses Sorted by Street

Obs	Name	Street	City	State
1	Wong	2 A St.	Honolulu	Hawaii
2	Smith	10 A St. Apt. 2	honolulu	hawaii
3	Shaw	10 A St. Apt. 10	Juneau	Alaska
4	Seiki	100 A St.	juneau	alaska

Addresses Sorted by State

Obs	Name	Street	City	State
1	Seiki	100 A St.	juneau	alaska
2	Shaw	10 A St. Apt. 10	Juneau	Alaska
3	Wong	2 A St.	Honolulu	Hawaii
4	Smith	10 A St. Apt. 2	honolulu	hawaii

When you use the STRENGTH=PRIMARY option, then case will be ignored for BY groups. In this example, the values alaska and Alaska are in one BY group, and hawaii and Hawaii are in a second BY group.

---

[2] Other possible values for the SORTSEQ= option include DANISH, FINNISH, ITALIAN, NORWEGIAN, POLISH, SPANISH, and SWEDISH.

4.5 Printing Your Data with PROC PRINT

The PRINT procedure is perhaps the most widely used SAS procedure. You have seen this procedure used many times in this book to print the contents of a SAS data set. In its simplest form, PROC PRINT prints all variables for all observations in the SAS data set. SAS decides the best way to format the output, so you don't have to worry about things like how many variables will fit on a page. But there are a few more features of PROC PRINT that you might want to use.

The PRINT procedure requires just one statement:

```
PROC PRINT;
```

By default, SAS uses the SAS data set created most recently. If you do not want to print the most recent data set, then use the DATA= option to specify the data set. We recommend always using the DATA= option for clarity in your programs as it is not always easy to quickly determine which data set was created last.

```
PROC PRINT DATA = data-set;
```

Also, SAS prints the observation numbers along with the variables' values. If you don't want observation numbers, use the NOOBS option in the PROC PRINT statement. If you define variable labels with a LABEL statement, and you want to print the labels instead of the variable names, then add the LABEL option as well. The following statement shows all of these options together:

```
PROC PRINT DATA = data-set NOOBS LABEL;
```

The following are optional statements that sometimes come in handy:

BY *variable-list;*	The BY statement starts a new section in the output for each new value of the BY variables and prints the values of the BY variables at the top of each section. The data must be presorted by the BY variables.
ID *variable-list;*	When you use the ID statement, the observation numbers are not printed. Instead, the variables in the ID variable list appear on the left-hand side of the page.
SUM *variable-list;*	The sum statement prints sums for the variables in the list.
VAR *variable-list;*	The VAR statement specifies which variables to print and the order. Without a VAR statement, all variables in the SAS data set are printed in the order that they occur in the data set.

Example Students from two fourth-grade classes are selling candy to earn money for a special field trip. The class earning more money gets a free box of candy. The following are the data for the results of the candy sale. The students' names are followed by their classroom number, the date they turned in their money, the type of candy: mint patties or chocolate dinosaurs, and the number of boxes sold:

```
Adriana  21  3/21/2012  MP   7
Nathan   14  3/21/2012  CD  19
Matthew  14  3/21/2012  CD  14
Claire   14  3/22/2012  CD  11
Ian      21  3/24/2012  MP  18
Chris    14  3/25/2012  CD   6
Anthony  21  3/25/2012  MP  13
Erika    21  3/25/2012  MP  17
```

The class earns $1.25 for each box of candy sold. The teachers want a report giving the money earned for each classroom, the money earned by each student, the type of candy sold, and the date the students returned their money. The following program reads the data, computes money earned (Profit), and sorts the data by classroom using PROC SORT. Then, the PROC PRINT step uses a BY statement to print the data by Class and a SUM statement to give the totals for Profit. The VAR statement lists the variables to be printed:

```
DATA sales;
   INFILE 'c:\MyRawData\CandySales.dat';
   INPUT Name $ 1-11 Class @15 DateReturned MMDDYY10. CandyType $
      Quantity;
   Profit = Quantity * 1.25;
PROC SORT DATA = sales;
   BY Class;
PROC PRINT DATA = sales;
   BY Class;
   SUM Profit;
   VAR Name DateReturned CandyType Profit;
   TITLE 'Candy Sales for Field Trip by Class';
RUN;
```

Here are the results. Notice that the values for the variable DateReturned are printed as their SAS date values. You can use formats, covered in the next section, to print dates in readable forms.

Candy Sales for Field Trip by Class

Class=14

Obs	Name	DateReturned	CandyType	Profit
1	Nathan	19073	CD	23.75
2	Matthew	19073	CD	17.50
3	Claire	19074	CD	13.75
4	Chris	19077	CD	7.50
Class				62.50

Class=21

Obs	Name	DateReturned	CandyType	Profit
5	Adriana	19073	MP	8.75
6	Ian	19076	MP	22.50
7	Anthony	19077	MP	16.25
8	Erika	19077	MP	21.25
Class				68.75
				131.25

4.6 ▶ Changing the Appearance of Printed Values with Formats

0	1002
2	2012
31	4336

➡

Obs	Date	Sales
1	01/01/60	1,002
2	01/03/60	2,012
3	02/01/60	4,336

When SAS prints your data, it decides which format is best—how many decimal places to print, how much space to allow for each value, and so on. This is very convenient and makes your job much easier, but SAS doesn't always do what you want. Fortunately you're not stuck with the format SAS thinks is best. You can change the appearance of printed values using SAS formats.

SAS has many formats for character, numeric, and date values. For example, you can use the COMMA*w.d* format to print numbers with embedded commas, the $*w*. format to control the number of characters printed, and the MMDDYY*w*. format to print SAS date values (the number of days since January 1, 1960) in a readable form like 12/03/2003. You can even print your data in more obscure formats like hexadecimal, zoned decimal, and packed decimal, if you like.[3]

The general forms of a SAS format are

Character	**Numeric**	**Date**
`$formatw.`	`formatw.d`	`formatw.`

where the $ indicates character formats, *format* is the name of the format, *w* is the total width including any decimal point, and *d* is the number of decimal places. The period in the format is very important because it distinguishes a format from a variable name, which cannot, by default, contain any special characters except the underscore.

FORMAT statement You can associate formats with variables in a FORMAT statement. The FORMAT statement starts with the keyword FORMAT, followed by the variable name (or names if more than one variable is to be associated with the same format), followed by the format. For example, the following FORMAT statement associates the DOLLAR8.2 format with the variables Profit and Loss and associates the MMDDYY8. format with the variable SaleDate:

```
FORMAT Profit Loss DOLLAR8.2 SaleDate MMDDYY8.;
```

FORMAT statements can go in either DATA steps or PROC steps. If the FORMAT statement is in a DATA step, then the format association is permanent and is stored with the SAS data set. If the FORMAT statement is in a PROC step, then it is temporary—affecting only the results from that procedure.

PUT statement You can also use formats in PUT statements when writing raw data files or reports. Place a format after each variable name, as in the following example:

```
PUT Profit DOLLAR8.2 Loss DOLLAR8.2 SaleDate MMDDYY8.;
```

Example In the previous section, results from the fourth-grade candy sale were printed using the PRINT procedure. The names of the students were printed along with the date they turned in their money, the type of candy sold, and the profit. You may have noticed that the dates printed were numbers like 19073 and 19077. Using the FORMAT statement in the PRINT procedure, we can print the dates in a readable form. At the same time, we can print the variable Profit using the DOLLAR6.2 format so dollar signs appear before the numbers.

Here are the data, where the students' names are followed by their classroom, the date they turned in their money, the type of candy sold: mint patties or chocolate dinosaurs, and the number of boxes sold:

```
Adriana   21   3/21/2012   MP    7
Nathan    14   3/21/2012   CD   19
Matthew   14   3/21/2012   CD   14
Claire    14   3/22/2012   CD   11
Ian       21   3/24/2012   MP   18
Chris     14   3/25/2012   CD    6
Anthony   21   3/25/2012   MP   13
Erika     21   3/25/2012   MP   17
```

The following program reads the raw data and computes Profit. The FORMAT statement in the PRINT procedure associates the DATE9. format with the variable DateReturned and the DOLLAR6.2 format with the variable Profit:

```
DATA sales;
   INFILE 'c:\MyRawData\CandySales.dat';
   INPUT Name $ 1-11 Class @15 DateReturned MMDDYY10. CandyType $
         Quantity;
   Profit = Quantity * 1.25;
PROC PRINT DATA = sales;
   VAR Name DateReturned CandyType Profit;
   FORMAT DateReturned DATE9. Profit DOLLAR6.2;
   TITLE 'Candy Sale Data Using Formats';
RUN;
```

Here are the results:

Candy Sale Data Using Formats

Obs	Name	DateReturned	CandyType	Profit
1	Adriana	21MAR2012	MP	$8.75
2	Nathan	21MAR2012	CD	$23.75
3	Matthew	21MAR2012	CD	$17.50
4	Claire	22MAR2012	CD	$13.75
5	Ian	24MAR2012	MP	$22.50
6	Chris	25MAR2012	CD	$7.50
7	Anthony	25MAR2012	MP	$16.25
8	Erika	25MAR2012	MP	$21.25

---

[3] You can also create your own formats using the FORMAT procedure covered in section 4.8.

4.7 ▶ Selected Standard Formats

Format	Definition	Width range	Default width
Character			
$UPCASE*w*.	Converts character data to uppercase	1–32767	Length of variable or 8
$*w*.	Writes standard character data—does not trim leading blanks (same as $CHAR*w*.)	1–32767	Length of variable or 1
Date, Time, and Datetime[4]			
DATE*w*.	Writes SAS date values in form *ddmmmyy* or *ddmmmyyyy*	5–11	7
DATETIME*w.d*	Writes SAS datetime values in form *ddmmmyy:hh:mm:ss.ss*	7–40	16
DTDATE*w*.	Writes SAS datetime values in form *ddmmmyy* or *ddmmmyyyy*	5–9	7
EURDFDD*w*.	Writes SAS date values in form *dd.mm.yy* or *dd.mm.yyyy*	2–10	8
JULIAN*w*.	Writes SAS date values in Julian date form *yyddd* or *yyyyddd*	5–7	5
MMDDYY*w*.	Writes SAS date values in form *mm/dd/yy* or *mm/dd/yyyy*	2–10	8
TIME*w.d*	Writes SAS time values in form *hh:mm:ss.ss*	2–20	8
WEEKDATE*w*.	Writes SAS date values in form *day-of-week, month-name dd, yy,* or *yyyy*	3–37	29
WORDDATE*w*.	Writes SAS date values in form *month-name dd, yyyy*	3–32	18
Numeric			
BEST*w*.	SAS System chooses best format—default format for numeric data	1–32	12
COMMA*w.d*	Writes numbers with commas	2–32	6
DOLLAR*w.d*	Writes numbers with a leading $ and commas separating every three digits	2–32	6
E*w*.	Writes numbers in scientific notation	7–32	12
EUROX*w.d*	Writes numbers with a leading € and periods separating every three digits	2–32	6
PERCENT*w.d*	Writes numeric data as percentages	4–32	6
w.d	Writes standard numeric data	1–32	none

Format	Input data	PUT statement	Results
Character			
$UPCASE*w*.	my cat	PUT Animal $UPCASE6.;	MY CAT
$*w*.	my cat my snake	PUT Animal $8. '*';	my cat * my snak*
Date, Time, and Datetime[4]			
DATE*w*.	8966	PUT Birth DATE7.; PUT Birth DATE9.;	19JUL84 19JUL1984
DATETIME*w*.	12182	PUT Start DATETIME13.; PUT Start DATETIME18.1;	01JAN60:03:23 01JAN60:03:23:02.0
DTDATE*w*.	12182	PUT Start DTDATE7.; PUT Start DTDATE9.;	01JAN60 01JAN1960
EURDFDD*w*.	8966	PUT Birth EURDFDD8.; PUT Birth EURDFDD10.;	19.07.84 19.07.1984
JULIAN*w*.	8966	PUT Birth JULIAN5.; PUT Birth JULIAN7.;	84201 1984201
MMDDYY*w*.	8966	PUT Birth MMDDYY8.; PUT Birth MMDDYY6.;	7/19/84 071984
TIME*w.d*	12182	PUT Start TIME8.; PUT Start TIME11.2;	3:23:02 3:23:02.00
WEEKDATE*w*.	8966	PUT Birth WEEKDATE15.; PUT Birth WEEKDATE29.;	Thu, Jul 19, 84 Thursday, July 19, 1984
WORDDATE*w*.	8966	PUT Birth WORDDATE12.; PUT Birth WORDDATE18.;	Jul 19, 1984 July 19, 1984
Numeric			
BEST*w*.	1200001	PUT Value BEST6.; PUT Value BEST8.;	1.20E6 1200001
COMMA*w.d*	1200001	PUT Value COMMA9.; PUT Value COMMA12.2;	1,200,001 1,200,001.00
DOLLAR*w.d*	1200001	PUT Value DOLLAR10.; PUT Value DOLLAR13.2;	$1,200,001 $1,200,001.00
E*w*.	1200001	PUT Value E7.;	1.2E+06
EUROX*w.d*	1200001	PUT Value EUROX13.2;	€1.200.001,00
PERCENT*w.d*	0.05	PUT Value PERCENT9.2;	5.00%
w.d	23.635	PUT Value 6.3; PUT Value 5.2;	23.635 23.64

[4] SAS date values are the number of days since January 1, 1960. SAS time values are the number of seconds past midnight, and datetime values are the number of seconds since midnight January 1, 1960.

4.8 Creating Your Own Formats Using PROC FORMAT

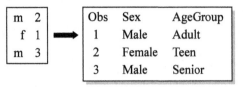

At some time you will probably want to create your own custom formats—especially if you use a lot of coded data. Imagine that you have just completed a survey for your company and to save disk space and time, all the responses to the survey questions are coded. For example, the age categories teen, adult, and senior are coded as numbers 1, 2, and 3. This is convenient for data entry and analysis but bothersome when it comes time to interpret the results. You could present your results along with a code book, and your company directors could look up the codes as they read the results. But this will probably not get you that promotion you've been looking for. A better solution is to create user-defined formats using PROC FORMAT and print the formatted values instead of the coded values.

The FORMAT procedure creates formats that will later be associated with variables in a FORMAT statement. The procedure starts with the statement PROC FORMAT and continues with one or more VALUE statements (other optional statements are available):

```
PROC FORMAT;
     VALUE name range-1 = 'formatted-text-1'
                 range-2 = 'formatted-text-2'
                     .
                     .
                     .
                 range-n = 'formatted-text-n';
```

The *name* in the VALUE statement is the name of the format you are creating. If the format is for character data, the *name* must start with a $. The *name* can't be longer than 32 characters (including the $ for character data), it must not start or end with a number, and cannot contain any special characters except the underscore. In addition, the *name* can't be the name of an existing format. Each *range* is the value of a variable that is assigned to the text given in quotation marks on the right side of the equal sign. The text can be up to 32,767 characters long, but some procedures print only the first 8 or 16 characters. The following are examples of valid range specifications:

```
            'A' = 'Asia'
1, 3, 5, 7, 9 = 'Odd'
500000 - HIGH = 'Not Affordable'
      13 -< 20 = 'Teenager'
   0 <- HIGH = 'Positive Non Zero'
        OTHER = 'Bad Data'
```

Character values should be enclosed in quotation marks ('A' for example). If there is more than one value in the range, then separate the values with a comma or use the hyphen (-) for a continuous range. The keywords LOW and HIGH can be used in ranges to indicate the lowest and the highest non-missing value for the variable. You can also use the less than symbol (<) in ranges to exclude either end point of the range. The OTHER keyword can be used to assign a format to any values not listed in the VALUE statement.

Example Universe Cars is surveying its customers as to their preferences for car colors. They have information about the customer's age, sex (coded as 1 for male and 2 for female), annual income, and preferred car color (yellow, gray, blue, or white). Here are the data:

```
19 1 14000 Y
45 1 65000 G
72 2 35000 B
31 1 44000 Y
58 2 83000 W
```

The following program reads the data; creates formats for age, sex, and car color using the FORMAT procedure; then prints the data using the new formats:

```
DATA carsurvey;
   INFILE 'c:\MyRawData\Cars.dat';
   INPUT Age Sex Income Color $;
PROC FORMAT;
   VALUE gender 1 = 'Male'
                2 = 'Female';
   VALUE agegroup 13 -< 20 = 'Teen'
                  20 -< 65 = 'Adult'
                  65 - HIGH = 'Senior';
   VALUE $col  'W' = 'Moon White'
               'B' = 'Sky Blue'
               'Y' = 'Sunburst Yellow'
               'G' = 'Rain Cloud Gray';
* Print data using user-defined and standard (DOLLAR8.) formats;
PROC PRINT DATA = carsurvey;
   FORMAT Sex gender. Age agegroup. Color $col. Income DOLLAR8.;
   TITLE 'Survey Results Printed with User-Defined Formats';
RUN;
```

This program creates two numeric formats: GENDER. for the variable Sex and AGEGROUP. for the variable Age. The program creates a character format, $COL., for the variable Color. Notice that the format names do not end with periods in the VALUE statement, but they do in the FORMAT statement.

Here is the output:

Survey Results Printed with User-Defined Formats

Obs	Age	Sex	Income	Color
1	Teen	Male	$14,000	Sunburst Yellow
2	Adult	Male	$65,000	Rain Cloud Gray
3	Senior	Female	$35,000	Sky Blue
4	Adult	Male	$44,000	Sunburst Yellow
5	Adult	Female	$83,000	Moon White

This example creates temporary formats that exist only for the current job or session. Creating and using permanent formats is discussed under the FORMAT Procedure in the SAS Help and Documentation.

4.9 Writing Simple Custom Reports

PROC PRINT is flexible and easy to use. Still, there are times when PROC PRINT just won't do: when your report to a state agency has to be spaced just like their fill-in-the-blank form, or when your client insists that the report contain complete sentences, or when you want one page per observation. At those times you can use the flexibility of the DATA step, and format to your heart's content.

You can write data in a DATA step the same way you read data—but in reverse. Instead of using an INFILE statement, you use a FILE statement; instead of INPUT statements, you use PUT statements. This is similar to writing a raw data file in a DATA step (section 10.5), but to write a report you use the PRINT option telling SAS to include the carriage returns and page breaks needed for printing. Here is the general form of a FILE statement for creating a report:

```
FILE 'file-specification' PRINT;
```

Like INPUT statements, PUT statements can be in list, column, or formatted style, but since SAS already knows whether a variable is numeric or character, you don't have to put a $ after character variables. If you use list format, SAS will automatically put a space between each variable. If you use column or formatted styles of PUT statements, SAS will put the variables wherever you specify. You can control spacing with the same pointer controls that INPUT statements use: @*n* to move to column *n*, +*n* to move *n* columns, / to skip to the next line, #*n* to skip to line *n*, and the trailing @ to hold the current line. In addition to printing variables, you can insert a text string by simply enclosing it in quotation marks.

Example To show how this differs from PROC PRINT, we'll use the candy sales data again. Two fourth-grade classes have sold candy to raise money for a field trip. Here are the data with each student's name, classroom number, the date they turned in their money, the type of candy: mint patties or chocolate dinosaurs, and the number of boxes sold:

```
Adriana   21   3/21/2012   MP    7
Nathan    14   3/21/2012   CD   19
Matthew   14   3/21/2012   CD   14
Claire    14   3/22/2012   CD   11
Ian       21   3/24/2012   MP   18
Chris     14   3/25/2012   CD    6
Anthony   21   3/25/2012   MP   13
Erika     21   3/25/2012   MP   17
```

The teachers want a report for each student showing how much money that student earned. They want each student's report on a separate page so it is easy to hand out. Lastly, they want it to be easy for fourth graders to understand, with complete sentences. Here is the program:

```
* Write a report with FILE and PUT statements;
DATA _NULL_;
   INFILE 'c:\MyRawData\CandySales.dat';
   INPUT Name $ 1-11 Class @15 DateReturned MMDDYY10.
         CandyType $ Quantity;
   Profit = Quantity * 1.25;
   FILE 'c:\MyRawData\Student.txt' PRINT;
   TITLE;

   PUT @5 'Candy sales report for ' Name 'from classroom ' Class
      // @5 'Congratulations!  You sold ' Quantity 'boxes of candy'
      / @5 'and earned ' Profit DOLLAR6.2 ' for our field trip.';
   PUT _PAGE_;
RUN;
```

Notice that the keyword _NULL_ appears in the DATA statement instead of a data set name. _NULL_ tells SAS not to bother writing a SAS data set (since the goal is to create a report not a data set), and makes the program run slightly faster. The FILE statement creates the output file for the report, and the PRINT option tells SAS to include carriage returns and page breaks. The null TITLE statement tells SAS to eliminate all automatic titles.

The first PUT statement in this program starts with a pointer, @5, telling SAS to go to column 5. Then it tells SAS to print the words Candy sales report for followed by the current value of the variable Name. The variables Name, Class, and Quantity are printed in list style whereas Profit is printed using formatted style and the DOLLAR6.2 format. A slash line pointer tells SAS to skip to the next line; two slashes skips two lines. You could use multiple PUT statements instead of slashes to skip lines because SAS goes to a new line every time there is a new PUT statement. The statement PUT _PAGE_ inserts a page break after each student's report. When the program is run, the log will contain these notes:

```
NOTE: 10 records were read from the infile 'c:\MyRawData\CandySales.dat'.
NOTE: 30 records were written to the file 'c:\MyRawData\Student.txt'.
```

The first three pages of the report look like this:

```
    Candy sales report for Adriana from classroom 21

    Congratulations!  You sold 7 boxes of candy
    and earned  $8.75 for our field trip.
```

```
    Candy sales report for Nathan from classroom 14

    Congratulations!  You sold 19 boxes of candy
    and earned $23.75 for our field trip.
```

```
    Candy sales report for Matthew from classroom 14

    Congratulations!  You sold 14 boxes of candy
    and earned $17.50 for our field trip.
```

4.10   Summarizing Your Data Using PROC MEANS

One of the first things people usually want to do with their data, after reading it and making sure it is correct, is look at some simple statistics. Statistics such as the mean value, standard deviation, and minimum and maximum values give you a feel for your data. These types of information can also alert you to errors in your data (a score of 980 in a basketball game, for example, is suspect). The MEANS procedure provides simple statistics for numeric variables.

The MEANS procedure starts with the keywords PROC MEANS, followed by options:

```
PROC MEANS options;
```

Some options control how your data are summarized.

MAXDEC = *n*   specifies the number of decimal places to be displayed
MISSING   treats missing values as valid summary groups

Other options request specific summary statistics :

MAX   maximum value
MIN   minimum value
MEAN   mean
MEDIAN   median
MODE   mode
N   number of non-missing values
NMISS   number of missing values
RANGE   range
STDDEV   standard deviation
SUM   sum

If you do not specify any summary statistics, SAS will print the number of non-missing values, the mean, the standard deviation, and the minimum and maximum values for each variable. More options for PROC MEANS are listed in section 9.3.

If you use the PROC MEANS statement with no other statements, then you will get statistics for all numeric variables in your data set. Here are some of the optional statements for controlling which variables are used:

BY *variable-list;*   The BY statement performs separate analyses for each level of the variables in the list. The data must first be sorted by these variables. (You can use PROC SORT to do this.)

CLASS *variable-list;*   The CLASS statement also performs separate analyses for each level of the variables in the list, but its output is more compact than with the BY statement, and the data do not have to be sorted first.

VAR *variable-list;*   The VAR statement specifies which numeric variables to use in the analysis. If it is absent, then SAS uses all numeric variables.

Example A wholesale nursery is selling garden flowers, and they want to summarize their sales figures by month. The data file which follows contains the customer ID, date of sale, and number of petunias, snapdragons, and marigolds sold:

```
756-01   05/04/2013 120   80 110
834-01   05/12/2013  90  160  60
901-02   05/18/2013  50  100  75
834-01   06/01/2013  80   60 100
756-01   06/11/2013 100  160  75
901-02   06/19/2013  60   60  60
756-01   06/25/2013  85  110 100
```

The following program reads the data; computes a new variable, Month, which is the month of the sale; sorts the data by Month using PROC SORT; and then summarizes the data by Month using PROC MEANS with a BY statement. The MAXDEC option is set to zero, so no decimal places will be printed.

```
DATA sales;
   INFILE 'c:\MyRawData\Flowers.dat';
   INPUT CustID $ @9 SaleDate MMDDYY10. Petunia SnapDragon
         Marigold;
   Month = MONTH(SaleDate);
PROC SORT DATA = sales;
   BY Month;
* Calculate means by Month for flower sales;
PROC MEANS DATA = sales MAXDEC = 0;
   BY Month;
   VAR Petunia SnapDragon Marigold;
   TITLE 'Summary of Flower Sales by Month';
RUN;
```

Here are the results of the PROC MEANS:

Summary of Flower Sales by Month

The MEANS Procedure

Month=5

Variable	N	Mean	Std Dev	Minimum	Maximum
Petunia	3	87	35	50	120
SnapDragon	3	113	42	80	160
Marigold	3	82	26	60	110

Month=6

Variable	N	Mean	Std Dev	Minimum	Maximum
Petunia	4	81	17	60	100
SnapDragon	4	98	48	60	160
Marigold	4	84	20	60	100

4.11 Writing Summary Statistics to a SAS Data Set

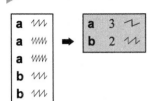

Sometimes you want to save summary statistics to a SAS data set for further analysis, or to merge with other data. For example, you might want to plot the hourly temperature in your office to show how it heats up every afternoon causing you to fall asleep, but the instrument you have records data for every minute. The MEANS procedure can condense the data by computing the mean temperature for each hour and then save the results in a SAS data set so it can be plotted.

There are two methods in PROC MEANS for saving summary statistics in a SAS data set. You can use the OUTPUT destination, which is covered in section 5.3, or you can use the OUTPUT statement. The OUTPUT statement has the following form:

```
OUTPUT OUT = data-set output-statistic-list;
```

Here, *data-set* is the name of the SAS data set which will contain the results (this can be either temporary or permanent), and *output-statistic-list* defines which statistics you want and the associated variable names. You can have more than one OUTPUT statement and multiple output statistic lists. The following is one of the possible forms for *output-statistic-list*:

```
statistic(variable-list) = name-list
```

Here, *statistic* can be any of the statistics available in PROC MEANS (SUM, N, MEAN, for example), *variable-list* defines which of the variables in the VAR statement you want to output, and *name-list* defines the new variable names for the statistics. The new variable names must be in the same order as their corresponding variables in *variable-list*. For example, the following PROC MEANS statements produce a new data set called ZOOSUM, which contains one observation with the variables LionWeight, the mean of the lions' weights, and BearWeight, the mean of the bears' weights:

```
PROC MEANS DATA = zoo NOPRINT;
   VAR Lions Tigers Bears;
   OUTPUT OUT = zoosum MEAN(Lions Bears) = LionWeight BearWeight;
RUN;
```

The NOPRINT option in the PROC MEANS statement tells SAS there is no need to produce any printed results since we are saving the results in a SAS data set.[5]

The SAS data set created in the OUTPUT statement will contain all the variables defined in the *output-statistic-list*; any variables listed in a BY or CLASS statement; plus two new variables, _TYPE_ and _FREQ_. If there is no BY or CLASS statement, then the data set will have just one observation. If there is a BY statement, then the data set will have one observation for each level of the BY group. CLASS statements produce one observation for each level of interaction of the class variables. The value of the _TYPE_ variable depends on the level of interaction. The observation where _TYPE_ has a value of zero is the grand total.[6]

Example The following are sales data for a wholesale nursery with the customer ID; date of sale; and the number of petunias, snapdragons, and marigolds sold:

```
756-01  05/04/2013 120  80 110
834-01  05/12/2013  90 160  60
901-02  05/18/2013  50 100  75
834-01  06/01/2013  80  60 100
756-01  06/11/2013 100 160  75
901-02  06/19/2013  60  60  60
756-01  06/25/2013  85 110 100
```

The nursery wants to summarize the data so that there is one observation per customer containing the sum and mean of the number of plants sold, and then save the results in a SAS data set for further analysis. The following program reads the data from the file; sorts by the variable, CustID; and then uses the MEANS procedure with the NOPRINT option to calculate the sums and means by CustID. The results are saved in a SAS data set named TOTALS in the OUTPUT statement. The sums are given the original variable names Petunia, SnapDragon, and Marigold, and the means are given new variable names MeanP, MeanSD, and MeanM. A PROC PRINT is used to show the TOTALS data set:

```
DATA sales;
   INFILE 'c:\MyRawData\Flowers.dat';
   INPUT CustID $ @9 SaleDate MMDDYY10. Petunia SnapDragon Marigold;
PROC SORT DATA = sales;
   BY CustID;
* Calculate means by CustomerID, output sum and mean to new data set;
PROC MEANS NOPRINT DATA = sales;
   BY CustID;
   VAR Petunia SnapDragon Marigold;
   OUTPUT OUT = totals
      MEAN(Petunia SnapDragon Marigold) = MeanP MeanSD MeanM
      SUM(Petunia SnapDragon Marigold) = Petunia SnapDragon Marigold;
PROC PRINT DATA = totals;
   TITLE 'Sum of Flower Data over Customer ID';
   FORMAT MeanP MeanSD MeanM 3.;
RUN;
```

Here are the results:

Sum of Flower Data over Customer ID

Obs	CustID	_TYPE_	_FREQ_	MeanP	MeanSD	MeanM	Petunia	SnapDragon	Marigold
1	756-01	0	3	102	117	95	305	350	285
2	834-01	0	2	85	110	80	170	220	160
3	901-02	0	2	55	80	68	110	160	135

---

[5] Using PROC MEANS with a NOPRINT option is the same as using PROC SUMMARY.

[6] For a more detailed explanation of the _TYPE_ variable, see the SAS Help and Documentation.

4.12 Counting Your Data with PROC FREQ

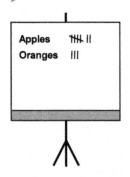

A frequency table is a simple list of counts answering the question "How many?" When you have counts for one variable, they are called one-way frequencies. When you combine two or more variables, the counts are called two-way frequencies, three-way frequencies, and so on. Tables combining two or more variables are also called cross-tabulations or contingency tables.

The most obvious reason for using PROC FREQ is to create tables showing the distribution of categorical data values, but PROC FREQ can also reveal irregularities in your data. You could get dizzy proofreading a large data set, but data entry errors are often glaringly obvious in a frequency table. The basic form of PROC FREQ is

```
PROC FREQ;
    TABLES variable-combinations;
```

To produce a one-way frequency table, just list the variable name. This statement produces a frequency table listing the number of observations for each value of YearsEducation:

```
TABLES YearsEducation;
```

To produce a cross-tabulation, list the variables separated by an asterisk. This statement produces a cross-tabulation showing the number of observations for each combination of Sex by YearsEducation:

```
TABLES Sex * YearsEducation;
```

You can specify any number of table requests in a single TABLES statement, and you can have as many TABLES statements as you wish. Be careful though; reading cross-tabulations of three or more levels is like playing three-dimensional tic-tac-toe without the benefit of a three-dimensional board.

Options, if any, appear after a slash in the TABLES statement. For a list of statistical options for PROC FREQ see section 9.6. Options for controlling the output of PROC FREQ include

LIST	prints cross-tabulations in list format rather than grid
MISSPRINT	includes missing values in frequencies but not in percentages
MISSING	includes missing values in frequencies and in percentages
NOCOL	suppresses printing of column percentages in cross-tabulations
NOPERCENT	suppresses printing of percentages
NOROW	suppresses printing of row percentages in cross-tabulations
OUT = data-set	writes a data set containing frequencies

The statement below, for instance, tells SAS to treat missing values as valid :

```
TABLES Sex * YearsEducation / MISSING;
```

Example The proprietor of a coffee shop keeps a record of sales. For each drink sold, she records the type of coffee (cappuccino, espresso, kona, or iced coffee), and whether the customer walked in or came to the drive-up window. Here are the data with ten observations per line:

```
esp w cap d cap w kon w ice w kon d esp d kon w ice d esp d
cap w esp d cap d Kon d .   d kon w esp d cap w ice w kon w
kon w kon w ice d esp d kon w esp d esp w kon w cap w kon w
```

The following program reads the data and produces one-way and two-way frequencies:

```
DATA orders;
   INFILE 'c:\MyRawData\Coffee.dat';
   INPUT Coffee $ Window $ @@;
* Print tables for Window and Window by Coffee;
PROC FREQ DATA = orders;
   TABLES Window  Window * Coffee;
RUN;
```

The output contains two tables. The first is a one-way frequency table for the variable Window. You can see that 13 customers came to the drive-up window while 17 walked into the restaurant.

The FREQ Procedure

Window	Frequency	Percent	Cumulative Frequency	Cumulative Percent
d	13	43.33	13	43.33
w	17	56.67	30	100.00

Table of Window by Coffee						
Window	**Coffee**					
Frequency Percent Row Pct Col Pct	Kon	cap	esp	ice	kon	Total
d	1	2	6	2	1	12
	3.45	6.90	20.69	6.90	3.45	41.38
	8.33	16.67	50.00	16.67	8.33	
	100.00	33.33	75.00	50.00	10.00	
w	0	4	2	2	9	17
	0.00	13.79	6.90	6.90	31.03	58.62
	0.00	23.53	11.76	11.76	52.94	
	0.00	66.67	25.00	50.00	90.00	
Total	1	6	8	4	10	29
	3.45	20.69	27.59	13.79	34.48	100.00
Frequency Missing = 1						

The second table is a two-way cross-tabulation of Window by Coffee. Inside each cell, SAS prints the frequency, percentage, percentage for that row, and percentage for that column; while cumulative frequencies and percents appear along the right side and bottom. Notice that the missing value is mentioned but not included in the statistics. (Use the MISSING or MISSPRINT options if you want missing values to be included in the table.) Also, there is one observation with a value of Kon for Coffee. This data entry error should be kon.

4.13 Producing Tabular Reports with PROC TABULATE

Every summary statistic the TABULATE procedure computes can also be produced by other procedures such as PRINT, MEANS, and FREQ, but PROC TABULATE is popular because its reports are pretty. If PROC TABULATE were a box, it would be gift-wrapped.

PROC TABULATE is so powerful that entire books have been written about it, but it is also so concise that you may feel like you're reading hieroglyphics. If you find the syntax of PROC TABULATE a little hard to get used to, that may be because it has roots outside of SAS. PROC TABULATE is based in part on the Table Producing Language, a complex and sophisticated language developed by the U.S. Department of Labor.

The general form of PROC TABULATE is

```
PROC TABULATE;
   CLASS classification-variable-list;
   TABLE page-dimension, row-dimension, column-dimension;
```

The CLASS statement tells SAS which variables contain categorical data to be used for dividing observations into groups, while the TABLE statement tells SAS how to organize your table and what numbers to compute. Each TABLE statement defines only one table, but you may have multiple TABLE statements. If a variable is listed in a CLASS statement, then, by default, PROC TABULATE produces simple counts of the number of observations in each category of that variable. PROC TABULATE offers many other statistics, and the next section describes how to request those.

Dimensions Each TABLE statement can specify up to three dimensions. Those dimensions, separated by commas, tell SAS which variables to use for the pages, rows, and columns in the report. If you specify only one dimension, then that becomes, by default, the column dimension. If you specify two dimensions, then you get rows and columns, but no page dimension. If you specify three dimensions, then you get pages, rows, and columns.

When you write a TABLE statement, start with the column dimension. Once you have that debugged, add the rows. Once you are happy with your rows and columns, then you are ready to add a page dimension, if you need one. Notice that the order of dimensions in the TABLE statement is page, then row, then column. So, to avoid scrambling your table when you add dimensions, insert the page and row specifications *in front* of the column dimension.

Missing data By default, observations are excluded from tables if they have missing values for variables listed in a CLASS statement. If you want to keep these observations, then simply add the MISSING option to your PROC statement like this:

```
PROC TABULATE MISSING;
```

Example Here are data about pleasure boats including the name of each boat, its home port, whether it is a sailing or power vessel, the type of boat (schooner, catamaran, or yacht), the price of an excursion, and the length of the boat in feet.

```
Silent Lady    Maalea    sail    sch    95.00    64
America II     Maalea    sail    yac    72.95    65
Aloha Anai     Lahaina   sail    cat   112.00    60
Ocean Spirit   Maalea    power   cat    62.00    65
Anuenue        Maalea    sail    sch   177.50    52
Hana Lei       Maalea    power   cat    88.99   110
Leilani        Maalea    power   yac    99.99    45
Kalakaua       Maalea    power   cat    69.50    70
Reef Runner    Lahaina   power   yac    59.95    50
Blue Dolphin   Maalea    sail    cat    92.95    65
```

Suppose you want a report showing the number of boats of each type that are sailing or power vessels for each port. The following DATA step reads the data from a raw data file named Boats.dat. Then PROC TABULATE creates a three-dimensional report with the values of Port for the pages, Locomotion for the rows, and Type for the columns.

```
DATA boats;
   INFILE 'c:\MyRawData\Boats.dat';
   INPUT Name $ 1-12 Port $ 14-20 Locomotion $ 22-26 Type $ 28-30
      Price 32-37 Length 39-41;
RUN;
* Tabulations with three dimensions;
PROC TABULATE DATA = boats;
   CLASS Port Locomotion Type;
   TABLE Port, Locomotion, Type;
   TITLE 'Number of Boats by Port, Locomotion, and Type';
RUN;
```

This report has two pages, one for each value of the page dimension. Here is the first page:

Number of Boats by Port, Locomotion, and Type

Port Maalea

	Type		
	cat	sch	yac
	N	N	N
Locomotion			
power	3	.	1
sail	1	2	1

The value of the page dimension appears in the top, left corner of the table. You can see that this is the page for the port of Maalea. The heading N tells you that the numbers in this table are simple counts, the number of boats in each group.

4.14 Adding Statistics to PROC TABULATE Output

By default, PROC TABULATE produces simple counts for variables listed in a CLASS statement, but you can request many other statistics in a TABLE statement. You can also concatenate or cross variables within dimensions. In fact, you can write TABLE statements so complicated that even *you* won't know what the report is going to look like until you run it.

While the CLASS statement lists categorical variables, the VAR statement tells SAS which variables contain continuous data. Here is the general form:

```
PROC TABULATE;
   VAR analysis-variable-list;
   CLASS classification-variable-list;
   TABLE page-dimension, row-dimension, column-dimension;
```

You may have both a CLASS statement and a VAR statement, or just one, but all variables listed in a TABLE statement must also appear in either a CLASS or a VAR statement.

Keywords In addition to variable names, each dimension can contain keywords. These are a few of the values TABULATE can compute.

ALL	adds a row, column, or page showing the total
MAX	highest value
MIN	lowest value
MEAN	arithmetic mean
MEDIAN	median
MODE	mode
N	number of non-missing values
NMISS	number of missing values
PCTN	percentage of observations for that group
PCTSUM	percentage of total represented by that group
STDDEV	standard deviation
SUM	sum

Concatenating, crossing, and grouping Within a dimension, variables and keywords can be concatenated, crossed, or grouped. To concatenate variables or keywords, simply list them separated by a space; to cross variables or keywords, separate then with an asterisk (*); and to group them, enclose the variables or keywords in parentheses. The keyword ALL is generally concatenated. To request other statistics, however, cross that keyword with the variable name.

Concatenating:	`TABLE Locomotion Type ALL;`
Crossing:	`TABLE MEAN * Price;`
Crossing, grouping, and concatenating:	`TABLE PCTN *(Locomotion Type);`

Example Here again are the boat data containing the name of each boat, its home port, whether it is a sailing or power vessel, the type of boat (schooner, catamaran, or yacht), the price of an excursion, and the boat's length.

```
Silent Lady    Maalea    sail    sch     95.00    64
America II      Maalea    sail    yac     72.95    65
Aloha Anai      Lahaina   sail    cat    112.00    60
Ocean Spirit    Maalea    power   cat     62.00    65
Anuenue         Maalea    sail    sch    177.50    52
Hana Lei        Maalea    power   cat     88.99   110
Leilani         Maalea    power   yac     99.99    45
Kalakaua        Maalea    power   cat     69.50    70
Reef Runner     Lahaina   power   yac     59.95    50
Blue Dolphin    Maalea    sail    cat     92.95    65
```

The following program is similar to the one in the previous section. However, this PROC TABULATE includes a VAR statement. The TABLE statement in this program contains only two dimensions; but it also concatenates, crosses, and groups variables and statistics.

```
DATA boats;
   INFILE 'c:\MyRawData\Boats.dat';
   INPUT Name $ 1-12 Port $ 14-20 Locomotion $ 22-26 Type $ 28-30
      Price 32-37 Length 39-41;
RUN;
* Tabulations with two dimensions and statistics;
PROC TABULATE DATA = boats;
   CLASS Locomotion Type;
   VAR Price;
   TABLE Locomotion ALL, MEAN*Price*(Type ALL);
   TITLE 'Mean Price by Locomotion and Type';
RUN;
```

The row dimension of this table concatenates the classification variable Locomotion with ALL to produce totals. The column dimension, on the other hand, crosses MEAN with the analysis variable Price and with the classification variable Type (which happens to be concatenated and grouped with ALL). Here are the results:

Mean Price by Locomotion and Type

	Mean			
	Price			
	Type			All
	cat	sch	yac	All
Locomotion				
power	73.50	.	79.97	76.09
sail	102.48	136.25	72.95	110.08
All	85.09	136.25	77.63	93.08

4.15 Enhancing the Appearance of PROC TABULATE Output

When you use PROC TABULATE, SAS wraps your data in tidy little boxes, but there may be times when they just don't look right. Using three simple options, you can enhance the appearance of your output. Think of it as changing the wrapping paper.

FORMAT= option To change the format of all the data cells in your table, use the FORMAT= option in your PROC statement. For example, if you needed the numbers in your table to have commas and no decimal places, you could use this PROC statement

```
PROC TABULATE FORMAT = COMMA10.0;
```

telling SAS to use the COMMA10.0 format for all the data cells in your table.

BOX= and MISSTEXT= options While the FORMAT= option must be used in your PROC statement, the BOX= and MISSTEXT= options go in TABLE statements. The BOX= option allows you to write a brief phrase in the normally empty box that appears in the upper left corner of every TABULATE report. Using this empty space can give your reports a nicely polished look. The MISSTEXT= option, on the other hand, specifies a value for SAS to print in empty data cells. The period that SAS prints, by default, for missing values can seem downright mysterious to someone, perhaps your CEO, who is not familiar with SAS output. You can give them something more meaningful with the MISSTEXT= option. This statement

```
TABLE Region, MEAN*Sales / BOX='Mean Sales by Region' MISSTEXT='No Sales';
```

tells SAS to print the title "Mean Sales by Region" in the upper left corner of the table, and to print the words "No Sales" in any cells of the table that have no data. The BOX= and MISSTEXT= options must be separated from the dimensions of the TABLE statement by a slash.

Example Here again are the boat data containing the name of each boat, its home port, whether it is a sailing or power vessel, the type of boat (schooner, catamaran, or yacht), the price of an excursion, and the boat's length.

```
Silent Lady   Maalea    sail    sch     95.00    64
America II    Maalea    sail    yac     72.95    65
Aloha Anai    Lahaina   sail    cat    112.00    60
Ocean Spirit  Maalea    power   cat     62.00    65
Anuenue       Maalea    sail    sch    177.50    52
Hana Lei      Maalea    power   cat     88.99   110
Leilani       Maalea    power   yac     99.99    45
Kalakaua      Maalea    power   cat     69.50    70
Reef Runner   Lahaina   power   yac     59.95    50
Blue Dolphin  Maalea    sail    cat     92.95    65
```

The following program is the same as the one in the previous section except that the FORMAT=, BOX=, and MISSTEXT= options have been added. Notice that the FORMAT= option goes in the PROC statement, while the BOX= and MISSTEXT= options go in the TABLE statement following a slash. Because the BOX= option serves as a title, a null TITLE statement is used to remove the usual title.

```
DATA boats;
   INFILE 'c:\MyRawData\Boats.dat';
   INPUT Name $ 1-12 Port $ 14-20 Locomotion $ 22-26 Type $ 28-30
      Price 32-37 Length 39-41;
RUN;
* PROC TABULATE report with options;
PROC TABULATE DATA = boats FORMAT=DOLLAR9.2;
   CLASS Locomotion Type;
   VAR Price;
   TABLE Locomotion ALL, MEAN*Price*(Type ALL)
      /BOX='Full Day Excursions' MISSTEXT='none';
   TITLE;
RUN;
```

Here is the enhanced output:

Full Day Excursions	Mean			
	Price			
	Type			
	cat	sch	yac	All
Locomotion				
power	$73.50	none	$79.97	$76.09
sail	$102.48	$136.25	$72.95	$110.08
All	$85.09	$136.25	$77.63	$93.08

Notice that all the data cells now use the DOLLAR9.2 format as specified in the FORMAT= option. The text "Full Day Excursions" now appears in the upper left corner which was empty in the previous section. In addition, the one data cell with no data now shows the word "none" instead of a period.

4.16 Changing Headers in PROC TABULATE Output

The TABULATE procedure produces reports with a lot of headers. Sometimes there are so many headers that your reports look cluttered; at other times you may simply feel that a different header would be more meaningful. Before you can change a header, though, you need to understand what type of header it is. TABULATE reports have two basic types of headers: headers that are the values of variables listed in a CLASS statement, and headers that are the names of variables and keywords. You use different methods to change different types of headers.

CLASS variable values To change headers which are the values of variables listed in a CLASS statement, use the FORMAT procedure to create a user-defined format. Then assign the format to the variable in a FORMAT statement (discussed in section 4.8).

Variable names and keywords To change headers which are the names of variables or keywords, put an equal sign after the variable or keyword followed by the new header enclosed in quotation marks.[7] You can eliminate a header entirely by setting it equal to blank (two quotation marks with nothing in between), and SAS will remove the box for that header. This TABLE statement

```
TABLE Region='', MEAN=''*Sales='Mean Sales by Region';
```

tells SAS to remove the headers for Region and MEAN, and to change the header for the variable Sales to "Mean Sales by Region".

In some cases SAS leaves the empty box when a row header is set to blank. This happens for statistics and analysis variables (but not class variables). To force SAS to remove the empty box, add the ROW=FLOAT option to the end of your TABLE statement like this:

```
TABLE MEAN=''*Sales='Mean Sales by Region', Region='' / ROW=FLOAT;
```

Example Here again are the boat data containing the name of each boat, its home port, whether it is a sailing or power vessel, the type of boat (schooner, catamaran, or yacht), the price of an excursion, and the boat's length.

```
Silent Lady    Maalea    sail    sch     95.00    64
America II     Maalea    sail    yac     72.95    65
Aloha Anai     Lahaina   sail    cat    112.00    60
Ocean Spirit   Maalea    power   cat     62.00    65
Anuenue        Maalea    sail    sch    177.50    52
Hana Lei       Maalea    power   cat     88.99   110
Leilani        Maalea    power   yac     99.99    45
Kalakaua       Maalea    power   cat     69.50    70
Reef Runner    Lahaina   power   yac     59.95    50
Blue Dolphin   Maalea    sail    cat     92.95    65
```

The following program is the same as the one in the previous section except that the headers have been changed. To start with, a FORMAT procedure creates a user-defined format named $typ. Then the $typ. format is assigned to the variable Type using a FORMAT statement. In the TABLE statement, more headers are changed. The headers for Locomotion, MEAN, and Type are all set to blank, while the header for Price is set to "Mean Price by Type of Boat".

```
DATA boats;
   INFILE 'c:\MyRawData\Boats.dat';
   INPUT Name $ 1-12 Port $ 14-20 Locomotion $ 22-26 Type $ 28-30
      Price 32-37 Length 39-41;
RUN;
* Changing headers;
PROC FORMAT;
   VALUE $typ   'cat' = 'catamaran'
                'sch' = 'schooner'
                'yac' = 'yacht';
PROC TABULATE DATA = boats FORMAT=DOLLAR9.2;
   CLASS Locomotion Type;
   VAR Price;
   FORMAT Type $typ.;
   TABLE Locomotion='' ALL,
      MEAN=''*Price='Mean Price by Type of Boat'*(Type='' ALL)
      /BOX='Full Day Excursions' MISSTEXT='none';
   TITLE;
RUN;
```

This program does not require the ROW=FLOAT option because the only variable being set to blank in the row dimension is a class variable. If you put an analysis variable or statistics keyword in the row dimension and set it equal to blank, then you would need to add the ROW=FLOAT option to remove empty boxes. Here is the output:

Full Day Excursions	Mean Price by Type of Boat			
	catamaran	schooner	yacht	All
power	$73.50	none	$79.97	$76.09
sail	$102.48	$136.25	$72.95	$110.08
All	$85.09	$136.25	$77.63	$93.08

This output is the same as the output in the preceding section, except for the new headers. Notice how much cleaner and more compact this report is.

---

[7] You can also change variable headers with a LABEL statement (section 4.1), and keyword headers with a KEYLABEL statement. However, the TABLE statement method used in this section is the only way that you can remove a variable header without leaving a blank box behind.

4.17 Specifying Multiple Formats for Data Cells in PROC TABULATE Output

Using the FORMAT= option in a PROC TABULATE statement, you can easily specify a format for the data cells; but you can only specify one format, and it must apply to all the data cells. If you want to use more than one format in your table, you can do that by putting the FORMAT= option in your TABLE statement.

To apply a format to an individual variable, cross it with the variable name like this:

```
variable-name*FORMAT=formatw.d
```

Then you insert this rather convoluted construction in your TABLE statement.

```
TABLE Region, MEAN*(Sales*FORMAT=COMMA8.0 Profit*FORMAT=DOLLAR10.2);
```

This TABLE statement applies the COMMA8.0 format to a variable named Sales, and the DOLLAR10.2 format to Profit.

Example Here again are the boat data containing the name of each boat, its home port, whether it is a sailing or power vessel, the type of boat (schooner, catamaran, or yacht), the price of an excursion, and the boat's length.

```
Silent Lady    Maalea    sail    sch    95.00    64
America II     Maalea    sail    yac    72.95    65
Aloha Anai     Lahaina   sail    cat   112.00    60
Ocean Spirit   Maalea    power   cat    62.00    65
Anuenue        Maalea    sail    sch   177.50    52
Hana Lei       Maalea    power   cat    88.99   110
Leilani        Maalea    power   yac    99.99    45
Kalakaua       Maalea    power   cat    69.50    70
Reef Runner    Lahaina   power   yac    59.95    50
Blue Dolphin   Maalea    sail    cat    92.95    65
```

Suppose you want to show the mean price and mean length of boats side-by-side in the same report. Using dollar signs makes sense for price, but not for length. In the program below, the format DOLLAR7.2 is applied to the variable Price, while the format 2.0 is applied to Length. Notice that the FORMAT= options are crossed with the variables using an asterisk.

```
DATA boats;
   INFILE 'c:\MyRawData\Boats.dat';
   INPUT Name $ 1-12 Port $ 14-20 Locomotion $ 22-26 Type $ 28-30
      Price 32-37 Length 39-41;
RUN;
* Using the FORMAT= option in the TABLE statement;
PROC TABULATE DATA = boats;
   CLASS Locomotion Type;
   VAR Price Length;
   TABLE Locomotion ALL,
      MEAN * (Price*FORMAT=DOLLAR7.2 Length*FORMAT=2.0) * (Type ALL);
   TITLE 'Price and Length by Type of Boat';
RUN;
```

Here is the resulting output:

Price and Length by Type of Boat

	Mean							
	Price				Length			
	Type				Type			
	cat	sch	yac	All	cat	sch	yac	All
Locomotion								
power	$73.50	.	$79.97	$76.09	82	.	48	68
sail	$102.48	$136.25	$72.95	$110.08	63	58	65	61
All	$85.09	$136.25	$77.63	$93.08	74	58	53	65

Notice that the values for Price are printed with dollar signs and decimal places, while the values for Length are printed without these.

4.18 Producing Simple Output with PROC REPORT

The REPORT procedure shares features with the PRINT, MEANS, TABULATE, and SORT procedures and the DATA step. With all those features rolled into one procedure, it's not surprising that PROC REPORT can be complex—in fact entire books have been written about it—but with all those features comes power.

Here is the general form of a basic REPORT procedure:

```
PROC REPORT NOWINDOWS;
     COLUMN variable-list;
```

In its simplest form, the COLUMN statement is similar to a VAR statement in PROC PRINT, telling SAS which variables to include and in what order. If you leave out the COLUMN statement, SAS will, by default, include all the variables in your data set. Before SAS 9.4 if you left out the NOWINDOWS option, SAS would open the interactive Report window. Starting with SAS 9.4, NOWINDOWS is the default so you can skip it.[8]

Numeric versus character data The type of report you get from PROC REPORT depends, in part, on the type of data you use. If you have at least one character variable in your report, then, by default, you will get a detail report with one row per observation. If, on the other hand, your report includes only numeric variables, then, by default, PROC REPORT will sum those variables. Even dates will be summed, by default, because they are numeric.[9]

Example Here are data about national parks and monuments in the USA. The variables are name, type (NP for national park or NM for national monument), region (East or West), number of museums (including visitor centers), and number of campgrounds.

```
Dinosaur                NM   West   2  6
Ellis Island            NM   East   1  0
Everglades              NP   East   5  2
Grand Canyon            NP   West   5  3
Great Smoky Mountains   NP   East   3 10
Hawaii Volcanoes        NP   West   2  2
Lava Beds               NM   West   1  1
Statue of Liberty       NM   East   1  0
Theodore Roosevelt      NP   .      2  2
Yellowstone             NP   West   2 11
Yosemite                NP   West   2 13
```

The following program reads the data in a DATA step, and then runs two reports. The first report has no COLUMN statement so SAS will use all the variables, while the second uses a COLUMN statement to select just the numeric variables.

```
DATA natparks;
   INFILE 'c:\MyRawData\Parks.dat';
   INPUT Name $ 1-21 Type $ Region $ Museums Camping;
RUN;
PROC REPORT DATA = natparks NOWINDOWS;
   TITLE 'Report with Character and Numeric Variables';
RUN;
PROC REPORT DATA = natparks NOWINDOWS;
   COLUMN Museums Camping;
   TITLE 'Report with Only Numeric Variables';
RUN;
```

While the two PROC steps are only slightly different, the reports they produced differ dramatically. The first report is almost identical to the output you would get from a PROC PRINT except for the absence of the OBS column. The second report, since it contained only numeric variables, was summed.

Report with Character and Numeric Variables

Name	Type	Region	Museums	Camping
Dinosaur	NM	West	2	6
Ellis Island	NM	East	1	0
Everglades	NP	East	5	2
Grand Canyon	NP	West	5	3
Great Smoky Mountains	NP	East	3	10
Hawaii Volcanoes	NP	West	2	2
Lava Beds	NM	West	1	1
Statue of Liberty	NM	East	1	0
Theodore Roosevelt	NP		2	2
Yellowstone	NP	West	9	11
Yosemite	NP	West	2	13

Report with Only Numeric Variables

Museums	Camping
33	50

---

[8] The Report window is a non-programming approach to using PROC REPORT. For more information, see the SAS Help and Documentation.

[9] You can override this default by assigning one of your numeric variables a usage type of DISPLAY in a DEFINE statement. See the next section.

4.19   Using DEFINE Statements in PROC REPORT

The DEFINE statement is a general purpose statement that specifies options for an individual variable. You can have a DEFINE statement for every variable, but you only need to have a DEFINE statement if you want to specify an option for that particular variable. The general form of a DEFINE statement is

```
DEFINE variable / options 'column-header';
```

In a DEFINE statement, you specify the variable name followed by a slash and any options for that particular variable.

Usage options   The most important option is a usage option that tells SAS how that variable is to be used. Possible values of usage options include:

ACROSS	creates a column for each unique value of the variable.
ANALYSIS	calculates statistics for the variable. This is the default usage for numeric variables, and the default statistic is sum.
COMPUTED	creates a new variable whose value you calculate in a compute block. See section 4.23 for a discussion of compute blocks.
DISPLAY	creates one row for each observation in the data set. This is the default usage for character variables.
GROUP	creates one row for each unique value of the variable.
ORDER	creates one row for each observation with rows arranged according to the values of the order variable.

Changing column headers   There are several ways to change column headers in PROC REPORT including using a LABEL statement as described in section 4.1, or specifying a column header in a DEFINE statement. The following statement tells SAS to arrange a report by the values of the variable Age, and use the words "Age at Admission" as the column header for that variable. Putting a slash in a column header tells SAS to split the header at that point.

```
DEFINE Age / ORDER 'Age at/Admission';
```

Missing data   By default, observations are excluded from reports if they have missing values for variables listed in ORDER, GROUP, or ACROSS statements. If you want to keep these observations, then simply add the MISSING option to your PROC statement like this:

```
PROC REPORT NOWINDOWS MISSING;
```

Example   Here again are the data about national parks and monuments in the USA. The variables are name, type (NP for national park or NM for national monument), region (East or West), number of museums (including visitor centers), and number of campgrounds.

```
Dinosaur                NM   West  2   6
Ellis Island            NM   East  1   0
Everglades              NP   East  5   2
Grand Canyon            NP   West  5   3
Great Smoky Mountains   NP   East  3  10
Hawaii Volcanoes        NP   West  2   2
Lava Beds               NM   West  1   1
Statue of Liberty       NM   East  1   0
Theodore Roosevelt      NP    .    2   2
Yellowstone             NP   West  9  11
Yosemite                NP   West  2  13
```

The following PROC REPORT contains two DEFINE statements. The first defines Region with a usage type of ORDER. The second specifies a column header for the variable Camping. Camping is a numeric variable and has a default usage of ANALYSIS, so the DEFINE statement does not change its usage. The MISSING option in the PROC statement tells SAS to include observations with missing values of Region.

```
DATA natparks;
   INFILE 'c:\MyRawData\Parks.dat';
   INPUT Name $ 1-21 Type $ Region $ Museums Camping;
RUN;
* PROC REPORT with ORDER variable, MISSING option, and column header;
PROC REPORT DATA = natparks NOWINDOWS MISSING;
   COLUMN Region Name Museums Camping;
   DEFINE Region / ORDER;
   DEFINE Camping / ANALYSIS 'Campgrounds';
   TITLE 'National Parks and Monuments Arranged by Region';
RUN;
```

Here are the results:

National Parks and Monuments Arranged by Region

Region	Name	Museums	Campgrounds
	Theodore Roosevelt	2	2
East	Ellis Island	1	0
	Everglades	5	2
	Great Smoky Mountains	3	10
	Statue of Liberty	1	0
West	Dinosaur	2	6
	Grand Canyon	5	3
	Hawaii Volcanoes	2	2
	Lava Beds	1	1
	Yellowstone	9	11
	Yosemite	2	13

4.20 Creating Summary Reports with PROC REPORT

Two different usage types cause the REPORT procedure to "roll up" data into summary groups based on the values of a variable. While the GROUP usage type produces summary rows, the ACROSS usage type produces summary columns.[10]

Group variables Defining a group variable is fairly simple. Just specify the GROUP usage option in a DEFINE statement. By default, analysis variables will be summed.[11] The following PROC REPORT tells SAS to produce a report showing the sum of Salary and of Bonus with a row for each value of Department.

Department	Salary	Bonus
A	~~~	~~
B	~~	~

```
PROC REPORT DATA = employees NOWINDOWS;
   COLUMN Department Salary Bonus;
   DEFINE Department / GROUP;
```

Across variables To define an across variable, you also use a DEFINE statement. However, by default SAS produces counts rather than sums. To obtain sums[11] for across variables, you must tell SAS which variables to summarize. You do that by putting a comma between the across variable and analysis variable (or variables if you enclose them in parentheses). The following PROC REPORT tells SAS to produce a report showing the sum of Salary and of Bonus with one column for each value of Department.

Department			
A		B	
Salary	Bonus	Salary	Bonus
~~	~~	~~	~

```
PROC REPORT DATA = employees NOWINDOWS;
   COLUMN Department , (Salary Bonus);
   DEFINE Department / ACROSS;
```

Example Here again are the data about national parks and monuments in the USA. The variables are name, type (NP for national park or NM for national monument), region (East or West), number of museums (including visitor centers), and number of campgrounds.

```
Dinosaur                NM   West   2    6
Ellis Island            NM   East   1    0
Everglades              NP   East   5    2
Grand Canyon            NP   West   5    3
Great Smoky Mountains   NP   East   3   10
Hawaii Volcanoes        NP   West   2    2
Lava Beds               NM   West   1    1
Statue of Liberty       NM   East   1    0
Theodore Roosevelt      NP   .      2    2
Yellowstone             NP   West   9   11
Yosemite                NP   West   2   13
```

The following program contains two PROC REPORTs. In the first, Region and Type are both defined as group variables. In the second, Region is still a group variable, but Type is an across variable. Notice that the two COLUMN statements are the same except for punctuation added to the second procedure to cross the across variable with the analysis variables.

```
DATA natparks;
   INFILE 'c:\MyRawData\Parks.dat';
   INPUT Name $ 1-21 Type $ Region $ Museums Camping;
RUN;

* Region and Type as GROUP variables;
PROC REPORT DATA = natparks NOWINDOWS;
   COLUMN Region Type Museums Camping;
   DEFINE Region / GROUP;
   DEFINE Type / GROUP;
   TITLE 'Summary Report with Two Group Variables';
RUN;
* Region as GROUP and Type as ACROSS with sums;
PROC REPORT DATA = natparks NOWINDOWS;
   COLUMN Region Type,(Museums Camping);
   DEFINE Region / GROUP;
   DEFINE Type / ACROSS;
   TITLE 'Summary Report with a Group and an Across Variable';
RUN;
```

Here is the resulting output:

Summary Report with Two Group Variables

Region	Type	Museums	Camping
East	NM	2	0
	NP	8	12
West	NM	3	7
	NP	18	29

Summary Report with a Group and an Across Variable

	Type			
	NM		NP	
Region	Museums	Camping	Museums	Camping
East	2	0	8	12
West	3	7	18	29

---

[10] If you have any display or order variables in the COLUMN statement, SAS will produce a detail report instead of consolidating data into summary groups.

[11] To request other statistics, see section 4.22.

4.21 Adding Summary Breaks to PROC REPORT Output

Two kinds of statements allow you to insert breaks into a report. The BREAK statement adds a break for each unique value of the variable you specify, while the RBREAK statement does the same for the entire report (or BY-group if you are using a BY statement). The general forms of these statements are

```
BREAK   location variable / options;
RBREAK  location / options;
```

where *location* has two possible values—BEFORE or AFTER—depending on whether you want the break to precede or follow that particular section of the report. The options that come after the slash tell SAS what kind of break to insert. Some of the possible options are

PAGE	starts a new page
SUMMARIZE	inserts summary statistics for numeric variables

Notice that the BREAK statement requires you to specify a variable, but the RBREAK statement does not. That's because the RBREAK statement produces only one break (at the beginning or end), while the BREAK statement produces one break for every unique value of the variable you specify. That variable must be either a group or order variable and therefore must also be listed in a DEFINE statement with either the GROUP or ORDER usage option. You can use an RBREAK statement in any report, but you can use BREAK only if you have at least one group or order variable.

Example Here again are the data about national parks and monuments in the USA. The variables are name, type (NP for national park or NM for national monument), region (East or West), number of museums (including visitor centers), and number of campgrounds.

```
Dinosaur               NM   West   2   6
Ellis Island           NM   East   1   0
Everglades             NP   East   5   2
Grand Canyon           NP   West   5   3
Great Smoky Mountains  NP   East   3  10
Hawaii Volcanoes       NP   West   2   2
Lava Beds              NM   West   1   1
Statue of Liberty      NM   East   1   0
Theodore Roosevelt     NP   .      2   2
Yellowstone            NP   West   9  11
Yosemite               NP   West   2  13
```

The following program defines Region as an order variable, and then uses both BREAK and RBREAK statements with the AFTER location. The SUMMARIZE option tells SAS to print totals for the numeric variables.

```
DATA natparks;
   INFILE 'c:\MyRawData\Parks.dat';
   INPUT Name $ 1-21 Type $ Region $ Museums Camping;
RUN;

* PROC REPORT with breaks;
PROC REPORT DATA = natparks NOWINDOWS;
   COLUMN Name Region Museums Camping;
   DEFINE Region / ORDER;
   BREAK AFTER Region / SUMMARIZE;
   RBREAK AFTER / SUMMARIZE;
   TITLE 'Detail Report with Summary Breaks';
RUN;
```

Here is the resulting output:

Detail Report with Summary Breaks

Name	Region	Museums	Camping
Ellis Island	East	1	0
Everglades		5	2
Great Smoky Mountains		3	10
Statue of Liberty		1	0
	East	*10*	*12*
Dinosaur	West	2	6
Grand Canyon		5	3
Hawaii Volcanoes		2	2
Lava Beds		1	1
Yellowstone		9	11
Yosemite		2	13
	West	*21*	*36*
		31	*48*

4.22 Adding Statistics to PROC REPORT Output

There are several ways to request statistics in the REPORT procedure. An easy method is to insert statistics keywords directly into the COLUMN statement along with the variable names. This is a little like requesting statistics in a TABLE statement in PROC TABULATE, except that instead of using an asterisk to cross a statistics keyword with a variable, you use a comma. In fact, PROC REPORT can produce all the same statistics as PROC TABULATE and PROC MEANS because it uses the same internal engine to compute those statistics. These are a few of the statistics PROC REPORT can compute:

MAX	highest value
MIN	lowest value
MEAN	arithmetic mean
MEDIAN	median
MODE	mode
N	number of non-missing values
NMISS	number of missing values
PCTN	percentage of observations for that group
PCTSUM	percentage of a total sum represented by that group
STD	standard deviation
SUM	sum

Applying statistics to variables To request a statistic for a particular variable, insert a comma between the statistic and variable in the COLUMN statement. One statistic, N, does not require a comma because it does not apply to a particular variable. If you insert N in a COLUMN statement, then SAS will print the number of observations that contributed to that row of the report. This statement tells SAS to print two columns of data: the median of a variable named Age, and the number of observations in that row.

```
COLUMN  Age,MEDIAN  N;
```

To request multiple statistics or statistics for multiple variables, put parentheses around the statistics or variables. This statement uses parentheses to request two statistics for the variable Age, and then requests one statistic for two variables, Height and Weight.

```
COLUMN Age,(MIN MAX) (Height Weight),MEAN;
```

Example Here again are the data about national parks and monuments in the USA. The variables are name, type, region, number of museums, and number of campgrounds.

```
Dinosaur               NM   West   2    6
Ellis Island           NM   East   1    0
Everglades             NP   East   5    2
Grand Canyon           NP   West   5    3
Great Smoky Mountains  NP   East   3   10
Hawaii Volcanoes       NP   West   2    2
Lava Beds              NM   West   1    1
Statue of Liberty      NM   East   1    0
Theodore Roosevelt     NP    .     2    2
Yellowstone            NP   West   9   11
Yosemite               NP   West   2   13
```

The following program contains two PROC REPORTs. Both procedures request the statistics N and MEAN, but the first report defines Type as a group variable, while the second defines Type as an across variable.

```
DATA natparks;
   INFILE 'c:\MyRawData\Parks.dat';
   INPUT Name $ 1-21 Type $ Region $ Museums Camping;
RUN;
*Statistics in COLUMN statement with two group variables;
PROC REPORT DATA = natparks NOWINDOWS;
   COLUMN Region Type N (Museums Camping),MEAN;
   DEFINE Region / GROUP;
   DEFINE Type / GROUP;
   TITLE 'Statistics with Two Group Variables';
RUN;
*Statistics in COLUMN statement with group and across variables;
PROC REPORT DATA = natparks NOWINDOWS;
   COLUMN Region N Type,(Museums Camping),MEAN;
   DEFINE Region / GROUP;
   DEFINE Type / ACROSS;
   TITLE 'Statistics with a Group and Across Variable';
RUN;
```

Here is the resulting output:

Statistics with Two Group Variables

			Museums	Camping
Region	Type	N	MEAN	MEAN
East	NM	2	1	0
	NP	2	4	6
West	NM	2	1.5	3.5
	NP	4	4.5	7.25

Statistics with a Group and Across Variable

		Type			
		NM		NP	
		Museums	Camping	Museums	Camping
Region	N	MEAN	MEAN	MEAN	MEAN
East	4	1	0	4	6
West	6	1.5	3.5	4.5	7.25

Notice that these reports are similar to the reports in section 4.20 except that these contain counts and means instead of sums.

4.23 Adding Computed Variables to PROC REPORT Output

Unlike most procedures, the REPORT procedure has the ability to compute not only statistics (like sums and means) but also new variables. You do this using a compute block. Compute blocks start with a COMPUTE statement and end with an ENDCOMP statement. In between, you put the programming statements to calculate your new variable. PROC REPORT uses a limited set of programming statements including assignment statements, IF-THEN/ELSE statements, and DO loops. You do not have to specify a DEFINE statement for the new variable, but if you do, then give it a usage type of COMPUTED. The general form of these statements is

```
DEFINE new-variable-name / COMPUTED;
COMPUTE new-variable-name / options;
   programming statements
ENDCOMP;
```

Computing a numeric variable For a numeric variable, simply name the new variable in the COMPUTE statement. If you use any variables with a type of analysis in the compute block, you must append the variable name with its statistic. The default statistic for an analysis variable is SUM. The following statements compute a variable named Income by adding Salary and Bonus.

```
DEFINE Income / COMPUTED;
COMPUTE  Income;
   Income = Salary.SUM + Bonus.SUM;
ENDCOMP;
```

Computing a character variable For a character variable, add the CHAR option to the COMPUTE statement. You will probably also want the LENGTH option. Lengths for computed character variables range from 1 to 200, with a default of 8. The following statements compute a variable named JobType using IF-THEN/ELSE statements.

```
DEFINE JobType / COMPUTED;
COMPUTE  JobType / CHAR LENGTH = 10;
   IF Title = 'Programmer' THEN JobType = 'Technical';
   ELSE JobType = 'Other';
ENDCOMP;
```

Example Here again are the data about national parks and monuments in the USA. The variables are name, type, region, number of museums, and number of campgrounds.

```
Dinosaur              NM   West   2    6
Ellis Island          NM   East   1    0
Everglades            NP   East   5    2
Grand Canyon          NP   West   5    3
Great Smoky Mountains NP   East   3   10
Hawaii Volcanoes      NP   West   2    2
Lava Beds             NM   West   1    1
Statue of Liberty     NM   East   1    0
Theodore Roosevelt    NP   .      2    2
Yellowstone           NP   West   9   11
Yosemite              NP   West   2   13
```

The following PROC REPORT computes two variables named Facilities and Note. Facilities is a numeric variable equal to the number of museums plus the number of campgrounds. Note is a character variable which is equal to "No Camping" for parks that have no campgrounds. Notice that the variables Museums and Camping must be listed in the COLUMN statement because they are used to compute the new variables. In order to exclude them from the results, the program uses the NOPRINT option in DEFINE statements.

```
DATA natparks;
   INFILE 'c:\MyRawData\Parks.dat';
   INPUT Name $ 1-21 Type $ Region $ Museums Camping;
RUN;

* COMPUTE new variables that are numeric and character;
PROC REPORT DATA = natparks NOWINDOWS;
   COLUMN Name Region Museums Camping Facilities Note;
   DEFINE Museums / ANALYSIS SUM NOPRINT;
   DEFINE Camping / ANALYSIS SUM NOPRINT;
   DEFINE Facilities / COMPUTED 'Camping/and/Museums';
   DEFINE Note / COMPUTED;
   COMPUTE Facilities;
      Facilities = Museums.SUM + Camping.SUM;
   ENDCOMP;
   COMPUTE Note / CHAR LENGTH = 10;
      IF Camping.SUM = 0 THEN Note = 'No Camping';
   ENDCOMP;
   TITLE 'Report with Two Computed Variables';
RUN;
```

Here is the resulting output:

Report with Two Computed Variables

Name	Region	Camping and Museums	Note
Dinosaur	West	8	
Ellis Island	East	1	No Camping
Everglades	East	7	
Grand Canyon	West	8	
Great Smoky Mountains	East	13	
Hawaii Volcanoes	West	4	
Lava Beds	West	2	
Statue of Liberty	East	1	No Camping
Theodore Roosevelt		4	
Yellowstone	West	20	
Yosemite	West	15	

4.24 Grouping Data in Procedures with User-Defined Formats

With user-defined formats you can group data in procedure output without creating a new variable. This is handy for cases where you have a lot of data, and it takes a long time to run a DATA step. Also, using this method it is easy to change the groupings by simply creating a new format. This method works for procedures that group data such as PROC FREQ, PROC TABULATE, PROC MEANS with a CLASS statement, and PROC REPORT with GROUP or ACROSS variables.

Grouping data this way is a two-step process. First, use the FORMAT procedure to define a format that assigns all the values that you want to group together to a text string. Second, use the FORMAT statement in the procedure to assign the format to the variable to be grouped.

Example The staff of the local library want to see the type of books people check out by age group. They have the age of the patron in years and the book type: fiction, mystery, science fiction, biography, non-fiction, and reference. Here are the data with nine observations per line:

```
17 sci  9 bio 28 fic 50 mys 13 fic 32 fic 67 fic 81 non 38 non
53 non 16 sci 15 bio 61 fic 52 ref 22 mys 76 bio 37 fic 86 fic
49 mys 78 non 45 sci 64 bio  8 fic 11 non 41 fic 46 ref 69 fic
34 fic 26 mys 23 sci 74 ref 15 sci 27 fic 23 mys 63 fic 78 non
40 bio 12 fic 29 fic 54 mys 67 fic 60 fic 38 sci 42 fic 80 fic
```

Here is the program that reads the data and creates two user-defined formats, one to group the age data, and one for the book type data. The FREQ procedures count the number of books by age group and book type. The Age variable is grouped into four categories using the AGEGPA. user-defined format in the first PROC FREQ while the second PROC FREQ groups age into two categories using the AGEGPB. format. In both PROC FREQs, BookType is grouped into two categories using the $TYP. user-defined format.

```
DATA books;
    INFILE 'c:\MyRawData\LibraryBooks.dat';
    INPUT Age BookType $ @@;
RUN;
*Define formats to group the data;
PROC FORMAT;
   VALUE agegpa
          0-18    = '0 to 18'
          19-25   = '19 to 25'
          26-49   = '26 to 49'
          50-HIGH = '  50+ ';
   VALUE agegpb
          0-25    = '0 to 25'
          26-HIGH = '  26+ ';
   VALUE $typ
          'bio','non','ref' = 'Non-Fiction'
          'fic','mys','sci' = 'Fiction';
RUN;
```

```
*Create two way table with Age grouped into four categories;
PROC FREQ DATA = books;
    TITLE 'Patron Age by Book Type: Four Age Groups';
    TABLES BookType * Age / NOPERCENT NOROW NOCOL;
    FORMAT Age agegpa. BookType $typ.;
RUN;
*Create two way table with Age grouped into two categories;
PROC FREQ DATA = books;
    TITLE 'Patron Age by Book Type: Two Age Groups';
    TABLES BookType * Age / NOPERCENT NOROW NOCOL;
    FORMAT Age agegpb. BookType $typ.;
RUN;
```

Because the NOPERCENT, NOROW, and NOCOL options were added to the TABLES statements, only frequencies appear in the results.

Patron Age by Book Type: Four Age Groups
The FREQ Procedure

Table of BookType by Age					
BookType	Age				
Frequency	0 to 18	19 to 25	26 to 49	50+	Total
Non-Fiction	3	0	3	8	14
Fiction	6	3	12	10	31
Total	9	3	15	18	45

Patron Age by Book Type: Two Age Groups
The FREQ Procedure

Table of BookType by Age			
BookType	Age		
Frequency	0 to 25	26+	Total
Non-Fiction	3	11	14
Fiction	9	22	31
Total	12	33	45

5

"Some men see things as they are and say, 'Why.' I dream things that never were and say, 'Why not.'"

ROBERT F. KENNEDY

From *Respectfully Quoted: A Dictionary of Quotations from the Library of Congress,* edited by Suzy Platt, copyright 1992 by Library of Congress. Based on George Bernard Shaw, *Back to Methuselah,* act 1, 1949.

CHAPTER 5

Enhancing Your Output with ODS

5.1 Concepts of the Output Delivery System

 You might think that procedures produce output. They don't. Technically, procedures produce only data. Then they send that data to the Output Delivery System (ODS) which determines where the output should go and what it should look like when it gets there. That means the question to ask yourself is not whether you want to use ODS—you always use ODS. The question is whether to accept default output or choose something else.

ODS is like a busy airport. Passengers arrive by car and bus. Once at the airport, passengers check baggage, pass security, eventually board a plane, and fly out to their destinations. In ODS, data are like passengers arriving from various procedures. ODS processes each set of data and sends it off to its proper destination. In fact, different types of ODS output are called destinations. What your data look like when they get to their destination is determined by templates. A template is a set of instructions telling ODS how to format your data. These two concepts—destinations and templates—are fundamental to understanding what you can do with ODS.

Destinations Starting with SAS 9.3 if you don't specify a destination, your output will be sent, by default, to HTML when you use the SAS windowing environment in Microsoft Windows or UNIX. With SAS 9.2 and earlier, the default destination was LISTING. LISTING is still the default for programs run in batch or in other operating environments. Here are the major destinations:

HTML	Hypertext Markup Language
LISTING	text output
PDF	Portable Document Format
PS	PostScript
PRINTER	high-resolution printer output
RTF	Rich Text Format
MARKUP	markup languages including XML
DOCUMENT	output document
OUTPUT	SAS data set

Most of these destinations are designed to create output for viewing on a screen or for printing. The LISTING destination is what appears in the Output window in the SAS windowing environment, or in the listing or output file if you use batch mode. The MARKUP destination is a general purpose tool for creating output in formats defined by tagsets. This includes XML (eXtensible Markup Language), EXCELXP, LaTeX, CSV (comma-separated values), and many other formats where data can be thought of as separated by tags. The OUTPUT destination creates SAS data sets. The DOCUMENT destination, on the other hand, allows you to create a reusable output "document" that you can re-render for any destination. So, if your boss decides he really wants that report in PDF, not RTF, you can replay the output document without having to rerun the entire SAS program that created the data. With an output document, you can also rearrange, duplicate, or delete tables to further customize your output.

Style and table templates   Templates tell ODS how to format and present your data. The two most common types of templates are table templates and style templates (also called table definitions and style definitions). A table template specifies the basic structure of your output (which variable will be in the first column?); while a style template specifies how the output will look (will the headers be blue or red?). ODS combines the data produced by a procedure with a table template and together they are called an output object. The output object is then combined with a style template and sent to a destination to create your final output.[1]

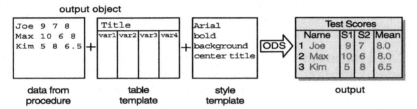

You can create your own table and style templates using the TEMPLATE procedure. However, PROC TEMPLATE's syntax is rather arcane. Fortunately, there are other, easier, ways to control and modify output. The quickest and easiest way to change the look of your output is to use one of the many built-in style templates. To view a list of the style templates available on your system, submit the following PROC TEMPLATE statements:

```
PROC TEMPLATE;
   LIST STYLES;
RUN;
```

A few of the built-in style templates are

```
ANALYSIS       D3D        MINIMAL      SASWEB
BARRETTSBLUE   HTMLBLUE   PRINTER      SANSPRINTER
BRICK          JOURNAL    RTF          STATISTICAL
```

Notice that RTF and PRINTER are names of both destinations and styles. Some styles work better with certain destinations than with others. HTMLBLUE is the default style for HTML output, RTF is the default style for RTF output, and PRINTER is the default style for output sent to the PRINTER, PDF, and PS destinations.

A few procedures, most notably PRINT, REPORT, and TABULATE, don't have ready-made table templates. Instead, the syntax for these procedures acts like a custom table template. While all procedures that produce printable output allow you to use style templates to control the overall look of that output, these three procedures also allow you to do something special. With PRINT, REPORT, and TABULATE, you can use the STYLE= option directly in the PROC step to control individual features of your output without having to create a whole new style template.

---

[1] In ODS Graphics, instead of a table template your data are combined with a graph template, and the final result is graphical output instead of tabular output. For the LISTING destination, style templates apply to graphical output but not tabular output because tabular output is rendered as plain text. See chapter 8 for information about ODS Graphics.

5.2 Tracing and Selecting Procedure Output

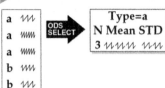

When ODS receives data from a procedure, it combines that data with a table template. Together the data and corresponding table template are called an output object. Many procedures produce just one output object, while others produce several. For most procedures when you use a BY statement, SAS produces one output object for each BY group. Every output object has a name. You can find the names of output objects by using the ODS TRACE statement. Then you can use an ODS SELECT (or ODS EXCLUDE) statement to choose just the output objects you want.

ODS TRACE statement The ODS TRACE statement tells SAS to print information about output objects in your SAS log. There are two ODS TRACE statements: one to turn on the trace, and one to turn it off. Here is how to use these statements in a program:

```
ODS TRACE ON;
the PROC steps you want to trace go here
RUN;
ODS TRACE OFF;
```

Notice that the RUN statement comes before the ODS TRACE OFF statement. Unlike most other SAS statements, the ODS statement executes immediately—without waiting for a RUN, PROC, or DATA statement. If you put the ODS TRACE OFF statement before the RUN statement, then the trace would turn off before the procedure completes.

Example Here are data about varieties of giant tomatoes. Each line of data includes the name of the variety, its color (red or yellow), the number of days from planting to harvest, and the weight (in pounds) of a typical tomato. Each line of data includes two varieties.

```
Big Zac, red, 80, 5, Delicious, red, 80, 3
Dinner Plate, red, 90, 2, Goliath, red, 85, 1.5
Mega Tom, red, 80, 2, Mortgage Lifter, red, 85, 2
Big Rainbow, yellow, 90, 1.5, Pineapple, yellow, 85, 2
```

The following program creates a data set named GIANT, and then traces PROC MEANS using ODS TRACE ON and ODS TRACE OFF statements:

```
DATA giant;
   INFILE 'c:\MyRawData\GiantTom.dat' DSD;
   INPUT Name :$15. Color $ Days Weight @@;
RUN;
* Trace PROC MEANS;
ODS TRACE ON;
PROC MEANS DATA = giant;
   BY Color;
RUN;
ODS TRACE OFF;
```

If you run this program, you will see the following trace in your SAS log. Because it contains a BY statement, the MEANS procedure produces one output object for each BY group (red and yellow). Notice that these two output objects have the same name, label, and template, but different paths.

```
Output Added:
-------------
Name:       Summary
Label:      Summary statistics
Template:   base.summary
Path:       Means.ByGroup1.Summary
-------------
NOTE: The above message was for the following by-group: Color=red

Output Added:
-------------
Name:       Summary
Label:      Summary statistics
Template:   base.summary
Path:       Means.ByGroup2.Summary
-------------
NOTE: The above message was for the following by-group: Color=yellow
```

ODS SELECT statement   Once you know the names of the output objects, you can use an ODS SELECT (or EXCLUDE) statement to choose just the output objects you want. The general form of an ODS SELECT statement is

```
The PROC step with the output objects you want to select
ODS SELECT output-object-list;
RUN;
```

where *output-object-list* is the name, label, or path of one or more output objects separated by spaces. By default, an ODS SELECT statement lasts for only one PROC step, so by placing the SELECT statement after the PROC statement and before the RUN, you are sure to capture the correct output. ODS EXCLUDE statements work the same way except you list output objects that you want to eliminate.

Example   This program runs PROC MEANS again using the GIANT data set, and an ODS SELECT statement to select just the first output object: Means.ByGroup1.Summary.

```
PROC MEANS DATA = giant;
   BY Color;
ODS SELECT Means.ByGroup1.Summary;
RUN;
```

Here are the results containing just the first BY group.

The MEANS Procedure

Color=red

Variable	N	Mean	Std Dev	Minimum	Maximum
Days	6	83.3333333	4.0824829	80.0000000	90.0000000
Weight	6	2.5833333	1.2812754	1.5000000	5.0000000

5.3 Creating SAS Data Sets from Procedure Output

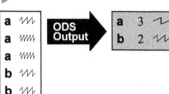

Sometimes you may want to put the results from a procedure into a SAS data set. Once the results are in a data set, you can merge them with another data set, compute new variables based on the results, or use the results as input for other procedures. Some procedures have OUTPUT statements, or OUT= options, allowing you to save the results as a SAS data set. But with ODS you can save almost any part of procedure output as a SAS data set by sending it to the OUTPUT destination. First you use an ODS TRACE statement (discussed in the previous section) to determine the name of the output object you want. Then you use an ODS OUTPUT statement to send that object to the OUTPUT destination.

ODS OUTPUT statement   Here is the general form of a basic ODS OUTPUT statement:

```
ODS OUTPUT output-object = new-data-set;
```

where *output-object* is the name, label, or path of the piece of output you want to save, and *new-data-set* is the name of the SAS data set you want to create.

The ODS OUTPUT statement does not belong to either a DATA or PROC step, but you need to be careful where you put it in your program. The ODS OUTPUT statement opens a SAS data set and waits for the correct procedure output. The data set remains open until the next encounter with the end of a PROC step. Because the ODS OUTPUT statement executes immediately, it will apply to whatever PROC is currently being processed, or it will apply to the next PROC if there is not a current PROC. To ensure that you get the correct output, we recommend that you put the ODS OUTPUT statement after your PROC statement, and before the next PROC, DATA, or RUN statement.

Example   Here again are data about varieties of giant tomatoes. Each line of data includes the name of the variety, its color (red or yellow), the number of days from planting to harvest, and the weight (in pounds) of a typical tomato. Each line of data includes two varieties.

```
Big Zac, red, 80, 5, Delicious, red, 80, 3
Dinner Plate, red, 90, 2, Goliath, red, 85, 1.5
Mega Tom, red, 80, 2, Mortgage Lifter, red, 85, 2
Big Rainbow, yellow, 90, 1.5, Pineapple, yellow, 85, 2
```

The following program creates a data set named GIANT, and then traces PROC TABULATE using ODS TRACE ON and ODS TRACE OFF statements:

```
DATA giant;
   INFILE 'c:\MyRawData\GiantTom.dat' DSD;
   INPUT Name :$15. Color $ Days Weight @@;
RUN;
ODS TRACE ON;
PROC TABULATE DATA = giant;
   CLASS Color;
   VAR Days Weight;
   TABLE Color ALL, (Days Weight) * MEAN;
RUN;
ODS TRACE OFF;
```

Here is an excerpt from the SAS log showing the trace produced by PROC TABULATE. PROC TABULATE produces one output object named Table.

```
Output Added:
-------------
Name:        Table
Label:       Table 1
Data Name:   Report
Path:        Tabulate.Report.Table
-------------
```

The following program uses an ODS OUTPUT statement to create a SAS data set named TABOUT from the Table output object. Then PROC PRINT prints the new data set.

```
PROC TABULATE DATA = giant;
   CLASS Color;
   VAR Days Weight;
   TABLE Color ALL, (Days Weight) * MEAN;
   TITLE 'Standard TABULATE Output';
ODS OUTPUT Table = tabout;
RUN;
PROC PRINT DATA = tabout;
   TITLE 'OUTPUT SAS Data Set from TABULATE';
RUN;
```

Here are the results showing two pieces of output. The first is the standard tabular result produced by PROC TABULATE. Below that is the TABOUT data set created by the ODS OUTPUT statement and printed by PROC PRINT.

Standard TABULATE Output

	Days	Weight
	Mean	Mean
Color		
red	83.33	2.58
yellow	87.50	1.75
All	84.38	2.38

OUTPUT SAS Data Set from TABULATE

Obs	Color	_TYPE_	_PAGE_	_TABLE_	Days_Mean	Weight_Mean
1	red	1	1	1	83.3333	2.58333
2	yellow	1	1	1	87.5000	1.75000
3		0	1	1	84.3750	2.37500

5.4 Creating Text Output

The LISTING destination creates simple text output. Text output consists of basic characters without the special formatting added by applications such as word processors or spreadsheets. Text output has some advantages. It is highly portable, compact when printed, and can be easily edited. LISTING is the default destination when you run SAS in batch or in the z/OS operating environment. If you want to produce LISTING output in the SAS windowing environment in Microsoft Windows or UNIX, then you must open the LISTING destination. There are two ways to do this, either by submitting an ODS LISTING statement or via the Tools menu.

Tools menu In the SAS windowing environment, you can open the LISTING destination by selecting **Tools ▶ Options ▶ Preferences** from the menu bar. Then click the **Results** tab and check the box next to **Create Listing**. SAS will continue to send output to the LISTING destination until you close it.

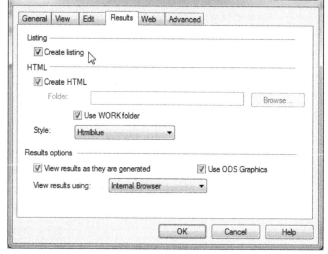

ODS statement You can also open the LISTING destination by submitting an ODS LISTING statement. The general form of this statement is

```
ODS LISTING;
```

If you submit this statement, then your output will be displayed in the Output window. If you add a FILE= option, then the output will be saved in a file instead, and will not appear in the Output window. The following statement tells SAS to send the output to the LISTING destination and save the results in a file named AnnualReport.lst.

```
ODS LISTING FILE = 'AnnualReport.lst';
```

Unlike most ODS destinations, you do not need to close the LISTING destination in order to see your output. The only reason to close the LISTING destination is if you want to stop producing text output. Here is the ODS statement which closes the LISTING destination.

```
ODS LISTING CLOSE;
```

Removing procedure titles Some procedures (such as PROC MEANS and PROC FREQ) include the name of the procedure in your output. You can remove procedure names by using the ODS NOPROCTITLE statement. This statement works for all destinations, not just LISTING.

```
ODS NOPROCTITLE;
```

Example This example uses data about average lengths, in feet, of selected whales and sharks. Notice that each line contains data for four observations.

```
beluga whale 15   dwarf shark .5    basking shark 30   humpback whale 50
whale  shark 40   blue  whale 100   killer  whale 30   mako    shark 12
```

The following program produces two pieces of output: one from the MEANS procedure, and one from the PRINT procedure. There are two ODS statements in the program. The first ODS statement opens the LISTING destination. The second ODS statement turns off procedure titles.

```
* Create the text output and remove procedure name;
ODS LISTING;
ODS NOPROCTITLE;
DATA marine;
   INFILE 'c:\MyRawData\Lengths8.dat';
   INPUT Name $ Family $ Length @@;
RUN;
PROC MEANS DATA = marine MEAN MIN MAX;
   CLASS Family;
   TITLE 'Whales and Sharks';
RUN;
PROC PRINT DATA = marine;
RUN;
```

Here is what the results looks like when viewed in the Output window in the SAS windowing environment. The LISTING destination does not use a style for tabular output. Instead the results are rendered as text using the SASMONOSPACE font.

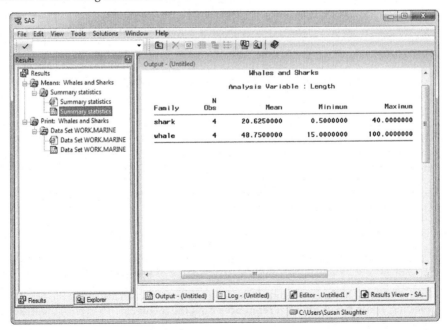

5.5 ## Creating HTML Output

When you send output to the HTML destination, you get files in Hypertext Markup Language (HTML) format. These files are ready to be posted on a Web site for viewing by your boss or colleagues, but HTML output has other uses too. It can be read into spreadsheets, and even printed or imported into word processors (though some formatting may change). Starting with SAS 9.3, HTML output is the default in the SAS windowing environment in Microsoft Windows and UNIX so you do not need to use ODS statements to open or close the destination. However, you may still want to use ODS statements to specify options. If you are running in batch or in other operating environments, then you will need to use ODS statements to produce HTML output.

ODS statement To open the HTML destination, use the ODS HTML statement. The general form of this statement is

```
ODS HTML BODY = 'body-filename.html' options;
```

The body file contains your results. The FILE= option is synonymous with BODY=. Other options available for this destination include

CONTENTS = 'filename' creates a table of contents with links to the body file.

PAGE = 'filename' creates a table of contents with links by page number.

FRAME = 'filename' creates a frame that allows you to view the body file and the contents or the page file at the same time. If you do not want either the contents or the page file, then you don't need to create a frame file.

STYLE = style-name specifies a style template. The default is HTMLBLUE.

You always want to create a body file, but the other files are optional. The following statement tells SAS to send output to the HTML destination, save the results in a file named AnnualReport.html, and use the BARRETTSBLUE style.

```
ODS HTML FILE = 'AnnualReport.html' STYLE = BARRETTSBLUE;
```

ODS statements are global, and do not belong to either DATA steps or PROC steps. However, if you put them in the wrong place, they won't capture the output that you want. A good place to put the first ODS statement is just before the step (or steps) whose output you wish to capture.

To close the HTML destination, put this statement after the step (or steps) whose output you wish to capture, and following a RUN statement:

```
ODS HTML CLOSE;
```

You do not need to include an ODS HTML CLOSE statement if you are only creating a body file and you are running in an operating environment that has HTML on by default.

Tools menu In the SAS windowing environment, you can also close the HTML destination by selecting **Tools ▶ Options ▶ Preferences** from the menu bar. Then click the **Results** tab and uncheck the box next to **Create HTML**.

Example Here again are data about average lengths, in feet, of selected whales and sharks.

```
beluga whale 15  dwarf shark .5   basking shark 30  humpback whale 50
whale  shark 40  blue  whale 100  killer  whale 30  mako  shark 12
```

The following program produces two pieces of output: one from PROC MEANS and one from PROC PRINT. There are three ODS statements. The first ODS statement selects the style D3D and then opens files for the body, frame, and table of contents. The second ODS statement turns off procedure titles. The third ODS statement closes the files.

```
* Create the HTML files and remove procedure name;
ODS HTML STYLE = D3D  BODY = 'c:\MyHTMLFiles\Marine.html'
      FRAME = 'c:\MyHTMLFiles\MarineFrame.html'
      CONTENTS = 'c:\MyHTMLFiles\MarineTOC.html';
ODS NOPROCTITLE;
DATA marine;
   INFILE 'c:\MyRawData\Lengths8.dat';
   INPUT Name $ Family $ Length @@;
RUN;
PROC MEANS DATA = marine MEAN MIN MAX;
   CLASS Family;
   TITLE 'Whales and Sharks';
RUN;
PROC PRINT DATA = marine;
RUN;
ODS HTML CLOSE;
```

Here is what the MarineFrame.html file looks like when viewed in a browser. The table of contents appears on the left and the procedure results appear on the right.

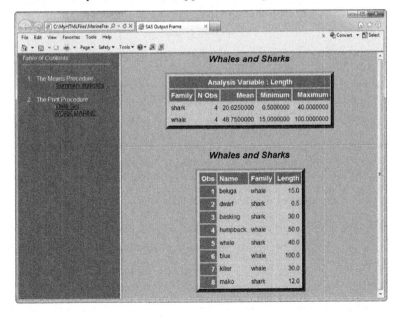

5.6 Creating RTF Output

Rich Text Format (RTF) was developed by Microsoft for document interchange. When you create RTF output, you can copy it into a Word document and edit or resize it like other Word tables. Sending output to the RTF destination is similar to sending it to the HTML destination except you use the ODS RTF statement.

ODS statement The general form of the ODS statement to open RTF files is

```
ODS RTF FILE = 'filename.rtf' options;
```

Unlike HTML, there is only one kind of RTF file, a file containing output. Here are some of the most commonly used options for this destination:

BODYTITLE	puts titles and footnotes in the main part of the RTF document instead of in Word headers or footers.
COLUMNS = n	requests columnar output where *n* is the number of columns.
SASDATE	by default, the date and time that appear at the top of RTF output indicate when the file was last opened or printed in Word. This option tells SAS to use the date and time when the current SAS session or job started running.[2]
STARTPAGE = value	controls page breaks. The default value, YES, inserts a page break between procedures. A value of NO turns off page breaks. A value of NOW inserts a page break at that point.
STYLE = style-name	specifies a style template. The default is RTF.

The following statement tells SAS to send output to the RTF destination, save the results in a file named AnnualReport.rtf, and use the SANSPRINTER style:

```
ODS RTF FILE = 'AnnualReport.rtf' STYLE = SANSPRINTER;
```

ODS statements are global, and do not belong to either DATA steps or PROC steps. However, if you put them in the wrong place, they won't capture the output that you want. A good place to put the first ODS statement is just before the step (or steps) whose output you wish to capture.

Here is the ODS statement which closes the RTF file.

```
ODS RTF CLOSE;
```

Put this statement after the step (or steps) whose output you wish to capture, and following a RUN statement.

Example Here again are data about average lengths, in feet, of selected whales and sharks.

```
beluga whale 15  dwarf shark .5   basking shark 30  humpback whale 50
whale  shark 40  blue  whale 100  killer  whale 30  mako   shark 12
```

The following program produces two pieces of output: one from PROC MEANS and one from PROC PRINT. There are three ODS statements in the program: one to open the RTF file, one to turn off procedure titles, and one to close the RTF file.

```
* Create an RTF file;
ODS RTF FILE = 'c:\MyRTFFiles\Marine.rtf' BODYTITLE STARTPAGE = NO;
ODS NOPROCTITLE;
DATA marine;
    INFILE 'c:\MyRawData\Lengths8.dat';
    INPUT Name $ Family $ Length @@;
RUN;
PROC MEANS DATA = marine MEAN MIN MAX;
    CLASS Family;
    TITLE 'Whales and Sharks';
RUN;
PROC PRINT DATA = marine;
RUN;
* Close the RTF file;
ODS RTF CLOSE;
```

Here is what the Marine.rtf file looks like when viewed in Microsoft Word. Because the BODYTITLE option was specified, the titles appear with the tables instead of in a Word header. The STARTPAGE=NO option told SAS not to insert a page break between the two tables. Since no style was specified, SAS used the default style, RTF.

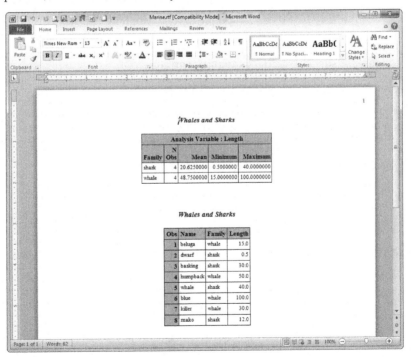

---

[2] If you have the system option DTRESET turned on and you use the SASDATE option, then SAS will use the date and time when the program ran instead of when SAS started.

5.7 Creating PDF Output

The PDF destination creates output in Portable Document Format, a format that was developed by Adobe Systems but then became an open standard for document exchange. The PDF destination is a member of the PRINTER family of ODS destinations which produces output for high-resolution printers. Like most other destinations, you need two statements to generate PDF output—one to open the destination and one to close it.

ODS statement The general form of the ODS statement to open the PDF destination is

```
ODS PDF FILE = 'filename.pdf' options;
```

Like the RTF destination, the PDF destination produces only one kind of file, a file containing output.

The options available for this destination include

COLUMNS = *n*   requests columnar output where *n* is the number of columns.

STARTPAGE = *value*   controls page breaks. The default value, YES, inserts a break between procedures. A value of NO turns off breaks. A value of NOW inserts a break at that point.

STYLE = *style-name*   specifies a style template. The default is PRINTER.

The following statement tells SAS to create PDF output, save the results in a file named AnnualReport.pdf, and use the SANSPRINTER style.

```
ODS PDF FILE = 'AnnualReport.pdf' STYLE = SANSPRINTER;
```

ODS statements are global, and do not belong to either DATA steps or PROC steps. However, if you put them in the wrong place, they won't capture the output that you want. A good place to put the first ODS statement is just before the step (or steps) whose output you wish to capture.

Here is the ODS statement which closes the PDF file.

```
ODS PDF CLOSE;
```

Put this statement after the step (or steps) whose output you wish to capture, and following a RUN statement.

Example Here again are data about average lengths, in feet, of selected whales and sharks.

```
beluga whale 15  dwarf shark .5   basking shark 30  humpback whale 50
whale  shark 40  blue  whale 100  killer  whale 30  mako   shark 12
```

The following program produces output with the MEANS and PRINT procedures. There are three ODS statements in the program: one to open the PDF file, one to turn off procedure titles, and one to close the PDF file.

```
* Create the PDF file;
ODS PDF FILE = 'c:\MyPDFFiles\Marine.pdf' STARTPAGE = NO;
ODS NOPROCTITLE;
DATA marine;
    INFILE 'c:\MyRawData\Lengths8.dat';
    INPUT Name $ Family $ Length @@;
RUN;
PROC MEANS DATA = marine MEAN MIN MAX;
    CLASS Family;
    TITLE 'Whales and Sharks';
RUN;
PROC PRINT DATA = marine;
RUN;
* Close the PDF file;
ODS PDF CLOSE;
```

Here is what the Marine.pdf file looks like when viewed in Adobe Reader. Because the option STARTPAGE=NO was specified, the output from both procedures appears on the same page. Since no style was specified, SAS used the default style, PRINTER.

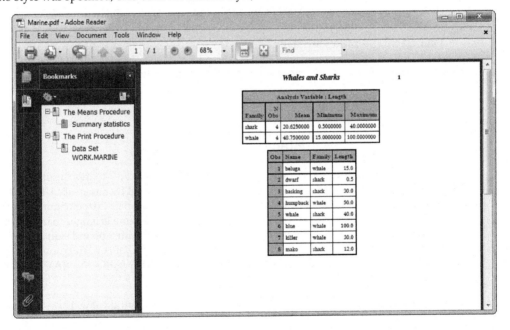

5.8 ▶ Customizing Titles and Footnotes

In ODS output, your style template tells SAS how titles and footnotes should look. However, you can easily change the appearance of titles and footnotes by inserting a few simple options in your TITLE and FOOTNOTE statements.

The general form for a TITLE or FOOTNOTE statement is

```
TITLE options 'text-string-1' options 'text-string-2' ... options 'text-string-n';

FOOTNOTE options 'text-string-1' options 'text-string-2' ...options 'text-string-n';
```

Text can be broken into pieces with different options for each piece. SAS will concatenate text strings just the way you type them, so be sure to include any necessary blanks. Each option applies to the text string that follows, and stays in effect until another value is specified for that option, or until the end of the statement. Here are the main options that you can choose:

COLOR=	specifies a color for the text.
BCOLOR=	specifies a color for the background of the text.
HEIGHT=	specifies the height of the text.
JUSTIFY=	requests justification.
FONT=	specifies a font for the text.
BOLD	makes text bold.
ITALIC	makes text italic.

Color The COLOR= option specifies the color of the text. This statement

```
TITLE COLOR=BLACK 'Black  ' COLOR=GRAY 'Gray  ' COLOR=LTGRAY 'Light Gray';
```

would produce this title:

Black Gray Light Gray

SAS supports hundreds of colors ranging from primary colors—red—to more esoteric colors— LIGRPR (light grayish purplish red). These colors can be specified by name—BLUE—or by hexadecimal code—#0000FF. In fact, SAS recognizes more than a half-dozen naming schemes for specifying color.[3] Names of colors need quotation marks if the name is longer than 8 characters or contains embedded spaces. RGB hexadecimal codes beginning with a pound sign also require quotation marks. If you want to specify colors by name, here is a list of basic colors you can start with: AQUA, BLACK, BLUE, FUCHSIA, GREEN, GRAY, LIME, MAROON, NAVY, OLIVE, PURPLE, RED, SILVER, TEAL, WHITE, YELLOW.

Background color The BCOLOR= option specifies a background color. This statement uses an RGB hexadecimal code:

```
TITLE BCOLOR='#C0C0C0' 'This Title Has a Gray Background';
```

and produces this title:

This Title Has a Gray Background

You can choose among the same colors as with the COLOR= option.

Height To change the height of the text, use the HEIGHT= option where the value of HEIGHT is a number with units of PT, IN, or CM. This statement

```
TITLE HEIGHT=12PT 'Small  ' HEIGHT=.25IN 'Medium  ' HEIGHT=1CM 'Large';
```

would produce this title:

Small Medium Large

Justification You can control justification of text using the JUSTIFY= option which can have the values LEFT, CENTER, or RIGHT. You can even mix these options within a single statement. This statement

```
TITLE JUSTIFY=LEFT 'Left ' JUSTIFY=CENTER 'vs. ' JUSTIFY=RIGHT 'Right';
```

would produce this title:

Left   **vs.**   **Right**

Font Use the FONT= option to specify a font. This statement

```
TITLE 'Default   ' FONT=Arial 'Arial    '
    FONT='Times New Roman' 'Times New Roman   ' FONT=Courier 'Courier';
```

would produce this title:

Default Arial Times New Roman <code>Courier</code>

The particular fonts available to you depend on your operating environment and hardware. Courier, Arial, Times, and Helvetica work in most situations.

Bold and italic By default, titles are bold. When you change the font, you also turn off the bolding. To turn on bolding, use the BOLD option; to turn on italics use the ITALIC option. There is no option to turn off bolding or italics, so if you wish to turn them off, use the FONT= option. Here are the three options together:

```
TITLE FONT=Courier 'Courier  ' BOLD 'Courier Bold  '
    ITALIC 'Courier Bold and Italic';
```

This statement produces this title:

<code>Courier</code>   <code>Courier Bold</code>   <code>Courier Bold and Italic</code>

---

[3] See "Color-Naming Schemes" in the SAS/GRAPH section of the SAS Help and Documentation for details about how to specify colors. To see a list of Web-safe colors in the SAS windowing environment, type REGEDIT in the command box on the tool bar to open the Registry Editor. Double-click COLORNAMES. Then double-click HTML.

5.9 Customizing PROC PRINT with the STYLE= Option

If you want to change the overall look of any output, you can choose a different style template by specifying it in a STYLE= option in your ODS statement. But what if you want to change the appearance of just the headers, or just one column of your output? Well, you're in luck! The reporting procedures, PRINT, REPORT, and TABULATE, allow you to change the style of various parts of the table using the STYLE= option in the procedures' statements.[4]

The general form of the STYLE= option in the PROC PRINT statement is

```
PROC PRINT STYLE(location-list) = {style-attribute = value};
```

The *location-list* indicates which parts of the table should take on the style, the *style-attribute* indicates the attribute you want to change, and the *value* is the value of the attribute. (See section 5.13 for a table of attributes and possible values.) For example, the following statement tells SAS that the DATA location should have the BACKGROUND style attribute set to the value PINK.

```
PROC PRINT STYLE(DATA) = {BACKGROUND = pink};
```

You can have several STYLE= options on one PROC PRINT statement, and the same style can apply to several locations. Here are some of the locations you can specify.

Location	Table region affected
DATA	all the data cells
HEADER	the column headers (variable names)
OBS	the data in the OBS column, or ID column if using an ID statement
OBSHEADER	the header for the OBS or ID column
TOTAL	the data in the totals row produced by a SUM statement
GRANDTOTAL	the data for the grand total produced by a SUM statement

If you place the STYLE= option in the PROC PRINT statement, the entire table will be affected. For example, if you specify HEADER as the location, then all of the column headers will have the new style. If you want to change the header of just one column, then you put the STYLE= option in the VAR statement like this:

```
VAR variable-list / STYLE(location-list) = {style-attribute = value};
```

Only the variables listed in the VAR statement will have the specified style. If you want different variables to have different styles, then use multiple VAR statements. Only the DATA and HEADER locations are valid on the VAR statement.

Example The following data are the Olympic gold medal winners for the women's 5000 meter speed skating event. The Olympic year is followed by the skater's name, country, time, and record (WR is world record) if any.

```
1994,Claudia Pechstein,GER,7:14.37
1998,Claudia Pechstein,GER,6:59.61,WR
2002,Claudia Pechstein,GER,6:46.91,WR
2006,Clara Hughes,CAN,6:59.07
2010,Martina Sablikova,CZE,6:50.92
```

This program uses the default destination (HTML) and style template (HTMLBLUE).

```
DATA skating;
    INFILE 'c:\MyRawData\Women5000.csv' DSD MISSOVER;
    INPUT Year Name :$20. Country $ Time $ Record $;
RUN;
PROC PRINT DATA = skating;
    TITLE 'Women''s 5000 Meter Speed Skating';
    ID Year;
RUN;
```

Here are the results:

Women's 5000 Meter Speed Skating

Year	Name	Country	Time	Record
1994	Claudia Pechstein	GER	7:14.37	
1998	Claudia Pechstein	GER	6:59.61	WR
2002	Claudia Pechstein	GER	6:46.91	WR
2006	Clara Hughes	CAN	6:59.07	
2010	Martina Sablikova	CZE	6:50.92	

The next program also uses the default style template, but the STYLE= option has been added to the PROC PRINT statement giving all the data cells a gray background and white foreground, and to a VAR statement making the data cells for the Record column centered and italic.

```
PROC PRINT DATA = skating
              STYLE(DATA) = {BACKGROUND = GRAY FOREGROUND = WHITE};
    TITLE 'Women''s 5000 Meter Speed Skating';
    VAR Name Country Time;
    VAR Record/STYLE(DATA) = {FONT_STYLE = ITALIC JUST = CENTER};
    ID Year;
RUN;
```

Here are the results:

Women's 5000 Meter Speed Skating

Year	Name	Country	Time	Record
1994	Claudia Pechstein	GER	7:14.37	
1998	Claudia Pechstein	GER	6:59.61	*WR*
2002	Claudia Pechstein	GER	6:46.91	*WR*
2006	Clara Hughes	CAN	6:59.07	
2010	Martina Sablikova	CZE	6:50.92	

---

[4] To change the style of specific parts of output from other procedures, you need to create a new style template using PROC TEMPLATE, then apply the new style using a STYLE= option in an ODS statement. See the SAS Help and Documentation for more information on the TEMPLATE procedure.

5.10 Customizing PROC REPORT with the STYLE= Option

Using the STYLE= option in PROC REPORT is similar to the PRINT procedure because you have to specify a location. The general form of the STYLE= option in the PROC REPORT statement is

```
PROC REPORT STYLE(location-list) = {style-attribute = value};
```

where *location-list* specifies the parts of the table that should take on the style, *style-attribute* is the characteristic you wish to change, and *value* is the way you want the style attribute to look. (See section 5.13 for a table of attributes and possible values.) For example, to give column headers a green background, you could use this statement:

```
PROC REPORT DATA = mysales STYLE(HEADER) = {BACKGROUND = GREEN};
```

You can specify more than one location in a single STYLE= option, and you can have several STYLE= options in one PROC REPORT statement. Here are some of the locations whose appearance you can control in PROC REPORT:

Location	Table region affected
HEADER	column headings
COLUMN	data cells
SUMMARY	totals created by SUMMARIZE option in BREAK or RBREAK statements

If you put a STYLE= option in a PROC REPORT statement, then it will affect the whole table, for example, all the column headings, all the data cells, or all the summary breaks. You can change part of a report by using the STYLE= option in other statements. To specify a style for a particular variable, put the STYLE= option in a DEFINE statement. If you use a GROUP variable, you may want to add the SPANROWS option to the PROC statement. The SPANROWS option combines cells in the same group into a single cell. These statements tell SAS to use Month as a group variable, and make the background blue for both the header and data:

```
PROC REPORT DATA = mysales SPANROWS;
   DEFINE Month / GROUP STYLE(HEADER COLUMN) = {BACKGROUND = BLUE};
```

To specify a style for particular summary breaks, use the STYLE= option in a BREAK or RBREAK statement. This statement tells SAS to use a red background for summary breaks for each value of Month.

```
BREAK AFTER Month / SUMMARIZE STYLE(SUMMARY) = {BACKGROUND = RED};
```

Example The following data show women who have won three or more gold medals in Olympic speed skating. The variables are name, country, the number of years in which gold medals were won, and the total number of gold medals. Each line contains two records.

```
Lydia Skoblikova, URS, 2, 6, Karin Enke, GDR, 2, 3
Bonnie Blair, USA, 3, 5, Gunda Nieman, GDR, 2, 3
Claudia Pechstein, GER, 4, 5, Marianne Timmer, NED, 2, 3
```

This program uses the default destination (HTML) and style template (HTMLBLUE).

```
DATA skating;
   INFILE 'c:\MyRawData\Speed.dat' DSD;
   INPUT Name :$20. Country $ NumYears NumGold @@;
RUN;
PROC REPORT DATA = skating NOWINDOWS;
   COLUMN Country Name NumGold;
   DEFINE Country / GROUP;
   TITLE 'Olympic Women''s Speed Skating';
RUN;
```

Here are the results:

Olympic Women's Speed Skating

Country	Name	NumGold
GDR	Karin Enke	3
	Gunda Nieman	3
GER	Claudia Pechstein	5
NED	Marianne Timmer	3
URS	Lydia Skoblikova	6
USA	Bonnie Blair	5

The next program also uses the default style template, but adds a STYLE= option in the PROC REPORT statement to change the background of all the data cells to gray and the foreground to white. The SPANROWS option combines the two lines for GDR into one cell. Then a STYLE= option in the DEFINE statement centers and italicizes the values of Country.

```
* STYLE= option in PROC and DEFINE statements;
PROC REPORT DATA = skating NOWINDOWS SPANROWS
      STYLE(COLUMN) = {BACKGROUND = GRAY FOREGROUND = WHITE};
   COLUMN Country Name NumGold;
   DEFINE Country / GROUP
      STYLE(COLUMN) = {FONT_STYLE = ITALIC JUST = CENTER};
   TITLE 'Olympic Women''s Speed Skating';

RUN;
```

Here are the results:

Olympic Women's Speed Skating

Country	Name	NumGold
GDR	Karin Enke	3
	Gunda Nieman	3
GER	Claudia Pechstein	5
NED	Marianne Timmer	3
URS	Lydia Skoblikova	6
USA	Bonnie Blair	5

5.11 Customizing PROC TABULATE with the STYLE= Option

Using the STYLE= option in the TABULATE procedure, you can customize the look of the table that TABULATE produces. There are a number of different style attributes you can change, affecting things like color and font of text. (See section 5.13 for a table of style attributes and their possible values.) The part of the table affected depends on where you place the STYLE= option. Here are some of the TABULATE statements that accept the STYLE= option:

Statement	Table region affected
PROC TABULATE	all the data cells
CLASS	class variable name headings
CLASSLEV	class level value headings
TABLE (crossed with elements)[5]	element's data cell
VAR	analysis variable name headings

PROC TABULATE statement If you place the STYLE= option on the PROC TABULATE statement, all the table's data cells will have the style. For example, if you wanted all the data cells in your table created from the MYSALES SAS data set to have a yellow background, then you would use the following statement:

```
PROC TABULATE DATA = mysales STYLE = {BACKGROUND = YELLOW};
```

TABLE statement If you want some of the data cells to have a different style from the rest, then you need to add the STYLE= option to the TABLE statement and cross the style with the variable or keyword you want to change (similar to having different formats for different parts of the table as discussed in section 4.17). Any style assigned in a TABLE statement will override styles assigned in the PROC TABULATE statement. For example the following TABLE statement produces a table where the data cells in the ALL column have a red background:

```
TABLE City, Month ALL*{STYLE = {BACKGROUND = RED}};
```

CLASSLEV, VAR, and CLASS statements The CLASSLEV, VAR, and CLASS statements all require that you place the STYLE= option after a slash (/). Any variable that appears in a CLASSLEV statement must also appear in a CLASS statement. For example, suppose you had a table with a class variable Month, and you wanted all the values of Month to have a foreground color of green, then you would use the CLASSLEV statement as follows:

```
CLASSLEV Month / STYLE = {FOREGROUND = GREEN};
```

Example The following data are for men's speed skating events in the winter Olympics. The Olympic year is followed by the event and the record for that event. OR is an Olympic record, WR is a world record, and None indicates that neither an Olympic nor world record was set that year. Note that there are four observations per line of data.

```
1998 500 OR 2002 500 OR 2006 500 None 2010 500 None
1998 1000 OR 2002 1000 WR 2006 1000 None 2010 1000 None
1998 1500 WR 2002 1500 WR 2006 1500 None 2010 1500 None
1998 5000 WR 2002 5000 WR 2006 5000 None 2010 5000 OR
1998 10000 WR 2002 10000 WR 2006 10000 None 2010 10000 OR
```

This program uses the default destination (HTML) and style template (HTMLBLUE).

```
DATA skating;
   INFILE 'c:\MyRawData\Records.dat';
   INPUT Year  Event $ Record $ @@;
RUN;
PROC TABULATE DATA = skating;
   CLASS Year Record;
   TABLE Year = '',Record*N = '';
   TITLE 'Men''s Speed Skating Olympic Records';
RUN;
```

Here are the results:

Men's Speed Skating Olympic Records

	Record		
	None	OR	WR
1998	.	2	3
2002	.	1	4
2006	5	.	.
2010	3	2	.

The next program uses the default style template, but adds a STYLE= option to the PROC statement making the data cells centered with a white foreground and gray background.

```
PROC TABULATE DATA = skating
      STYLE = {BACKGROUND = GRAY FOREGROUND = WHITE JUST = CENTER};
   CLASS Year Record;
   TABLE Year = '',Record*N = '';
   TITLE 'Men''s Speed Skating Olympic Records';
RUN;
```

Here are the results:

Men's Speed Skating Olympic Records

	Record		
	None	OR	WR
1998	.	2	3
2002	.	1	4
2006	5	.	.
2010	3	2	.

---

[5] You can also use STYLE= as an option on the TABLE statement and then it affects the structural parts of the table (such as borders and cell widths). See the SAS Help and Documentation for more information.

5.12 Adding Traffic-Lighting to Your Output

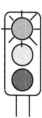

Traffic-lighting is a feature that allows you to control the style of cells in the table based on the value of the data in the cell. This way you can draw attention to important values in your report, or highlight relationships between values. Traffic-lighting can be used in any of the three reporting procedures: PRINT, REPORT, and TABULATE.

To implement traffic-lighting you need to do two things. First, create a user-defined format specifying different values for the style attribute you want to change over the range in data values. (See the next section for a table of style attributes and possible values.) Then set the style attribute equal to the format you defined in the STYLE= option. For example, if you had a FORMAT procedure that created a format as follows:

```
PROC FORMAT;
   VALUE posneg
      LOW -< 0 = 'red'
      0-HIGH = 'black';
```

Then in a VAR statement in a PRINT procedure, you could set the value of the attribute equal to the format in the STYLE= option as follows:

```
VAR Balance / STYLE = {FOREGROUND = posneg.};
```

Then all the data cells for the variable Balance would have red numbers if they are negative and black numbers if they are positive.

Example The following data are the top five finishers in the men's 5000 meter speed skating event at the 2002 Winter Olympics. The skater's place is followed by his name, country, and time in seconds.

```
1,Jochem Uytdehaage, Netherlands,374.66
2,Derek Parra, United States,377.98
3,Jens Boden, Germany,381.73
4,Dmitry Shepel, Russia,381.85
5,KC Boutiette, United States,382.97
```

The following program reads and prints the data using PROC PRINT. The resulting output uses the default destination (HTML) and the default style (HTMLBLUE).

```
DATA results;
   INFILE 'c:\MyRawData\Mens5000.dat' DSD;
   INPUT Place Name :$20. Country :$15. Time ;
RUN;
PROC PRINT DATA = results;
   ID Place;
   TITLE 'Men''s 5000m Speed Skating';
RUN;
```

Here are the results:

Men's 5000m Speed Skating

Place	Name	Country	Time
1	Jochem Uytdehaage	Netherlands	374.66
2	Derek Parra	United States	377.98
3	Jens Boden	Germany	381.73
4	Dmitry Shepel	Russia	381.85
5	KC Boutiette	United States	382.97

To give an idea of how these times compare with previous times skaters set for this event, we can use traffic lighting. Prior to the 2002 Olympics, the world record for the 5000 meter speed skating was 378.72 seconds and the Olympic record was 382.20 seconds. To show which skaters skated faster than these records, the following PROC FORMAT creates a user-defined format, named REC. which assigns the color light gray to times less than the world record, very light gray to times less than the Olympic record, and white to other times. The second VAR statement in the PROC PRINT uses the STYLE= option to set the BACKGROUND attribute of the values for the variable Time equal to the REC. format.

```
PROC FORMAT;
   VALUE rec 0 -< 378.72 = 'LIGHT GRAY'
             378.72 -< 382.20 = 'VERY LIGHT GRAY'
             382.20 - HIGH = 'WHITE';
RUN;
PROC PRINT DATA = results;
   ID Place;
   VAR Name Country;
   VAR Time / STYLE = {BACKGROUND = rec.};
   TITLE 'Men''s 5000m Speed Skating';
RUN;
```

Here is the output showing the different color backgrounds based on the value of Time. Those skaters who broke the previous world record have a light gray background for Time, those who broke the Olympic record have a very light gray background, and the fifth skater who didn't break any records has a white background.

Men's 5000m Speed Skating

Place	Name	Country	Time
1	Jochem Uytdehaage	Netherlands	374.66
2	Derek Parra	United States	377.98
3	Jens Boden	Germany	381.73
4	Dmitry Shepel	Russia	381.85
5	KC Boutiette	United States	382.97

5.13 Selected Style Attributes

Attribute	Description	Possible Values
BACKGROUND	Specifies the background color of the table or cell.	Any valid color [6]
BACKGROUNDIMAGE	Specifies a background image to be used for the table or cell. Not valid for RTF.	Any GIF, JPEG, or PNG image file [7]
FLYOVER	Specifies the pop-up text displayed when the cursor is held over the text (HTML) or if you double-click on the text (PDF).	Any text string enclosed in quotation marks
FONT_FACE	Specifies the font to use for the text in the cells.	Any valid font (Most devices support Times, Courier, Arial, and Helvetica)
FONT_SIZE	Specifies the relative size of the font for the text in cells.[8]	1 to 7
FONT_STYLE	Specifies the style of the font used in the cells.	ITALIC, ROMAN, or SLANT (Italic and slant may map to the same font)
FONT_WEIGHT	Specifies the weight of the font used in the cells.	BOLD, MEDIUM, or LIGHT
FOREGROUND	Specifies the color of the text in the cells.	Any valid color [6]
JUST	Specifies the justification of the text in the cells.	R | RIGHT, C | CENTER, L | LEFT, or D (decimal)
PRETEXT or POSTTEXT	Specifies text that goes either before (PRETEXT) or after (POSTTEXT) the text in the cells.	Any text string enclosed in quotation marks
PREIMAGE or POSTIMAGE	Specifies an image that will be inserted either before (PREIMAGE) or after (POSTIMAGE) the text in the cells.	Any GIF, JPEG, or PNG image file (JPEG and PNG only for RTF) [7]
URL	Specifies the URL to link to from the text in the cell. HTML, PDF, and RTF only.	Any URL

Attribute	STYLE= code	Result
BACKGROUND	`STYLE(DATA)=` `    {BACKGROUND=white};`	speed skating

BACKGROUNDIMAGE	`STYLE(DATA)=`
	`    {BACKGROUNDIMAGE=`
	`'c:\MyImages\snow.gif'};`
		speed skating

FLYOVER	`STYLE(DATA)=` `    {FLYOVER='Try it!'};`	speed skating Try it!
FONT_FACE	`STYLE(DATA)=` `    {FONT_FACE=courier};`	speed skating
FONT_SIZE	`STYLE(DATA)=` `    {FONT_SIZE=2};`	speed skating
FONT_STYLE	`STYLE(DATA)=` `    {FONT_STYLE=italic};`	*speed skating*
FONT_WEIGHT	`STYLE(DATA)=` `    {FONT_WEIGHT=bold};`	**speed skating**
FOREGROUND	`STYLE(DATA)=` `    {FOREGROUND=white};`	speed skating
JUST	`STYLE(DATA)=` `    {JUST=right};`	speed skating
PRETEXT or POSTTEXT	`STYLE(DATA)=` `    {POST_TEXT=' is fun'};`	speed skating is fun
PREIMAGE or POSTIMAGE	`STYLE(DATA)=` `    {PREIMAGE='SS2.gif'};`	speed skating
URL	`STYLE(DATA)=` `{URL='http://skating.org'};`	speed skating

---

[6] There are several ways that you can specify color and these are discussed in the SAS/GRAPH documentation. If you want an exact color, you may use the RGB notation (e.g. #00FF00 is green), or if you want to use colors by name, then the following are some colors you may choose: AQUA, BLACK, BLUE, FUCHSIA, GREEN, GRAY, LIME, MAROON, NAVY, OLIVE, PURPLE, RED, SILVER, TEAL, WHITE, YELLOW.

[7] For HTML, if you use a simple filename, then the SAS internal browser may not be able to find the file. If you use a complete path and then move the files to a new location, be sure to edit the HTML file to reflect the new location.

[8] For some destinations, you can specify size in units of measure: cm, in, mm, pt, px (pixels). For example, if you want text that is 24 points, then you would specify FONT_SIZE=24pt.

6

"I usually say, 'The computer is the dumbest thing on campus. It does exactly what you tell it to; not necessarily what you want. Logic is up to you.'"

NECIA A. BLACK, R.N., PH.D.

From the SAS-L Listserv, May 6, 1994. Reprinted by permission of the author.

CHAPTER 6

Modifying and Combining SAS Data Sets

6.1 ▶ Modifying a Data Set Using the SET Statement

 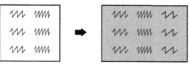

The SET statement in the DATA step allows you to read a SAS data set so you can add new variables, create a subset, or otherwise modify the data set. If you were short on disk space, for example, you might not want to store your computed variables in a permanent SAS data set. Instead, you might want to calculate them as needed for analysis. Likewise, to save processing time, you might want to create a subset of a SAS data set when you only want to look at a small portion of a large data set. The SET statement brings a SAS data set, one observation at a time, into the DATA step for processing.[1]

To read a SAS data set, start with the DATA statement specifying the name of the new data set. Then follow with the SET statement specifying the name of the old data set you want to read. If you don't want to create a new data set, you can specify the same name in the DATA and SET statements. Then the results of the DATA step will overwrite the old data set named in the SET statement.[2] The following shows the general form of the DATA and SET statements:

```
DATA new-data-set;
   SET data-set;
```

Any assignment, subsetting IF, or other DATA step statements usually follow the SET statement. For example, the following creates a new data set, FRIDAY, which is a replica of the SALES data set, except FRIDAY has only the observations for Fridays, and it has an additional variable, Total:

```
DATA friday;
   SET sales;
   IF Day = 'F';
   Total = Popcorn + Peanuts;
RUN;
```

Example The Fun Times Amusement Park is collecting data about their train ride. They can add more cars on the train during peak hours to shorten the wait, or take them off when they're not needed to save fuel costs. The raw data file contains data for the time of day, the number of cars on the train, and the total number of people on the train:

```
10:10   6 21
12:15  10 56
15:30  10 25
11:30   8 34
13:15   8 12
10:45   6 13
20:30   6 32
23:15   6 12
```

The data are read into a permanent SAS data set, TRAINS, stored in the MySASLib directory on the park's central computer by means of the following program:

```
* Create permanent SAS data set trains;
DATA 'c:\MySASLib\trains';
   INFILE 'c:\MyRawData\Train.dat';
   INPUT Time TIME5. Cars People;
RUN;
```

This example uses direct referencing to tell SAS where to store the permanent SAS data set, but you could use a LIBNAME statement instead.

Each train car holds a maximum of six people. After collecting the data, the Fun Times management decides they want to know the average number of people per car on each ride. This number was not calculated in the original DATA step which created the permanent SAS data set, but can be calculated by the following program:

```
* Read the SAS data set trains with a SET statement;
DATA averagetrain;
   SET 'c:\MySASLib\trains';
   PeoplePerCar = People / Cars;
RUN;
PROC PRINT DATA = averagetrain;
   TITLE 'Average Number of People per Train Car';
   FORMAT Time TIME5.;
RUN;
```

The DATA statement defines a new temporary SAS data set named AVERAGETRAIN. Then the SET statement reads the permanent SAS data set TRAINS, and an assignment statement creates the new variable PeoplePerCar. Here are the results of the PROC PRINT:

Average Number of People per Train Car

Obs	Time	Cars	People	PeoplePerCar
1	10:10	6	21	3.50000
2	12:15	10	56	5.60000
3	15:30	10	25	2.50000
4	11:30	8	34	4.25000
5	13:15	8	12	1.50000
6	10:45	6	13	2.16667
7	20:30	6	32	5.33333
8	23:15	6	12	2.00000

---

[1] The MODIFY statement also allows you to modify a single data set. See the SAS Help and Documentation for more information.

[2] By default, SAS will not overwrite a data set in a DATA step that has errors.

6.2 ► Stacking Data Sets Using the SET Statement

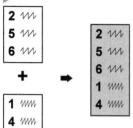

The SET statement with one SAS data set allows you to read and modify the data. With two or more data sets, in addition to reading and modifying the data, the SET statement concatenates or stacks the data sets one on top of the other. This is useful when you want to combine data sets with all or most of the same variables but different observations. You might, for example, have data from two different locations or data taken at two separate times, but you need the data together for analysis.

In a DATA step, first specify the name of the new SAS data set in the DATA statement, then list the names of the old data sets you want to combine in the SET statement:[3]

```
DATA new-data-set;
   SET data-set-1 data-set-n;
```

The number of observations in the new data set will equal the sum of the number of observations in the old data sets. The order of observations is determined by the order of the list of old data sets. If one of the data sets has a variable not contained in the other data sets, then the observations from the other data sets will have missing values for that variable.

Example The Fun Times Amusement Park has two entrances where they collect data about their customers. The data file for the south entrance has an S (for south) followed by the customers' Fun Times pass numbers, the sizes of their parties, and their ages. The file for the north entrance has an N (for north), the same data as the south entrance, plus one more column for the parking lot where they left their cars (the south entrance has only one lot). The following shows samples of the two data files:

Data for South Entrance	Data for North Entrance
S 43 3 27	N 21 5 41 1
S 44 3 24	N 87 4 33 3
S 45 3 2	N 65 2 67 1
	N 66 2 7 1

The first two parts of the following program read the raw data for the south and north entrances into SAS data sets and print them to make sure they are correct. The third part combines the two SAS data sets using a SET statement. The same DATA step creates a new variable, AmountPaid, which tells how much each customer paid based on their age. This final data set is printed using PROC PRINT:

```
DATA southentrance;
   INFILE 'c:\MyRawData\South.dat';
   INPUT Entrance $ PassNumber PartySize Age;
PROC PRINT DATA = southentrance;
   TITLE 'South Entrance Data';
RUN;
DATA northentrance;
   INFILE 'c:\MyRawData\North.dat';
   INPUT Entrance $ PassNumber PartySize Age Lot;
PROC PRINT DATA = northentrance;
   TITLE 'North Entrance Data';
RUN;
```

```
* Create a data set, both, combining northentrance and southentrance;
* Create a variable, AmountPaid, based on value of variable Age;
DATA both;
   SET southentrance northentrance;
   IF Age = . THEN AmountPaid = .;
      ELSE IF Age < 3  THEN AmountPaid = 0;
      ELSE IF Age < 65 THEN AmountPaid = 35;
      ELSE AmountPaid = 27;
RUN;
PROC PRINT DATA = both;
   TITLE 'Both Entrances';
RUN;
```

The following are the results of the three PRINT procedures in the program. Notice that the final data set has missing values for the variable Lot for all the observations which came from the south entrance. Because the variable Lot was not in the SOUTHENTRANCE data set, SAS assigned missing values to those observations.

South Entrance Data

Obs	Entrance	PassNumber	PartySize	Age
1	S	43	3	27
2	S	44	3	24
3	S	45	3	2

North Entrance Data

Obs	Entrance	PassNumber	PartySize	Age	Lot
1	N	21	5	41	1
2	N	87	4	33	3
3	N	65	2	67	1
4	N	66	2	7	1

Both Entrances

Obs	Entrance	PassNumber	PartySize	Age	Lot	AmountPaid
1	S	43	3	27	.	35
2	S	44	3	24	.	35
3	S	45	3	2	.	0
4	N	21	5	41	1	35
5	N	87	4	33	3	35
6	N	65	2	67	1	27
7	N	66	2	7	1	35

---

[3] Starting with SAS 9.2, you can also use numbered range lists and name prefix lists for data set lists in SET statements. This is similar to the variable name lists covered in section 3.12. See the SAS Help and Documentation for details.

6.3 ▶ Interleaving Data Sets Using the SET Statement

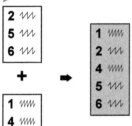

The previous section explained how to stack data sets that have all or most of the same variables but different observations. However, if you have data sets that are already sorted by some important variable, then simply stacking the data sets may unsort the data sets. You could stack the two data sets and then re-sort them using PROC SORT. But if your data sets are already sorted, it is more efficient to preserve that order, than to stack and re-sort. All you need to do is use a BY statement with your SET statement. Here's the general form:

```
DATA new-data-set;
    SET data-set-1 data-set-n;
    BY variable-list;
```

In a DATA statement, you specify the name of the new SAS data set you want to create. In a SET statement, you list the data sets to be interleaved. Then in a BY statement, you list one or more variables that SAS should use for ordering the observations. The number of observations in the new data set will be equal to the sum of the number of observations in the old data sets. If one of the data sets has a variable not contained in the other data sets, then values of that variable will be set to missing for observations from the other data sets.

Before you can interleave observations, the data sets must be sorted by the BY variables. If one or the other of your data sets is not already sorted, then use PROC SORT to do the job.

Example To show how this is different from stacking data sets, we'll use the amusement park data again. There are two data sets, one for the south entrance and one for the north. For every customer, the park collects the following data: the entrance (S or N), the customer's Fun Times pass number, size of that customer's party, and age. For customers entering from the north, the data set also includes parking lot number. Notice that the data for the south entrance are already sorted by pass number, but the data for the north entrance are not.

Data for South Entrance	Data for North Entrance
S 43 3 27	N 21 5 41 1
S 44 3 24	N 87 4 33 3
S 45 3 2	N 65 2 67 1
	N 66 2 7 1

Instead of stacking the two data sets, this program interleaves the data sets by pass number. This program first reads the data for the south entrance and prints them to make sure they are correct. Then the program reads the data for the north entrance, sorts them, and prints them. Then in the final DATA step, SAS combines the two data sets, NORHTENTRANCE and SOUTHENTRANCE, creating a new data set named INTERLEAVE. The BY statement tells SAS to combine the data sets by PassNumber:

```
DATA southentrance;
    INFILE 'c:\MyRawData\South.dat';
    INPUT Entrance $ PassNumber PartySize Age;
PROC PRINT DATA = southentrance;
    TITLE 'South Entrance Data';
RUN;
```

```
 DATA northentrance;
    INFILE 'c:\MyRawData\North.dat';
    INPUT Entrance $ PassNumber PartySize Age Lot;
PROC SORT DATA = northentrance;
    BY PassNumber;
PROC PRINT DATA = northentrance;
    TITLE 'North Entrance Data';
RUN;
* Interleave observations by PassNumber;
DATA interleave;
    SET northentrance southentrance;
    BY PassNumber;
RUN;
PROC PRINT DATA = interleave;
    TITLE 'Both Entrances, By Pass Number';
RUN;
```

Here are the results of the three PRINT procedures. Notice how the observations have been interleaved so that the new data set is sorted by PassNumber:

South Entrance Data

Obs	Entrance	PassNumber	PartySize	Age
1	S	43	3	27
2	S	44	3	24
3	S	45	3	2

North Entrance Data

Obs	Entrance	PassNumber	PartySize	Age	Lot
1	N	21	5	41	1
2	N	65	2	67	1
3	N	66	2	7	1
4	N	87	4	33	3

Both Entrances, By Pass Number

Obs	Entrance	PassNumber	PartySize	Age	Lot
1	N	21	5	41	1
2	S	43	3	27	.
3	S	44	3	24	.
4	S	45	3	2	.
5	N	65	2	67	1
6	N	66	2	7	1
7	N	87	4	33	3

6.4 ▸ Combining Data Sets Using a One-to-One Match Merge

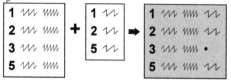

When you want to match observations from one data set with observations from another, use the MERGE statement in the DATA step. If you know the two data sets are in EXACTLY the same order, you don't have to have any common variables between the data sets. Typically, however, you will want to have, for matching purposes, a common variable or several variables which taken together uniquely identify each observation. This is important. Having a common variable to merge by ensures that the observations are properly matched. For example, to merge patient data with billing data, you would use the patient ID as a matching variable. Otherwise you risk getting Mary Smith's visit to the obstetrician mixed up with Matthew Smith's visit to the optometrist.

Merging SAS data sets is a simple process. First, if the data are not already sorted, use the SORT procedure to sort all data sets by the common variables. Then, in the DATA statement, name the new SAS data set to hold the results and follow with a MERGE statement listing the data sets to be combined.[4] Use a BY statement to indicate the common variables:

```
DATA new-data-set;
   MERGE data-set-1 data-set-n;
   BY variable-list;
```

If you merge two data sets, and they have variables with the same names—besides the BY variables—then variables from the second data set will overwrite any variables having the same name in the first data set.

Example A Belgian chocolatier keeps track of the number of each type of chocolate sold each day. The code number for each chocolate and the number of pieces sold that day are kept in a file. In a separate file she keeps the names and descriptions of each chocolate as well as the code number. In order to print the day's sales along with the descriptions of the chocolates, the two files must be merged together using the code number as the common variable. Here is a sample of the data:

Sales data
```
C865 15
K086  9
A536 21
S163 34
K014  1
A206 12
B713 29
```

Description
```
A536 Walnoot    Walnut halves in bed of dark chocolate
B713 Frambozen  Raspberry marzipan covered in milk chocolate
C865 Vanille    Vanilla-flavored rolled in ground hazelnuts
K014 Kroon      Milk chocolate with a mint cream center
K086 Koning     Hazelnut paste in dark chocolate
M315 Pyramide   White with dark chocolate trimming
S163 Orbais     Chocolate cream in dark chocolate
```

The first two parts of the following program read the descriptions and sales data. The descriptions data are already sorted by CodeNum, so we don't need to use PROC SORT. The sales data are not sorted, so a PROC SORT follows the DATA step. (If you attempt to merge data which are not sorted, SAS will refuse and give you this error message: ERROR: BY variables are not properly sorted.)

```
DATA descriptions;
    INFILE 'c:\MyRawData\chocolate.dat' TRUNCOVER;
    INPUT CodeNum $ 1-4 Name $ 6-14 Description $ 15-60;
RUN;
DATA sales;
    INFILE 'c:\MyRawData\chocsales.dat';
    INPUT CodeNum $ 1-4 PiecesSold 6-7;
PROC SORT DATA = sales;
    BY CodeNum;
RUN;
* Merge data sets by CodeNum;
DATA chocolates;
    MERGE sales descriptions;
    BY CodeNum;
RUN;
PROC PRINT DATA = chocolates;
    TITLE "Today's Chocolate Sales";
RUN;
```

The final part of the program creates a data set named CHOCOLATES by merging the SALES data set and the DESCRIPTIONS data set. The common variable CodeNum in the BY statement is used for matching purposes. The following output shows the final data set after merging:

Today's Chocolate Sales

Obs	CodeNum	PiecesSold	Name	Description
1	A206	12	Mokka	Coffee buttercream in dark chocolate
2	A536	21	Walnoot	Walnut halves in bed of dark chocolate
3	B713	29	Frambozen	Raspberry marzipan covered in milk chocolate
4	C865	15	Vanille	Vanilla-flavored rolled in ground hazelnuts
5	K014	1	Kroon	Milk chocolate with a mint cream center
6	K086	9	Koning	Hazelnut paste in dark chocolate
7	M315	.	Pyramide	White with dark chocolate trimming
8	S163	34	Orbais	Chocolate cream in dark chocolate

Notice that the final data set has a missing value for PiecesSold in the seventh observation. This is because there were no sales for the Pyramide chocolate. All observations from both data sets were included in the final data set whether they had a match or not.

---

[4] Starting with SAS 9.2, you can use numbered range lists and prefix name lists for data set lists in MERGE statements. This is similar to the variable name lists covered in section 3.12. See the SAS Help and Documentation for details.

6.5 ▶ Combining Data Sets Using a One-to-Many Match Merge

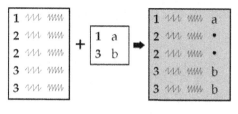

Sometimes you need to combine two data sets by matching one observation from one data set with more than one observation in another. Suppose you had data for every state in the U.S. and wanted to combine it with data for every county. This would be a one-to-many match merge because each state observation matches with many county observations.

The statements for a one-to-many match merge are identical to the statements for a one-to-one match merge:

```
DATA new-data-set;
   MERGE data-set-1 data-set-2;
   BY variable-list;
```

The order of the data sets in the MERGE statement does not affect the matching. In other words, a one-to-many merge will match the same observations as a many-to-one merge.

Before you merge two data sets, they must be sorted by one or more common variables. If your data sets are not already sorted in the proper order, then use PROC SORT to do the job.

You cannot do a one-to-many merge without a BY statement. SAS uses the variables listed in the BY statement to decide which observations belong together. Without a BY statement, SAS simply joins together the first observation from each data set, then the second observation from each data set, and so on. In other words, SAS performs a one-to-one unmatched merge, which is probably not what you want.

If you merge two data sets, and they contain variables with the same name—besides the BY variables—then you should either rename the variables or drop one of the duplicate variables. Otherwise variables from the second data set may overwrite variables having the same name in the first data set. For example, if you merge two data sets that each contain a variable named BirthDate, then you could rename the variables (perhaps as BirthDate1 and BirthDate2), or you could simply drop BirthDate from one data set. Then the values of BirthDate will not overwrite each other. You can use the RENAME= and DROP= data set options (discussed in section 6.11) to prevent the overwriting of data values.

Example A distributor of athletic shoes is putting all its shoes on sale at 20 to 30% off the regular price. The distributor has two data files, one with information about each type of shoe and one with the discount factors. The first file contains one record for each shoe with values for style, type of exercise (running, walking, or cross-training), and regular price. The second file contains one record for each type of exercise and its discount. Here are the two raw data files:

Shoes data			Discount data	
Max Flight	running	142.99	c-train	.25
Zip Fit Leather	walking	83.99	running	.30
Zoom Airborne	running	112.99	walking	.20
Light Step	walking	73.99		
Max Step Woven	walking	75.99		
Zip Sneak	c-train	92.99		

To find the sale price, the following program combines the two data files:

```
DATA regular;
   INFILE 'c:\MyRawData\Shoe.dat';
   INPUT Style $ 1-15 ExerciseType $ RegularPrice;
RUN;
PROC SORT DATA = regular;
   BY ExerciseType;
RUN;
DATA discount;
   INFILE 'c:\MyRawData\Disc.dat';
   INPUT ExerciseType $ Adjustment;
RUN;
* Perform many-to-one match merge;
DATA prices;
   MERGE regular discount;
   BY ExerciseType;
   NewPrice = ROUND(RegularPrice - (RegularPrice * Adjustment), .01);
RUN;
PROC PRINT DATA = prices;
   TITLE 'Price List for May';
RUN;
```

The first DATA step reads the regular prices, creating a data set named REGULAR. That data set is then sorted by ExerciseType using PROC SORT. The second DATA step reads the price adjustments, creating a data set named DISCOUNT. This data set is already arranged by ExerciseType, so it doesn't have to be sorted. The third DATA step creates a data set named PRICES, merging the first two data sets by ExerciseType, and computes a variable called NewPrice. The output looks like this:

Price List for May

Obs	Style	ExerciseType	RegularPrice	Adjustment	NewPrice
1	Zip Sneak	c-train	92.99	0.25	69.74
2	Max Flight	running	142.99	0.30	100.09
3	Zoom Airborne	running	112.99	0.30	79.09
4	Zip Fit Leather	walking	83.99	0.20	67.19
5	Light Step	walking	73.99	0.20	59.19
6	Max Step Woven	walking	75.99	0.20	60.79

Notice that the values for Adjustment from the DISCOUNT data set are repeated for every observation in the REGULAR data set with the same value of ExerciseType.

6.6 ▶ Merging Summary Statistics with the Original Data

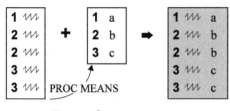

Once in a while you need to combine summary statistics with your data, such as when you want to compare each observation to the group mean, or when you want to calculate a percentage using the group total. To do this, summarize your data using PROC MEANS, and put the results in a new data set. Then merge the summarized data back with the original data using a one-to-many match merge.

Example A distributor of athletic shoes is considering doing a special promotion for the top selling styles. The vice-president of marketing has asked you to produce a report. The report should be divided by type of exercise (running, walking, or cross-training) and show the percentage of sales for each style within its type. For each shoe, the raw data file contains the style name, type of exercise, and total sales for the last quarter:

```
Max Flight      running 1930
Zip Fit Leather walking 2250
Zoom Airborne   running 4150
Light Step      walking 1130
Max Step Woven  walking 2230
Zip Sneak       c-train 1190
```

Here is the program:

```
DATA shoes;
   INFILE 'c:\MyRawData\Shoesales.dat';
   INPUT Style $ 1-15 ExerciseType $ Sales;
RUN;
PROC SORT DATA = shoes;
   BY ExerciseType;
RUN;
* Summarize sales by ExerciseType and print;
PROC MEANS NOPRINT DATA = shoes;
   VAR Sales;
   BY ExerciseType;
   OUTPUT OUT = summarydata SUM(Sales) = Total;
RUN;
PROC PRINT DATA = summarydata;
   TITLE 'Summary Data Set';
RUN;
* Merge totals with the original data set;
DATA shoesummary;
   MERGE shoes summarydata;
   BY ExerciseType;
   Percent = Sales / Total * 100;
RUN;
```

```
PROC PRINT DATA = shoesummary;
   BY ExerciseType;
   ID ExerciseType;
   VAR Style Sales Total Percent;
   TITLE 'Sales Share by Type of Exercise';
RUN;
```

This program is long but straightforward. It starts by reading the raw data in a DATA step and sorting them with PROC SORT. Then it summarizes the data with PROC MEANS by the variable ExerciseType. The OUTPUT statement tells SAS to create a new data set named SUMMARYDATA, containing a variable named Total, which equals the sum of the variable Sales. The NOPRINT option tells SAS not to print the standard PROC MEANS report. Instead, the summary data set is printed by PROC PRINT:

Summary Data Set

Obs	ExerciseType	_TYPE_	_FREQ_	Total
1	c-train	0	1	1190
2	running	0	2	6080
3	walking	0	3	5610

In the last part of the program, the original data set, SHOES, is merged with SUMMARYDATA to make a new data set, SHOESUMMARY. This DATA step computes a new variable called Percent. Then the last PROC PRINT writes the final report with percentage of sales by ExerciseType for each title. Using a BY and an ID statement together gives this report a little different look:

Sales Share by Type of Exercise

ExerciseType	Style	Sales	Total	Percent
c-train	Zip Sneak	1190	1190	100.000

ExerciseType	Style	Sales	Total	Percent
running	Max Flight	1930	6080	31.743
	Zoom Airborne	4150	6080	68.257

ExerciseType	Style	Sales	Total	Percent
walking	Zip Fit Leather	2250	5610	40.107
	Light Step	1130	5610	20.143
	Max Step Woven	2230	5610	39.750

6.7 Combining a Grand Total with the Original Data

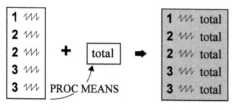

You can use the MEANS procedure to create a data set containing a grand total rather than BY group totals. But you cannot use a MERGE statement to combine a grand total with the original data because there is no common variable to merge by. Luckily, there is another way. You can use two SET statements like this:

```
DATA new-data-set;
   IF _N_ = 1 THEN SET summary-data-set;
   SET original-data-set;
```

In this DATA step, *original-data-set* is the data set with more than one observation (the original data) and *summary-data-set* is the data set with a single observation (the grand total). SAS reads *original-data-set* in a normal SET statement, simply reading the observations in a straightforward way. SAS also reads *summary-data-set* with a SET statement but only in the first iteration of the DATA step (when _N_ equals 1).[5] SAS then retains the values of variables from *summary-data-set* for all observations in *new-data-set*.

This works because variables read with a SET statement are automatically retained. Normally you don't notice this because the retained values are overwritten by the next observation. But in this case the variables from *summary-data-set* are read once at the first iteration of the DATA step and then retained for all other observations. The effect is similar to a RETAIN statement (discussed in section 3.10). This technique can be used any time you want to combine a single observation with many observations, without a common variable.

Example To show how this is different from merging BY group summary statistics with original data, we'll use the same data as in the previous section. A distributor of athletic shoes is considering doing a special promotion for the top-selling styles. The vice-president of marketing asks you to produce a report showing the percentage of total sales for each style. For each style of shoe the raw data file contains the style name, type of exercise, and sales for the last quarter:

```
Max Flight       running 1930
Zip Fit Leather  walking 2250
Zoom Airborne    running 4150
Light Step       walking 1130
Max Step Woven   walking 2230
Zip Sneak        c-train 1190
```

Here is the program:

```
DATA shoes;
   INFILE 'c:\MyRawData\Shoesales.dat';
   INPUT Style $ 1-15 ExerciseType $ Sales;
RUN;
* Output grand total of sales to a data set and print;
PROC MEANS NOPRINT DATA = shoes;
   VAR Sales;
   OUTPUT OUT = summarydata SUM(Sales) = GrandTotal;
RUN;
PROC PRINT DATA = summarydata;
   TITLE 'Summary Data Set';
RUN;
* Combine the grand total with the original data;
DATA shoesummary;
   IF _N_ = 1 THEN SET summarydata;
   SET shoes;
   Percent = Sales / GrandTotal * 100;
RUN;
PROC PRINT DATA = shoesummary;
   VAR Style ExerciseType Sales GrandTotal Percent;
   TITLE 'Overall Sales Share';
RUN;
```

This program starts with a DATA step to input the raw data. Then PROC MEANS creates an output data set named SUMMARYDATA with one observation containing a variable named GrandTotal, which is equal to the sum of Sales. This will be a grand total because there is no BY or CLASS statement. The second DATA step combines the original data with the grand total using two SET statements and then computes the variable Percent using the grand total data.

The output looks like this:

Summary Data Set

Obs	_TYPE_	_FREQ_	GrandTotal
1	0	6	12880

Overall Sales Share

Obs	Style	ExerciseType	Sales	GrandTotal	Percent
1	Max Flight	running	1930	12880	14.9845
2	Zip Fit Leather	walking	2250	12880	17.4689
3	Zoom Airborne	running	4150	12880	32.2205
4	Light Step	walking	1130	12880	8.7733
5	Max Step Woven	walking	2230	12880	17.3137
6	Zip Sneak	c-train	1190	12880	9.2391

---

[5] See section 6.15 for an explanation of _N_.

6.8 Updating a Master Data Set with Transactions

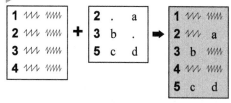

The UPDATE statement is used far less than the MERGE statement, but it is just right for those times when you have a master data set that must be updated with bits of new information. A bank account is a good example of this type of transaction-oriented data, since it is regularly updated with credits and debits.

The UPDATE statement is similar to the MERGE statement, because both combine data sets by matching observations on common variables.[6] However, there are critical differences:

- ♦ First, with UPDATE the resulting master data set always has just one observation for each unique value of the common variables. That way, you don't get a new observation for your bank account every time you deposit a paycheck.

- ♦ Second, missing values in the transaction data set do not overwrite existing values in the master data set. That way, you are not obliged to enter your address and tax ID number every time you make a withdrawal.

The basic form of the UPDATE statement is

```
DATA master-data-set;
   UPDATE master-data-set transaction-data-set;
   BY variable-list;
```

Here are a few points to remember about the UPDATE statement. You can specify only two data sets: one master and one transaction. Both data sets must be sorted by their common variables. Also, the values of those BY variables must be unique in the master data set. Using the bank example, you could have many transactions for a single account, but only one observation per account in the master data set.

Example A hospital maintains a master database with information about patients. A sample appears below. Each record contains the patient's account number, last name, address, date of birth, sex, insurance code, and the date that patient's information was last updated.

```
620135 Smith    234 Aspen St.    12-21-1975 m CBC 02-16-1998
645722 Miyamoto 65 3rd Ave.      04-03-1936 f MCR 05-30-1999
645739 Jensvold 505 Glendale Ave. 06-15-1960 f HLT 09-23-2006
874329 Kazoyan  76-C La Vista       .         . MCD 01-15-2011
```

Whenever a patient is admitted to the hospital, the admissions staff check the data for that patient. They create a transaction record for every new patient and for any returning patients whose status has changed. Here are three transactions:

```
620135 .        .                   .         . HLT 06-15-2012
874329 .        .                 04-24-1954 m . 06-15-2012
235777 Harman   5656 Land Way     01-18-2000 f MCD 06-15-2012
```

The first transaction is for a returning patient whose insurance has changed. The second transaction fills in missing information for a returning patient. The last transaction is for a new patient who must be added to the database.

Since master data sets are updated frequently, they are usually saved as permanent SAS data sets. To make this example more realistic, this program puts the master data into a permanent data set named PATIENTMASTER in the MySASLib directory on the C drive (Windows).

```
LIBNAME perm 'c:\MySASLib';
DATA perm.patientmaster;
    INFILE 'c:\MyRawData\Admit.dat';
    INPUT Account LastName $ 8-16 Address $ 17-34
        BirthDate MMDDYY10. Sex $ InsCode $ 48-50 @52 LastUpdate MMDDYY10.;
RUN;
```

The next program reads the transaction data and sorts them with PROC SORT. Then it adds the transactions to PATIENTMASTER with an UPDATE statement. The master data set is already sorted by Account and, therefore, doesn't need to be sorted again:

```
LIBNAME perm 'c:\MySASLib';
DATA transactions;
    INFILE 'c:\MyRawData\NewAdmit.dat';
    INPUT Account LastName $ 8-16 Address $ 17-34 BirthDate MMDDYY10.
        Sex $ InsCode $ 48-50 @52 LastUpdate MMDDYY10.;
RUN;
PROC SORT DATA = transactions;
    BY Account;
RUN;
* Update patient data with transactions;
DATA perm.patientmaster;
    UPDATE perm.patientmaster transactions;
    BY Account;
RUN;
PROC PRINT DATA = perm.patientmaster;
    FORMAT BirthDate LastUpdate MMDDYY10.;
    TITLE 'Admissions Data';
RUN;
```

The results of the PROC PRINT look like this:

Admissions Data

Obs	Account	LastName	Address	BirthDate	Sex	InsCode	LastUpdate
1	235777	Harman	5656 Land Way	01/18/2000	f	MCD	06/15/2012
2	620135	Smith	234 Aspen St.	12/21/1975	m	HLT	06/15/2012
3	645722	Miyamoto	65 3rd Ave.	04/03/1936	f	MCR	05/30/1999
4	645739	Jensvold	505 Glendale Ave.	06/15/1960	f	HLT	09/23/2006
5	874329	Kazoyan	76-C La Vista	04/24/1954	m	MCD	06/15/2012

---

[6] The MODIFY statement is another way to update a master data set. See the SAS Help and Documentation for more information.

6.9 ▸ Writing Multiple Data Sets Using the OUTPUT Statement

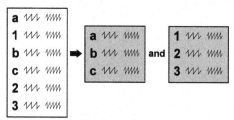

Up to this point, all the DATA steps in this book have created a single data set, except for DATA _NULL_ statements which produce no data set at all. Normally you want to make only one data set in each DATA step. However, there may be times when it is more efficient or more convenient to create multiple data sets in a single DATA step. You can do this by simply putting more than one data set name in your DATA statement. The statement below tells SAS to create three data sets named LIONS, TIGERS, and BEARS:

```
DATA lions tigers bears;
```

If that is all you do, then SAS will write all the observations to all the data sets, and you will have three identical data sets. Normally, of course, you want to create different data sets. You can do that with an OUTPUT statement.

Every DATA step has an implied OUTPUT statement at the end which tells SAS to write the current observation to the output data set before returning to the beginning of the DATA step to process the next observation. You can override this implicit OUTPUT statement with your own OUTPUT statement. The basic form of the OUTPUT statement is

```
OUTPUT data-set-name;
```

If you leave out the data set name, then the observation will be written to all data sets named in the DATA statement. OUTPUT statements can be used alone or in IF-THEN or DO-loop processing.

```
IF family = 'Ursidae' THEN OUTPUT bears;
```

Example A local zoo maintains a database about the feeding of the animals. A portion of the data appears below. For each group of animals the data include the scientific class, the enclosure those animals live in, and whether they get fed in the morning, afternoon, or both:

```
bears       Mammalia   E2   both
elephants   Mammalia   W3   am
flamingos   Aves       W1   pm
frogs       Amphibia   S2   pm
kangaroos   Mammalia   N4   am
lions       Mammalia   W6   pm
snakes      Reptilia   S1   pm
tigers      Mammalia   W9   both
zebras      Mammalia   W2   am
```

To help with feeding the animals, the following program creates two lists, one for morning feedings and one for afternoon feedings.

```
DATA morning afternoon;
   INFILE 'c:\MyRawData\Zoo.dat';
   INPUT Animal $ 1-9 Class $ 11-18 Enclosure $ FeedTime $;
   IF FeedTime = 'am' THEN OUTPUT morning;
      ELSE IF FeedTime = 'pm' THEN OUTPUT afternoon;
      ELSE IF FeedTime = 'both' THEN OUTPUT;
RUN;
PROC PRINT DATA = morning;
   TITLE 'Animals with Morning Feedings';
PROC PRINT DATA = afternoon;
   TITLE 'Animals with Afternoon Feedings';
RUN;
```

This DATA step creates two data sets named MORNING and AFTERNOON. Then the IF-THEN/ELSE statements tell SAS which observations to put in each data set. Because the final OUTPUT statement does not specify a data set, SAS adds those observations to both data sets. The log contains these notes saying that SAS read one input file and wrote two data sets:

```
NOTE: 9 records were read from the infile 'c:\MyRawData\Zoo.dat'.
NOTE: The data set WORK.MORNING has 5 observations and 4 variables.
NOTE: The data set WORK.AFTERNOON has 6 observations and 4 variables.
```

Here are the two reports, one for each data set:

Animals with Morning Feedings

Obs	Animal	Class	Enclosure	FeedTime
1	bears	Mammalia	E2	both
2	elephants	Mammalia	W3	am
3	kangaroos	Mammalia	N4	am
4	tigers	Mammalia	W9	both
5	zebras	Mammalia	W2	am

Animals with Afternoon Feedings

Obs	Animal	Class	Enclosure	FeedTime
1	bears	Mammalia	E2	both
2	flamingos	Aves	W1	pm
3	frogs	Amphibia	S2	pm
4	lions	Mammalia	W6	pm
5	snakes	Reptilia	S1	pm
6	tigers	Mammalia	W9	both

OUTPUT statements have other uses besides writing multiple data sets in a single DATA step and can be used any time you want to explicitly control when SAS writes observations to a data set.

6.10 Making Several Observations from One Using the OUTPUT Statement

Usually SAS writes an observation to a data set at the end of the DATA step, but you can override this default using the OUTPUT statement. If you want to write several observations for each pass through the DATA step, you can put an OUTPUT statement in a DO loop or just use several OUTPUT statements. The OUTPUT statement gives you control over when an observation is written to a SAS data set. If your DATA step doesn't have an OUTPUT statement, then it is implied at the end of the step. Once you put an OUTPUT statement in your DATA step, it is no longer implied, and SAS writes an observation only when it encounters an OUTPUT statement.

Example The following program demonstrates how you can use an OUTPUT statement in a DO loop to generate data. Here we have a mathematical equation ($y=x^2$) and we want to generate data points for later plotting:

```
* Create data for variables x and y;
DATA generate;
   DO x = 1 TO 6;
      y = x ** 2;
      OUTPUT;
   END;
PROC PRINT DATA = generate;
   TITLE 'Generated Data';
RUN;
```

This program has no INPUT or SET statement—so there is only one iteration of the entire DATA step—but it has a DO loop with six iterations. Because the OUTPUT statement is inside the DO loop, an observation is created each time through the loop. Without the OUTPUT statement, SAS would have written only one observation at the end of the DATA step when it reached the implied OUTPUT. The following are the results of the PROC PRINT:

Generated Data

Obs	x	y
1	1	1
2	2	4
3	3	9
4	4	16
5	5	25
6	6	36

Example Here's how you can use OUTPUT statements to create several observations from a single pass through the DATA step. The following data are for ticket sales at three movie theaters. After the month are the theaters' names and sales for all three theaters:

```
Jan Varsity 56723 Downtown 69831 Super-6 70025
Feb Varsity 62137 Downtown 43901 Super-6 81534
Mar Varsity 49982 Downtown 55783 Super-6 69800
```

For the analysis you want to do, you need to have the theater name as one variable and the ticket sales as another variable. The month should be repeated three times, once for each theater.

The following program has three INPUT statements all reading from the same raw data file. The first INPUT statement reads values for Month, Location, and Tickets, and then holds the data line using the trailing at sign (@). The OUTPUT statement that follows writes an observation. The next INPUT statement reads the second set of data for Location and Tickets, and again holds the data line. Another OUTPUT statement writes another observation. Month still has the same value because it isn't in the second INPUT statement. The last INPUT statement reads the last values for Location and Tickets, this time releasing the data line for the next iteration through the DATA step. The final OUTPUT statement writes the third observation for that iteration of the DATA step. The program has three OUTPUT statements for the three observations created in each iteration of the DATA step:

```
* Create three observations for each data line read
*    using three OUTPUT statements;
DATA theaters;
    INFILE 'c:\MyRawData\Movies.dat';
    INPUT Month $ Location $ Tickets @;
    OUTPUT;
    INPUT Location $ Tickets @;
    OUTPUT;
    INPUT Location $ Tickets;
    OUTPUT;
RUN;
PROC PRINT DATA = theaters;
    TITLE 'Ticket Sales';
RUN;
```

The following are the results of the PROC PRINT. Notice that there are three observations in the data set for each line in the raw data file, and that the value for Month is repeated:

Ticket Sales

Obs	Month	Location	Tickets
1	Jan	Varsity	56723
2	Jan	Downtown	69831
3	Jan	Super-6	70025
4	Feb	Varsity	62137
5	Feb	Downtown	43901
6	Feb	Super-6	81534
7	Mar	Varsity	49982
8	Mar	Downtown	55783
9	Mar	Super-6	69800

6.11 Using SAS Data Set Options

In this book, you have already seen a lot of options. It may help to keep them straight if you realize that the SAS language has three basic types of options: system options, statement options, and data set options. System options have the most global influence, followed by statement options, with data set options having the most limited effect.

System options are those that stay in effect for the duration of your job or session. These options affect how SAS operates, and are usually issued when you invoke SAS or via an OPTIONS statement. System options include the CENTER option, which tells SAS to center all output, and the YEARCUTOFF= option, which tells SAS how to intrepret two-digit dates.[7]

Statement options appear in individual statements and influence how SAS runs that particular DATA or PROC step. The NOPRINT option in PROC MEANS, for example, tells SAS not to produce a printed report. DATA= is a statement option that tells SAS which data set to use for a procedure. You can use DATA= in any procedure that reads a SAS data set. Without it, SAS defaults to the most recently created data set.

In contrast, data set options affect only how SAS reads or writes an individual data set. You can use data set options in DATA steps (in DATA, SET, MERGE, or UPDATE statements) or in PROC steps (in conjuction with a DATA= statement option). To use a data set option, you simply put it between parentheses directly following the data set name. These are the most frequently used data set options:

KEEP = *variable-list*	tells SAS which variables to keep.
DROP = *variable-list*	tells SAS which variables to drop.
RENAME = (*oldvar = newvar*)	tells SAS to rename certain variables.
FIRSTOBS = *n*	tells SAS to start reading at observation *n*.
OBS = *n*	tells SAS to stop reading at observation *n*.
LABEL = '*data-set-label*'	specifies a descriptive label for a SAS data set.
IN = *new-var-name*	creates a temporary variable for tracking whether that data set contributed to the current observation (discussed in section 6.12).
WHERE = *condition*	selects observations that meet a specified condition (discussed in section 6.13).

Selecting and renaming variables Here are examples of the KEEP=, DROP=, and RENAME= data set options:

```
DATA selectedvars;
   SET animals (KEEP = Class Species Status);

PROC PRINT DATA = animals (DROP = Habitat);

DATA animals (RENAME = (Class = Type Habitat = Home));
   SET animals;

PROC PRINT DATA = animals (RENAME =(Class = Type Habitat = Home));
```

You could probably get by without these options, but they play an important role in fine tuning SAS programs. Data sets, for example, have a way of accumulating unwanted variables. Dropping unwanted variables will make your program run faster and use less disk space. Likewise, when you read a large data set, you often need only a few variables. By using the KEEP= option, you can avoid reading a lot of variables you don't intend to use.

The DROP=, KEEP=, and RENAME= options are similar to the DROP, KEEP, and RENAME statements. However, the statements apply to all data sets named in the DATA statement, while the options apply only to the particular data set whose name they follow. Also, the statements are more limited than the options since they can be used only in DATA steps, and apply only to the data set being created. In contrast, the data set options can be used in DATA or PROC steps and can apply to input or output data sets. Please note that these options do not change input data sets; they change only what is read from input data sets.

Selecting observations by observation number You can use the FIRSTOBS= and OBS= data set options together to tell SAS which observations to read from a data set. The options in the following statements tell SAS to read just 20 observations:

```
DATA animals;
   SET animals (FIRSTOBS = 101 OBS = 120);

PROC PRINT DATA = animals (FIRSTOBS = 101 OBS = 120);
```

If you use large data sets, you can save development time by testing your programs with a subset of your data with the FIRSTOBS= and OBS= options.

The FIRSTOBS= and OBS= data set options are similar to statement and system options with the same name. The statement options apply only to raw data files being read with an INFILE statement, whereas the data set options apply only to existing SAS data sets that you read in a DATA or PROC step. The system options apply to all files and data sets. If you use similar system and data set options, the data set option will override the system option for that particular data set.

Labeling SAS data sets The LABEL= option is somewhat different from other options covered here. All the other options affect your data, but not LABEL=. Instead, LABEL= adds a text string to the descriptor portion of your data set. In this example, SAS creates a data set named RARE, and gives it the label "Endangered Species Data":

```
DATA rare (LABEL = 'Endangered Species Data');
   SET animals;
   IF Status = 'Endangered';
```

The LABEL= data set option is similar to the LABEL statement used in DATA and PROC steps. However, the LABEL statement applies labels to individual variables, while the LABEL= data set option applies a label to an entire data set. Using data set labels is a good habit because it helps to document your work. Data set labels are displayed in the output of PROC CONTENTS and at the top of the Viewtable window.

---

[7] Other system options are discussed in section 1.13.

6.12 Tracking and Selecting Observations with the IN= Option

Select matching observations

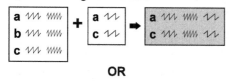

OR

Select non-matching observations

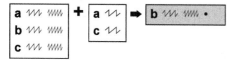

When you combine two data sets, you can use IN= options to track which of the original data sets contributed to each observation in the new data set. You can think of the IN= option as a sort of tag. Instead of saying "Product of Canada," the tag says something like "Product of data set one." Once you have that information, you can use it in many ways including selecting matching or non-matching observations during a merge.

The IN= data set option can be used any time you read a SAS data set in a DATA step—with SET, MERGE, or UPDATE—but is most often used with MERGE. To use the IN= option, you simply put the option in parentheses directly following the data set you want to track, and specify a name for the IN= variable. The names of IN= variables must follow standard SAS naming conventions—start with a letter or underscore; be 32 characters or fewer in length; and contain only letters, numerals, or underscores.

The DATA step below creates a data set named BOTH by merging two data sets named STATE and COUNTY. Then the IN= options create two variables named InState and InCounty:

```
DATA both;
   MERGE state (IN = InState) county (IN = InCounty);
   BY StateName;
```

Unlike most variables, IN= variables are temporary, existing only during the current DATA step. SAS gives the IN= variables a value of 0 or 1. A value of 1 means that data set did contribute to the current observation, and a value of 0 means the data set did not contribute. Suppose the COUNTY data set above contained no data for Louisiana. (Louisiana has parishes, not counties.) In that case, there would be one observation for Louisiana which would have a value of 1 for the variable InState and a value of 0 for InCounty because the STATE data set contributed to that observation, but the COUNTY data set did not.

You can use this variable like any other variable in the current DATA step, but it is most often used in subsetting IF or IF-THEN statements such as these:

```
Subsetting IF:   IF InState = 1;
                 IF InCounty = 0;
                 IF InState = 1 AND InCounty = 1;
   IF-THEN:      IF InCounty = 1 THEN Origin = 1;
                 IF InState = 1 THEN State = 'Yes';
```

Example A sporting goods manufacturer wants to send a sales rep to contact all customers who did not place any orders during the third quarter of the year. The company has two data files, one that contains all customers and one that contains all orders placed during the third quarter. To compile a list of customers without orders, you merge the two data sets using the IN= option, and then select customers who had no observations in the orders data set. The customer data file contains the customer number, name, and address. The orders data file contains the customer number and total price, with one observation for every order placed during the third quarter. Here are samples of the two raw data files:

Customer data		Orders data
101 Murphy's Sports	115 Main St.	102 562.01
102 Sun N Ski	2106 Newberry Ave.	104 254.98
103 Sports Outfitters	19 Cary Way	104 1642.00
104 Cramer & Johnson	4106 Arlington Blvd.	101 3497.56
105 Sports Savers	2708 Broadway	102 385.30

Here is the program that finds customers who did not place any orders:

```
DATA customer;
   INFILE 'c:\MyRawData\CustAddress.dat' TRUNCOVER;
   INPUT CustomerNumber Name $ 5-21 Address $ 23-42;
DATA orders;
   INFILE 'c:\MyRawData\OrdersQ3.dat';
   INPUT CustomerNumber Total;
PROC SORT DATA = orders;
   BY CustomerNumber;
RUN;
* Combine the data sets using the IN= option;
DATA noorders;
   MERGE customer orders (IN = Recent);
   BY CustomerNumber;
   IF Recent = 0;
RUN;
PROC PRINT DATA = noorders;
   TITLE 'Customers with No Orders in the Third Quarter';
RUN;
```

The customer data are already sorted by customer number and so do not need to be sorted with PROC SORT. The orders data, however, are in the order received and must be sorted by customer number before merging. In the final DATA step, the IN= option creates a variable named Recent, which equals 1 if the ORDERS data set contributed to that observation and 0 if it did not. Then a subsetting IF statement keeps only the observations where Recent is equal to 0—those observations with no orders data. Notice that there is no IN= option on the CUSTOMER data set. Only one IN= option was needed to identify customers who did not place any orders. Here is the list that can be given to sales reps:

Customers with No Orders in the Third Quarter

Obs	CustomerNumber	Name	Address	Total
1	103	Sports Outfitters	19 Cary Way	.
2	105	Sports Savers	2708 Broadway	.

The values for the variable Total are missing because these customers did not have observations in the ORDERS data set. The variable Recent does not appear in the output because, as a temporary variable, it was not added to the NOORDERS data set.

6.13 Selecting Observations with the WHERE= Option

By this point, you've probably realized that with SAS programing there is usually more than one way to perform any particular task. Of all the things you can do with SAS, subsetting your data probably presents you with the most choices. The idea is simple: you have a data set, but you want to use only part of it. Maybe you have census data for the entire U.S., but you want data only for Arkansas, or for males, or for households with more than 10 people. In any particular case, the best way to subset your data depends on the type of data file you have, and what you want to do after you subset the data. That's why SAS offers you so many ways to do this.

This book has already covered several ways to subset a data set. If your data are in a raw data file, then you can read part of the file using multiple INPUT statements (section 2.13). If your data are in a SAS data set, you can use a subsetting IF statement in a DATA step (section 3.7). If you are using a procedure, you can subset your data using a WHERE statement (section 4.2). WHERE statements can also be used in DATA steps (appendix). You can use OUTPUT statements to control which observations are written to a data set (section 6.9). Even with all these ways to subset your data, there is another way worth knowing: the WHERE= data set option.

The WHERE= data set option is the most flexible of all ways to subset data. You can use it in DATA steps or PROC steps, when you read existing data sets and when you write new data sets. The basic form of a WHERE= data set option is

```
WHERE = (condition)
```

Only observations satisfying the condition will be used by SAS. The WHERE= data set option is, not surprisingly, similar to the WHERE statement, and uses the same symbolic and mnemonic operators listed in section 4.2. To use the WHERE= data set option in a DATA step, you simply put it between parentheses following the name of the data set to which it applies. If used in a SET, MERGE, or UPDATE statement, the WHERE= option will be applied to the data set that is being read. If used in a DATA statement, the WHERE= option will be applied to the data set that is being written.

```
DATA gone;
   SET animals (WHERE = (Status = 'Extinct'));

DATA uncommon (WHERE = (Status IN ('Endangered', 'Threatened')));
   SET animals;
```

The following procedures will use only observations that satisfy the WHERE= condition.

```
PROC IMPORT DATAFILE = 'c:\MyRawData\Wildlife.csv'
   OUT = animals (WHERE = (Class = 'Mammalia')) REPLACE;

PROC PRINT DATA = animals (WHERE = (Habitat='Riparian'));

PROC EXPORT DATA = animals (WHERE = (Status='Threatened'))
   OUTFILE = 'c:\MyRawData\Wildlife.xls';
```

Note that in order to use a WHERE= option with a PROC IMPORT you must know—ahead of time—the name that SAS will give your variables. See sections 2.16 and 2.17 for more information about the IMPORT procedure and sections 10.3 and 10.4 for the EXPORT procedure.

Example The following data contain information about the Seven Summits, the highest mountains on each continent. Each line of data includes the name of a mountain, its continent, and height in meters.

```
Kilimanjaro    Africa         5895
Vinson Massif  Antarctica     4897
Everest        Asia           8848
Elbrus         Europe         5642
McKinley       North America  6194
Aconcagua      South America  6962
Kosciuszuko    Australia      2228
```

This program reads the data with an INPUT statement, and creates two data sets named TALLPEAKS and AMERICAN. The WHERE= data set options control which observations are included in each data set.

```
*Input the data and create two subsets;
DATA tallpeaks (WHERE = (Height > 6000))
     american (WHERE = (Continent CONTAINS ('America')));
   INFILE 'c:\MyRawData\Mountains.dat';
   INPUT Name $1-14 Continent $15-28 Height;
RUN;
PROC PRINT DATA = tallpeaks;
   TITLE 'Members of the Seven Summits above 6,000 Meters';
RUN;
PROC PRINT DATA = american;
   TITLE 'Members of the Seven Summits in the Americas';
RUN;
```

Here are the results:

Members of the Seven Summits above 6,000 Meters

Obs	Name	Continent	Height
1	Everest	Asia	8848
2	McKinley	North America	6194
3	Aconcagua	South America	6962

Members of the Seven Summits in the Americas

Obs	Name	Continent	Height
1	McKinley	North America	6194
2	Aconcagua	South America	6962

6.14   Changing Observations to Variables Using PROC TRANSPOSE

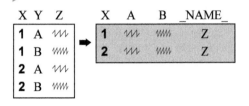

We have already seen ways to combine data sets, create new variables, and sort data. Now, using PROC TRANSPOSE, we will flip data—so get your spatulas ready.

The TRANSPOSE procedure transposes SAS data sets, turning observations into variables or variables into observations. In most cases, to convert observations into variables, you can use the following statements:

```
PROC TRANSPOSE DATA = old-data-set OUT = new-data-set;
   BY variable-list;
   ID variable-list;
   VAR variable-list;
```

In the PROC TRANSPOSE statement, *old-data-set* refers to the SAS data set you want to transpose, and *new-data-set* is the name of the newly transposed data set.

BY statement You can use the BY statement if you have any grouping variables that you want to keep as variables. These variables are included in the transposed data set, but they are not themselves transposed. The transposed data set will have one observation for each BY level per variable transposed. For example, in the figure above, the variable X is the BY variable. The data set must be sorted by these variables before transposing.

ID statement The ID statement names the variable whose formatted values will become the new variable names. If more than one variable is listed, then the values of all variables in the ID statement will be concatenated to form the new variable names. The ID values must occur only once in the data set; or if a BY statement is present, then the values must be unique within BY-groups. If the first ID variable is numeric, then the new variable names have an underscore for a prefix (_1 or _2, for example). If you don't use an ID statement, then the new variables will be named COL1, COL2, and so on. In the figure above, the variable Y is the ID variable. Notice how its values are the names of the new variables in the transposed data set.

VAR statement The VAR statement names the variables whose values you want to transpose. In the figure above, the variable Z is the VAR variable. SAS creates a new variable, _NAME_, which has as values the names of the variables in the VAR statement. If there is more than one VAR variable, then _NAME_ will have more than one value.

Example Suppose you have the following data about players for minor league baseball teams. You have the team name, player's number, the type of data (salary or batting average), and the entry:

```
Garlics 10 salary 43000
Peaches  8 salary 38000
Garlics 21 salary 51000
Peaches 10 salary 47500
Garlics 10 batavg .281
Peaches  8 batavg .252
Garlics 21 batavg .265
Peaches 10 batavg .301
```

You want to look at the relationship between batting average and salary. To do this, salary and batting average must be variables. The following program reads the raw data into a SAS data set and sorts the data by team and player. Then the data are transposed using PROC TRANSPOSE.

```
DATA baseball;
    INFILE 'c:\MyRawData\Transpos.dat';
    INPUT Team $ Player Type $ Entry;
PROC SORT DATA = baseball;
    BY Team Player;
PROC PRINT DATA = baseball;
    TITLE 'Baseball Data After Sorting and Before Transposing';
RUN;
* Transpose data so salary and batavg are variables;
PROC TRANSPOSE DATA = baseball OUT = flipped;
    BY Team Player;
    ID Type;
    VAR Entry;
PROC PRINT DATA = flipped;
    TITLE 'Baseball Data After Transposing';
RUN;
```

In the PROC TRANSPOSE step, the BY variables are Team and Player. You want those variables to remain in the data set, and they define the new observations (you want only one observation for each team and player combination). The ID variable is Type, whose values (salary and batavg) will be the new variable names. The variable to be transposed, Entry, is specified in the VAR statement. Notice that its name, Entry, now appears as a value under the variable _NAME_. The TRANSPOSE procedure automatically generates the _NAME_ variable, but in this application it is not very meaningful and could be dropped. Here are the results:

Baseball Data After Sorting and Before Transposing

Obs	Team	Player	Type	Entry
1	Garlics	10	salary	43000.00
2	Garlics	10	batavg	0.28
3	Garlics	21	salary	51000.00
4	Garlics	21	batavg	0.27
5	Peaches	8	salary	38000.00
6	Peaches	8	batavg	0.25
7	Peaches	10	salary	47500.00
8	Peaches	10	batavg	0.30

Baseball Data After Transposing

Obs	Team	Player	_NAME_	salary	batavg
1	Garlics	10	Entry	43000	0.281
2	Garlics	21	Entry	51000	0.265
3	Peaches	8	Entry	38000	0.252
4	Peaches	10	Entry	47500	0.301

6.15 Using SAS Automatic Variables

In addition to the variables you create in your SAS data set, SAS creates a few more called automatic variables. You don't ordinarily see these variables because they are temporary and are not saved with your data. But they are available in the DATA step, and you can use them just like you use any variable that you create yourself.

_N_ and _ERROR_ The _N_ and _ERROR_ variables are always available to you in the DATA step. _N_ indicates the number of times SAS has looped through the DATA step. This is not necessarily equal to the observation number, since a simple subsetting IF statement can change the relationship between observation number and the number of iterations of the DATA step. The _ERROR_ variable has a value of 1 if there is a data error for that observation and 0 if there isn't. Things that can cause data errors include invalid data (such as characters in a numeric field), conversion errors (like division by zero), and illegal arguments in functions (including log of zero).

FIRST.*variable* and LAST.*variable* Other automatic variables are available only in special circumstances. The FIRST.*variable* and LAST.*variable* automatic variables are available when you are using a BY statement in a DATA step. The FIRST.*variable* will have a value of 1 when SAS is processing an observation with the first occurrence of a new value for that variable and a value of 0 for the other observations. The LAST.*variable* will have a value of 1 for an observation with the last occurrence of a value for that variable and the value 0 for the other observations.

Example Your hometown is having a walk around the town square to raise money for the library. You have the following data: entry number, age group, and finishing time. (Notice that there is more than one observation per line of data.)

```
54 youth  35.5 21 adult   21.6   6 adult   25.8 13 senior 29.0
38 senior 40.3 19 youth   39.6   3 adult   19.0 25 youth   47.3
11 adult  21.9  8 senior  54.3 41 adult   43.0 32 youth   38.6
```

The first thing you want to do is create a new variable for overall finishing place and print the results. The first part of the following program reads the raw data, and sorts the data by finishing time (Time). Then another DATA step creates the new Place variable and gives it the current value of _N_. The PRINT procedure produces the list of finishers:

```
DATA walkers;
   INFILE 'c:\MyRawData\Walk.dat';
   INPUT Entry AgeGroup $ Time @@;
PROC SORT DATA = walkers;
   BY Time;
* Create a new variable, Place;
DATA ordered;
   SET walkers;
   Place = _N_;
PROC PRINT DATA = ordered;
  TITLE 'Results of Walk';
RUN;
```

```
PROC SORT DATA = ordered;
   BY AgeGroup Time;
* Keep the first observation in each age group;
DATA winners;
   SET ordered;
   BY AgeGroup;
   IF FIRST.AgeGroup = 1;
PROC PRINT DATA = winners;
   TITLE 'Winners in Each Age Group';
RUN;
```

The second part of this program produces a list of the top finishers in each age category. The ORDERED data set containing the new Place variable is sorted by AgeGroup and Time. In the DATA step, the SET statement reads the ORDERED data set. The BY statement in the DATA step generates the FIRST.AgeGroup and LAST.AgeGroup temporary variables. The subsetting IF statement, IF FIRST.AgeGroup = 1, keeps only the first observation in the BY group. Since the Winners data set is sorted by AgeGroup and Time, the first observation in each BY group is the top finisher of that group.

Here are the results of the two PRINT procedures. The first page shows the data after sorting by Time and including the new variable Place. Notice that the _N_ temporary variable does not appear in the printout. The second page shows the results of the second part of the program—the winners for each age category and their overall place:

Results of Walk

Obs	Entry	AgeGroup	Time	Place
1	3	adult	19.0	1
2	21	adult	21.6	2
3	11	adult	21.9	3
4	6	adult	25.8	4
5	13	senior	29.0	5
6	54	youth	35.5	6
7	32	youth	38.6	7
8	19	youth	39.6	8
9	38	senior	40.3	9
10	41	adult	43.0	10
11	25	youth	47.3	11
12	8	senior	54.3	12

Winners in Each Age Group

Obs	Entry	AgeGroup	Time	Place
1	3	adult	19.0	1
2	13	senior	29.0	5
3	54	youth	35.5	6

7

"Nobody is too old to learn—but a lot of people keep putting it off."

WILLIAM O'NEILL

CHAPTER 7

Writing Flexible Code with the SAS Macro Facility

7.1 Macro Concepts

Not so long ago the SAS macro facility was considered an advanced topic relevant only to experienced SAS users. Over time, however, macros have become more prevalent so that now even new SAS users would do well to know a little about the SAS macro facility. Fortunately, the basic macro concepts are not difficult to understand. This chapter introduces the most commonly used features of the SAS macro language.

Because macros take longer to write and debug than standard SAS code, you generally won't want macros in programs that will be run only a few times. But used properly, macros can make the development and maintenance of production programs much easier. They do this in several ways. First, with macros you can make one small change in your program and have SAS echo that change throughout your program. Second, macros allow you to write a piece of code once and use it over and over, in the same program or in different programs. You can even store macros in a central location—an autocall library—and share them between programs and between programmers. Third, you can make your programs data driven, letting SAS decide what to do based on actual data values.

The macro processor When you submit a standard SAS program, SAS compiles and then immediately executes it. But when you write a macro, there is an additional step. Before SAS can compile and execute your program, SAS must pass your macro statements to the macro processor which "resolves" your macros, generating standard SAS code. Because you are writing a program that writes a program, this is sometimes called meta-programming.

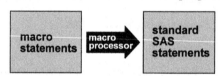

Macros and macro variables SAS macro code consists of two basic parts: macros and macro variables. The names of macro variables are prefixed with an ampersand (&) while the names of macros are prefixed with a percent sign (%).[1] A macro variable is like a standard data variable except that, having only a single value, it does not belong to a data set, and its value is always character. This value could be a variable name, a numeral, or any text that you want substituted into your program. A macro, on the other hand, is a larger piece of a program that may contain complex logic including complete DATA and PROC steps and macro statements such as %DO, %END, and %IF-%THEN/%ELSE.

When SAS users talk about "macros" they sometimes mean macros, and sometimes mean macro processing in general. Macro variables are usually called *macro variables*.

Local versus global Macro variables can have two kinds of "scope"—either local or global. Generally, a macro variable is local if it is defined inside a macro. A macro variable is generally global if it is defined in "open code" which is everything outside a macro. You can use a global macro variable anywhere in your program, but you can use a local macro variable only inside its own macro. [2] If you keep this in mind as you write your programs, you will avoid two common errors: trying to use a local macro variable outside its macro and accidentally creating local and global macro variables with the same name.

Turning on the macro processor Before you can use macros you must have the MACRO system option turned on. This option is usually turned on by default, but may be turned off, especially on mainframes, because SAS runs slightly faster when it doesn't have to bother with checking for macros. If you are not sure whether the MACRO option is on, you can find out by submitting these statements:

```
PROC OPTIONS OPTION = MACRO;
RUN;
```

Check your SAS log. If you see the option MACRO, then the macro processor is turned on, and you can use it. If you see NOMACRO there, you need to specify the MACRO option at invocation or in a configuration file. Specifying this type of option is system dependent. For details about how to do this, see the SAS Help and Documentation for your operating environment.

Avoiding macro errors There's no question about it, macros can make your head hurt. You can avoid the macro migraine by developing your program in a piecewise fashion. First, write your program in standard SAS code. Then, when it's bug-free, convert it to macro logic adding one feature at a time. This modular approach to programming is always a good idea, but it's critical with macros.

---

[1] There are exceptions. Macro names prefixed with a % are called name-style macros. Two other types of macros do not start with a %: command-style and statement-style. In general, macros starting with a prefix are superior both because they are more efficient (the macro processor recognizes them more quickly), and because they are less easily confused with SAS keywords.

Also the %INCLUDE, %LIST, and %RUN statements are NOT part of the macro facility despite their % prefix.

[2] There are ways to force a local macro variable to become global and vice versa. See the SAS Help and Documentation for the SAS Macro Language if you need to change the scope of your macro variables.

7.2 Substituting Text with Macro Variables

Macro variables may be the most straightforward and easy-to-use part of the macro facility, yet if you master only this one feature of macro programming you will have greatly increased your flexibility as a SAS programmer. Suppose you have a SAS program that you run once a week. Each time you run it you have to edit the program so it will select data for the correct range of dates and print the correct dates in the title. This process is time-consuming and prone to errors. (What if you accidentally delete a semicolon?!) Instead, you can use a macro variable to insert the correct date. Then you can have another cup of coffee while someone else, someone who knows very little about SAS, runs this program for you.

When SAS encounters the name of a macro variable, the macro processor simply replaces the name with the value of that macro variable. That value is a character constant that you specify.

Creating a macro variable with %LET The simplest way to assign a value to a macro variable is with the %LET statement. The general form of this statement is

```
%LET macro-variable-name = value;
```

where *macro-variable-name* must follow the rules for SAS variable names (32 characters or fewer in length; start with a letter or underscore; and contain only letters, numerals, and underscores). *Value* is the text to be substituted for the macro variable name, and can be longer than you are ever likely to need—over 65,000 characters long. The following statements each create a macro variable.

```
%LET iterations = 10;

%LET country = New Zealand;
```

Notice that unlike an ordinary assignment statement, *value* does not require quotation marks even when it contains characters. Except for blanks at the beginning and end, which are trimmed, everything between the equals sign and the semicolon becomes part of the value for that macro variable.

Using a macro variable To use a macro variable you simply add the ampersand prefix (&) and stick the macro variable name wherever you want its value to be substituted. Keep in mind that the macro processor doesn't look for macros inside *single* quotation marks. To get around this, simply use double quotation marks. The following statements show possible ways to use the macro variables defined above.

```
DO i = 1 to &iterations;

TITLE "Addresses in &country";
```

After being resolved by the macro processor, these statements would become

```
DO i = 1 to 10;

TITLE "Addresses in New Zealand";
```

Example   A grower of tropical flowers records information about each sale in a raw data file. The data include customer ID, date of sale, variety of flower, sale quantity, and sale amount.

```
240W 02-07-2012 Ginger     120  960
240W 02-10-2012 Protea     180 1710
356W 02-10-2012 Heliconia   60  720
356W 02-15-2012 Anthurium  300 1050
188R 02-16-2012 Ginger      24  192
188R 02-18-2012 Anthurium   24   96
240W 02-21-2012 Heliconia   48  600
240W 02-27-2012 Protea      48  456
356W 02-29-2012 Ginger     240 1980
```

Periodically, the grower needs a report about sales of a single variety. The macro variable in this program allows the grower to choose one variety without editing the DATA or PROC step. Instead, he just types the name of the variety once, in the %LET statement.

```
%LET flowertype = Ginger;

* Read the data and subset with a macro variable;
DATA flowersales;
    INFILE 'c:\MyRawData\TropicalFlowers.dat';
    INPUT CustomerID $4. @6 SaleDate MMDDYY10. @17 Variety $9.
        SaleQuantity SaleAmount;
    IF Variety = "&flowertype";
RUN;
* Print the report using a macro variable;
PROC PRINT DATA = flowersales;
    FORMAT SaleDate WORDDATE18. SaleAmount DOLLAR7.;
    TITLE "Sales of &flowertype";
RUN;
```

The program starts with a %LET statement that creates a macro variable named &FLOWERTYPE, assigning to it a value of Ginger. Because the variable &FLOWERTYPE is defined outside a macro, it is a global macro variable and can be used anywhere in this program. In this case, the value Ginger is substituted for &FLOWERTYPE in a subsetting IF statement and a TITLE statement. Here are the results:

Sales of Ginger

Obs	CustomerID	SaleDate	Variety	SaleQuantity	SaleAmount
1	240W	February 7, 2012	Ginger	120	$960
2	188R	February 16, 2012	Ginger	24	$192
3	356W	February 29, 2012	Ginger	240	$1,980

This is a short program, so using a macro variable didn't save much trouble. However, if you had a program 100 or even 1,000 lines long, a macro variable could be a blessing.

7.3 Concatenating Macro Variables with Other Text

The previous section described how you can use macro variables to increase the flexibility of your SAS programs. Macro variables hold pieces of text that you can use later to insert into your program. These pieces of text can be used alone, or they can be combined with other text.

Combining text with macro variables When SAS encounters the ampersand (&) embedded in text, it will look for macro variable names starting with the first character after the ampersand until it encounters either a space, a semicolon, another ampersand, or a period. So, if you want to add text before your macro variable, simply concatenate the text with an ampersand and the macro variable name. If you want to add text after the macro variable, then you need to insert a period between the end of the macro variable name and the text. The period signals the end of the macro variable and will not be included in the resolved text. Concatenating two macro variables together does not require a period between the names because the ampersand for the second macro variable signals the end of the first macro variable.

Here are some examples with two macro variables, &REGION and &MYNAME, defined as follows:

```
%LET Region = West;
%LET MyName = Sam;
```

SAS statement before resolution	SAS statement after resolution
`Office = "NorthAmerica&Region";`	`Office = "NorthAmericaWest";`
`Office = "&Region.Coast";`	`Office = "WestCoast";`
`DATA &MyName..Sales;`	`DATA Sam.Sales;`
`DATA &MyName&Region.ern_Sales;`	`DATA SamWestern_Sales;`

Automatic macro variables Every time you invoke SAS, the macro processor automatically creates certain macro variables. Some examples of automatic macro variables are

Variable name	Example	Description
&SYSDATE	28MAY12	the character value of the date that job or session began
&SYSDAY	Wednesday	the day of the week that job or session began
&SYSNOBS	312	number of observations in last SAS dataset created

These macro variables can be used in your programs just like macro variables that you create.

Example Here are the tropical flower sales data from the previous section. The data include customer ID, date of sale, variety of flower, sale quantity, and sale amount.

```
240W 02-07-2012 Ginger     120  960
240W 02-10-2012 Protea     180 1710
356W 02-10-2012 Heliconia   60  720
356W 02-15-2012 Anthurium  300 1050
188R 02-16-2012 Ginger      24  192
188R 02-18-2012 Anthurium   24   96
240W 02-21-2012 Heliconia   48  600
240W 02-27-2012 Protea      48  456
356W 02-29-2012 Ginger     240 1980
```

This program creates a macro variable named &SUMVAR which, when used with the prefix Sale, determines which variable will be summarized. When the macro variable has the value Quantity, as in this example, then variable in the VAR statement of the PROC MEANS becomes SaleQuantity. The &SUMVAR macro variable also appears in the TITLE statement.

```
%LET SumVar = Quantity;

* Read the data and subset with a macro variable;
DATA flowersales;
    INFILE 'c:\MyRawData\TropicalFlowers.dat';
    INPUT CustomerID $4. @6 SaleDate MMDDYY10. @17 Variety $9.
        SaleQuantity SaleAmount;
RUN;
* Create RTF file with today's date in the file name;
ODS RTF FILE="c:\MyRTFFiles\FlowerSales_&SYSDATE..rtf";
* Summarize the sales for the selected variable;
PROC MEANS DATA = flowersales SUM MIN MAX MAXDEC=0;
    VAR Sale&SumVar;
    CLASS Variety;
    TITLE "Summary of Sales &SumVar by Variety";
RUN;
* Close the RTF file;
ODS RTF CLOSE;
```

The program creates an RTF file, and the name of the file depends on the date the SAS job or session begins. If the session begins on October 25, 2013, then the filename will be FlowerSales_25OCT2013.rtf. Notice that there are two periods in the file specification in the ODS RTF statement. The first period signals the end of the macro variable name &SYSDATE, while the second period becomes part of the filename. Here is what the RTF file looks like opened in Microsoft Word.

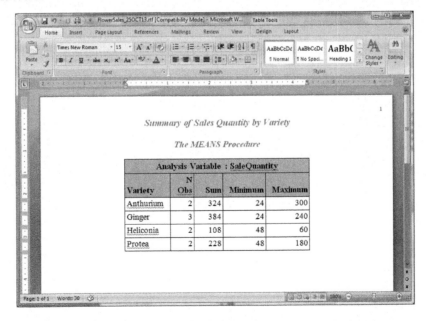

7.4 Creating Modular Code with Macros

Anytime you find yourself writing the same or similar SAS statements over and over, you should consider using a macro. A macro lets you package a piece of bug-free code and use it repeatedly within a single SAS program or in many SAS programs.

You can think of a macro as a kind of sandwich. The %MACRO and %MEND statements are like two slices of bread. Between those slices you can put any statements you want. The general form of a macro is

```
%MACRO macro-name;
   macro-text
%MEND macro-name;
```

The %MACRO statement tells SAS that this is the beginning of a macro, while %MEND marks the end. *Macro-name* is a name you make up, and can be up to 32 characters in length, start with a letter or underscore, and contain only letters, numerals, and underscores. The *macro-name* in the MEND statement is optional, but your macros will be easier to debug and maintain if you include it. That way there's no question which %MACRO statement goes with which %MEND. *Macro-text* (also called a macro definition) is a set of SAS statements.

Invoking a macro After you have defined a macro, you can invoke it by adding the percent sign prefix to its name like this:

```
%macro-name
```

A semicolon is not required when invoking a macro, though adding one generally does no harm.

Example Using the data from the previous section, this example creates a simple macro. The data include customer ID, date of sale, variety of flower, sale quantity, and sale amount.

```
240W 02-07-2012 Ginger     120   960
240W 02-10-2012 Protea     180  1710
356W 02-10-2012 Heliconia   60   720
356W 02-15-2012 Anthurium  300  1050
188R 02-16-2012 Ginger      24   192
188R 02-18-2012 Anthurium   24    96
240W 02-21-2012 Heliconia   48   600
240W 02-27-2012 Protea      48   456
356W 02-29-2012 Ginger     240  1980
```

The following program creates a macro named %SAMPLE to sort the data by SaleQuantity and print the five observations with the largest sales. Then the program reads the data in a standard DATA step, and invokes the macro.

```
* Macro to print 5 largest sales;
%MACRO sample;
   PROC SORT DATA = flowersales;
      BY DESCENDING SaleQuantity;
   RUN;
   PROC PRINT DATA = flowersales (OBS = 5);
       FORMAT SaleDate WORDDATE18. SaleAmount DOLLAR7.;
       TITLE 'Five Largest Sales by Quantity';
   RUN;
%MEND sample;

* Read the flower sales data;
DATA flowersales;
   INFILE 'c:\MyRawData\TropicalFlowers.dat';
   INPUT CustomerID $4. @6 SaleDate MMDDYY10. @17 Variety $9.
       SaleQuantity SaleAmount;
RUN;

* Invoke the macro;
%sample
```

Here is the output:

Five Largest Sales by Quantity

Obs	CustomerID	SaleDate	Variety	SaleQuantity	SaleAmount
1	356W	February 15, 2012	Anthurium	300	$1,050
2	356W	February 29, 2012	Ginger	240	$1,980
3	240W	February 10, 2012	Protea	180	$1,710
4	240W	February 7, 2012	Ginger	120	$960
5	356W	February 10, 2012	Heliconia	60	$720

This macro is fairly limited because it does the same thing every time. To increase the flexibility of macros, combine them with %LET statements or add parameters as described in the next section.

Macro autocall libraries The macros in this book are defined and invoked inside a single program, but you can also store macros in a central location, called an autocall library. Macros in a library can be shared by programs and programmers. Basically you save your macros as files in a directory or as members of a partitioned data set (depending on your operating environment), and use the MAUTOSOURCE and SASAUTOS= system options to tell SAS where to look for macros. Then you can invoke a macro even though the original macro does not appear in your program. For more information see the SAS Help and Documentation.

7.5 Adding Parameters to Macros

Macros can save you a lot of trouble, allowing you to write a set of statements once and then use them over and over. However, you usually don't want to repeat exactly the same statements. You may want the same report, but for a different data set, or product, or patient. Parameters allow you to do this.

Parameters are macro variables whose value you set when you invoke a macro. The simplest macros, like the macro in the previous section, have no parameters. To add parameters to a macro, you simply list the macro-variable names between parentheses in the %MACRO statement. Here is one of the possible forms of the parameter-list.

```
%MACRO macro-name (parameter-1= ,parameter-2= , . . . parameter-n=);
   macro-text
%MEND macro-name;
```

For example, a macro named %QUARTERLYREPORT might start like this:

```
%MACRO quarterlyreport(quarter=,salesrep=);
```

This macro has two parameters: &QUARTER and &SALESREP. You could invoke the macro with this statement:

```
%quarterlyreport(quarter=3,salesrep=Smith)
```

The SAS macro processor would replace each occurrence of the macro variable &QUARTER with the value 3, and would substitute Smith for &SALESREP.

Example Using the tropical flower data again, suppose the grower often needs a report showing sales to an individual customer. The following program defines a macro that lets the grower select sales for a single customer and then sort the results. As before, the data contain the customer ID, date of sale, variety of flower, sale quantity, and sale amount.

```
240W 02-07-2012 Ginger     120  960
240W 02-10-2012 Protea     180 1710
356W 02-10-2012 Heliconia   60  720
356W 02-15-2012 Anthurium  300 1050
188R 02-16-2012 Ginger      24  192
188R 02-18-2012 Anthurium   24   96
240W 02-21-2012 Heliconia   48  600
240W 02-27-2012 Protea      48  456
356W 02-29-2012 Ginger     240 1980
```

The following program defines a macro named %SELECT, and then invokes the macro twice. This macro sorts and prints the FlowerSales data, using parameters to create two macro variables named &CUSTOMER and &SORTVAR.

```
* Macro with parameters;
%MACRO select(customer=,sortvar=);
   PROC SORT DATA = flowersales OUT = salesout;
      BY &sortvar;
      WHERE CustomerID = "&customer";
   RUN;
   PROC PRINT DATA = salesout;
      FORMAT SaleDate WORDDATE18. SaleAmount DOLLAR7.;
      TITLE1 "Orders for Customer Number &customer";
      TITLE2 "Sorted by &sortvar";
   RUN;
%MEND select;

* Read all the flower sales data;
DATA flowersales;
   INFILE 'c:\MyRawData\TropicalFlowers.dat';
   INPUT CustomerID $4. @6 SaleDate MMDDYY10. @17 Variety $9.
         SaleQuantity SaleAmount;
RUN;

*Invoke the macro;
%select(customer = 356W, sortvar = SaleQuantity)
%select(customer = 240W, sortvar = Variety)
```

Here is the output:

Orders for Customer Number 356W
Sorted by SaleQuantity

Obs	CustomerID	SaleDate	Variety	SaleQuantity	SaleAmount
1	356W	February 10, 2012	Heliconia	60	$720
2	356W	February 29, 2012	Ginger	240	$1,980
3	356W	February 15, 2012	Anthurium	300	$1,050

Orders for Customer Number 240W
Sorted by Variety

Obs	CustomerID	SaleDate	Variety	SaleQuantity	SaleAmount
1	240W	February 7, 2012	Ginger	120	$960
2	240W	February 21, 2012	Heliconia	48	$600
3	240W	February 10, 2012	Protea	180	$1,710
4	240W	February 27, 2012	Protea	48	$456

7.6 Writing Macros with Conditional Logic

Combining macros and macro variables gives you a lot of flexibility, but you can increase
that flexibility even more by adding macro statements such as %IF. Fortunately, many macro
statements have parallel statements in standard SAS code so they should feel familiar. Here are
the general forms of the statements used for conditional logic in macros:

```
%IF condition %THEN action;
   %ELSE %IF condition %THEN action;
   %ELSE action;

%IF condition %THEN %DO;
   SAS statements
%END;
```

These macro statements can be used only inside a macro.

You may be wondering why anyone needs these statements. Why not just use the standard
IF-THEN? You may indeed use standard IF-THEN statements in your macros, but you will
use them for different actions. %IF statements can contain actions that standard IF statements
can't contain, such as complete DATA or PROC steps and even other macro statements. The
%IF-%THEN statements don't appear in the standard SAS code generated by your macro.
Remember you are writing a program that writes a program.

For example, you could combine conditional logic with the &SYSDAY automatic variable like this:

```
%IF &SYSDAY = Tuesday %THEN %LET country = Belgium;
   %ELSE %LET country = France;
```

If you run the program on Tuesday, the macro processor resolves the statements to:

```
%LET country = Belgium;
```

If you run the program on any other day, then the macro processor resolves the statements to:

```
%LET country = France;
```

Example Using the tropical flower data again, this example shows a macro with conditional
logic. The grower wants to print one report on Monday and a different report on Tuesday. You can
write one program that will run either report using the &SYSDAY automatic macro variable. The
raw data contain the customer ID, date of sale, variety of flower, sale quantity, and sale amount.

```
240W 02-07-2012 Ginger    120   960
240W 02-10-2012 Protea    180  1710
356W 02-10-2012 Heliconia  60   720
356W 02-15-2012 Anthurium 300  1050
188R 02-16-2012 Ginger     24   192
188R 02-18-2012 Anthurium  24    96
240W 02-21-2012 Heliconia  48   600
240W 02-27-2012 Protea     48   456
356W 02-29-2012 Ginger    240  1980
```

Here is the program:

```
%MACRO dailyreports;
   %IF &SYSDAY = Monday %THEN %DO;
      PROC PRINT DATA = flowersales;
         FORMAT SaleDate WORDDATE18. SaleAmount DOLLAR7.;
         TITLE 'Monday Report: Current Flower Sales';
      RUN;
   %END;
   %ELSE %IF &SYSDAY = Tuesday %THEN %DO;
      PROC MEANS DATA = flowersales MEAN MIN MAX;
         CLASS Variety;
         VAR SaleQuantity;
         TITLE 'Tuesday Report: Summary of Flower Sales';
      RUN;
   %END;
%MEND dailyreports;

DATA flowersales;
   INFILE 'c:\MyRawData\TropicalFlowers.dat';
   INPUT CustomerID $4. @6 SaleDate MMDDYY10. @17 Variety $9.
      SaleQuantity SaleAmount;
RUN;

%dailyreports
```

When the program is submitted on Tuesday, the macro processor will write this program:

```
DATA flowersales;
   INFILE 'c:\MyRawData\TropicalFlowers.dat';
   INPUT CustomerID $4. @6 SaleDate MMDDYY10. @17 Variety $9.
      SaleQuantity SaleAmount;
RUN;

PROC MEANS DATA = flowersales MEAN MIN MAX;
   CLASS Variety;
   VAR SaleQuantity;
   TITLE 'Tuesday Report: Summary of Flower Sales';
RUN;
```

If you run this program on Tuesday the output will look like this:

Tuesday Report: Summary of Flower Sales
The MEANS Procedure

Analysis Variable : SaleQuantity				
Variety	N Obs	Mean	Minimum	Maximum
Anthurium	2	162.0000000	24.0000000	300.0000000
Ginger	3	128.0000000	24.0000000	240.0000000
Heliconia	2	54.0000000	48.0000000	60.0000000
Protea	2	114.0000000	48.0000000	180.0000000

7.7   Writing Data-Driven Programs with CALL SYMPUT

When you submit a SAS program containing macros it goes first to the macro processor which generates standard SAS code from the macro references. Then SAS compiles and executes your program. Not until execution—the final stage—does SAS see any actual data values. This is the tricky part of writing data-driven programs: SAS doesn't know the values of your data until the execution phase, and by that time it is ordinarily too late. However, there is a way to have your digital cake and eat it too—CALL SYMPUT.

CALL SYMPUT takes a value from a DATA step and assigns it to a macro variable. You can then use this macro variable in later steps. To assign a value to a single macro variable, you use CALL SYMPUT with this general form:

```
CALL SYMPUT("macro-variable-name",value);
```

where *macro-variable-name*, enclosed in quotation marks, is the name of a macro variable, either new or old, and *value* is the value you want to assign to that macro variable. *Value* can be the name of a variable whose value SAS will use, or it can be a constant value enclosed in quotation marks.

CALL SYMPUT is often used in IF-THEN statements such as this:

```
IF Age >= 18 THEN CALL SYMPUT("status", "Adult");
   ELSE CALL SYMPUT("status", "Minor");
```

These statements create a macro variable named &STATUS and assign to it a value of Adult or Minor depending on the variable Age. The following CALL SYMPUT uses a variable as its *value*:

```
IF TotalSales > 1000000 THEN CALL SYMPUT("bestseller", BookTitle);
```

This statement tells SAS to create a macro variable named &BESTSELLER which is equal to the value of the variable BookTitle when TotalSales exceed 1,000,000.

Caution   You cannot create a macro variable with CALL SYMPUT and use it in the same DATA step because SAS does not assign a value to the macro variable until the DATA step executes. DATA steps execute when SAS encounters a step boundary such as a subsequent DATA, PROC, or RUN statement.

Example   Here are the flower sales data consisting of customer ID, date of sale, variety of flower, sale quantity, and sale amount.

```
240W 02-07-2012 Ginger     120   960
240W 02-10-2012 Protea     180  1710
356W 02-10-2012 Heliconia   60   720
356W 02-15-2012 Anthurium  300  1050
188R 02-16-2012 Ginger      24   192
188R 02-18-2012 Anthurium   24    96
240W 02-21-2012 Heliconia   48   600
240W 02-27-2012 Protea      48   456
356W 02-29-2012 Ginger     240  1980
```

In this example, the grower wants a program that will find the customer with the single largest order in dollars, and print all the orders for that customer.

```
* Read the raw data;
DATA flowersales;
    INFILE 'c:\MyRawData\TropicalFlowers.dat';
    INPUT CustomerID $4. @6 SaleDate MMDDYY10. @17 Variety $9.
        SaleQuantity SaleAmount;
PROC SORT DATA = flowersales;
    BY DESCENDING SaleAmount;
RUN;
* Find biggest order and pass the customer id to a macro variable;
DATA _NULL_;
    SET flowersales;
    IF _N_ = 1 THEN CALL SYMPUT("selectedcustomer",CustomerID);
    ELSE STOP;
RUN;
PROC PRINT DATA = flowersales;
    WHERE CustomerID = "&selectedcustomer";
    FORMAT SaleDate WORDDATE18. SaleAmount DOLLAR7.;
    TITLE "Customer &selectedcustomer Had the Single Largest Order";
RUN;
```

This program has a lot of steps, but each step is fairly simple. The first DATA step reads the data from the raw data file. Then PROC SORT sorts the data by descending SaleAmount. That way, the largest single order will be the first observation in the newly sorted data set.

The second DATA step then uses CALL SYMPUT to assign the value of the variable CustomerID to the macro variable &SELECTEDCUSTOMER when _N_ equals 1 (the first iteration of the DATA step). Since that is all we need from this DATA step, we can use the STOP statement to tell SAS to end this DATA step. The STOP statement is not necessary, but it is efficient because it prevents SAS from reading the remaining observations for no reason.

When SAS reaches the RUN statement, SAS knows that the DATA step has ended so SAS executes the DATA step. At this point the macro variable &SELECTEDCUSTOMER has the value 356W (the customer ID with the largest single order in dollars) and can be used in the PROC PRINT. The output looks like this:

Customer 356W Had the Single Largest Order

Obs	CustomerID	SaleDate	Variety	SaleQuantity	SaleAmount
1	356W	February 29, 2012	Ginger	240	$1,980
3	356W	February 15, 2012	Anthurium	300	$1,050
5	356W	February 10, 2012	Heliconia	60	$720

For more information on CALL routines, see the SAS Help and Documentation.

7.8 Debugging Macro Errors

Many people find that writing macros is not that hard. Debugging them, however, is another matter. This section covers techniques to ease the debugging process.

Avoiding macro errors As much as possible, develop your program in standard SAS code first. Then, when it is bug-free, add the macro logic one feature at a time. Add your %MACRO and %MEND statements. When that's working, add your macro variables, one at a time, and so on, until your macro is complete and bug-free.

Quoting problems The macro processor doesn't resolve macros inside single quotation marks. To get around this, use double quotation marks whenever you refer to a macro or macro variable and you want SAS to resolve it. For example, below are two TITLE statements containing a macro variable named &MONTH. If the value of &MONTH is January, then SAS will substitute January in the title with the double quotation marks, but not the title with single quotation marks.

Original statement	Statement after resolution
`TITLE 'Report for &month';`	`TITLE 'Report for &month';`
`TITLE "Report for &month";`	`TITLE "Report for January";`

System options for debugging macros These five system options affect the kinds of messages SAS writes in your log. The default settings appear in bold.

MERROR | NOMERROR	When this option is on, SAS will issue a warning if you invoke a macro that SAS cannot find.
SERROR | NOSERROR	When this option is on, SAS will issue a warning if you use a macro variable that SAS cannot find.
MLOGIC | **NOMLOGIC**	When this option is on, SAS prints in your log details about the execution of macros.
MPRINT | **NOMPRINT**	When this option is on, SAS prints in your log the standard SAS code generated by macros.
SYMBOLGEN | **NOSYMBOLGEN**	When this option is on, SAS prints in your log the values of macro variables.

While you want the MERROR and SERROR options to be on at all times, you will probably want to turn on MLOGIC, MPRINT, and SYMBOLGEN one at a time and only while you are debugging since they tend to make your log hard to read. To turn them on (or off), use the OPTIONS statement, for example:

```
OPTIONS MPRINT NOSYMBOLGEN NOMLOGIC;
```

MERROR message If SAS has trouble finding a macro, and the MERROR option is on, then SAS will print this message:

```
WARNING: Apparent invocation of macro SAMPL not resolved.
```

Check for a misspelled macro name.

SERROR message If SAS has trouble resolving a macro variable in open code, and the SERROR option is on, then SAS will print this message:

```
WARNING: Apparent symbolic reference FLOWER not resolved.
```

Check for a misspelled macro variable name. If the name is spelled right, then the scope may be wrong. Check to see if you are using a local variable outside of its macro. See section 7.1 for definitions of local and global macro variables.

MLOGIC messages When the MLOGIC option is on, SAS prints messages in your log describing the actions of the macro processor. Here is a macro named %SAMPLE:

```
%MACRO sample(flowertype=);
   PROC PRINT DATA = flowersales;
      WHERE Variety = "&flowertype";
   RUN;
%MEND sample;
```

If you run %SAMPLE with the MLOGIC option, your log will look like this:

```
24   OPTIONS MLOGIC;
25   %sample(flowertype=Anthurium)
MLOGIC(SAMPLE):  Beginning execution.
MLOGIC(SAMPLE):  Parameter FLOWERTYPE has value Anthurium
MLOGIC(SAMPLE):  Ending execution.
```

MPRINT messages When the MPRINT option is on, SAS prints messages in your log showing the SAS statements generated by your macro. If you run %SAMPLE with the MPRINT option, your log will look like this:

```
36   OPTIONS MPRINT;
37   %sample(flowertype=Anthurium)
MPRINT(SAMPLE):   PROC PRINT DATA = flowersales;
MPRINT(SAMPLE):   WHERE Variety = "Anthurium";
MPRINT(SAMPLE):   RUN;
```

SYMBOLGEN messages When the SYMBOLGEN option is on, SAS prints messages in your log showing the value of each macro variable after resolution. If you run %SAMPLE with the SYMBOLGEN option, your log will look like this:

```
30   OPTIONS SYMBOLGEN;
31   %sample(flowertype=Anthurium)
SYMBOLGEN:  Macro variable FLOWERTYPE resolves to Anthurium
```

8 ▶

> "Graphs reveal discoveries
> as the bud unfolds the flower."

Henry D. Hubbard

From Graphic Presentation by Willard Cope Brinton, 1939.

CHAPTER 8

Visualizing Your Data

8.1 Concepts of ODS Graphics

ODS Graphics is designed to give you high-quality graphs with a minimum of effort. As you might expect, ODS Graphics is an extension of the Output Delivery System, but instead of creating tabular output, ODS Graphics creates graphs, and it produces them using the same destinations and styles as ODS tabular output. Starting with SAS 9.3, ODS Graphics is part of Base SAS, so you do not need to license any additional products.[1]

Using ODS Graphics in statistical procedures Over 80 statistical procedures have the ability to produce graphs using ODS Graphics. Included are procedures from Base SAS, SAS/STAT, SAS/ETS, and SAS/QC.[2] When you run these procedures, ODS Graphics will produce graphs that are specially designed for that type of anaylsis.

Starting with SAS 9.3, ODS Graphics is turned on by default in the SAS windowing environment in Microsoft Windows and UNIX. ODS Graphics is turned off by default when you run in batch mode or in other operating environments. To turn this feature on, insert this statement into your program before any statistical procedures:

```
ODS GRAPHICS ON;
```

Statistical procedures that support ODS Graphics will then create appropriate graphs.

You do not need to turn ODS Graphics off, but if you wish to turn it off (either to make your programs run faster, or simply because you do not want the graphs) use this statement:

```
ODS GRAPHICS OFF;
```

Note that ODS GRAPHICS is not a destination (like HTML or PDF). You open and close ODS destinations; you turn ODS GRAPHICS on or off.

Using ODS Graphics for stand-alone graphs ODS Graphics also includes a family of procedures designed to create stand-alone graphs (graphs that are not embedded in the output of a statistical procedure). The SGPLOT and SGPANEL procedures are two of these. Because these procedures always produce graphs, you do not need to specify the ODS GRAPHICS ON statement even in batch mode. However, there may still be times when you want to use this statement to specify graphics options.

The SGPLOT procedure creates single-celled graphs while SGPANEL can create multi-celled graphs based on classification variables. The various types of graphs fall into three general categories.

Category	Types of Graphs
X Y plots	band, bubble, ellipse, high-low, loess, needle, penalized B-spline, regression, scatter, series, step, and vector
Continuous Distributions	box, density, and histogram
Categorical Distributions	dot, bar, and line

Within a category, you can overlay multiple graphs as long as combining them makes sense. This chapter covers the most common types of graphs. Other graphs use similar syntax and options.

ODS destinations Starting with SAS 9.3, your graphs will be rendered, by default, in HTML for the SAS windowing environment on Microsoft Windows or UNIX. The traditional LISTING destination remains the default when you run in batch and in other operating environments. See chapter 5 for information about controlling destinations.

Saving graphs Also starting with SAS 9.3, graphs are written in your WORK library and will therefore be deleted when you exit SAS. This is good because it prevents your disks from becoming cluttered with old graphs. For information about how to save graphs, see section 8.12.

Styles for graphs ODS style templates control the overall appearance of your output. You can use the same style templates for graphs as for tabular output. However, some styles are better suited to statistical graphics than others. The following table lists styles that are recommended for statistical results.

Desired Output	Style Name	Default for Destination
Color	ANALYSIS	
	HTMLBLUE	HTML
	LISTING	LISTING (graphs only)
	PRINTER	PRINTER, PDF, PS
	RTF	RTF
	STATISTICAL	
Gray scale	JOURNAL	
Black and white	JOURNAL2	

You can specify a style for your graphs using the STYLE= option in the ODS statement for a destination. For example, to produce gray-scale graphics in the LISTING destination you would use this statement:

```
ODS LISTING STYLE = JOURNAL;
```

For the LISTING destination, the STYLE= option applies only to graphical output; tabular output is still rendered as text. Also keep in mind that every destination has a default style associated with it, so if you change the destination for a graph, its appearance may change too.

Viewing ODS Graphics When you produce ODS Graphics in the SAS windowing environment, the Results Viewer window generally opens displaying your results. However, when you use the LISTING destination, graphs are not automatically displayed. You can view any graph by double-clicking its graph icon in the Results window.[3]

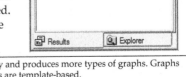

8.2 Creating Bar Charts

Bar charts show the distribution of a categorical variable where the length of each bar is proportional to the number of observations in that category. To create a chart with vertical bars, use a VBAR statement with this general form:

```
PROC SGPLOT;
    VBAR variable-name / options;
```

For horizontal bars, replace the keyword VBAR with HBAR. Possible options include

ALPHA = *n*	specifies the level for the confidence limits. The value of n must be between 0 (100% confidence) and 1 (0% confidence). The default is 0.05 (95% confidence limits).
BARWIDTH = *n*	sets the width of bars. Values range from 0.1 to 1 with a default of 0.8.
DATALABEL = *variable-name*	displays a label for each bar. If you specify a variable name, then values of that variable will be used. Otherwise, SAS will calculate appropriate values.
DISCRETEOFFSET = *n*	offsets bars from midpoints which is useful for overlaying bar charts. The value must be between –0.5 (left) and +0.5 (right). The default is 0 (no offset).
LIMITSTAT = *statistic*	specifies the type of limit lines to be shown. Possible values are CLM, STDDEV (standard deviation), or STDERR (standard error). This option cannot be used with the GROUP= option. You must specify a RESPONSE= option and STAT=MEAN.
MISSING	includes a bar for missing values.
GROUP = *variable-name*	specifies a variable used to group the data.
GROUPDISPLAY = *type*	specifies how to display grouped bars, either STACK (the default) or CLUSTER.
RESPONSE = *variable-name*	specifies a numeric variable to be summarized.
STAT = *statistic*	specifies a statistic, either FREQ, MEAN, or SUM. FREQ is the default if there is no response variable. SUM is the default when you specify a response variable.
TRANSPARENCY = *n*	specifies the degree of transparency for the bars. The value of n must be between 0 (the default) and 1, with 1 being completely transparent and 0 being completely opaque.

Example A chocolate manufacturer is considering whether to add four new varieties of chocolate to its line of products. The company asked volunteers to taste the new flavors. The data contain each person's age group (A for adult, C for child) followed by their favorite flavor (80%Cacao, Earl Grey, Ginger, or Pear). Notice that each line of data contains six responses.

```
A Pear A 80%Cacao A EarlGrey C 80%Cacao A Ginger C Pear
C 80%Cacao C Pear C Pear A EarlGrey A 80%Cacao C 80%Cacao
A Ginger A Pear C EarlGrey C 80%Cacao A 80%Cacao A EarlGrey
A 80%Cacao C Pear C Pear A 80%Cacao C Pear C 80%Cacao
```

The following program reads the raw data and creates a user-defined format. Then PROC SGPLOT creates a bar chart using the GROUP= and GROUPDISPLAY= options.

```
DATA chocolate;
   INFILE 'c:\MyRawData\Choc.dat';
   INPUT AgeGroup $ FavoriteFlavor $ @@;
RUN;
PROC FORMAT;
   VALUE $AgeGp 'A' = 'Adult' 'C' = 'Child';
RUN;
* Bar chart for favorite flavor;
PROC SGPLOT DATA = chocolate;
   VBAR FavoriteFlavor / GROUP = AgeGroup GROUPDISPLAY = CLUSTER;
   FORMAT AgeGroup $AgeGp.;
   LABEL FavoriteFlavor = 'Flavor of Chocolate';
   TITLE 'Favorite Chocolate Flavors by Age';
RUN;
```

This chart has clustered bars showing the number of respondents in each age group who chose each flavor. The LABEL statement replaced the name of the variable FavoriteFlavor with the words "Flavor of Chocolate" in the X axis label. The FORMAT statement replaced the data values (A and C) with more descriptive values (Adult and Child) in the legend.

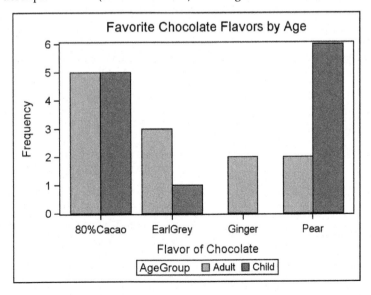

8.3 Creating Histograms and Density Curves

The bar charts in the preceding section show the distribution of categorical data. To show the distribution of continuous data, you can use histograms (or box plots which are described in the next section). In a histogram, the data are divided into discrete intervals called bins. Each bin is represented by a rectangle which makes histograms look similar to bar charts. However, bar charts typically have a gap between the bars while histograms do not.

Histograms To create a histogram, use a HISTOGRAM statement with this basic form:

```
PROC SGPLOT;
   HISTOGRAM variable-name / options;
```

Possible options include

BINSTART = *n*	specifies the midpoint for the first bin.
BINWIDTH = *n*	specifies the bin width (in units of the horizontal axis). SAS determines the number of bins. This option is ignored if you specify the NBINS= option.
NBINS = *n*	specifies the number of bins. SAS determines the bin width.
SCALE = *scaling-type*	specifies the scale for the vertical axis, either PERCENT (the default), COUNT, or PROPORTION.
SHOWBINS	places tick marks at the midpoints of the bins. By default, tick marks are placed at regular intervals based on minimum and maximum values.
TRANSPARENCY = *n*	specifies the degree of transparency for the histogram. The value of n must be between 0 (the default) and 1, with 1 being completely transparent and 0 being completely opaque.

Density curves You can also plot density curves for your data. The basic form of a DENSITY statement is

```
PROC SGPLOT;
   DENSITY variable-name / options;
```

Common options are

TYPE = *distribution-type*	specifies the type of distribution curve, either NORMAL (the default) or KERNEL.
TRANSPARENCY = *n*	specifies the degree of transparency for the density curve. The value of n must be between 0 (the default) and 1, with 1 being completely transparent and 0 being completely opaque.

The HISTOGRAM and DENSITY statements can be used together, but not with other types of graphs. Keep in mind that when you overlay graphs, the order of statements is important because the second graph will be drawn on top of the first and could hide it.

Example A fourth grade class has a competition to see who can read the most books in one month. For each student, the teacher records the student's name and the number of books read. Notice that each line of data includes six students.

```
Bella 4 Anthony  9 Joe 10 Chris 6 Beth 5 Daniel 2
David 7 Emily 7 Josh 7 Will 9 Olivia 7 Matt 8
Maddy 8 Sam 13  Jessica 6 Jose 6 Mia 12 Elliott 8
Tyler 15 Lauren 10 Cate 14 Ava 11 Mary 9 Eric 10
Megan 13 Michael 9 John 18 Alex 5 Cody 11 Amy 4
```

The DATA step below reads the raw data from a file named Reading.dat. Then an SGPLOT procedure creates a histogram for the number of books. The bins will have a width of two, the horizontal axis will have a tick mark at the center of each bin, and the vertical axis will show the count (in this case, the number of students). Two density distributions will be overlaid on the histogram: the normal distribution and the kernel density estimate.

```
DATA contest;
   INFILE 'c:\MyRawData\Reading.dat';
   INPUT Name $ NumberBooks @@;
RUN;
* Create histogram and density curves;
PROC SGPLOT DATA = contest;
   HISTOGRAM NumberBooks / BINWIDTH = 2 SHOWBINS SCALE = COUNT;
   DENSITY NumberBooks;
   DENSITY NumberBooks / TYPE = KERNEL;
   TITLE 'Reading Contest';
RUN;
```

Here are the results:

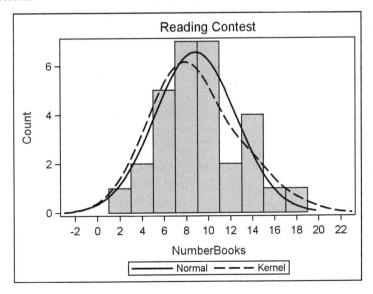

8.4 Creating Box Plots

Like histograms, box plots show the distribution of continuous data. This type of graph is also called a box-and-whisker plot because of the way it looks. Every part of a box plot tells you something about the distribution of your data.

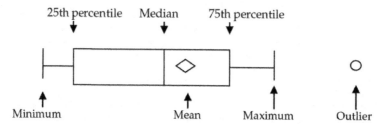

The ends of the box indicate the 25th and 75th pecentiles (also called the interquartile range). The line inside the box indicates the 50th percentile (the median), and the marker indicates the mean. By default the whiskers cannot be longer than 1.5 times the length of the box. Any points beyond the whiskers are considered outliers and are marked with circles. If you specify the EXTREME option, then the whiskers will extend the entire range.

To create a vertical box plot , use a VBOX statement like this:

```
PROC SGPLOT;
   VBOX variable-name / options;
```

For horizontal box plots, replace the keyword VBOX with HBOX. Possible options include

CATEGORY = variable-name	specifies a categorical variable. One box plot will be created for each value of this variable.
EXTREME	specifies that the whiskers should extend to the true minimum and maximum values so outliers will not be identified.
GROUP = variable-name	specifies a second categorical variable. One box plot will be created for each value of this variable within the categorical variable.
MISSING	includes a box for missing values for the group or category variable.
TRANSPARENCY = n	specifies the degree of transparency for the box plot. The value of n must be between 0 (the default) and 1, with 1 being completely transparent and 0 being completely opaque.

The VBOX and HBOX statements cannot be used with statements that create other types of plots.

Example A small town sponsors an annual bicycle criterium. That's a race where bicyclists go round and round a loop. The racers compete in three divisions: Youth, Adult, and Masters. The data include each bicyclist's division and the number of laps they completed in one hour. Notice that each line of data contains results for five competitors.

```
Adult    44 Adult    33 Youth    33 Masters 38 Adult    40
Masters 32 Youth    32 Youth    38 Youth    33 Adult    47
Masters 37 Masters 46 Youth    34 Adult    42 Youth    24
Masters 33 Adult    44 Youth    35 Adult    49 Adult    38
Adult    39 Adult    42 Adult    32 Youth    42 Youth    31
Masters 33 Adult    33 Masters 32 Youth    37 Masters 40
```

The DATA step below reads the raw data from a file named Criterium.dat. Then an SGPLOT procedure creates vertical box plots of the number of laps. The CATEGORY= option tells SAS to create a separate box plot for each division.

```
DATA bikerace;
   INFILE 'c:\MyRawData\Criterium.dat';
   INPUT Division $ NumberLaps @@;
RUN;
* Create box plot;
PROC SGPLOT DATA = bikerace;
   VBOX NumberLaps / CATEGORY = Division;
   TITLE 'Bicycle Criterium Results by Division';
RUN;
```

Here is the box plot showing the number of laps by division.

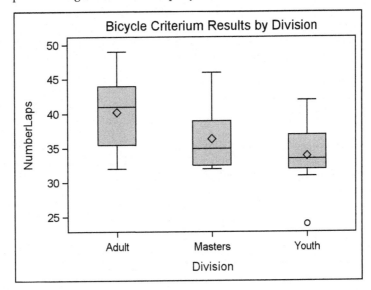

8.5 Creating Scatter Plots

Scatter plots are an effective way to show the relationship between two continuous variables. For experimental data, the independent variable is traditionally assigned to the horizontal axis while the dependent variable is assigned to the vertical axis. To create scatter plots, use the SCATTER statement like this:

```
PROC SGPLOT;
   SCATTER X=horizontal-variable Y=vertical-variable / options;
```

Possible options include

DATALABEL = *variable-name*	displays a label for each data point. If you specify a variable name, the values of that variable will be used as labels. If you do not specify a variable name, then the values of the Y variable will be used.
GROUP = *variable-name*	specifies a variable to be used for grouping data.
NOMISSINGGROUP	specifies that observations with missing values for the group variable should not be included.
TRANSPARENCY = *n*	specifies the degree of transparency for the markers. The value of n must be between 0 (the default) and 1, with 1 being completely transparent and 0 being completely opaque.

Example To illustrate the use of scatter plots, here are data about birds. For each species, there are four variables: name, type (S for songbirds or R for raptors), length in cm (from tip of beak to tip of tail), and wingspan in cm. Note that each line of data includes several birds.

```
Robin         S   28   41 Bald Eagle   R 102 244 Barn Owl    R   50 110
Osprey        R   66 180 Cardinal      S  23  31 Goldfinch   S   11  19
Golden Eagle  R 100 234 Crow           S  53 100 Magpie      S   60  60
Elf Owl       R   15  27 Condor        R 140 300
```

The following program reads the data and produces a scatter plot grouped by type. Since the values S and R are not very descriptive, PROC FORMAT is used to create a user-defined format that is then specified in a FORMAT statement in the SGPLOT procedure to change S to Songbirds and R to Raptors.

```
DATA wings;
   INFILE 'c:\MyRawData\Birds.dat';
   INPUT Name $12. Type $ Length Wingspan @@;
RUN;
* Plot Wingspan by Length;
PROC FORMAT;
   VALUE $birdtype
      'S' = 'Songbirds'
      'R' = 'Raptors';
RUN;
PROC SGPLOT DATA = wings;
   SCATTER X = Wingspan Y = Length / GROUP = Type;
   FORMAT Type $birdtype.;
   TITLE 'Comparison of Wingspan vs. Length';
RUN;
```

Here is the scatter plot.[4]

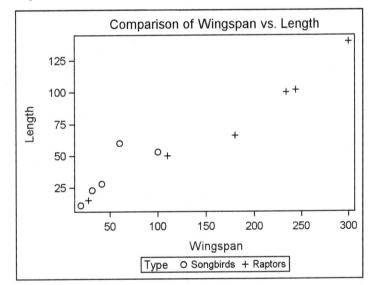

---

[4] If you create this plot using the default (HTMLBLUE) style template, the markers will be circles of different colors instead of circles and plus signs. For this example, the style template was changed to JOURNAL so that the markers would have different shapes. For information about how to change marker attributes or style templates, see sections 8.10 and 8.12.

8.6 Creating Series Plots

A series plot is similar to a scatter plot except that instead of marking each data point, SAS connects the data points with a line. Series plots make sense whenever data must be displayed in a particular order. Dates and times of any kind are good candidates for series plots. To create a series plot, use a SERIES statement with this basic form:

```
PROC SGPLOT;
    SERIES X=horizontal-variable Y=vertical-variable / options;
```

Possible options include

CURVELABEL = 'text-string'	adds a label for the curve. If you do not specify a text string, then SAS uses the label from the Y variable.
DATALABEL = variable-name	displays a label for each data point. If you specify a variable name, the values of that variable will be used as labels. If you do not specify a variable name, then the values of the Y variable will be used.
GROUP = variable-name	specifies a variable to be used for grouping the data. A separate line is created for each unique value of the grouping variable.
MARKERS	adds a marker for each data point.
NOMISSINGGROUP	specifies that observations with missing values for the group variable should not be included.
TRANSPARENCY = n	specifies the degree of transparency for plot line. The value of n must be between 0 (the default) and 1, with 1 being completely transparent and 0 being completely opaque.

Note that SAS will connect the points in the order in which they appear in the data set. To have the points connected properly, your data must be sorted by the horizontal variable. If your data are not already sorted, then use PROC SORT before plotting your data.

Example A technical writer collects data about her use of electricity for one day. Each hour she checks her meter and records the number of kilowatt hours used since the last reading. The data include the time (on a 24 hour clock) and the number of kilowatt hours. Note that each line of data contains six readings.

```
0 .22 1 .15 2 .17 3 .18 4 .19 5 .23
6 .5 7 .63 8 .61 9 .6 10 .48 11 .45
12 .44 13 .44 14 .39 15 .35 16 .42 17 .47
18 .7 19 .66 20 .7 21 .69 22 .6 23 .4
```

She could use a scatter plot to display these data, but since one of the variables is time, using a series plot makes sense. The following program reads the data from a raw data file named Hourly.dat and then creates a series plot of time versus kilowatt hours. The MARKERS option tells SAS to add a maker for each data point on the line.

```
DATA electricity;
    INFILE 'c:\MyRawData\Hourly.dat';
    INPUT Time kWh @@;
RUN;
* Plot temperatures by time;
PROC SGPLOT DATA = electricity;
    SERIES X = Time Y = kWh / MARKERS;
    TITLE 'Hourly Use of Electricity';
RUN;
```

The plot looks like this:

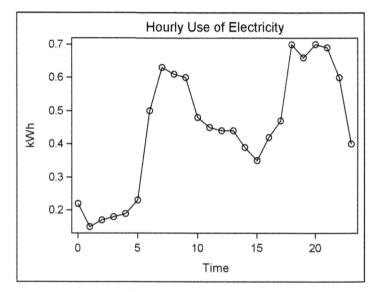

Note that the data did not need to be sorted because they were already ordered by the variable on the X axis (Time).

8.7 Creating Fitted Curves

Scatter plots show the relationship between two variables. One way to explore that relationship further is to plot a fitted curve. The SGPLOT procedure produces several kinds of fitted curves including regression lines, loess curves, and penalized B-spline curves. To create any of these types of fitted curves, use a statement with this general form:

```
PROC SGPLOT;
   statement-name X=horizontal-variable Y=vertical-variable / options;
```

Where the *statement-name* can be

REG	regression line or curve
LOESS	loess curve
PBSPLINE	penalized B-spline curve

Options for fitted curves include

ALPHA = *n*	specifies the level for the confidence limits. The value of n must be between 0 (100% confidence) and 1 (0% confidence). The default is 0.05 (95% confidence limits).
CLI	adds prediction limits for individual predicted values (for REG and PBSPLINE only).
CLM	adds confidence limits for mean predicted values.
CURVELABEL = *'text-string'*	adds a label for the curve. If you do not specify a text string, then SAS uses the label from the Y variable.
GROUP = *variable-name*	specifies a variable to be used for grouping the data. A separate line is created for each unique value of the grouping variable.
NOLEGCLI	removes legend entry for CLI band.
NOLEGCLM	removes legend entry for CLM band.
NOLEGFIT	removes legend entry for fit curve.
NOMARKERS	removes markers for data points.
CLMTRANSPARENCY = *n*	specifies the degree of transparency for the confidence limits. The value of n must be between 0 (the default) and 1, with 1 being completely transparent and 0 being completely opaque.

Each of the types of fitted curves offers additional options for controlling the parameters for the interpolation. See the SAS Help and Documentation for more information.

Example The following data show the winning race times for the men's 1500 meter run at the Olympics. The Olympic year is followed by the time rounded to the nearest second. Note that each line of data contains several observations.

```
1896 273 1900 246 1904 245 1906 252 1908 243 1912 237 1920 242
1924 234 1928 233 1932 231 1936 228 1948 230 1952 225 1956 221
1960 216 1964 218 1968 215 1972 216 1976 219 1980 218 1984 213
1988 216 1992 220 1996 216 2000 212 2004 214 2008 213 2012 215
```

This program reads the data and overlays two fitted curves for the race times: a loess plot and a regression plot. The CLM option on the LOESS statement generates the 95% confidence limit band for the mean predicted values, while the NOLEGCLM option tells SAS not to include the confidence limit band in the legend.

```
DATA Olympic1500;
    INFILE 'C:\MyRawData\Olympic1500.dat';
    INPUT Year Men @@;
RUN;
PROC SGPLOT DATA = Olympic1500;
    LOESS X = Year Y = Men / NOMARKERS CLM NOLEGCLM;
    REG X = Year Y = Men;
    LABEL Men = 'Time in Seconds';
    TITLE "Olympic Times for Men's 1500 Meter Run";
RUN;
```

Here is the result:

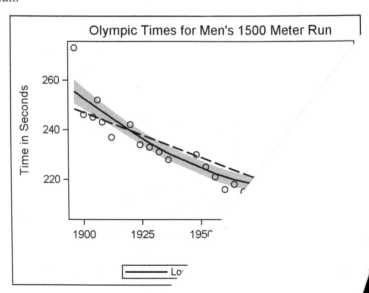

This graph shows the data points with both ⟨
NOMARKERS option was included on th⟨
The confidence limits for mean predicted v⟨
surrounding the loess line.

8.8 ▶ Controlling Axes and Reference Lines

Statements like VBAR and LOESS tell SAS the type of graph to create. However, the SGPLOT procedure also has supporting statements that allow you to control other features of your graph such as axes and reference lines.

Axes To specify options for the horizontal axis, use a statement with this general form:

```
PROC SGPLOT;
   XAXIS options;
```

For the vertical axis, replace the keyword XAXIS with YAXIS . Options include

GRID	creates a line at each tick mark on the axis.
LABEL = 'text-string'	specifies a text string enclosed in quotes to be used as the label for the axis. You can also use an ordinary LABEL statement, but a label specified using an AXIS statement will override one from any other source. If there is no variable label, then SAS uses the variable name.
TYPE = axis-type	specifies the type of axis. DISCRETE is the default for character variables. LINEAR is the default for numeric variables. TIME is the default for variables that have date, time, or datetime formats associated with them. LOG specifies a logarithmic scale.
VALUES = (values-list)	specifies values for tick marks on axes. Values must be enclosed in parentheses, and can be specified either as a list (0 5 10 15 20) or a range (0 TO 20 BY 5).

Reference lines Adding reference lines to a graph shows which points are above or below important levels. To add a horizontal or vertical reference line, use a REFLINE statement.[5]

```
PROC SGPLOT;
   REFLINE values / options;
```

The values are the points at which the reference lines should be drawn. Values can be specified either as a list, 0 5 10 15 20, or a range, 0 TO 20 BY 5.[6] Options include

AXIS = axis	specifies the axis that contains the reference line values, either X or Y. The default is Y for horizontal lines.
LABEL = (label-list)	specifies one or more text strings (each enclosed in quotes and separated by spaces) to be used as labels for the reference lines.
TRANSPARENCY = n	specifies the degree of transparency for the reference line. The value of n must be between 0 (the default) and 1, with 1 being completely transparent and 0 being completely opaque.

If the REFLINE statement comes before any plot statements, then the line will be drawn behind the plot elements. If it comes afterwards, then the line will be drawn in front of the plot elements.

Example This example compares average high temperatures in three cities: International Falls, Minnesota; Raleigh, North Carolina; and Yuma, Arizona. The variables are month and the high temperatures for each city. Temperatures are in Fahrenheit. There are three months in each line.

```
1  12.2 50.7  68.5   2  20.1 54.5   74.1   3  32.4 63.7  79.0
4  49.6 72.7  86.7   5  64.4 79.7   94.1   6  73.0 85.8 103.1
7  78.1 88.7 106.9   8  75.6 87.4  105.6   9  64.0 82.6 101.5
10 52.2 72.9  91.0  11  32.5 63.9   77.5  12  17.8 54.1  68.9
```

To compare the three cities, there are three SERIES statements, one for each city. Reference lines will be drawn at 32 and 75 degrees. In this data set, the variable Month is simply a number (1–12) rather than a SAS date value. In order to avoid having values of month such as 3.5, the axis type has been set to DISCRETE using an XAXIS statement. A YAXIS statement specifies an axis label.

```
DATA cities;
   INFILE 'c:\MyRawData\ThreeCities.dat';
   INPUT Month IntFalls Raleigh Yuma @@;
RUN;
* Plot average high and low temperatures by city;
PROC SGPLOT DATA = cities;
   SERIES X = Month Y = IntFalls;
   SERIES X = Month Y = Raleigh;
   SERIES X = Month Y = Yuma;
   REFLINE 32 75 / LABEL = ('32 degrees' '75 degrees') TRANSPARENCY = 0.5;
   XAXIS TYPE = DISCRETE;
   YAXIS LABEL = 'Average High Temperature (F)';
   TITLE 'Temperatures for International Falls, Raleigh, and Yuma';
RUN;
```

The plot looks like this.

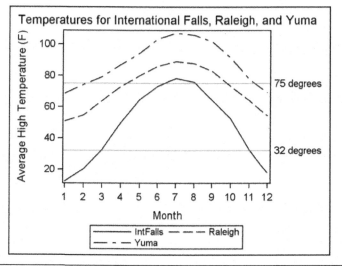

---

[5] To draw sloped lines, use the LINEPARM statement. See the SAS Help and Documentation for more information.

[6] Instead of values, you can also specify a variable name, and SAS will draw reference lines for each value of that variable.

8.9 Controlling Legends and Insets

The SGPLOT and SGPANEL procedures generate legends automatically for your plots when appropriate. This is great because then you don't have to think about them. But sometimes you may want to remove the legend, or move it to a different place, or add a note or comment of your own.

Changing legends You can change many aspects of a legend using the KEYLEGEND statement with this general form.[7]

```
KEYLEGEND / options;
```

Options for legends include

ACROSS = *n*	specifies the number of columns in the legend.
DOWN = *n*	specifies the number of rows in the legend.
LOCATION = *value*	specifies the location for the legend, either INSIDE the axis area or OUTSIDE (the default).
NOBORDER	removes the border.
POSITION = *value*	specifies the position of the legend, either TOP, TOPLEFT, TOPRIGHT, BOTTOM (the default), BOTTOMLEFT, BOTTOMRIGHT, LEFT, or RIGHT.

Removing legends Sometimes you don't want a legend. To remove it, simply add the NOAUTOLEGEND to the PROC SGPLOT statement.

```
PROC SGPLOT DATA = data-set NOAUTOLEGEND;
```

If you have both a KEYLEGEND statement and the NOAUTOLEGEND option, then the option will be ignored.

Adding Insets To place text in the axis area use an INSET statement with this general form.[8]

```
INSET 'text-string-1' 'text-string-2' ... 'text-string-n' / options;
```

If you have more than one text string, then the strings will be placed one below the other. Options for insets include

BORDER	adds a border.
POSITION = *value*	specifies the position of the inset, either TOP, TOPLEFT, TOPRIGHT, BOTTOM (the default), BOTTOMLEFT, BOTTOMRIGHT, LEFT, or RIGHT.

Example The following data show the winning times in seconds for the men's 1500 meter run at the Olympics along with the world record time for each year. The Olympic year is followed by the Olympic time and world record time rounded to the nearest second. Each line contains several observations.

```
1896 273 250 1900 246 246 1904 245 245 1906 252 245 1908 243 240
1912 237 236 1920 242 235 1924 234 233 1928 233 231 1932 231 229
1936 229 229 1948 230 223 1952 225 223 1956 221 221 1960 216 216
1964 218 216 1968 215 213 1972 216 213 1976 219 212 1980 218 211
1984 213 211 1988 216 209 1992 220 209 1996 216 207 2000 212 206
2004 214 206 2008 213 206 2012 215 206
```

In this program, a SCATTER statement plots the Olympic time for each year. Then a SERIES statement plots the world record time for each year. The KEYLEGEND statement specifies that the legend should be located inside the graph area in the top right corner. The INSET statement places a note in the bottom left corner of the graph.

```
DATA Olympic1500;
   INFILE 'c:\MyRawData\OlympicWithWR1500.dat';
   INPUT Year OlympicTime WorldRecord @@;
RUN;
PROC SGPLOT DATA = Olympic1500;
   SCATTER X = Year Y = OlympicTime;
   SERIES X = Year Y = WorldRecord;
   KEYLEGEND / LOCATION = INSIDE POSITION = TOPRIGHT;
   INSET 'Olympics not held in' '1940 and 1944' / POSITION = BOTTOMLEFT;
   YAXIS LABEL = 'Time in Seconds';
   TITLE "Times for Men's 1500 Meter Run";
RUN;
```

Here is the output.

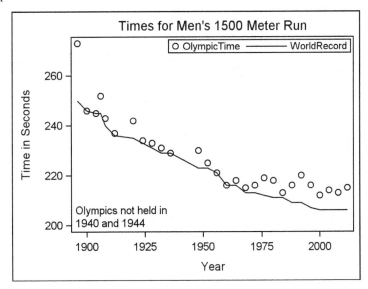

---

[7] If you have multiple plot statements, you can use multiple KEYLEGEND statements to control each legend independently. To do this, use a NAME= option in your plot and KEYLEGEND statements. See the SAS Help and Documentation for details.

[8] There are other ways to add text to a graph. You can make one-time changes using the ODS Graphics Editor, or you can use an annotation data set with the SGANNO= option in your program. See the SAS Help and Documentation for more information.

8.10 Customizing Graph Attributes

When you create graphs, you want them to be attractive and easy to read. That's why SAS has style templates that have been designed specifically for use with graphs (listed in section 8.1). Still there may be times when you want stars instead of circles, or thicker lines, or a different color. Fortunately, the SGPLOT procedure includes options for controlling graph attributes. [9]

To use these options, put them after a slash at the end of a basic plot statement. For example,

```
PROC SGPLOT;
   SCATTER X = Score Y = HoursOfStudy / MARKERATTRS = (SYMBOL = STAR);
```

There are many options for controlling graph attributes. Some common ones are

FILLATTRS = (*attribute* = *value*) — specifies the appearance of a filled area. The only attribute is COLOR=.

LABELATTRS = (*attribute* = *value*) — specifies the appearance of axis labels. Attributes include COLOR=, SIZE=, STYLE=, and WEIGHT=.

LINEATTRS = (*attribute* = *value*) — specifies the appearance of a line. Attributes are COLOR=, PATTERN=, and THICKNESS=.

MARKERATTRS = (*attribute* = *value*) — specifies the appearance of a marker. Attributes are COLOR=, SIZE=, and SYMBOL=.

VALUEATTRS = (*attribute* = *value*) — specifies the appearance of axis tick labels. Attributes include COLOR=, SIZE=, STYLE=, and WEIGHT=.

Each attribute has many possible values. Here are just a few:

Attribute	Possible Values
COLOR=	RGB notation such as #FF0000 (red) or named values such as RED, plus many others
PATTERN=	SOLID, DASH, SHORTDASH, LONGDASH, DOT, DASHDASHDOT, or DASHDOTDOT
SIZE=	numbers with the units CM, IN, MM, PCT, PT, or PX (the default)
STYLE=	ITALIC or NORMAL (the default)
SYMBOL=	CIRCLE, CIRCLEFILLED, DIAMOND, DIAMONDFILLED, PLUS, SQUARE, SQUAREFILLED, STAR, STARFILLED, TRIANGLE, or TRIANGLEFILLED
THICKNESS=	numbers with the units CM, IN, MM, PCT, PT, or PX (the default)
WEIGHT=	BOLD or NORMAL

Of course, not all types of plots support all graph attributes. For example, you cannot use FILLATTRS= with a scatter plot because scatter plots don't have any filled areas. There are additional graph attributes. For a complete list, check the SAS Help and Documentation.

Example The following data show the winning race times for the men's 1500 meter run at the Olympics along with the world record time for each year. The Olympic year is followed by the Olympic time and world record time in seconds. Each line contains several observations.

```
1896 273 250 1900 246 246 1904 245 245 1906 252 245 1908 243 240
1912 237 236 1920 242 235 1924 234 233 1928 233 231 1932 231 229
1936 229 229 1948 230 223 1952 225 223 1956 221 221 1960 216 216
1964 218 216 1968 215 213 1972 216 213 1976 219 212 1980 218 211
1984 213 211 1988 216 209 1992 220 209 1996 216 207 2000 212 206
2004 214 206 2008 213 206 2012 215 206
```

Here is the program that reads the data and produces two plots. First a SCATTER statement plots the Olympic times using a filled circle 2mm in size. Then a SERIES statement plots the world record times with a line that is 2mm thick and 75% transparent. The axis labels and title are bold.

```
DATA Olympic1500;
   INFILE 'c:\MyRawData\OlympicWithWR1500.dat';
   INPUT Year OlympicTime WorldRecord @@;
RUN;
PROC SGPLOT DATA = Olympic1500;
   SCATTER X = Year Y = OlympicTime /
      MARKERATTRS = (SYMBOL = CIRCLEFILLED SIZE = 2MM);
   SERIES X = Year Y = WorldRecord /
      LINEATTRS = (THICKNESS = 2MM) TRANSPARENCY = .75;
   XAXIS LABELATTRS = (WEIGHT = BOLD);
   YAXIS LABEL = 'Time in Seconds' LABELATTRS = (WEIGHT = BOLD);
   TITLE BOLD "Times for Men's 1500 Meter Run";
RUN;
```

Here is the output.

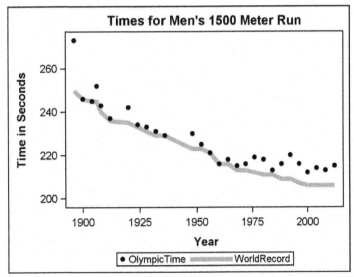

---

[9] You can also use the ODS Graphics Editor to make one-time changes. See the SAS Help and Documentation for details.

8.11 Creating Paneled Graphs

The SGPANEL procedure is a close cousin of the SGPLOT procedure. The SGPANEL procedure produces nearly all the same types of graphs as the SGPLOT procedure, but while SGPLOT produces single-celled graphs, SGPANEL can produce multi-celled graphs. PROC SGPANEL produces a separate cell for each combination of values of the classifcation variables that you specify. Each of those cells uses the same variables on their X and Y axes.[10]

The syntax for PROC SGPANEL is almost identical to PROC SGPLOT, so it is easy to convert one to the other by making just a couple changes to your code. You simply replace the keyword SGPLOT with SGPANEL, and add a PANELBY statement like this:

```
PROC SGPANEL;
   PANELBY variable-list / options;
   plot-statement;
```

The PANELBY statement must appear before any statements that create plots. Possible options include

COLUMNS = *n*	specifies the number of columns in the panel.
MISSING	specifies that observations with missing values for the PANELBY variable should be included.
NOVARNAME	removes the variable name from cell headings.
ROWS = *n*	specifies the number of rows in the panel.
SPACING = *n*	specifies the number of pixels between rows and columns in the panel. The default is 0.
UNISCALE = *value*	specifies which axes will share the same range of values. Possible values are COLUMN, ROW, and ALL (the default).

Instead of XAXIS and YAXIS statements, the SGPANEL procedure uses COLAXIS and ROWAXIS statements to control axes. See section 8.8 for axis options.

Example To illustrate a paneled graph, here are data about birds. For each species, there are four variables: name, type (S for songbirds or R for raptors), length in cm (from tip of beak to tip of tail), and wingspan in cm. Note that each line of data includes several birds.

```
Robin         S   28  41 Bald Eagle  R 102 244 Barn Owl   R   50 110
Osprey        R   66 180 Cardinal    S   23  31 Goldfinch  S   11  19
Golden Eagle  R 100 234 Crow         S   53 100 Magpie     S   60  60
Elf Owl       R   15  27 Condor       R 140 300
```

The following program produces a paneled plot. This plot is similar to the grouped plot shown in section 8.5. In that graph, data for songbirds and raptors are overlaid in a single cell. In this example, the two groups are plotted in separate cells. The NOVARNAME option removes the word "Type=" from the column headings, and the SPACING= option inserts a little space between the two cells. This example also uses PROC FORMAT to create a user-defined format for the variable Type so that the column headings are words instead of the coded values R and S.

```
DATA wings;
    INFILE 'c:\MyRawData\Birds.dat';
    INPUT Name $12. Type $ Length Wingspan @@;
RUN;
* Plot Wingspan by Length;
PROC FORMAT;
    VALUE $birdtype
        'S' = 'Songbirds'
        'R' = 'Raptors';
RUN;
PROC SGPANEL DATA = wings;
   PANELBY Type / NOVARNAME SPACING = 5;
   SCATTER X = Wingspan Y = Length;
    FORMAT Type $birdtype.;
    TITLE 'Comparison of Wingspan vs. Length';
RUN;
```

Here are the results.

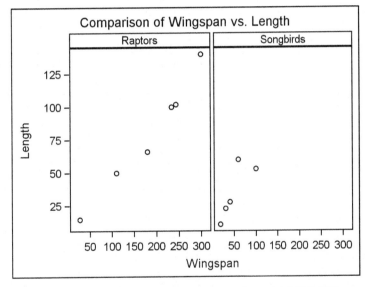

Note that you could have used a standard BY statement with PROC SGPLOT instead of a PANELBY statement with PROC SGPANEL, but then SAS would have produced two completely separate graphs (one for raptors and another for songbirds) instead of two cells within a single graph. Also, when you use a BY statement, the data must be pre-sorted by the values of the BY variables, but when you use a PANELBY statement, the data do not need to be sorted.

---

[10] To produce a paneled plot with cells that have different axes, use the SGSCATTER procedure. The SGSCATTER procedure uses different syntax than the SGPLOT and SGPANEL procedures. For more information, see the SAS Help and Documentation.

8.12 Specifying Image Properties and Saving Graphics Output

If you are writing a paper or creating a presentation, you may need to access individual graphs. In the Windows operating environment, you can simply copy and paste images when you view them in SAS. Sometimes that may be all you need. However, at other times you may wish to specify the properties of your graphs or save them in files for later use.

Specifying properties of images To specify properties for your images, use the ODS GRAPHICS statement with this general form:

```
ODS GRAPHICS / options;
```

Options include

`HEIGHT = n`	specifies the image height in CM, IN, MM, PT, or PX.
`IMAGENAME = 'filename'`	specifies the base image filename. The default name for an image file is the name of its ODS output object. See section 5.2 for a discussion of output objects.
`OUTPUTFMT = file-type`	specifies the graph format. The default varies by destination. Possible values include BMP, GIF, JPEG, PDF, PNG, PS, SVG, TIFF, and many others.
`RESET`	resets options to their defaults.
`WIDTH = n`	specifies the image width in CM, IN, MM, PT, or PX.

In most cases, the default size for graphs is 640 pixels wide by 480 pixels high. If you specify only one dimension (width but not height, or vice versa), then SAS will adjust the other dimension to maintain a default aspect ratio of 4:3.

When you save image files, SAS will append numerals to the end of the image name. For example, if you specify an image name of Final, then your files will be named Final, Final1, Final2, and so on. If you rerun your code, SAS will, by default, continue counting so that the new files will not overwrite the old. Specifying the RESET option before the IMAGENAME= option tells SAS to start over each time.

Saving graphical output For some destinations (including PDF and RTF), graphs and tabular output are integrated together in a single file. For other destinations (including LISTING and HTML), graphs are saved separately from tabular output. The option you use to save graphs depends on whether graphs are separate or integrated. But either way, you use an ODS destination statement with this general form:

```
ODS destination-name options;
```

where *destination-name* is your ODS destination such as HTML, LISTING, PDF, or RTF. Options include

`FILE = 'path/filename'`	specifies a path and filename for saving output images from the PDF and RTF destinations. Images will be saved in a single file along with tabular output.

`GPATH = 'path'`	specifies a path for saving output images from the LISTING and HTML destinations. Images will be saved in individual files.
`DPI = n`	specifies the image resolution for the PDF destination. The default is 200.
`IMAGE_DPI = n`	specifies image resolution for the HTML, LISTING, and RTF destinations. The default is 100.
`STYLE = style-name`	specifies a style template. See section 8.1 for a list of styles.

LISTING is generally a good destination for capturing individual graphs since it offers the most image formats and saves images in separate files. This statement would save ODS Graphics images in individual files in a folder named MyGraphics on the C drive (Windows) using the STATISTICAL style and 300 dots per inch:

```
ODS LISTING GPATH = 'c:\MyGraphics' STYLE = STATISTICAL IMAGE_DPI = 300;
```

Example Here again are data about birds. For each species, there are four variables: name, type (S for songbirds or R for raptors), length in cm (from tip of beak to tip of tail), and wingspan in cm. Note that each line of data includes several birds.

```
Robin        S  28  41 Bald Eagle   R 102 244 Barn Owl   R  50 110
Osprey       R  66 180 Cardinal     S  23  31 Goldfinch  S  11  19
Golden Eagle R 100 234 Crow         S  53 100 Magpie     S  60  60
Elf Owl      R  15  27 Condor       R 140 300
```

The following program produces a scatter plot, sends it to the ODS LISTING destination, saves the graph output, and uses options to control the style, image name, format, height, and width.

```
DATA wings;
   INFILE 'c:\MyRawData\Birds.dat';
   INPUT Name $12. Type $ Length Wingspan @@;
RUN;
* Plot Wingspan by Length;
ODS LISTING GPATH =
 'c:\MyGraphs' STYLE =
JOURNAL;
ODS GRAPHICS / RESET
   IMAGENAME = 'BirdGraph'
   OUTPUTFMT = BMP
   HEIGHT = 2IN WIDTH = 3IN;
PROC SGPLOT DATA = wings;
   SCATTER X =
   Wingspan Y = Length;
   TITLE 'Comparison of '
      'Wingspan vs. Length';
RUN;
```

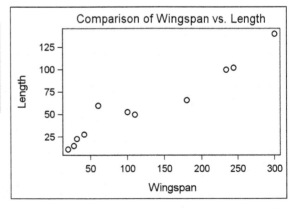

9 ▶

"33⅓% of the mice used in the experiment were cured by the test drug; 33⅓% of the test population were unaffected by the drug and remained in a moribund condition; the third mouse got away."

ERWIN NETER

From "How to Write a Scientific Paper" by Robert A. Day, ASM News, vol. 41, no. 7, pp 486-494, July 1975. Reprinted by permission of publisher and author. Also appears in *How to Write and Publish a Scientific Paper* 4th edition by Robert A. Day, copyright 1994 by Oryx Press.

CHAPTER 9

Using Basic Statistical Procedures

9.1 Examining the Distribution of Data with PROC UNIVARIATE

When you are doing statistical analysis, you usually have a goal in mind, a question you are trying to answer, or a hypotheses you want to test. But before you jump into statistical tests, it is a good idea to pause and do a little exploration. A good procedure to use at this point is PROC UNIVARIATE.

PROC UNIVARIATE, which is part of Base SAS software, produces statistics and graphs describing the distribution of a single variable. The statistics include the mean, median, mode, standard deviation, skewness, and kurtosis.

Using PROC UNIVARIATE is fairly simple. After the PROC statement, you specify one or more numeric variables in a VAR statement:

```
PROC UNIVARIATE;
   VAR variable-list;
```

Without a VAR statement, SAS will calculate statistics for all numeric variables in your data set. You can specify other options in the PROC statement, if you wish, such as NORMAL which produces tests of normality:

```
PROC UNIVARIATE NORMAL;
```

Example The following data consist of test scores from a statistics class. Each line contains scores for 10 students.

```
56 78 84 73 90 44 76 87 92 75
85 67 90 84 74 64 73 78 69 56
87 73 100 54 81 78 69 64 73 65
```

This program reads the data from a file called Scores.dat and then runs PROC UNIVARIATE:

```
DATA class;
   INFILE 'c:\MyRawData\Scores.dat';
   INPUT Score @@;
RUN;
PROC UNIVARIATE DATA = class;
   VAR Score;
   TITLE;
RUN;
```

The output appears on the next page. The output starts with basic information about your distribution: number of observations (N), mean, and standard deviation. Skewness indicates how asymmetrical the distribution is (whether it is more spread out on one side), while kurtosis indicates how flat or peaked the distribution is. The normal distribution has values of 0 for both skewness and kurtosis.[1] Other sections of the output contain three measures of central tendency: mean, median, and mode; tests of the hypothesis that the population mean is 0; quantiles; and extreme observations (in case you have outliers).

The UNIVARIATE Procedure
Variable: Score

Moments			
N	30	Sum Weights	30
Mean	74.6333333	Sum Observations	2239
Std Deviation	12.5848385	Variance	158.378161
Skewness	-0.3495061	Kurtosis	0.10385765
Uncorrected SS	171697	Corrected SS	4592.96667
Coeff Variation	16.8622222	Std Error Mean	2.29766665

Basic Statistical Measures			
Location		Variability	
Mean	74.63333	Std Deviation	12.58484
Median	74.50000	Variance	158.37816
Mode	73.00000	Range	56.00000
		Interquartile Range	17.00000

Tests for Location: Mu0=0				
Test		Statistic	p Value	
Student's t	t	32.48223	Pr > |t|	<.0001
Sign	M	15	Pr >= |M|	<.0001
Signed Rank	S	232.5	Pr >= |S|	<.0001

Quantiles (Definition 5)	
Quantile	Estimate
100% Max	100.0
99%	100.0
95%	92.0
90%	90.0
75% Q3	84.0
50% Median	74.5
25% Q1	67.0
10%	56.0
5%	54.0
1%	44.0
0% Min	44.0

Extreme Observations			
Lowest		Highest	
Value	Obs	Value	Obs
44	6	87	21
54	24	90	5
56	20	90	13
56	1	92	9
64	28	100	23

---

[1] There are two formulas for kurtosis. SAS software uses the formula that has a value of 0 for a normal distribution. For details about the formula that SAS uses to compute kurtosis, see the SAS Help and Documentation.

9.2 Creating Statistical Graphics with PROC UNIVARIATE

The UNIVARIATE procedure can produce several graphs that are useful for data exploration. For example, histograms are a good way to visualize the distribution of a variable, while probability and quantile-quantile plots can show how the data compare to theoretical distributions. To produce these graphs, include the desired plot request statement. Here is the general form of PROC UNIVARIATE with plot requests:

```
PROC UNIVARIATE;
   VAR variable-list;
   Plot-request variable-list / options;
RUN;
```

Plot requests The following graphs can be created with PROC UNIVARIATE:

CDFPLOT	requests a cumulative distribution function plot.
HISTOGRAM	requests a histogram.
PPPLOT	requests a probability-probability plot.
PROBPLOT	requests a probability plot.
QQPLOT	requests a quantile-quantile plot.

If no variable list is specified, then plots will be produced for all variables in the VAR statement. If there is no VAR statement or variable list, then plots will be produced for all numeric variables.

Plot options The CDFPLOT and HISTOGRAM plots show the distribution of the specified variable. To overlay a curve showing a standard distribution, specify the desired distribution with a plot option. Available distributions options include: BETA, EXPONENTIAL, GAMMA, LOGNORMAL, NORMAL, and WEIBULL. The PPPLOT, PROBPLOT, and QQPLOT statements use the normal distribution as the default. If you would like to use a different distribution, specify it with a plot option. For example, to create a probability plot of the variable Score using the exponential distribution, use the following:

```
PROBPLOT Score / EXPONENTIAL;
```

Example The following data from the previous section consist of test scores from a statistics class. Each line contains scores for 10 students.

```
56 78 84 73 90 44 76 87 92 75
85 67 90 84 74 64 73 78 69 56
87 73 100 54 81 78 69 64 73 65
```

The following program reads the data and creates a histogram of the Score variable with the normal distribution overlaid, and a probability plot using the normal distribution:

```
DATA class;
   INFILE 'c:\MyRawData\Scores.dat';
   INPUT Score @@;
RUN;
```

```
PROC UNIVARIATE DATA = class;
   VAR Score;
   HISTOGRAM Score / NORMAL;
   PROBPLOT Score;
   TITLE;
RUN;
```

Here are the two plots: a histogram and a probability plot. (The NORMAL option on the HISTOGRAM statement produces additional tabular results that are not shown.) The relatively linear pattern formed by the points in the probability plot indicate that the data are closely matched to the normal distribution.

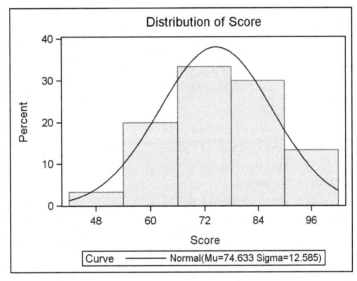

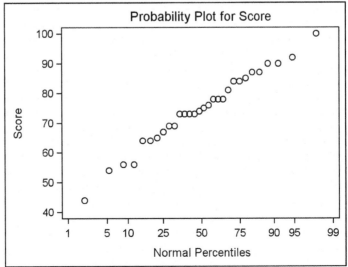

9.3 Producing Statistics with PROC MEANS

Most of the descriptive statistics that you produce with PROC UNIVARIATE you can also produce with PROC MEANS. UNIVARIATE is useful when you want an in-depth statistical analysis of the data distribution. But if you know you want only a few statistics, then MEANS is a better way to go. With MEANS you can ask for just the statistics you want. The MEANS procedure does not produce any ODS Graphics.

The MEANS procedure requires only one statement:

```
PROC MEANS statistic-keywords;
```

If you do not include any statistic keywords, then MEANS will produce the mean, the number of non-missing values, the standard deviation, the minimum value, and the maximum value for each numeric variable. The following table shows statistics you can request. (Some statistics have two names; the alternate name is shown in parentheses.) If you add any statistic keywords in the PROC MEANS statement, then MEANS will no longer produce the default statistics—you must request them.

CLM	two-sided confidence limits	RANGE	the range
CSS	corrected sum of squares	SKEWNESS	skewness
CV	coefficient of variaton	STDDEV	standard deviation
KURTOSIS	kurtosis	STDERR	standard error of the mean
LCLM	lower confidence limit	SUM	the sum
MAX	maximum value	SUMWGT	sum of weighted variables
MEAN	mean	UCLM	upper confidence limit
MIN	minimum value	USS	uncorrected sum of squares variance
MODE	mode	VAR	variance
N	number of non-missing values	PROBT	probability for Student's *t*
NMISS	number of missing values	T	Student's *t*
MEDIAN(P50)	median	Q3(P75)	75% quantile
Q1(P25)	25% quantile	P5	5% quantile
P1	1% quantile	P90	90% quantile
P10	10% quantile	P99	99% quantile
P95	95% quantile		

Confidence limits The default confidence level for the confidence limits is .05 or 95%. If you want a different confidence level, then request it with the ALPHA= option in the PROC MEANS statement. For example, if you want 90% confidence limits, then specify ALPHA=.10 along with the CLM option. Then the PROC MEANS statement would look like this:

```
PROC MEANS ALPHA = .10 CLM;
```

VAR statement By default MEANS will produce statistics for all numeric variables in your data set. If you do not want all the variables, then specify the ones you want in the VAR statement. Here is the general form of the MEANS procedure with the VAR statement:

```
PROC MEANS options;
   VAR variable-list;
```

Example Your friend is an aspiring author of children's books. To increase her chances of getting her books published, she wants to know how many pages her books should have. At the local library, she counts the number of pages in a random selection of children's picture books. Here are the data:

```
34 30 29 32 52 25 24 27 31 29
24 26 30 30 30 29 21 30 25 28
28 28 29 38 28 29 24 24 29 31
30 27 45 30 22 16 29 14 16 29
32 20 20 15 28 28 29 31 29 36
```

To determine the average number of pages in children's picture books, use the MEANS procedure. PROC MEANS can also produce the median number of pages as well as the 90% confidence limits. Here is the program that will read the data and produce the desired statistics:

```
DATA booklengths;
   INFILE 'c:\MyRawData\Picbooks.dat';
   INPUT NumberOfPages @@;
RUN;
*Produce summary statistics;
PROC MEANS DATA = booklengths N MEAN MEDIAN CLM ALPHA = .10;
   TITLE 'Summary of Picture Book Lengths';
RUN;
```

Here are the results of the MEANS procedure:

Summary of Picture Book Lengths
The MEANS Procedure

Analysis Variable : NumberOfPages				
N	Mean	Median	Lower 90% CL for Mean	Upper 90% CL for Mean
50	28.0000000	29.0000000	26.4419136	29.5580864

The average number of pages in the children's books sampled was 28. The median value of 29 says that half the books sampled had 29 pages or fewer. The confidence limits tell us that we are 90% certain that the true population mean (all children's picture books) falls between 26.44 and 29.56 pages. From this analysis your friend concludes that she should make her books between 26 and 30 pages long to maximize her chances of getting published (of course subject matter and writing style might also help).

9.4 Testing Means with PROC TTEST

As you would expect from its name, the TTEST procedure, which is part of SAS/STAT software, computes *t* tests. You use *t* tests when you want to compare means. Suppose, for example, that a statistics instructor selected a random sample of students to have extra tutoring. She could test whether the true mean of their scores was above a specific level (called a one sample test), she could compare the scores of students who had tutoring to those who did not (a two independent sample test), and she could compare the scores of students before and after tutoring (a paired test). PROC TTEST performs all these types of tests.

One sample comparisons To compute a *t* test for a single mean, you list that variable in a VAR statement. SAS will test whether the mean is significanlty different from H_0, a specified null value. The default value of H_0 is zero. You can specify a different value using the H0= option.

```
PROC TTEST H0 = n options;
   VAR variable;
```

Two independent sample comparisons To compare two independent groups, you use a CLASS and a VAR statement. In the CLASS statement, you list the variable that distinguishes the two groups. In the VAR statement, you list the response variable.

```
PROC TTEST options;
   CLASS variable;
   VAR variable;
```

Paired comparisons When the variables you are comparing are paired, you use a PAIRED statement. The simplest form of this statement lists the two variables to be compared, separated by an asterisk.

```
PROC TTEST options;
   PAIRED variable1 * variable2;
```

Options Here are a few of the options available:

ALPHA = n	specifies the level for the confidence limits. The value of *n* must be between 0 (100% confidence) and 1 (0% confidence). The default is 0.05 (95% confidence limits).
CI = type	specifies the type of confidence interval for the standard deviation. If you don't specify this option, then by default the value of type is EQUAL which produces an equal-tailed confidence interval. Other possible values are UMPU for an interval based on the uniformly most powerful unbiased test, and NONE to request no confidence interval for the standard deviation.
H0 = n	requests a test of the hypothesis $H_0 = n$. The default value is 0.
NOBYVAR	moves the names of the variables from the title to the output table.
SIDES = type	specifies whether the p-value and confidence interval are one or two-tailed. Possible values of *type* are 2 (the default) for two-tailed, L (for a lower one-sided test) or U (for an upper one-sided test).

Example The following data give the finishing times for semifinal and final races of the women's 50 meter freestyle swim. Each swimmer's initials are followed by their final time and semifinal time in seconds. Each line of data contains times for four swimmers.

```
RK 24.05 24.07 AH 24.28 24.45 MV 24.39 24.50 BS 24.46 24.57
FH 24.47 24.63 TA 24.61 24.71 JH 24.62 24.68 AV 24.69 24.64
```

The following program reads the raw data and uses a paired *t* test to test the mean difference between the semifinal and final times:

```
DATA Swim;
   INFILE 'c:\MyRawData\Olympic50mSwim.dat';
   INPUT Swimmer $ FinalTime SemiFinalTime @@;
RUN;
PROC TTEST DATA=Swim;
  TITLE '50m Freestyle Semifinal vs. Final Results';
  PAIRED SemiFinalTime * FinalTime;
RUN;
```

Here are the tabular results produced by PROC TTEST. Graphical results are shown in the next section.

50m Freestyle Semifinal vs. Final Results

The TTEST Procedure

Difference: SemiFinalTime - FinalTime

N	Mean	Std Dev	Std Err	Minimum	Maximum
8	0.0850	0.0731	0.0258	-0.0500	0.1700

Mean	95% CL Mean		Std Dev	95% CL Std Dev	
0.0850	0.0239	0.1461	0.0731	0.0483	0.1488

DF	t Value	Pr > |t|
7	3.29	0.0133

In this example, the mean difference between each swimmer's semifinal time and their final time is 0.0850 seconds. The *t* test shows significant evidence ($t_{df=7}$ = 3.29, p = 0.0133) of a difference between the mean semifinal and final times .

9.5 ▶ Creating Statistical Graphics with PROC TTEST

The TTEST procedure uses ODS Graphics to produce several plots that help you visualize your data including histograms, box plots, and Q-Q plots. Many plots are generated by default, but you can control which plots are created using the PLOTS option on the PROC TTEST statement. Here is the general form of the PROC TTEST statement with plot options:

```
PROC TTEST PLOTS = (plot-request-list);
```

Plot requests The plots available to you depend on the type of comparison you request. Here are plots you can request for one sample, two sample, and paired *t* tests:

ALL	requests all appropriate plots.
BOXPLOT	creates box plots.
HISTOGRAM	creates histograms overlaid with normal and kernel density curves.
INTERVALPLOT	creates plots of confidence interval of means.
NONE	suppresses all plots.
QQPLOT	creates a normal quantile-quantile (Q-Q) plot.
SUMMARYPLOT	creates one plot that includes both histograms and box plots.

The following plots are also available for paired *t* tests:

AGREEMENTPLOT	creates agreement plots.
PROFILESPLOT	creates a profiles plot.

Excluding automatic plots By default the QQPLOT and SUMMARYPLOT plots are generated automatically for one sample, two sample and paired *t* tests. For paired *t* tests, the AGREEMENTPLOT and PROFILESPLOT are also generated by default. If you choose specific plots in the plot-list, the default plots will still be created unless you add the ONLY global option:

```
PROC TTEST PLOTS(ONLY) = (plot-request-list);
```

Example The following data give the finishing times for semifinal and final races of the women's 50 meter freestyle swim. Each swimmer's initials are followed by their final time and semifinal time in seconds. Each line of data contains times for four swimmers.

```
RK 24.05 24.07 AH 24.28 24.45 MV 24.39 24.50 BS 24.46 24.57
FH 24.47 24.63 TA 24.61 24.71 JH 24.62 24.68 AV 24.69 24.64
```

The following program reads the raw data, uses a paired *t* test to test the mean difference between the semifinal and final times, and requests just the Summary and QQ plots.

```
DATA Swim;
   INFILE 'c:\MyRawData\Olympic50mSwim.dat';
   INPUT Swimmer $ FinalTime SemiFinalTime @@;
RUN;
PROC TTEST DATA=Swim PLOTS(ONLY) = (SUMMARYPLOT QQPLOT);
   TITLE '50m Freestyle Semifinal vs. Final Results';
   PAIRED SemiFinalTime * FinalTime;
RUN;
```

Here are the results for the Q-Q and Summary plots. The tabular results for the paired *t* test were shown in the preceding section.

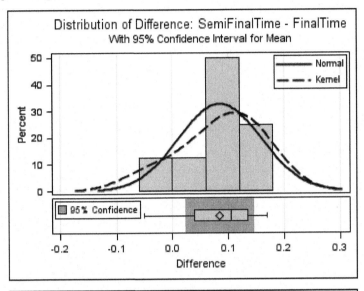

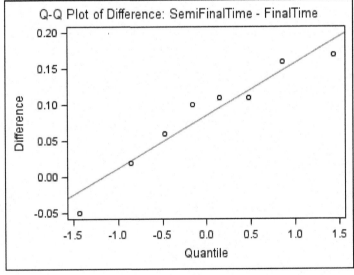

9.6 Testing Categorical Data with PROC FREQ

PROC FREQ, which is part of Base SAS software, produces many statistics for categorical data. The best known of these is chi-square. One of the most common uses of PROC FREQ is to test the hypothesis of no association between two variables. Another use is to compute measures of association, which indicate the strength of the relationship between the variables. The basic form of PROC FREQ is

```
PROC FREQ;
   TABLES variable-combinations / options;
```

Options Here are a few of the statistical options available:

AGREE	requests tests and measures of classification agreement including McNemar's test, Bowker's test, Cochran's Q test, and kappa statistics.
CHISQ	requests chi-square tests of independence and measures of association.
CL	requests confidence limits for measures of association.
CMH	requests Cochran-Mantel-Haenszel statistics, typically for stratified two-way tables.
EXACT	requests Fisher's exact test for tables larger than 2X2.
MEASURES	requests measures of association including Pearson and Spearman correlation coefficients, gamma, Kendall's tau-b, Stuart's tau-c, Somer's D, lambda, odds ratios, risk ratios, and confidence intervals.
RELRISK	requests relative risk measures for 2X2 tables.
TREND	requests the Cochran-Armitage test for trend.

Example One day your neighbor, who rides the bus to work, complains that the regular bus is usually late. He says the express bus is usually on time. Realizing that this is categorical data, you decide to test whether there really is a relationship between the type of bus and arriving on time. You collect data for type of bus (E for express or R for regular) and promptness (L for late or O for on time). Each line of data contains several observations.

```
E O E L E L R O E O E O E O R L R O R L R O E O R L E O R L R O E O
E O R L E L E O R L E O R L E O R L E O R O E L E O E O E O E O E L
E O E O R L R L R O R L E L E O R L R O E O E O E O E L R O R L
```

The following program reads the raw data and runs PROC FREQ with the CHISQ option:

```
DATA bus;
   INFILE 'c:\MyRawData\Bus.dat';
   INPUT BusType $  OnTimeOrLate $ @@;
RUN;
PROC FREQ DATA = bus;
   TABLES BusType * OnTimeOrLate / CHISQ;
   TITLE;
RUN;
```

Here are the results showing that the regular bus is late 61.90% of the time, while the express bus is late only 24.14% of the time. Assuming that bus type and arrival time are independent, the probability of obtaining a chi-square this large or larger by chance alone is 0.0071. So the data do support the idea that there is an association between type of bus and arrival time. The Fisher's exact test provides the same conclusion with a p-value of 0.0097.

The FREQ Procedure

Table of BusType by OnTimeOrLate			
BusType	**OnTimeOrLate**		
Frequency Percent Row Pct Col Pct	**L**	**O**	**Total**
E	7 14.00 24.14 35.00	22 44.00 75.86 73.33	29 58.00
R	13 26.00 61.90 65.00	8 16.00 38.10 26.67	21 42.00
Total	20 40.00	30 60.00	50 100.00

Statistics for Table of BusType by OnTimeOrLate

Statistic	DF	Value	Prob
Chi-Square	1	7.2386	0.0071
Likelihood Ratio Chi-Square	1	7.3364	0.0068
Continuity Adj. Chi-Square	1	5.7505	0.0165
Mantel-Haenszel Chi-Square	1	7.0939	0.0077
Phi Coefficient		-0.3805	
Contingency Coefficient		0.3556	
Cramer's V		-0.3805	

Fisher's Exact Test	
Cell (1,1) Frequency (F)	7
Left-sided Pr <= F	0.0081
Right-sided Pr >= F	0.9987
Table Probability (P)	0.0067
Two-sided Pr <= P	0.0097

Sample Size = 50

9.7 ▶ Creating Statistical Graphics with PROC FREQ

The FREQ procedure uses ODS Graphics to produce several plots that help you visualize your data including frequency plots, odds ratio plots, agreement plots, deviation plots, and two types of plots with Kappa statistics and confidence limits. Here is the general form of PROC FREQ with plot options:

```
PROC FREQ;
   TABLES variable-combinations / options PLOTS = (plot-list);
RUN;
```

Plot requests The plots available to you depend on the type of table you request. For example, the DEVIATIONPLOT is only available for one-way tables when using the CHISQ option on the TABLES statement. Here are the plots you can request along with the required option, if any, and type of table request:

Plot Name	Table type	Require option on TABLES statement
AGREEPLOT	two-way	AGREE
CUMFREQPLOT	one-way	
DEVIATIONPLOT	one-way	CHISQ
FREQPLOT	any request	
KAPPAPLOT	three-way	AGREE
ODDSRATIOPLOT	hx2x2	MEASURES or RELRISK
RELREISKPLOT	hx2x2	MEASURES or RELRISK
RISKDIFFPLOT	hx2x2	RISKDIFF
WTKAPPAPLOT	hxrxr (r>2)	AGREE

To produce a CUMFREQPLOT or FREQPLOT, you must specify it in the PLOTS= option of the TABLES statement. Otherwise if you do not specify any plots in the TABLE statement, then all plots associated with the table you request will be produced by default.

Plot options Many options are available that control the look of the plots generated. For a complete list of options, see the SAS Help and Documentation. For example, the FREQPLOT has options for controlling the layout of the plots for two-way tables. By default, the bars are grouped vertically. To group the bars horizontally, use

```
TABLES variable1 * variable2 / PLOTS = FREQPLOT(TWOWAY = GROUPHORIZONTAL);
```

To stack the bars, use the TWOWAY=STACKED option.

Example This example uses the same data as the previous section about promptness of busses. Each line of data contains several observations for type of bus (E for express or R for regular) and promptness (L for late or O for on time).

```
E O E L E L R O E O E O E O R L R O R L R O E O R L E O R L R O E O
E O R L E L E O R L E O R L E O R L E O R O E L E O E O E O E O E L
E O E O R L R L R O R L E L E O R L R O E O E O E O E L R O R L
```

The following program reads the data and uses PROC FREQ to request a two-way frequency table. The PLOTS=FREQPLOT option in the TABLES statement produces a frequency plot. Adding the TWOWAY=GROUPHORIZONTAL option to FREQPLOT produces bars that are grouped horizontally instead of vertically. The FORMAT procedure creates formats that are applied to the BusType and OnTimeOrLate variables using a FORMAT statement in the FREQ procedure. This gives more descriptive labels to the plot.

```
DATA bus;
   INFILE 'c:\MyRawData\Bus.dat';
   INPUT BusType $  OnTimeOrLate $ @@;
RUN;
PROC FORMAT;
  VALUE $type 'R'='Regular'
              'E'='Express';
  VALUE $late 'O'='On Time'
              'L'='Late';
RUN;
PROC FREQ DATA = bus;
   TABLES BusType * OnTimeOrLate / PLOTS=FREQPLOT(TWOWAY=GROUPHORIZONTAL);
   FORMAT BusType $Type. OnTimeOrLate $Late.;
RUN;
```

Here is the plot. Note that the tabular portion of the output, the frequency table, is not shown.

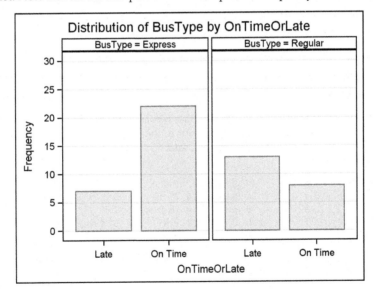

Examining Correlations with PROC CORR

The CORR procedure, which is included with Base SAS software, computes correlations. A correlation coefficient measures the strength of the linear relationship between two variables. If two variables are completely unrelated, they will have a correlation of 0. If two variables have a perfect linear relationship, they will have a correlation of 1.0 or –1.0. In real life, correlations fall somewhere between these numbers. The basic statement for PROC CORR is rather simple:

```
PROC CORR;
```

These two words tell SAS to compute correlations between all possible pairs of the numeric variables. You can add the VAR and WITH statements to specify variables:

```
VAR variable-list;
WITH variable-list;
```

Variables listed in the VAR statement appear across the top of the table of correlations, while variables listed in the WITH statement appear down the side of the table. If you use a VAR statement but no WITH statement, then the variables appear both across the top and down the side.

By default, PROC CORR computes Pearson product-moment correlation coefficients. You can add options to the PROC statement to request non-parametric correlation coefficients. The SPEARMAN option in the statement below tells SAS to compute Spearman's rank correlations instead of Pearson's correlations:

```
PROC CORR  SPEARMAN;
```

Other options include HOEFFDING (for Hoeffding's D statistic) and KENDALL (for Kendall's tau-b coefficient).

Example Each student in a statistics class recorded three values: test score, the number of hours spent watching television in the week prior to the test, and the number of hours spent exercising during the same week. Here are the raw data:

```
56 6 2    78 7 4    84 5 5    73 4 0    90 3 4
44 9 0    76 5 1    87 3 3    92 2 7    75 8 3
85 1 6    67 4 2    90 5 5    84 6 5    74 5 2
64 4 1    73 0 5    78 5 2    69 6 1    56 7 1
87 8 4    73 8 3   100 0 6    54 8 0    81 5 4
78 5 2    69 4 1    64 7 1    73 7 3    65 6 2
```

Notice that each line contains data for five students. The following program reads the raw data from a file called Exercise.dat, and then uses PROC CORR to compute the correlations:

```
DATA class;
    INFILE 'c:\MyRawData\Exercise.dat';
    INPUT Score Television Exercise @@;
RUN;

PROC CORR DATA = class;
    VAR Television Exercise;
    WITH Score;
    TITLE 'Correlations for Test Scores';
    TITLE2 'With Hours of Television and Exercise';
RUN;
```

Here is the report from PROC CORR:

Correlations for Test Scores
With Hours of Television and Exercise
The CORR Procedure

1 With Variables:	Score
2 Variables:	Television Exercise

Simple Statistics						
Variable	N	Mean	Std Dev	Sum	Minimum	Maximum
Score	30	74.63333	12.58484	2239	44.00000	100.00000
Television	30	5.10000	2.33932	153.00000	0	9.00000
Exercise	30	2.83333	1.94906	85.00000	0	7.00000

❶ Pearson Correlation Coefficients, N = 30 ❷ Prob > |r| under H0: Rho=0	Television	Exercise
Score	❶ -0.55390 ❷ 0.0015	❶ 0.79733 ❷ <.0001

This report starts with descriptive statistics for each variable, and then lists the correlation matrix which contains: ❶ correlation coefficients (in this case, Pearson), and ❷ the probability of getting a larger absolute value for each correlation assuming the population correlation is zero.

In this example, both hours of television and hours of exercise are correlated with test score, but exercise is positively correlated while television is negatively correlated. This means students who watched more television tended to have lower scores, while the students who spent more time exercising tended to have higher scores.

9.9 ▶ Creating Statistical Graphics with PROC CORR

The CORR procedure evaluates the strength of the linear relationship between pairs of variables. The tabular output gives the correlation coefficients and other simple statistics, and using ODS Graphics you can also visualize the relationship. Plots are not generated by default, so you need to specify the desired plots using the PLOTS= option. Here is the general form of PROC CORR with the PLOTS option:

```
PROC CORR PLOTS = (plot-list);
   VAR variable-list;
   WITH variable-list;
RUN;
```

Plot requests The CORR procedure can produce two types of plots:

SCATTER	creates scatter plots for pairs of variables. Prediction or confidence ellipses are overlaid on the plot.
MATRIX	creates a matrix of scatter plots for all variables.

Plot options By default, the scatter plots include prediction ellipses for new observations. If you want confidence ellipses for means, then specify the ELLIPSE=CONFIDENCE option on the scatter plot:

```
PROC CORR PLOTS = SCATTER(ELLIPSE = CONFIDENCE);
```

If you do not want any ellipses on your scatter plots, then use the ELLIPSE=NONE option.

If you do not have a WITH statement, then matrix plots will show a symmetrical plot with all variable combinations appearing twice. By default the diagonal cells in the matrix will be empty. If you use the HISTOGRAM option for the matrix plot, then a histogram will be produced for each variable and displayed along the diagonal.

```
PROC CORR PLOTS = MATRIX(HISTOGRAM);
```

Example Here are the data from the previous section about students in a statistics class. For each student we have the test score, the number of hours spent watching television in the week prior to the test, and the number of hours spent exercising during the same week. Each line contains data for five students.

```
56 6 2    78 7 4    84 5 5    73 4 0    90 3 4
44 9 0    76 5 1    87 3 3    92 2 7    75 8 3
85 1 6    67 4 2    90 5 5    84 6 5    74 5 2
64 4 1    73 0 5    78 5 2    69 6 1    56 7 1
87 8 4    73 8 3   100 0 6    54 8 0    81 5 4
78 5 2    69 4 1    64 7 1    73 7 3    65 6 2
```

The following program reads the data and uses the same PROC CORR statements shown in the previous section except both the scatter and matrix plots are requested:

```
DATA class;
   INFILE 'c:\MyRawData\Exercise.dat';
   INPUT Score Television Exercise @@;
RUN;
PROC CORR DATA = class PLOTS = (SCATTER MATRIX);
   VAR Television Exercise;
   WITH Score;
   TITLE 'Correlations for Test Scores';
   TITLE2 'With Hours of Television and Exercise';
RUN;
```

The program produces three plots: a scatter plot for Score by Television, a scatter plot for Score by Exercise (not shown), and the Scatter Plot Matrix.

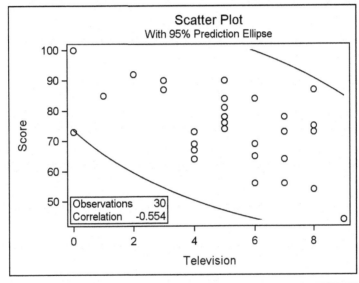

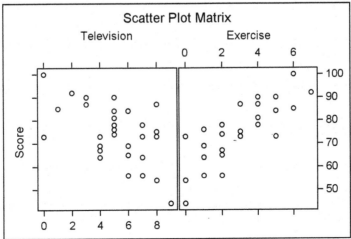

9.10 Using PROC REG for Simple Regression Analysis

The REG procedure fits linear regression models by least-squares and is one of many SAS procedures which perform regression analysis. PROC REG is part of SAS/STAT, which is licensed separately from Base SAS software. We will show an example of a simple regression analysis using continuous numeric variables with only one regressor variable. However, PROC REG is capable of analyzing models with many regressor variables using a variety of model-selection methods including stepwise regression, forward selection, and backward elimination. Other procedures in SAS/STAT will perform non-linear and logistic regression. In SAS/ETS you will find procedures for time series analysis. If you are unsure about what type of analysis you need, or are unfamiliar with basic statistical principles, we recommend that you seek advice from a trained statistician, or consult a good statistical textbook.

The REG procedure has only two required statements. It must start with the PROC REG statement and have a MODEL statement specifying the analysis model. The following shows the general form of the REG procedure:

```
PROC REG;
   MODEL dependent = independent;
```

In the MODEL statement, the dependent variable is listed on the left side of the equal sign and the independent, or regressor, variable is listed on the right.

Example At your young neighbor's T-ball game (that's where the players hit the ball from the top of a tee instead of having the ball pitched to them), he said to you, "You can tell how far they'll hit the ball by how tall they are." To give him a little practical lesson in statistics, you decide to test his hypothesis. You gather data from 30 players, measuring their height in inches and their longest of three hits in feet. The following are the data. Notice that data for several players are listed on one line:

```
50 110   49 135   48 129   53 150   48 124 50 143   51 126   45 107
53 146   50 154   47 136   52 144   47 124 50 133   50 128   50 118
48 135   47 129   45 126   48 118   45 121 53 142   46 122   47 119
51 134   49 130   46 132   51 144   50 132 50 131
```

The following program reads the data and performs the regression analysis. In the MODEL statement, Distance is the dependent variable, and Height is the independent variable.

```
DATA hits;
   INFILE 'c:\MyRawData\Baseball.dat';
   INPUT Height Distance @@;
RUN;
* Perform regression analysis;
PROC REG DATA = hits;
   MODEL Distance = Height;
   TITLE 'Results of Regression Analysis';
RUN;
```

The REG procedure produces tabular results and several graphs by default. Only the tabular results are shown here; see the next section for an example showing the graphical results. The first section of the tabular output is the analysis of variance section, which gives information about how well the model fits the data:

Results of Regression Analysis

The REG Procedure
Model: MODEL1
Dependent Variable: Distance

Number of Observations Read	30
Number of Observations Used	30

Analysis of Variance					
Source	❶ DF	Sum of Squares	❷ Mean Square	❸ F Value	❹ Pr > F
Model	1	1365.50831	1365.50831	16.86	0.0003
Error	28	2268.35836	81.01280		
Corrected Total	29	3633.86667			

❺ Root MSE	9.00071	R-Square	0.3758
Dependent Mean	130.73333	❼ Adj R-Sq	0.3535
❻ Coeff Var	6.88479		

❶ **DF**	degrees of freedom associated with the source
❷ **Mean Square**	mean square (sum of squares divided by the degrees of freedom)
❸ **F value**	F value for testing the null hypothesis (all parameters are zero except intercept)
❹ **Pr > F**	significance probability or p-value
❺ **Root MSE**	root mean square error
❻ **Coeff Var**	the coefficient of variation
❼ **Adj R-sq**	the R-square value adjusted for degrees of freedom

The parameter estimates follow the analysis of variance section and give the parameters for each term in the model, including the intercept:

Parameter Estimates					
Variable	❶ DF	Parameter Estimate	Standard Error	❷ t Value	❸ Pr > |t|
Intercept	1	-11.00859	34.56363	-0.32	0.7525
Height	1	2.89466	0.70506	4.11	0.0003

❶ **DF**	degrees of freedom for the variable
❷ **t Value**	t test for the parameter equal to zero
❸ **Pr > |t|**	two-tailed significance probability

From the parameter estimates you can construct the regression equation:

```
Distance = -11.00859 + (2.89466 * Height)
```

In this example, the distance the ball was hit did increase with the player's height. The slope of the model is significant ($p = 0.0003$) but the relationship is not very strong (R-square = 0.3758). Perhaps age or years of experience are better predictors of how far the ball will go.

9.11 Creating Statistical Graphics with PROC REG

There are many plots that are useful for visualizing the results of regression analysis and for assessing how well the model fits the data. PROC REG uses ODS Graphics to produce many such plots including a diagnostic panel that contains up to nine plots in one figure. Some plots are produced automatically while others need to be specified. Here is the general form of PROC REG with the PLOTS option:

```
PROC REG PLOTS(options) = (plot-request-list);
   MODEL dependent = independent;
RUN;
```

Plot requests Here are some plots you can request for simple linear regression:

FITPLOT	scatter plot with regression line and confidence and prediction bands
RESIDUALS	residuals plotted against independent variable
DIAGNOSTICS	diagnostics panel including all of the following plots
COOKSD	Cook's D statistic by observation number
OBSERVEDBYPREDICTED	dependent variable by predicted values
QQPLOT	normal quantile plot of residuals
RESIDUALBYPREDICTED	residuals by predicted values
RESIDUALHISTOGRAM	histogram of residuals
RFPLOT	residual fit plot
RSTUDENTBYLEVERAGE	studentized residuals by leverage
RSTUDENTBYPREDICTED	studentized residuals by predicted values

Excluding automatic plots By default the RESIDUALS and DIAGNOSTICS plots are generated automatically. Additional plots may also be produced by default depending on the type of model. For example, a FITPLOT is automatically generated when there is one regressor variable. If you choose specific plots in the plot-request-list, the default plots will still be created unless you use the ONLY global option:

```
PROC REG PLOTS(ONLY) = (plot-request-list);
```

Example The following example uses the same data as the previous section about T-ball players. The player's height in inches is followed by their longest of three hits in feet. Notice that data for several players are listed on one line:

```
50 110   49 135   48 129   53 150   48 124 50 143   51 126   45 107
53 146   50 154   47 136   52 144   47 124 50 133   50 128   50 118
48 135   47 129   45 126   48 118   45 121 53 142   46 122   47 119
51 134   49 130   46 132   51 144   50 132 50 131
```

The following program reads the data and performs the regression analysis as in the previous section. However, in this program only the FITPLOT and DIAGNOSTICS plots are requested:

```
DATA hits;
   INFILE 'c:\MyRawData\Baseball.dat';
   INPUT Height Distance @@;
RUN;
PROC REG DATA = hits PLOTS(ONLY) = (DIAGNOSTICS FITPLOT);
   MODEL Distance = Height;
   TITLE 'Results of Regression Analysis';
RUN;
```

Here are the results for the Fit Diagnostics panel and the Fit Plot. The tabular results are not shown here, but are the same as in the previous section.

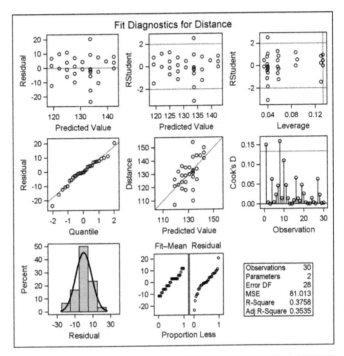

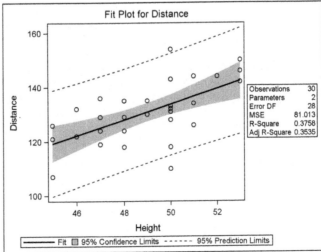

9.12 Using PROC ANOVA for One-Way Analysis of Variance

The ANOVA procedure is one of many in SAS that perform analysis of variance. PROC ANOVA is part of SAS/STAT, which is licensed separately from Base SAS software. PROC ANOVA is specifically designed for balanced data—data where there are equal numbers of observations in each combination of the classification factors. An exception is for one-way analysis of variance where the data do not need to be balanced. If you are not doing one-way analysis of variance and your data are not balanced, then you should use the GLM procedure, whose statements are almost identical to those of PROC ANOVA. Although we are discussing only simple one-way analysis of variance in this section, PROC ANOVA can handle multiple classification variables and models that include nested and crossed effects as well as repeated measures. If you are unsure of the appropriate analysis for your data, or are unfamiliar with basic statistical principles, we recommend that you seek advice from a trained statistician or consult a good statistical textbook.

The ANOVA procedure has two required statements: the CLASS and MODEL statements. The following is the general form of the ANOVA procedure:

```
PROC ANOVA;
   CLASS variable-list;
   MODEL dependent = effects;
```

The CLASS statement must come before the MODEL statement and defines the classification variables. For one-way analysis of variance, only one variable is listed. The MODEL statement defines the dependent variable and the effects. For one-way analysis of variance, the effect is the classification variable.

As you might expect, there are many optional statements for PROC ANOVA. One of the most useful is the MEANS statement, which calculates means of the dependent variable for any of the main effects in the MODEL statement. In addition, the MEANS statement can perform several types of multiple comparison tests including Bonferroni *t* tests (BON), Duncan's multiple-range test (DUNCAN), Scheffe's multiple-comparison procedure (SCHEFFE), pairwise *t* tests (T), and Tukey's studentized range test (TUKEY). The MEANS statement has the following general form:

```
   MEANS effects / options;
```

The effects can be any effect in the MODEL statement, and options include the name of the desired multiple comparison test (DUNCAN for example).

Example Your daughter plays basketball on a team that travels throughout the state. She complains that it seems like the girls from the other regions in the state are all taller than the girls from her region. You decide to test her hypothesis by getting the heights for a sample of girls from the four regions and performing one-way analysis of variance to see if there are any differences. Each data line includes region and height for eight girls:

```
West 65 West 58 West 63 West 57 West 61 West 53 West 56 West 66
West 55 West 56 West 65 West 54 West 55 West 62 West 55 West 58
East 65 East 55 East 57 East 66 East 59 East 63 East 58 East 57
East 58 East 63 East 61 East 62 East 58 East 57 East 65 East 57
South 63 South 63 South 68 South 56 South 60 South 65 South 64 South 62
South 59 South 67 South 59 South 65 South 66 South 67 South 64 South 68
North 63 North 65 North 58 North 55 North 57 North 66 North 59 North 61
North 65 North 56 North 57 North 63 North 61 North 60 North 64 North 62
```

You want to know which, if any, regions have taller girls than the rest, so you use the MEANS statement in your program and choose Scheffe's multiple-comparison procedure to compare the means. Here is the program to read the data and perform the analysis of variance:

```
DATA heights;
   INFILE 'c:\MyRawData\GirlHeights.dat';
   INPUT Region $ Height @@;
RUN;
* Use ANOVA to run one-way analysis of variance;
PROC ANOVA DATA = heights;
   CLASS Region;
   MODEL Height = Region;
   MEANS Region / SCHEFFE;
   TITLE "Girls' Heights from Four Regions";
RUN;
```

In this case, Region is the classification variable and also the effect in the MODEL statement. Height is the dependent variable. The MEANS statement will produce means of the girls' heights for each region, and the SCHEFFE option will test which regions are different from the others.

Here is the box plot that is created automatically. The small p-value (p=0.0051) indicates that at least two of the four regions differ in mean height. The tabular output is shown and discussed in the next section.

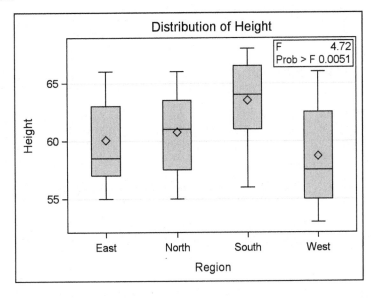

9.13 Reading the Output of PROC ANOVA

The tabular output from PROC ANOVA has at least two parts. First ANOVA produces a table giving information about the classification variables: number of levels, values, and number of observations. Next it produces an analysis of variance table. If you use optional statements like MEANS, then their output will follow.

The example from the previous section used the following PROC ANOVA statements:

```
PROC ANOVA DATA = heights;
   CLASS Region;
   MODEL Height = Region;
   MEANS Region / SCHEFFE;
   TITLE "Girls' Heights from Four Regions";
RUN;
```

The graph produced by the ANOVA procedure is shown in the previous section. The first page of the tabular output (shown below) gives information about the classification variable Region. It has four levels with values East, North, South, and West; and there are 64 observations.

Girls' Heights from Four Regions
The ANOVA Procedure

Class Level Information		
Class	**Levels**	**Values**
Region	4	East North South West

Number of Observations Read	64
Number of Observations Used	64

The second part of the output is the analysis of variance table:

Girls' Heights from Four Regions
The ANOVA Procedure

Dependent Variable: Height

❶ Source	❷ DF	❸ Sum of Squares	❹ Mean Square	❺ F Value	❻ Pr > F
Model	3	196.625000	65.541667	4.72	0.0051
Error	60	833.375000	13.889583		
Corrected Total	63	1030.000000			

❼ R-Square	❽ Coeff Var	❾ Root MSE	❿ Height Mean
0.190898	6.134771	3.726873	60.75000

Source	DF	Anova SS	Mean Square	F Value	Pr > F
Region	3	196.6250000	65.5416667	4.72	0.0051

Highlights of the output are

❶	**Source**	source of variation
❷	**DF**	degrees of freedom for the model, error, and total
❸	**Sum of Squares**	sum of squares for the portion attributed to the model, error, and total
❹	**Mean Square**	mean square (sum of squares divided by the degrees of freedom)
❺	**F Value**	F value (mean square for model divided by the mean square for error)
❻	**Pr > F**	significance probability associated with the F statistic
❼	**R-Square**	R-square
❽	**Coeff Var**	coefficient of variation
❾	**Root MSE**	root mean square error
❿	**Height Mean**	mean of the dependent variable

Because the effect of Region is significant ($p = .0051$), we conclude that there are differences in the mean heights of girls from the four regions. The SCHEFFE option in the MEANS statement compares the mean heights between the regions. Letters are used to group means, and means with the same letters are not significantly different from each other (at the 0.05 level). The following results show that your friend's daughter is partially correct—one region (South) has taller girls than her region (West) but no other two regions differ significantly in mean height.

Girls' Heights from Four Regions

The ANOVA Procedure

Scheffe's Test for Height

Note: This test controls the Type I experimentwise error rate.

Alpha	0.05
Error Degrees of Freedom	60
Error Mean Square	13.88958
Critical Value of F	2.75808
Minimum Significant Difference	3.7902

Means with the same letter are not significantly different.				
Scheffe Grouping		**Mean**	**N**	**Region**
	A	63.500	16	South
	A			
B	A	60.750	16	North
B	A			
B	A	60.063	16	East
B				
B		58.688	16	West

10

"When we try to pick out anything by itself, we find it hitched to everything in the Universe."

JOHN MUIR

From *My First Summer in the Sierra* by John Muir. Public domain.

CHAPTER 10

Exporting Your Data

10.1   Methods for Exporting Your Data

In our ever increasingly complex world, people often need to transfer data from one application to another. Fortunately, SAS gives you many options for doing this. The types of files that you can create and the methods available for creating those files depend on what operating environment you are using and whether you have SAS/ACCESS software.

Methods for exporting data to other applications fall into these general categories:

+ creating delimited or text files that the other software can read

+ creating files in formats like HTML, RTF, or XML that the other software can read

+ writing the data in the other software's native format

Creating delimited and text files No matter what your environment, you can always create delimited or text files and most software has the ability to read these types of data files.

+ The DATA step, discussed in section 10.5, gives you the most control over the format of your files, but requires the most steps.

+ The Export Wizard, discussed in section 10.2, and the EXPORT procedure, discussed in section 10.3, are easy to use, but you have less control over the result and not everyone has access to these tools.

+ The Output Delivery System (ODS), discussed in section 10.6, can create comma-separated values (CSV) files from any procedure output and a simple PROC PRINT will produce a reasonable file for importing into other programs.

Creating HTML, RTF, and XML files Using ODS, discussed in section 10.6, you can create HTML, RTF, and XML files from any procedure output. Many applications can read data in these types of files. Although we do not cover creating RTF and XML files for this purpose, the general method is the same as creating HTML files.

Creating files in native formats There are several methods for creating files in the native format of other software applications. Not all methods are available for all software applications, and some methods depend on what SAS software products you have installed, which operating environment, and what version of SAS you are using. We do not attempt to cover all methods, so see the SAS Help and Documentation for complete information.

+ For PC files including Microsoft Excel, Microsoft Access, dBase, Paradox, SPSS, Stata, and JMP, you can create files using the Export Wizard discussed in section 10.2, or the EXPORT procedure discussed in section 10.4 (the example is for Excel). However, to create files in most of these formats you need SAS/ACCESS Interface to PC Files. Support for JMP files is now included in Base SAS. This method is only available for the Windows or UNIX operating systems.

♦   You may have a PC Files Server application running in your SAS environment. The PC
    Files Server facilitates sharing of some PC files between different Windows computers,
    between Windows and UNIX computers, or even on a single Windows computer. The PC
    Files Server application requires that SAS/ACCESS Interface to PC Files be installed. You
    can use the PC Files Server through either the Export Wizard or the EXPORT procedure.

♦   If you don't have SAS/ACCESS Interface to PC Files, and you are using Windows, you
    may be able to use Dynamic Data Exchange (DDE) to move data from SAS to some PC
    applications without creating any intermediate files.

♦   For database management systems that are not PC based including ORACLE, DB2,
    INGRES, MYSQL, and SYBASE, there are SAS/ACCESS products that allow you to create
    files in the native formats of these applications.

10.2   Writing Files Using the Export Wizard

The Export Wizard, available in the Windows and UNIX operating environments, provides an easy way to produce files that can be imported into other software. The Export Wizard is a graphical user interface (GUI) to the EXPORT procedure (discussed in sections 10.3 and 10.4), and if you need to export data only once in a while, then it's easier than trying to remember the PROC EXPORT statements. The Export Wizard can write data files in many different formats including delimited files, column formatted files and, if you have SAS/ACCESS Interface to PC Files, many popular PC file formats.

Start the Export Wizard by selecting **File ▶ Export Data...** from the menu bar.

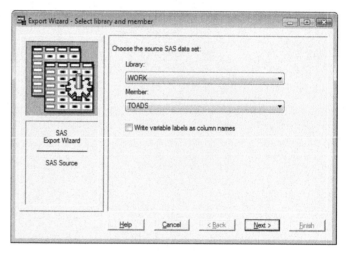

In the first Export Wizard window, choose the library and member name for the SAS data set that you want to export. If you are exporting a temporary SAS data set, then the library is WORK. If you are exporting a permanent SAS data set, then make sure your library is defined before you start the Export Wizard. Then choose the library from the drop-down list. The member name is the name of the SAS data set. In this window you can also choose to use the variable labels instead of the variable names as the column names.

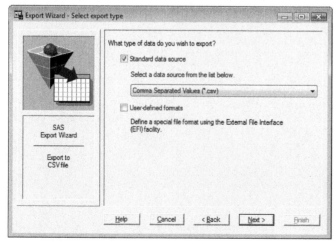

In the next window, choose the type of file you would like to create. Either choose from the pull-down list of standard data sources, or check the box next to **User-defined formats**. The User-defined formats option takes you to the External File Interface (EFI) facility which enables you to assign formats to your variables, as well as choose either a delimited file structure, or a file that is arranged into columns. Some data source choices will lead you to additional windows specific to that data source. In this example, the data set will be exported as a comma-separated values (CSV) file.

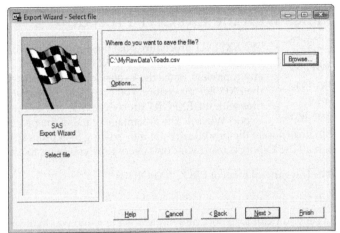

In the next window you choose the location for the exported data to be saved. If you are exporting CSV, tab delimited, or other types of delimited files, clicking the **Options...** button opens the Delimited File Options window where you may choose more options.

For delimited files, specify which delimiter to use in the in the Delimiter box. For CSV or tab-delimited files, the delimiter is already determined so that section of the window is grayed out. If any of your data values contains the delimiter, then that value will be enclosed in double quotation marks. Also in this window you can choose to write variable names or variable labels in the first row of the file, or write the data only.

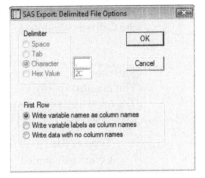

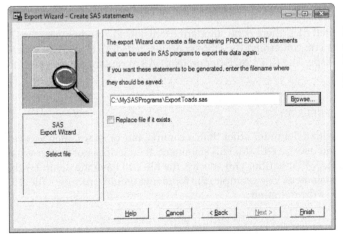

In the final window you have the option to save the PROC EXPORT statements that are generated through the Export Wizard.

10.3 Writing Delimited Files with the EXPORT Procedure

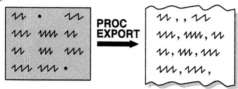

The EXPORT procedure, like the Export Wizard, is available for Windows and UNIX operating environments. Since the Export Wizard is an interface to the EXPORT procedure, you can create the same types of files with the EXPORT procedure that you can with the Export Wizard. The advantage of using the procedure over the wizard is that you can incorporate the procedure code into existing SAS programs, and you don't need to step through all the Export Wizard windows every time you want to create a file.

The EXPORT procedure The general form of PROC EXPORT is

```
PROC EXPORT DATA = data-set OUTFILE = 'filename';
```

where *data-set* is the SAS data set you want to export, and *filename* is the name you make up for the output data file. The following statement tells SAS to read a temporary SAS data set named HOTELS and write a comma-delimited file named Hotels.csv in a directory named MyRawData on the C drive (Windows):

```
PROC EXPORT DATA = hotels OUTFILE = 'c:\MyRawData\Hotels.csv';
```

SAS uses the last part of the filename, called the file extension, to decide what type of file to create. You can also specify the file type by adding the DBMS= option to the PROC EXPORT statement. The following table shows the filename extensions and DBMS identifiers currently available for delimited files. If you specify the DBMS= option, then it takes precedence over the file extension.

Type of file	Extension	DBMS Identifier
Comma-delimited	.csv	CSV
Tab-delimited	.txt	TAB
Space-delimited		DLM

Notice that for space-delimited files, there is no standard extension so you must use the DBMS= option. The following statement, containing the DBMS= option, tells SAS to create a space-delimited file named Hotels.spc. The REPLACE option tells SAS to replace any file with the same name.

```
PROC EXPORT DATA = hotels OUTFILE = 'c:\MyRawData\Hotels.spc'
       DBMS = DLM REPLACE;
```

If you want to create a file with a delimiter other than a comma, tab, or space, then you can add the DELIMITER statement. If you use the DELIMITER statement, then it does not matter what file extension you use, or what DBMS identifier you specify, the file will have the delimiter that you specify in the DELIMITER statement. For example, the following would produce a file, Hotels.txt, that has the ampersand (&) as the delimiter:

```
PROC EXPORT DATA = hotels OUTFILE = 'c:\MyRawData\Hotels.txt'
       DBMS = DLM REPLACE;
   DELIMITER='&';
```

Example A travel company maintains a SAS data set containing information about golf courses. For each golf course the file includes its name, number of holes, par, yardage, and greens fees.

```
Kapalua Plantation    18   73   7263    125.00
Pukalani              18   72   6945     55.00
Sandlewood            18   72   6469     35.00
Silversword           18   71    .       57.00
Waiehu Municipal      18   72   6330     25.00
Grand Waikapa         18   72   6122    200.00
```

The following program uses INFILE and INPUT statements to read the data and put them in a permanent SAS data set named GOLF in the MySASLib directory on the C drive (Windows). This example uses a LIBNAME statement to tell SAS where to store the permanent SAS data set, but you could use direct referencing instead:

```
LIBNAME travel 'c:\MySASLib';
DATA travel.golf;
    INFILE 'c:\MyRawData\Golf.dat';
    INPUT CourseName $18. NumberOfHoles Par Yardage GreenFees;
RUN;
```

Now, suppose you want to write a letter to a potential customer and insert the golf data. The following program writes a plain text, tab-delimited file that you can read with any text editor or word processor:

```
LIBNAME travel 'c:\MySASLib';
* Create Tab-delimited file;
PROC EXPORT DATA = travel.golf OUTFILE = 'c:\MyRawData\Golf.txt' REPLACE;
RUN;
```

Because the name of the output file ends with .txt and there is no DELIMITER statement, SAS will write a tab-delimited file. If you run this program, your log will contain the following note about the output file:

```
NOTE: 7 records were written to the file 'c:\MyRawData\Golf.txt'.
```

Notice that while the data set contained six observations, SAS wrote seven records. The extra record contains the variable names. If you read this file into a word processor and set the tabs, it will look like this:

Any format that you have assigned to variables in the SAS data set will be used by PROC EXPORT when creating the delimited file. If you want to change a format, use a FORMAT statement (discussed in section 4.6) in a DATA step before running PROC EXPORT.

10.4 **Writing Microsoft Excel Files with the EXPORT Procedure**

If you are using the Windows or UNIX operating environment, and you have SAS/ACCESS Interface to PC Files, then you can use the EXPORT procedure to create Microsoft Excel files.

Here is the general form of PROC EXPORT for writing Excel files:

```
PROC EXPORT DATA = data-set OUTFILE = 'filename' DBMS = identifier
        REPLACE;
```

where *data-set* is the SAS data set you want to export, and *filename* is the name you make up for the output data file. The DBMS= option tells SAS what type of Excel file to create. The REPLACE option tells SAS to replace the file if it already exists.

DBMS identifiers There are several DBMS identifiers you can use to create Excel files. Three commonly used identifiers are EXCEL, XLS, and XLSX. The EXCEL identifier is available only on Windows. The XLS identifier creates older style files (.xls extension) and is available on Windows and UNIX. The XLSX[1] identifier creates newer style files (.xlsx extension) and is available on both Windows and UNIX. Not all of these identifiers may work for you if your Windows computer has a mixture of 64-bit and 32-bit applications. In addition, some computer configurations may require that a PC Files Server be installed. The PC Files Server uses the EXCELCS identifier. See the SAS Help and Documentation for more information.

Naming sheets By default, the name of the Microsoft Excel sheet will be the same as the name of the SAS data set. If you want the sheet to have a different name, then specify it in the SHEET= statement. Special characters in sheet names will be converted to underscores, and the $ is not allowed at the end of the sheet name. The following statement creates a sheet named Golf_Hotels:

```
SHEET = 'Golf Hotels';
```

You can create Excel files with multiple sheets by submitting multiple EXPORT procedures, specifying the same file name in the OUTFILE= option, but using a different name in the SHEET= statement. If a sheet by that name already exists in the file, it will not be overwritten unless you also specify the REPLACE option.

Example A travel company maintains a SAS data set containing information about golf courses. For each golf course the file includes its name, number of holes, par, yardage, and greens fees.

```
Kapalua Plantation   18   73   7263  125.00
Pukalani             18   72   6945   55.00
Sandlewood           18   72   6469   35.00
Silversword          18   71    .     57.00
Waiehu Municipal     18   72   6330   25.00
Grand Waikapa        18   72   6122  200.00
```

The following program uses INFILE and INPUT statements to read the data and put them in a permanent SAS data set named GOLF in the MySASLib directory on the C drive (Windows):

```
LIBNAME travel 'c:\MySASLib';
DATA travel.golf;
   INFILE 'c:\MyRawData\Golf.dat';
   INPUT CourseName $18. NumberOfHoles Par Yardage GreenFees;
RUN;
```

Now suppose your office mate needs that information, but she wants it in a Microsoft Excel file. The following program writes a Microsoft Excel file from the SAS data set GOLF:

```
LIBNAME travel 'c:\MySASLib';
* Create Microsoft Excel file';
PROC EXPORT DATA=travel.golf OUTFILE = 'c:\MyExcel\Golf.xls' DBMS=EXCEL
   REPLACE;
RUN;
```

Here is what the Microsoft Excel file looks like. Notice that the name of the sheet is the same as the name of the SAS data set.

A1		f_x	'CourseName		
	A	B	C	D	E
1	CourseName	NumberOfHoles	Par	Yardage	GreenFees
2	Kapalua Plantation	18	73	7263	125
3	Pukalani	18	72	6945	55
4	Sandlewood	18	72	6469	35
5	Silversword	18	71		57
6	Waiehu Municipal	18	72	6330	25
7	Grand Waikapa	18	72	6122	200
8					

GOLF

If you have user-defined formats which have been associated with variables, only the unformatted values will be exported to Excel. The FORMAT statement is not supported in the EXPORT procedure.

---

[1] The XLSX identifier is available for the EXPORT procedure starting with SAS version 9.3M1.

10.5 Writing Raw Data Files with the DATA Step

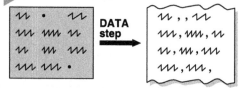

When you need total control over the contents and format of raw data files that you are creating, then the DATA step is the way to go. Using FILE and PUT statements in the DATA step, you can write almost any form of raw data file. This method has, to some extent, been replaced by the easier-to-use PROC EXPORT and Export Wizard,[2] but while PROC EXPORT gives you only a few options in formatting your files, the DATA step gives you flexibility to create raw data files just the way you want.

You can write raw data the same way that you read raw data, with just a few changes. Instead of naming the external file in an INFILE statement, you name it in a FILE statement. Instead of reading variables with an INPUT statement, you write them with a PUT statement. To say it another way, you use INFILE and INPUT statements to get raw data into SAS, and FILE and PUT statements to get raw data out.

PUT statements can be in list, column, or formatted style, just like INPUT statements, but since SAS already knows whether a variable is numeric or character, you don't have to put a $ after character variables. If you use list style PUT statements, SAS will automatically put one space between each variable, creating a space-delimited file. To write files with other delimiters, use a list-style PUT statement and the DSD and DLM= options in your FILE statement.[3]

```
FILE 'file-specification' DSD DLM = 'delimiter';
```

If you use column or formatted styles of PUT statements, SAS will put the variables wherever you specify. You can control spacing with the same pointer controls that INPUT statements use: @n to move to column n, +n to move n columns, / to skip to the next line, #n to skip to line n, and the trailing @ to hold the current line. In addition to printing variables, you can insert a text string by simply enclosing it in quotation marks.

Example To show how much more control you have using the DATA step as opposed to PROC EXPORT, this example uses the same data containing information about golf courses. For each course the file includes the course name, number of holes, par, yardage, and greens fees.

```
Kapalua Plantation   18   73   7263   125.00
Pukalani             18   72   6945    55.00
Sandlewood           18   72   6469    35.00
Silversword          18   71   .       57.00
Waiehu Municipal     18   72   6330    25.00
Grand Waikapa        18   72   6122   200.00
```

The following program uses INFILE and INPUT statements to read the data from a file called Golf.dat and put it in a permanent SAS data set named GOLF in the MySASLib directory on the C drive (Windows):

```
LIBNAME travel 'c:\MySASLib';
DATA travel.golf;
   INFILE 'c:\MyRawData\Golf.dat';
   INPUT CourseName $18. NumberOfHoles Par Yardage GreenFees;
RUN;
```

Suppose you want to put the data in a raw data file, but with only three variables, in a new order, and with dollar signs added to the variable GreenFees. The following program reads the SAS data set and writes a raw data file using FILE and PUT statements:

```
LIBNAME travel 'c:\MySASLib';
DATA _NULL_;
   SET travel.golf;
   FILE 'c:\MyRawData\Newfile.dat';
   PUT CourseName 'Golf Course' @32 GreenFees DOLLAR7.2 @40 'Par ' Par;
RUN;
```

The word _NULL_ appears in the DATA statement instead of a SAS data set name. You could put a data set name there, but _NULL_ is a special keyword that tells SAS not to bother making a new SAS data set. By not writing a new SAS data set, you save computer resources.

The SET statement simply tells SAS to read the permanent SAS data set GOLF. The FILE statement tells SAS the name of the output file you want to create. Then the PUT statement tells SAS what to write and where. The PUT statement contains two quoted strings, "Golf Course" and "Par" which SAS inserts in the raw data file. The PUT statement also tells SAS exactly where to place the data values for each variable using the @ column pointer, and to use the DOLLAR7.2 format to write the values for the GreenFees variable. Using the PUT statement you have complete control over the content of your raw data files.

If you run this program, your log will contain the following note telling how many records were written to the output file:

```
NOTE: 6 records were written to the file 'c:\MyRawData\Newfile.dat'.
```

Here is what the output file looks like in the text editor Microsoft Notepad:

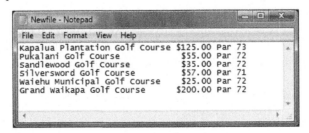

---

[2] In the z/OS operating environment you cannot use EXPORT, but you can use the DATA step to write raw data files.

[3] See section 2.15 for a discussion of the DSD= and DLM= options.

10.6   Writing Delimited and HTML Files Using ODS

The Output Delivery System (ODS) is a powerful tool for creating all sorts of output formats. Some of the output formats that ODS can create are useful for transferring data from SAS to other applications. Many applications can read data that are in either CSV or HTML format, and the great thing is that you can use this method in any operating environment and it's included in Base SAS software.

Since all procedure output goes to ODS, you can use ODS to export data by choosing the appropriate output destination for your application, and using PROC PRINT to get a listing of your data. By default, SAS will print a period for any missing numeric data. If you would rather have SAS print nothing for missing numeric data, then you can use the MISSING='' system option. Also by default, PROC PRINT includes observation numbers. If you don't want observation numbers in your output file, then use the NOOBS option on the PROC PRINT statement.

CSV files   The CSV destination puts commas between data values and double quotation marks around character values. The double quotation marks allow data values to contain commas. To create a CSV file containing your data, use the following ODS statements:

```
ODS CSV FILE = 'filename.csv';
  Your PROC PRINT statements go here
RUN;
ODS CSV CLOSE;
```

where *filename.csv* is the name of the CSV file that you are creating, and you insert the appropriate PROC PRINT statements for your data. The CSV output destination does not include titles or footnotes; if you want titles and footnotes to appear in the CSV file, then use the CSVALL output destination instead of CSV.

HTML files   Use the following statements to produce an HTML file of your data (and any titles or footnotes) with the default style. You can choose a different style by adding the STYLE= option to the ODS HTML statement. Or, if you do not want any styling, then use the CHTML (compact HTML) output destination instead of HTML. The FILE= option on the ODS HTML statement is synonymous with the BODY= option.

```
ODS HTML FILE = 'filename.html';
  Your PROC PRINT statements go here
RUN;
ODS HTML CLOSE;
```

Example   This example uses the permanent SAS data set, GOLF (created in the previous section), which has information about golf courses in Hawaii. The following program uses ODS to create a CSV file, golfinfo.csv, from the results of the PRINT procedure:

```
LIBNAME travel 'c:\MySASLib';
ODS CSV FILE='c:\MyCSVFiles\golfinfo.csv';
PROC PRINT DATA = travel.golf;
  TITLE 'Golf Course Information';
RUN;
ODS CSV CLOSE;
```

This is what the CSV file, golfinfo.csv, looks like if you open it in a simple editor such as Microsoft Notepad:

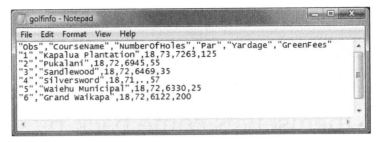

If you open the same file, golfinfo.csv, using Microsoft Excel, this is what you see:

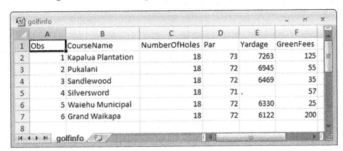

The following program creates an HTML file, golfinfo.html,[4] of the GOLF data, this time using the NOOBS option on the PROC PRINT statement to eliminate the Obs column:

```
LIBNAME travel 'c:\MySASLib';
ODS HTML FILE='c:\MyHTMLFiles\golfinfo.html';
PROC PRINT DATA = travel.golf NOOBS;
   TITLE 'Golf Course Information';
RUN;
ODS HTML CLOSE;
```

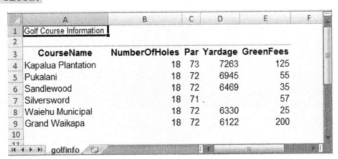

This is what the HTML file looks like when you open it in Microsoft Excel. You can see that although the data are the same as in the CSV file, the HTML file also includes the title and the default HTML styling.

---

[4] If you want the HTML file to be automatically recognized as a Microsoft Excel file, then give the file the .xls extension instead of the .html extension.

11

> " Problems that go away by themselves come back by themselves. "

Marcy E. Davis

CHAPTER 11

Debugging Your SAS Programs

11.1   Writing SAS Programs That Work

It's not always easy to write a program that works the first time you run it. Even experienced SAS programmers will tell you it's a delightful surprise when their programs run on the first try. The longer and more complicated the program, the more likely it is to have syntax or logic errors. But don't despair, there are a few guidelines you can follow that can make your programs run correctly sooner and help you discover errors more easily.

Make programs easy to read   One simple thing you can do is develop the habit of writing programs in a neat and consistent manner. Programs that are easy to read are easier to debug and will save you time in the long run. The following are suggestions on how to write your programs:

♦   Put only one SAS statement on a line. SAS allows you to put as many statements on a line as you wish, which may save some space in your program, but the saved space is rarely worth the sacrifice in readability.

♦   Use indention to show the different parts of the program. Indent all statements within the DATA and PROC steps. This way you can tell at a glance how many DATA and PROC steps there are in a program and which statement belongs to which step. It's also helpful to further indent any statements between a DO statement and its END statement.

♦   Use comment statements generously to document your programs. This takes some discipline but is important, especially if anyone else is likely to read or use your program. Everyone has a different programming style, and it is often impossible to figure out what someone else's program is doing and why. Comment statements take the mystery out of the program.

Test each part of the program   You can increase your programming efficiency tremendously by making sure each part of your program is working before moving on to write the next part. If you were building a house, you would make sure the foundation was level and square before putting up the walls. You would test the plumbing before finishing the bathroom. You are required to have each stage of the house inspected before moving on to the next. The same should be done for your SAS program. But you don't have to wait for the inspector to come out; you can do it yourself.

If you are reading data from a file, use Viewtable or PROC PRINT to check the SAS data set at least once to make sure it is correct before moving on. Sometimes, even though there are no errors or even suspicious notes in your SAS log, the SAS data set is not correct. This could happen because SAS did not read the data the way you imagined (after all it does what you say, not what you're thinking) or because the data had some peculiarities you did not realize. For example, a researcher who received two data files from Taiwan wanted to merge them together by date. She could not figure out why they refused to merge correctly until she printed both data sets and realized one of the files used Taiwanese dates, which are offset by 11 years.

It's a good habit to look at all the SAS data sets you create in a program at least once to make sure they are correct. As with reading raw data files, sometimes merging and setting data sets can produce the wrong result even though there were no error messages. So when in doubt, use Viewtable or PROC PRINT.

Test programs with small data sets Sometimes it's not practical to test your program with your entire data set. If your data files are very large, you may not want to print all the data and it may take a long time for your programs to run. In these cases, you can test your program with a subset of your data.

If you are reading data from a file, you can use the OBS= option in the INFILE statement to tell SAS to stop reading when it gets to that line in the file. This way you can read only the first 50 or 100 lines of data or however many it takes to get a good representation of your data. The following statement will read only the first 100 lines of the raw data file Mydata.dat:

```
INFILE 'Mydata.dat' OBS = 100;
```

You can also use the FIRSTOBS= option to start reading from the middle of the data file. So, if the first 100 data lines are not a good representation of your data but 101 through 200 are, you can use the following statement to read just those lines:

```
INFILE 'Mydata.dat' FIRSTOBS = 101 OBS = 200;
```

Here FIRSTOBS= and OBS= relate to the records of raw data in the file. These do not necessarily correspond to the observations in the SAS data set created. If, for example, you are reading two records for each observation, then you would need to read 200 records to get 100 observations.

If you are reading a SAS data set instead of a raw data file, you can use the OBS= and FIRSTOBS= data set options in the SET, MERGE, or UPDATE statements.[1] This controls which observations are processed in the DATA step. For example, the following DATA step will read the first 50 observations in the CATS data set. Note that when reading SAS data sets, OBS= and FIRSTOBS= truly do correspond to the observations and not to data lines:

```
DATA sampleofcats;
   SET cats (OBS = 50);
```

Test with representative data Using OBS= and FIRSTOBS= is an easy way to test your programs, but sometimes it is difficult to get a good representation of your data this way. You may need to create a small test data set by extracting representative parts of the larger data set. Or you may want to make up representative data for testing purposes. Making up data has the advantage that you can simplify the data and make sure you have every possible combination of values to test.

Sometimes you may want to make up data and write a small program just to test one aspect of your larger program. This can be extremely useful for narrowing down possible sources of error in a large, complicated program.

Syntax sensitive editors Both the SAS windowing environment and Enterprise Guide have editors that color code your program as you write it. SAS keywords appear in one color, variables in another. All text within quotation marks appears in the same color, so it is immediately obvious when you forget to close your quotation marks. Similarly, missing semicolons are much easier to discover because the colors in your program are not right. Catching errors as you type them can be a real time saver.

---

[1] Data set options are discussed in section 6.11.

11.2 Fixing Programs That Don't Work

In spite of your best efforts, sometimes programs just don't work. More often than not, programs don't run the first time. Even with simple programs it is easy to forget a semicolon or misspell a keyword—everyone does sometimes. If your program doesn't work, the source of the problem may be obvious like an error message with the offending part of your program underlined, or not so obvious as when you have no errors but still don't have the expected results. Whatever the problem, here are a few guidelines you can follow to help fix your program.

Read the SAS log The SAS log has a wealth of information about your program. In addition to listing the program statements, it tells you things like how many lines were read from your raw data file and what were the minimum and maximum line lengths. It gives the number of observations and variables in each SAS data set you create. Information like this may seem inconsequential at first but can be very helpful in finding the source of your errors.

The SAS log has three types of messages about your program: errors, warnings, and notes.

Errors These are hard to ignore. Not only do they come up in red on your screen, but your program will not run with errors. Usually errors are some kind of syntax or spelling mistake. The following shows the error message when you accidentally add a slash between the PROC PRINT and DATA= keywords. SAS underlines the problem (the slash) and tells you there is a syntax error. Sometimes SAS will tell you what is expected in the location where the error occurred and often this is very revealing.

```
1    PROC PRINT / DATA=one;
               -
               22
               200
ERROR 22-322: Syntax error, expecting one of the following: ;, BLANKLINE,
              DATA, DOUBLE, HEADING, LABEL, N, NOOBS, OBS, ROUND, ROWS,
              SPLIT, STYLE, UNIFORM, WIDTH.
ERROR 200-322: The symbol is not recognized and will be ignored.
```

The location of the error is easy to find, because it is usually underlined, but the source of the error can sometimes be tricky. Sometimes what is wrong is not what is underlined but something else earlier in the program.

Warnings These are less serious than errors because your program will run with warnings. But beware, a warning may mean that SAS has done something you have not intended. For example, SAS will attempt to correct your spelling of certain keywords. If you misspell INPUT as IMPUT, you will get the following message in your log:

```
WARNING 1-322: Assuming the symbol INPUT was misspelled as IMPUT.
```

Usually you would think, "SAS is so smart—it knows what I meant to say," but occasionally that may not be what you meant at all. Make sure that you know what all the warnings are about and that you agree with them.

Notes   These are less straightforward than either warnings or errors. Sometimes notes just give you information, like telling you the execution time of each step in your program. But sometimes notes can indicate a problem. Suppose, for example, that you have the following note in your SAS log:

```
NOTE: SAS went to a new line when INPUT statement reached past the end of a
      line.
```

This could mean that SAS did exactly what you wanted, or it could indicate a problem with your program or your data. Make sure that you know what each note means and why it is there.

Start at the beginning   Whenever you read the SAS log, start at the beginning. This seems like a ridiculous statement—why wouldn't you start at the beginning? Well, if you are using the SAS windowing environment, the SAS log rolls by in the Log window. When the program is finished, you are left looking at the end of the log. If you happen to see an error at the end of the log, it is natural to try to fix that error first—the first one you see. Avoid this temptation. Often errors at the end of the log are caused by earlier ones. If you fix the first error, often most or all of the other errors will disappear. If your lawnmower is out of gas and won't start, it's probably better to add gas before trying to figure out why it won't start. The same logic applies to debugging SAS programs; fixing one problem will often fix others.

Look for common mistakes first   More often than not there is a simple reason why your program doesn't work. Look for simple reasons before trying to find something more complicated. The remainder of this chapter consists of sections discussing the most common errors encountered in SAS programming. When you see this little bug in the upper-right corner of a section, you'll know that the material deals with how to debug your program.

Sometimes error messages just don't make any sense. For example, you may get an error message saying the INPUT statement is not valid. This doesn't make much sense because you know INPUT is a valid SAS statement. In cases like these, look for missing semicolons in the statements before the error. If SAS has underlined an item, be sure to look not only at the underlined item but also at the previous few statements.

Finally, if you just can't figure out why you are not getting the results you expect, make sure to use Viewtable or PROC PRINT to check any new SAS data sets you create. This can really help you discover errors in your logic, and sometimes uncover surprising details about your data.

Check your syntax   If you have large data sets, you may want to check for syntax errors in your program before processing your data. To do this, add the following line to your program and submit it in the usual way:

```
OPTIONS OBS=0 NOREPLACE;
```

The OBS=0 option tells SAS not to process any data, while the NOREPLACE option tells SAS not to replace existing SAS data sets with empty ones. Once you know your syntax is correct, you can resubmit your program without the OPTIONS statement in batch mode, or replace the OPTIONS with the following if you are using the SAS windowing environment.

```
OPTIONS OBS=MAX REPLACE;
```

Remember that this syntax check will not uncover any errors related to your data or logic.

11.3 Searching for the Missing Semicolon

Missing semicolons are the most common source of errors in SAS programs. For whatever reason, we humans can't seem to remember to put a semicolon at the end of all our statements. (Maybe we all have rebellious right pinkies—who knows.) This is unfortunate because, while it is easy to forget the semicolon, it is not always easy to find the missing semicolon. The error messages produced are often misleading, making it difficult to find the error.

SAS reads statements from one semicolon to the next without regard to the layout of the program. If you leave off a semicolon, you in effect concatenate two SAS statements. Then SAS gets confused because it seems as though you are missing statements, or it tries to interpret entire statements as options in the previous statement. This can produce some very puzzling messages. So, if you get an error message that just doesn't make sense, look for missing semicolons.

Example The following program is missing a semicolon on the comment statement before the DATA statement:

```
* Read the data file ToadJump.dat using list input
DATA toads;
    INFILE 'c:\MyRawData\ToadJump.dat';
    INPUT ToadName $ Weight Jump1 Jump2 Jump3;
RUN;
```

Here is the SAS log after the program has run:

```
1      * Read the data file ToadJump.dat using list input
2      DATA toads;
3          INFILE 'c:\MyRawData\ToadJump.dat';
           ------
           180
ERROR 180-322: Statement is not valid or it is used out of proper order.
4          INPUT ToadName $ Weight Jump1 Jump2 Jump3;
           -----
           180
ERROR 180-322: Statement is not valid or it is used out of proper order.
5      RUN;
```

In this case, DATA toads becomes part of the comment statement. Because there is now no DATA statement, SAS underlines the INFILE and INPUT keywords and says, "Hey these statements are in the wrong place; they have to be part of a DATA step." This doesn't make much sense to you because you know INFILE and INPUT are valid statements, and you did put them in a DATA step (or so you thought). That's when you should suspect a missing semicolon.

Example The next example shows the same program, but now the semicolon is missing from the DATA statement. The INFILE statement becomes part of the DATA statement, and SAS tries to create a SAS data set named INFILE. SAS also tries to interpret the filename, 'c:\MyRawData\ToadJump.dat' as a SAS data set name, but the .dat extension is not valid for SAS data sets. It also gives you an error saying that there is no DATALINES or INFILE statement. In addition, you get some warnings about data sets being incomplete. This is a good example of how one simple mistake can produce a lot of confusing messages:

```
30    * Read the data file ToadJump.dat using list input;
31    DATA toads
32      INFILE 'C:\MyRawData\ToadJump.dat';
33      INPUT ToadName $ Weight Jump1 Jump2 Jump3;
34    RUN;
ERROR: No DATALINES or INFILE statement.
ERROR: Extension for physical file name 'C:\MyRawData\ToadJump.dat' does
       not correspond to a valid member type.
NOTE: The SAS System stopped processing this step because of errors.
WARNING: The data set WORK.TOADS may be incomplete.  When this step was
         stopped there were 0 observations and 5 variables.
WARNING: Data set WORK.TOADS was not replaced because this step was stopped.
WARNING: The data set WORK.INFILE may be incomplete.  When this step was
         stopped there were 0 observations and 5 variables.
```

Missing semicolons can produce a variety of error messages. Usually the messages say that either a statement is not valid, or an option or parameter is not valid or recognized. Sometimes you don't get an error message, but the results are still not right. If you leave off the semicolon from the last RUN statement when submitting programs in the SAS windowing environment, you won't get an error. But SAS won't run the last part of your program either.

The DATASTMTCHK system option Some missing semicolons, such as the one in the last example, are easier to find if you use the DATASTMTCHK system option. This option controls which names you can use for SAS data sets in a DATA statement. By default it is set so that you cannot use the words: MERGE, RETAIN, SET, or UPDATE as a SAS data set name. This prevents you from accidentally overwriting an existing data set just because you forget a semicolon at the end of a DATA statement. You can make all SAS keywords invalid SAS data set names by setting the DATASTMTCHK option to ALLKEYWORDS. The partial log below again shows a missing semicolon at the end of the DATA statement, but this time DATASTMTCHK is set to ALLKEYWORDS:

```
35    OPTIONS DATASTMTCHK=ALLKEYWORDS;
36    * Read the data file ToadJump.dat using list input;
37    DATA toads
38      INFILE 'C:\MyRawData\ToadJump.dat';
        ------
        57
ERROR 57-185: INFILE is not allowed in the DATA statement when option
              DATASTMTCHK=ALLKEYWORDS.  Check for a missing semicolon in
              the DATA statement, or use DATASTMTCHK=NONE.
39      INPUT ToadName $ Weight Jump1 Jump2 Jump3;
40    RUN;
```

11.4 Note: INPUT Statement Reached Past the End of a Line

The note "SAS went to a new line when INPUT statement reached past the end of a line" is rather innocent looking, but its presence can indicate a problem. This note often goes unnoticed. It doesn't come up in red or even green lettering. It doesn't cause your program to stop. But look for it in your SAS log because it is a common note that usually means there is a problem.

This note means that as SAS was reading your data, it got to the end of the data line before it read values for all the variables in your INPUT statement. When this happens, SAS goes by default to the next line of data to get values for the remaining variables. Sometimes this is exactly what you want SAS to do, but if it's not, take a good look at your SAS log and output to be sure you know why this is happening.

Look in your SAS log where it tells you the number of lines it read from the data file and the number of observations in the SAS data set. If you have fewer observations than lines read, and you planned to have one observation per line, then you know you have a problem. Check the SAS data set using PROC PRINT or Viewtable. This can be very helpful in determining the source of the problem.

Example This example shows what can happen if you are using list input, and don't have periods for missing values. The following data come from a toad-jumping contest, where the toad's number is followed by its weight and distances for each of three jumps. When a toad was disqualified from a jump, no entry was made for that jump:

```
13   65 1.9 3.0
25  131 2.5 3.1 .5
10  202 3.8
8   128 3.2 1.9 2.6
3   162
21   99 2.4 1.7 3.0
```

Here is the SAS log from a program that reads the raw data using list input:

```
1    DATA toads;
2        INFILE 'c:\MyRawData\ToadJmp2.dat';
3        INPUT ToadNumber Weight Jump1 Jump2 Jump3;
4    RUN;
NOTE: The infile 'c:\MyRawData\ToadJmp2.dat' is:
      File Name=c:\MyRawData\ToadJmp2.dat,
      RECFM=V,LRECL=256
❶ NOTE: 6 records were read from the infile 'c:\MyRawData\ToadJmp2.dat'.
      The minimum record length was 6.
      The maximum record length was 18.
❸ NOTE: SAS went to a new line when INPUT statement reached past the end of a line.
❷ NOTE: The data set WORK.TOADS has 3 observations and 5 variables.
  NOTE: DATA statement used (Total process time):
      real time           0.37 seconds
```

❶ Notice that there were six records read from the raw data file.

❷ But there are only three observations in the SAS data set.

❸ The note, "...INPUT statement reached...," should alert you that there may be a problem.

If you look at the data set in Viewtable, you can see that there is a problem. The numbers don't look at all correct. (Can a toad jump 128 meters?)

	ToadNumber	Weight	Jump1	Jump2	Jump3
1	13	65	1.9	3	25
2	10	202	3.8	8	128
3	3	162	21	99	2.4

VIEWTABLE: Work.Toads

Here SAS went to a new line when you didn't want it to. To fix this problem, the simplest thing to do is use the MISSOVER option in the INFILE statement. MISSOVER instructs SAS to assign missing values to any variables for which there were no data instead of going to the next line for data. The INFILE statement would look like this:

```
INFILE 'c:\MyRawData\Toadjmp2.dat' MISSOVER;
```

Possible causes Other reasons for receiving a note informing you that the INPUT statement reached past the end of the line include

♦ You planned for SAS to go to the next data line when it ran out of data.

♦ Blank lines in your data file, usually at the beginning or end, can cause this note. Look at the minimum line length in the SAS log. If it is zero, then you have blank lines. Edit out the blank lines and rerun your program.

♦ If you are using list input and you do not have a space between every data value, you can get this note. For example, if you try to read the following data using list input, SAS will run out of data for the Gilroy Garlics because there is no space between the 15 and the 1035. SAS will read it as one number, then read the 12 where it should have been reading the 1035, and so on. To correct this problem, either add a space between the two numbers, or use column or formatted input.

```
Columbia Peaches      35  67  1 10  2  1
Gilroy Garlics        151035 12 11  7  6
Sacramento Tomatoes   124  85 15  4  9  1
```

♦ If you have some data lines which are shorter than the rest, and you are using column or formatted input, this can cause a problem. If you try to read a name, for example, in columns 60 through 70 when some of the names extend only to column 68, and you didn't add spaces at the end of the line to fill it out to column 70, then SAS will go to the next line to read the name. To avoid this problem, use the TRUNCOVER option in the INFILE statement (discussed in section 2.14). For example:

```
INFILE 'c:\MyRawData\Addresses.dat' TRUNCOVER;
```

11.5 Note: Lost Card

Lost card? You thought you were writing SAS programs, not playing a card game. This note makes more sense if you remember that computer programs and data used to be punched out on computer cards. A lost card means that SAS was expecting another line (or card) of data and didn't find it.

If you are reading multiple lines of data for each observation, then a lost card could mean you have missing or duplicate lines of data. If you are reading two data lines for each observation, then SAS will expect an even number of lines in the data file. If you have an odd number, then you will get the lost-card message. It can often be difficult to locate the missing or duplicate lines, especially with large data files. Printing the SAS data set as well as careful proofreading of the data file can be helpful in identifying problem areas.

Example The following example shows what can happen if you have a missing line of data. The raw data show the normal high and low temperatures and the record high and low for the month of July for each city, but the last city is missing a data line:

```
Nome AK
55 44
88 29
Miami FL
90 75
97 65
Raleigh NC
88 68
```

The following shows the SAS log from a program which reads the data, three lines per observation:

```
1    DATA highlow;
2      INFILE 'c:\MyRawData\Temps1.dat';
3      INPUT City $ State $ / NormalHigh NormalLow / RecordHigh RecordLow;
NOTE: The infile 'c:\MyRawData\Temps1.dat' is:
      File Name=c:\MyRawData\Temps1.dat,
      RECFM=V,LRECL=256
NOTE: LOST CARD.
City=Raleigh State=NC NormalHigh=88 NormalLow=68 RecordHigh=. RecordLow=.
_ERROR_=1 _N_=3
NOTE: 8 records were read from the infile 'c:\MyRawData\Temps1.dat'.
      The minimum record length was 5.
      The maximum record length was 10.
NOTE: The data set WORK.HIGHLOW has 2 observations and 6 variables.
NOTE: DATA statement used (Total process time):
      real time           0.03 seconds
      cpu time            0.03 seconds
```

In this case, you get the lost-card note, and SAS prints the data values it read for the observation with the missing data. You can see from the log that SAS read eight records from the file but the SAS data set has only two observations. The incomplete observation was not included.

Example It is very common to get other messages along with the lost-card note. The invalid-data note is a common byproduct of the lost card. If the second line were missing from the temperature data, then you would get invalid data because SAS will try to read Miami FL as the record high and low for Nome AK.

```
Nome AK
88 29
Miami FL
90 75
97 65
Raleigh NC
88 68
105 50
```

Here is the SAS log showing the invalid-data note:

```
NOTE: Invalid data for RecordHigh in line 3 1-5.
NOTE: Invalid data for RecordLow in line 3 7-8.
RULE:     ----+----1----+----2----+----3----+----4----+----5----+----6----+
3         Miami FL
City=Nome State=AK NormalHigh=88 NormalLow=29 RecordHigh=. RecordLow=.
_ERROR_=1 _N_=1
```

Example In addition to getting the lost-card note, it is also common to get a note indicating that the INPUT statement reached past the end of a line. If you forgot the last number in the file, as in the following example, then you would get these two notes together:

```
Nome AK
55 44
88 29
Miami FL
90 75
97 65
Raleigh NC
88 68
105
```

When a program uses list input, SAS will try to go to the next line to get the data for the last variable. Since there isn't another line of data, you get the lost-card note.

```
NOTE: LOST CARD.
City=Raleigh State=NC NormalHigh=88 NormalLow=68 RecordHigh=105 RecordLow=. _ERROR_=1
_N_=3
NOTE: 9 records were read from the infile
      'c:\MyRawData\Temps3.dat'.
      The minimum record length was 3.
      The maximum record length was 10.
NOTE: SAS went to a new line when INPUT statement reached past the end of
      a line.
NOTE: The data set WORK.HIGHLOW has 2 observations and 6 variables.
```

11.6 Note: Invalid Data

The typical new SAS user, upon seeing the invalid-data note, will ignore it, hoping perhaps that it will simply go away by itself. That's rather ironic considering that the message is explicit and easy to interpret once you know how to read it.

Interpreting the message The invalid-data note appears when SAS is unable to read from a raw data file because the data are inconsistent with the INPUT statement. This note almost always indicates a problem. For example, one common mistake is typing in the letter O instead of the number 0. If the variable is numeric, then SAS is unable to interpret the letter O. In response, SAS does two things; it sets the value of this variable to missing and prints out a message like this for the problematic observation:

```
❶ NOTE: Invalid data for IDNumber in line 8 1-5.
❷ RULE:----+----1----+----2----+----3----+----4----+----5----+----6----+
❷ 8     OO7  James Bond    SA341
❸ IDNumber=. Name=James Bond Class=SA Q1=3 Q2=4 Q3=1 _ERROR_=1 _N_=8
```

❶ The first line tells you where the problem occurred. Specifically, it states the name of the variable SAS got stuck on and the line number and columns of the raw data file that SAS was trying to read. In this example, the error occurred while SAS was trying to read a variable named IDNumber from columns 1 through 5 in line 8 of the input file.

❷ The next line is a ruler with columns as the increments. The numeral 1 marks the tenth column, 2 marks the twentieth, and so on. Below the ruler, SAS dumps the actual line of raw data so you can see the little troublemaker for yourself. Using the ruler as a guide, you can count over to the column in question. At this point you can compare the actual raw data to your INPUT statement, and the error is usually obvious. The value of IDNumber should be zero-zero-seven, but looking at the line of actual data you can see that a careless typist has typed zero-letter O-seven. Such an error may seem minor to you, but you'll soon learn that computers are hopelessly persnickety.

❸ As if this weren't enough, SAS prints one more piece of information: the value of each variable for that observation as SAS read it. In this case, you can see that IDNumber equals missing, Name equals James Bond, and so on. Two automatic variables appear at the end of the line: _ERROR_ and _N_. The _ERROR_ variable has a value of 1 if there is a data error for that observation, and 0 if there is not. In an invalid-data note, _ERROR_ always equals 1. The automatic variable _N_ is the number of times SAS has looped through the DATA step.

Unprintable characters Occasionally invalid data contain unprintable characters. In these cases, SAS shows you the raw data in hexadecimal format.

```
NOTE: Invalid data for IDNumber in line 10 1-5.
   RULE: ----+----1----+----2----+----3----+----4----+----5----+----6----+
❶ CHAR  ..   Indiana Jones PI83.
❷ ZONE  20222466666624666725433222222222222222222222222222222222222222222
❷ NUMR  E90009E491E10AFE5300983E0000000000000000000000000000000000000000000
IdNumber=. Name=Indiana Jones Class=PI Q1=8 Q2=3 Q3=. _ERROR_=1 _N_=10
```

❶ As before, SAS prints the line of raw data that contains the invalid data.

❷ Directly below the line of raw data, SAS prints two lines containing the hexadecimal equivalent of the data. You needn't understand hexadecimal values to be able to read this. SAS prints the data this way because the normal 10 numerals and 26 letters don't provide enough values to represent all computer symbols uniquely. Hexadecimal uses two characters to represent each symbol. To read hexadecimal, take a digit from the first line (labeled ZONE) together with the corresponding digit from the second line (labeled NUMR). In this case, a tab slipped into column 2 and appears as a harmless-looking period in the line of data. In hexadecimal, however, the tab appears as 09, while a real period in column 1 is 2E in hex. [2]

Possible causes Common reasons for receiving the invalid-data note include

♦ character values in a field that should be numeric (including using the letter O instead of the numeral zero)

♦ forgetting to specify that a variable is character (SAS assumes it is numeric)

♦ incorrect column specifications producing embedded spaces in numeric data

♦ list-style input with two periods in a row and no space in between

♦ missing data not marked with a period for list-style input causing SAS to read the next data value

♦ special characters such as tab, carriage-return-line-feed, or form-feed in numeric data

♦ using the wrong informat such as MMDDYY. instead of DDMMYY.

♦ invalid dates (such as September 31) read with a date informat

Double question mark informat modifier Sometimes you have invalid data, and there is nothing you can do about it. You know the data are bad, and you just want SAS to go ahead and set those values to missing without filling your log with notes. At those times, you can use the ?? informat modifier. The ?? informat modifier suppresses the invalid-data note, and prevents the automatic variable _ERROR_ from being set to 1. Just insert the two question marks after the name of the problematic variable and before any informat or column specifications. For example, to prevent the preceding invalid-data notes for the variable IdNumber, you would add ?? to the INPUT statement like this:

```
INPUT IdNumber ?? 1-5 Name $ 6-18 Class $ 20-21 Q1 22 Q2 23 Q3 24;
```

---

[2] In z/OS the hexadecimal representation of a tab is 05.

11.7 Note: Missing Values Were Generated

The missing-values note appears when SAS is unable to compute the value of a variable because of preexisting missing values in your data. This is not necessarily a problem. It is possible that your data contain legitimate missing values and that setting a new variable to missing is a desirable response. But it is also possible that the missing values result from an error and that you need to fix your program or your data. A good rule is to think of the missing-values note as a flag telling you to check for an error.

Example Here again are the data from the toad-jumping contest including the toad's name, weight, and the distance jumped in each of three trials:

```
Lucky 2.3 1.9 . 3.0
Spot 4.6 2.5 3.1 .5
Tubs 7.1 . . 3.8
Hop 4.5 3.2 1.9 2.6
Noisy 3.8 1.3 1.8
1.5
Winner 5.7 . . .
```

Notice that several of the toads have missing values for one or more jumps. To compute the average distance jumped, the program in the following SAS log reads the raw data, adds together the values for the three jumps, and divides by three:

```
1     DATA toads;
2        INFILE 'c:\MyRawData\ToadJump.dat';
3        INPUT ToadName $ Weight Jump1 Jump2 Jump3;
4        AverageJump = (Jump1 + Jump2 + Jump3) / 3;
5     RUN;
NOTE: The infile 'c:\MyRawData\ToadJump.dat' is:
      FILE NAME=c:\MyRawData\ToadJump.dat,
      RECFM=V,LRECL=256
NOTE: 7 records were read from the infile 'c:\MyRawData\ToadJump.dat'.
      The minimum record length was 3.
      The maximum record length was 19.
NOTE: SAS went to a new line when INPUT statement reached past the end of
      a line.
NOTE: ❶ Missing values were generated as a result of performing an
         operation on missing values.
      ❷ Each place is given by: (Number of times) at (Line):(Column)
         3 at 4:25
NOTE: The data set WORK.TOADS has 6 observations and 6 variables.
```

Because of missing values in the data, SAS was unable to compute AverageJump for some of the toads. In response, SAS printed the missing-values note which has two parts:

❶ The first part of the note says that SAS was forced to set some values to missing.

❷ The second part is a bit more cryptic. SAS lists the number of times values were set to missing. This generally corresponds to the number of observations that generated missing values, unless the problem occurs within a DO-loop. Next SAS states where in the program it encountered the problem. In the preceding example, SAS set three values to missing: at line 4, column 25. Looking at the program, you can see that line 4 is the line which calculates AverageJump, and column 25 contains the first plus sign. Looking at the raw data, you can see that three observations have missing values for Jump1, Jump2, or Jump3. Those observations are the three times mentioned in the missing-values note.

Finding the missing values In this case it was easy to find the observations with missing values. But if you had a data set with hundreds, or millions, of observations, then you couldn't just glance at the data. In that case, you could subset the problematic observations with a subsetting IF statement like this:

```
DATA missing;
   INFILE 'c:\MyRawData\ToadJump.dat';
   INPUT ToadName $ Weight Jump1 Jump2 Jump3;
   AverageJump = (Jump1 + Jump2 + Jump3) / 3;
   IF AverageJump = .;
RUN;
```

Once you have selected just the observations that have missing values, you can use Viewtable or PROC PRINT to examine them. Here is Viewtable showing the observations with missing values for AverageJump:

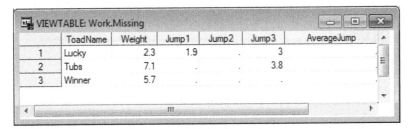

Using the SUM and MEAN functions You may be able to circumvent this problem when you are computing a sum or mean by using the SUM or MEAN function instead of an arithmetic expression. In the preceding program, you could remove this line:

```
AverageJump = (Jump1 + Jump2 + Jump3) / 3;
```

And substitute this line:

```
AverageJump = MEAN(Jump1, Jump2, Jump3);
```

The SUM and MEAN functions use only non-missing values for the computation. In this example, you would still get the missing-values note for one toad, Winner, because it had missing values for all three jumps.

11.8 Note: Numeric Values Have Been Converted to Character (or Vice Versa)

Even with only two data types, numeric and character, SAS programmers sometimes get their variables mixed up. When you accidentally mix numeric and character variables, SAS tries to fix your program by converting variables from numeric to character or vice versa, as needed. Programmers sometimes ignore this problem, but that is not a good idea. If you ignore this message, it may come back to haunt you as you find new incompatibilities resulting from the fix. If, indeed, a variable needs to be converted, you should do it yourself, explicitly, so you know what your variables are doing.

Example To show how SAS handles this kind of incompatibility, here are data about a class. Each line of data contains a student's ID number, name, and scores on two tests.

```
110 Linda    53 60
203 Derek    72 64
105 Kathy    98 82
224 Michael 80 55
```

The instructor runs the following program to read the data and create a permanent SAS data set named SCORES.

```
LIBNAME students 'c:\MySASLib';
DATA students.scores;
   INFILE 'c:\MyRawData\TestScores.dat';
   INPUT StudentID Name $ Score1 Score2 $;
RUN;
```

After creating the permanent SAS data set, the instructor runs a program to compute the total score and substring the first digit of StudentID. (Students in section 1 of the class have IDs starting with 1 while students in section 2 have IDs starting with 2.) Here is the log from the program:

```
2      DATA grades;
3         SET students.scores;
4         TotalScore = Score1 + Score2;
5         Class = SUBSTR(StudentID,1,1);
6      RUN;
NOTE: Character values have been converted to numeric values at the places
      given by: (Line):(Column).
      4:26
NOTE: Numeric values have been converted to character values at the places
      given by: (Line):(Column).
      5:19
NOTE: There were 4 observations read from the data set STUDENTS.SCORES.
NOTE: The data set WORK.GRADES has 4 observations and 6 variables.
NOTE: DATA statement used (Total process time):
      real time           0.04 seconds
      cpu time            0.04
```

This program produces two values-have-been-converted notes. The first conversion occurred in line 4, column 26. Looking at line 4 of the log, you can see that the variable name Score2 appears in column 26. Score2 was accidentally input as a character variable, so SAS had to convert it to numeric before adding it to Score1 to compute TotalScore.

The second conversion occurred in line 5, column 19. Looking at line 5 of the log, you can see that the variable StudentID appears in column 19. StudentID was input as a numeric variable, but the SUBSTR function requires character variables, so SAS was forced to convert StudentID to character.

Converting variables You could go back and input the raw data with the correct types, but sometimes that's just not practical. Instead you can convert the variables from one type to another. To convert variables from character to numeric, you use the INPUT function. To convert from numeric to character, you use the PUT function. Most often, you would use these functions in an assignment statement with the following syntax:

Character to Numeric	**Numeric to Character**
`newvar = INPUT(oldvar, informat);`	`newvar = PUT(oldvar, format);`

These two slightly eccentric functions are first cousins of the PUT and INPUT statements. Just as an INPUT statement uses informats, the INPUT function uses informats; and just as PUT statements use formats, the PUT function uses formats. These functions can be confusing because they are similar but different. In the case of the INPUT function, the informat must be the type you are converting to—numeric. In contrast, the format for the PUT function must be the type you are converting from—numeric.[3] To convert the troublesome variables in the preceding program, you would use these statements:

Character to Numeric	**Numeric to Character**
`NewScore2 = INPUT(Score2, 2.);`	`NewID = PUT(StudentID, 3.);`

Here is a log showing the program with the statements to convert Score2 and StudentID:

```
7      DATA grades;
8         SET students.scores;
9         NewScore2 = INPUT(Score2, 2.);
10        TotalScore = Score1 + NewScore2;
11        NewID = PUT(StudentID,3.);
12        Class = SUBSTR(NewID,1,1);
13     RUN;
NOTE: There were 4 observations read from the data set STUDENTS.SCORES.
NOTE: The data set WORK.GRADES has 4 observations and 8 variables.
NOTE: DATA statement used (Total process time):
      real time           0.03 seconds
      cpu time            0.03 seconds
```

Notice that this version of the program runs without any suspicious messages.

---

[3] In this discussion, we are talking about converting variables from numeric to character or vice versa, but you can also use the PUT function to change one character value to another character value. When you do this, *oldvar* and *newvar* would be character variables, and the format would be a character format.

11.9 DATA Step Produces Wrong Results but No Error Message

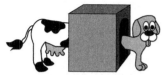 Some of the hardest errors to debug aren't errors at all, at least not to SAS. If you do complex programming, you may write a DATA step that runs just fine—without any errors or suspicious notes—but produces the wrong results. The more complex your programs are, the more likely you are to get this kind of error. Sometimes it seems like a DATA step is a black box. You know what goes in, and you know what comes out, but what happens in the middle is a mystery. This problem is actually a logic error; somewhere along the way, SAS got the wrong instruction.

Example Here is a program that illustrates this problem and how to debug it. The raw data file below contains information from a class. For each student there are three scores from tests, and one score from homework:

```
Linda    53 60  66 42
Derek    72 64  56 32
Kathy    98 82 100 48
Michael 80 55  95 50
```

This program is supposed to select students whose average score is below 70, but it doesn't work. Here is the log from the wayward program:

```
1      * Keep only students with mean below 70;
2      DATA lowscore;
3         INFILE 'c:\MyRawData\Class.dat';
4         INPUT Name $ Score1 Score2 Score3 Homework;
5         Homework = Homework * 2;
6         AverageScore = MEAN(Score1 + Score2 + Score3 + Homework);
7         IF AverageScore < 70;
8      RUN;
NOTE: The infile 'c:\MyRawData\Class.dat' is:
      File Name=c:\MyRawData\Class.dat,
      RECFM=V,LRECL=256
NOTE: 4 records were read from the infile 'c:\MyRawData\Class.dat'.
      The minimum record length was 20.
      The maximum record length was 20.
NOTE: The data set WORK.LOWSCORE has 0 observations and 6 variables.
```

First, the DATA step reads the raw data from a file named Class.dat. The highest possible score on homework is 50. To make the homework count the same as a test, the program doubles the value of Homework. Then the program computes the mean of the three test scores and Homework, and subsets the data by selecting only observations with a mean score below 70. Unfortunately, something went wrong. The LOWSCORE data set contains no observations. A glance at the raw data confirms that there should be students whose mean scores are below 70.

Using the PUT and PUTLOG statements to debug To debug a problem like this, you have to figure out exactly what is happening inside the DATA step. A good way to do this—especially if your DATA step is long and complex—is with PUT or PUTLOG statements. Elsewhere in this book, PUT statements are used along with FILE statements to write raw data files and custom reports. If you use a PUT statement without a FILE statement, then SAS writes in the

SAS log. PUTLOG statements are the same except that they always write to the log even when you have a FILE statement. PUT and PUTLOG statements can take many forms, but for debugging, a handy style is

```
PUTLOG _ALL_;
```

SAS will print all the variables in your data set. If you have a lot of variables, you can print just the relevant ones this way:

```
PUTLOG variable-1=   variable-2=   . . .   variable-n=;
```

The DATA step below is identical to the one shown earlier except that a PUTLOG statement was added. In a longer DATA step, you might choose to have PUTLOG statements at several points. In this case, one will suffice. This PUTLOG statement is placed before the subsetting IF, since in this particular program the subsetting IF eliminates all observations:

```
9    * Keep only students with mean below 70;
10   DATA lowscore;
11      INFILE 'c:\MyRawData\Class.dat';
12      INPUT Name $ Score1 Score2 Score3 Homework;
13      Homework = Homework * 2;
14      AverageScore = MEAN(Score1 + Score2 + Score3 + Homework);
15      PUTLOG Name= Score1= Score2= Score3= Homework= AverageScore=;
16      IF AverageScore < 70;
17   RUN;
NOTE: The infile 'c:\MyRawData\Class.dat' is:
      FILE NAME=c:\MyRawData\Class.dat,
      RECFM=V,LRECL=256
Name=Linda Score1=53 Score2=60 Score3=66 Homework=84 AverageScore=263
Name=Derek Score1=72 Score2=64 Score3=56 Homework=64 AverageScore=256
Name=Kathy Score1=98 Score2=82 Score3=100 Homework=96 AverageScore=376
Name=Michael Score1=80 Score2=55 Score3=95 Homework=100 AverageScore=330
NOTE: 4 records were read from the infile 'c:\MyRawData\Class.dat'.
      The minimum record length was 20.
      The maximum record length was 20.
NOTE: The data set WORK.LOWSCORE has 0 observations and 6 variables.
```

Looking at the the log, you can see the result of the PUTLOG statement. The data listed in the middle of the log show that the variables are being input properly, and the variable Homework is being adjusted properly. However, something is wrong with the values of AverageScore; they are much too high. There is a syntax error in the line that computes AverageScore. Instead of commas separating the three score variables in the MEAN function, there are plus signs. Since functions can contain arithmetic expressions, SAS simply added the four variables together, as instructed, and computed the mean of a single number. That's why no observations had values of AverageScore below 70.

11.10 Error: Invalid Option, Error: The Option Is Not Recognized, or Error: Statement Is Not Valid

If SAS cannot make sense out of one of your statements, it stops executing the current DATA or PROC step and prints one of these messages:

```
ERROR 22-7: Invalid option name.
ERROR 202-322: The option or parameter is not recognized and will be
     ignored.
ERROR 180-322: Statement is not valid or it is used out of proper order.
```

The invalid-option message and its cousin, the option-is-not-recognized message, tell you that you have a valid statement, but SAS can't make sense out of an apparent option. The statement-is-not-valid message, on the other hand, means that SAS can't understand the statement at all.

Thankfully, with all three messages SAS underlines the point at which it got confused so you know where to look for the problem.

Example The SAS log below contains an invalid option:

```
1      DATA scores (ROP = Score1);
                    ---
                    22
ERROR 22-7: Invalid option name ROP.
2          INFILE 'c:\MyRawData\Class.dat';
3          INPUT  Name $ Score1 Score2 Score3 Homework;
4      RUN;
NOTE: The SAS System stopped processing this step because of errors.
NOTE: DATA statement used (Total process time):
        real time           0.03 seconds
        cpu time            0.00 seconds
```

In this DATA step, the word DROP was misspelled as ROP. Since SAS cannot interpret this, it underlines the word ROP, prints the invalid-option message, and stops processing the DATA step.

Example The following log contains an option-is-not-recognized message:

```
5      PROC PRINT
6          VAR Score2;
           ---
           22
           202
ERROR 22-322:  Syntax error, expecting one of the following: ;, BLANKLINE,
     DATA, DOUBLE, HEADING, LABEL, N, NOOBS, OBS, ROUND, ROWS, SPLIT, STYLE,
     UNIFORM, WIDTH.
ERROR 202-322: The option or parameter is not recognized and will be ignored.
7      RUN;
NOTE: The SAS System stopped processing this step because of errors.
NOTE: PROCEDURE PRINT used (Total process time):
        real time           0.25 seconds
        cpu time            0.09 seconds
```

SAS underlined the VAR statement. This message may seem puzzling since VAR is not an option, but a statement, and a valid statement at that. But if you look at the previous statement, you will see that the PROC statement is missing one of those pesky semicolons. As a result, SAS tried to interpret the words VAR and Score2 as options in the PROC statement. Since no options exist with those names, SAS stopped processing the step and printed the option-is-not-recognized message. SAS also printed the syntax-error message listing all the valid options for a PROC PRINT statement.

Example Here is a log with the statement-is-not-valid message:

```
8     PROC PRINT;
9        SET class;
         ---
         180
ERROR 180-322: Statement is not valid or it is used out of proper order.
10    RUN;
NOTE: The SAS System stopped processing this step because of errors.
NOTE: PROCEDURE PRINT used (Total process time):
      real time             0.01 seconds
      cpu time              0.01 seconds
```

In this case, a SET statement was used in a PROC step. Since SET statements can be used only in DATA steps, SAS underlines the word SET and prints the statement-is-not-valid message.

Possible causes Generally, with these error messages, the cause of the problem is easy to detect. You should check the underlined item and the previous statement for possible errors. Possible causes include

- ♦ a misspelled keyword

- ♦ a missing semicolon

- ♦ a DATA step statement in a PROC step (or vice versa)

- ♦ a RUN statement in the middle of a DATA or PROC step (this does not cause errors for some procedures)

- ♦ the correct option with the wrong statement

- ♦ an unmatched quotation mark

- ♦ an unmatched comment

11.11 Note: Variable Is Uninitialized or Error: Variable Not Found

If you find one of these messages in your SAS log, then SAS is telling you that the variable named in the message does not exist:

```
NOTE: Variable X is uninitialized.

WARNING: Variable X not found.

ERROR: Variable X not found.
```

Generally, the first time you get one of these messages, it is quite a shock. You may be sure that the variable does exist. After all, you remember creating it. Fortunately, the problem is usually easy to fix once you understand what SAS is telling you.

If the problem happens in a DATA step, then SAS prints the variable-is-uninitialized note, initializes the variable, and continues to execute your program. Normally variables are initialized when they are read (via an INPUT, SET, MERGE, or UPDATE statement) or when they are created via an assignment statement. If you use a variable for the first time in a way that does not assign a value to the variable (such as on the right side of an assignment statement, in the condition of an IF statement, or in a DROP or KEEP option) then SAS tries to fix the problem by assigning a value of missing to the variable for all observations. This is very generous of SAS, but it almost never fixes the problem, since you probably don't want the variable to have missing values for all observations.

When the problem happens in a PROC step, the results are more grave. If the error occurs in a critical statement such as a VAR statement, then SAS prints the variable-not-found error and does not execute the step. If the error occurs in a less critical statement such as a LABEL statement, then SAS prints the variable-not-found warning message, and attempts to run the step.

Example Here is the log from a program with missing-variable problems in both a DATA and a PROC step:

```
1      DATA highscores (KEEP = Name Total);
2          INFILE 'c:\MyRawData\TestScores.dat';
3          INPUT StudentID Name $ Score1 Score2;
4          IF Scor1 > 90;
5          Total = Score1 + Score2;
6      RUN;
NOTE: Variable Scor1 is uninitialized.
NOTE: The data set WORK.HIGHSCORES has 0 observations and 2 variables.
NOTE: DATA statement used (Total process time):
      real time           0.04 seconds
      cpu time            0.03 seconds
7
```

```
8     PROC PRINT DATA = highscores;
9        VAR Name Score2 Total;
ERROR: Variable SCORE2 not found.
10    RUN;
NOTE: The SAS System stopped processing this step because of errors.
NOTE: PROCEDURE PRINT used (Total process time):
      real time           0.03 seconds
      cpu time            0.01 seconds
```

In this DATA step, the INPUT statement reads four variables: StudentID, Name, Score1, and Score2. But a misspelling in the subsetting IF statement causes SAS to initialize a new variable named Scor1. Because Scor1 has missing values, none of the observations satisfies the subsetting IF, and the data set HIGHSCORES is left with zero observations.

In the PROC PRINT, the VAR statement requests three variables: Name, Score2, and Total. Score2 did exist but was dropped from the data set by the KEEP= option in the DATA statement. That KEEP= option kept only two variables, Name and Total. As a result, SAS prints the variable-not-found error message, and does not execute the PROC PRINT.

Possible causes Common ways to "lose" variables include

♦ misspelling a variable name

♦ using a variable that was dropped at some earlier time

♦ using the wrong data set

♦ committing a logic error, such as using a variable before it is created

If the source of the problem is not immediately obvious, a look at the properties of the data set can often help you figure out what is going on. You can examine the properties of a data set using the Properties window or PROC CONTENTS. The Properties window (discussed in section 1.12) and PROC CONTENTS (discussed in section 2.21) give you information about what is in a SAS data set including variable names.

11.12 SAS Truncates a Character Variable

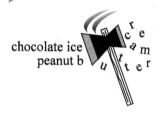

Sometimes you may notice that some, or all, of the values of a character variable are truncated. You may be expecting "peanut butter" and get "peanut b" or "chocolate ice cream" and get "chocolate ice." This usually happens when you use IF statements to create a new character variable, or when you are using list-style input and you have values longer than eight characters.

All character variables have a fixed length determined by one of the following methods.

INPUT statement If a variable's values are read from a raw data file, then the length is determined by the INPUT statement. If you are using list-style input, then the length defaults to 8. If you are using column or formatted input, then the length is determined by the number of columns, or informat. The following shows examples of INPUT statements that read values for the variable Food and the resulting lengths of Food:

INPUT statement	**Length of Food**
INPUT Food $;	8
INPUT Food $ 1-10;	10
INPUT Food $15.;	15

Assignment statement If you are creating the variable in an assignment statement, then the length is determined by the first occurrence of the new variable name. For example, the following program creates a variable, Status, whose values are determined by the Temperature variable:

```
DATA summer;
   SET temps;
   IF Temperature > 100 THEN Status = 'Hot';
      ELSE Status = 'Cold';
RUN;
```

Because the word Hot has three characters and that is the first statement which uses the variable, Status has a length of 3. Any other values for that variable would be truncated to three characters (Col instead of Cold, for example).

LENGTH statement The LENGTH statement in a DATA step defines variable lengths and, if it comes before the INPUT or assignment statement, will override either of the previous two methods of determining length. The following LENGTH statement sets the length of the Status variable to 4 and the Food variable to 15:

```
LENGTH Status $4 Food $15;
```

ATTRIB statement You can also assign variable lengths in an ATTRIB statement in a DATA step where you can associate formats, informats, labels, and lengths to variables in a single statement. Always place the LENGTH option before a FORMAT option in an ATTRIB statement to ensure that the variables are assigned proper lengths. For example, the following statement assigns the character variable Status a length of 4 and the label Hot or Cold:

```
ATTRIB Status LENGTH = $4 LABEL = 'Hot or Cold';
```

Example The following example shows what can happen if you let SAS determine the length of a character variable (in this case, using the assignment statement method). You have the following data for a consumer survey of car color preferences. Age is followed by sex (coded as 1 for male and 2 for female), annual income, and preferred car color (yellow, gray, blue, or white):

```
19 1 14000 Y
45 1 65000 G
72 2 35000 B
31 1 44000 Y
58 2 83000 W
```

You want to create a new variable, AgeGroup, which has these values: Teen for customers under 20, Adult for ages 20 through 64, and Senior for those 65 and over. In the following program, a series of IF-THEN/ELSE statements create AgeGroup:

```
DATA carsurvey;
    INFILE 'c:\MyRawData\Cars.dat';
    INPUT Age Sex Income Color $;
    IF Age < 20 THEN AgeGroup = 'Teen';
        ELSE IF Age < 65 THEN AgeGroup = 'Adult';
        ELSE AgeGroup = 'Senior';
PROC PRINT DATA = carsurvey;
    TITLE 'Car Color Survey Results';
RUN;
```

The following results of the PROC PRINT show how the values of AgeGroup are truncated to four characters—the number of characters in Teen.

Car Color Survey Results

Obs	Age	Sex	Income	Color	AgeGroup
1	19	1	14000	Y	Teen
2	45	1	65000	G	Adul
3	72	2	35000	B	Seni
4	31	1	44000	Y	Adul
5	58	2	83000	W	Adul

The addition of a LENGTH statement in the DATA step, as follows, would eliminate the truncation problem:

```
DATA carsurvey;
    INFILE 'c:\MyRawData\Cars.dat';
    INPUT Age Sex Income Color $;
    LENGTH AgeGroup $6;
    IF Age < 20 THEN AgeGroup = 'Teen';
        ELSE IF Age < 65 THEN AgeGroup = 'Adult';
        ELSE AgeGroup = 'Senior';
RUN;
```

11.13 SAS Stops in the Middle of a Program

One of the most disconcerting errors encountered by SAS users is having SAS stop in the middle of a program. It's as if your SAS code has suddenly dropped dead without so much as an error message to act as a smoking gun. Without an error message, you are left to sleuth this problem on your own. Often the problem has nothing to do with SAS. Instead the operating environment may have stopped your program in its tracks. Other times the problem results from errors that prevent SAS from seeing the entire program.

A number of completely unrelated reasons can cause SAS to stop. They are listed below, starting with the most general problems and ending with the ones that are specific to certain execution modes or operating environments.

An unmatched quotation mark Unmatched quotation marks wreak havoc on SAS programs, including making SAS stop in the middle of a program. In this case, SAS stops because, in effect, it thinks the remainder of the program is part of a quote. In batch mode, the solution is simple enough. Insert the missing quotation mark and resubmit the program. In the SAS windowing environment you can't just resubmit the program because SAS is still waiting for the other quotation mark. The solution is to submit a sacrificial quotation mark like this:

```
';
RUN;
```

Then edit your program, correct the problem (remembering to delete the extra quotation mark and RUN statement at the end), and rerun the program. Some prefer to exit SAS and start over. If you do, just remember to save your program before exiting.

An unmatched comment Unmatched comments can cause SAS to stop in the middle of a program, much like unmatched quotation marks. The problem is that SAS can't read the entire program because part of it is accidentally stuck in a comment. This isn't so likely to happen if you use the kind of comment that starts with an asterisk and ends with a semicolon since programs contain many semicolons, and any semicolon will do to end a comment. But if you use the style of comment that starts with /* and ends with */, and you forget to include the last */, then SAS will assume that the remainder of your program is one long comment. The solution, in batch mode, is to insert the missing end-of-comment and resubmit the program. In the SAS windowing environment, the solution is to submit a lone end-of-comment like this:

```
*/;
RUN;
```

Then edit your program, correct the problem (remembering to delete the extra end-of-comment and RUN statement at the end), and rerun the program. Some prefer to exit SAS and start over. If you do, just remember to save your program before exiting.

No RUN statement at the end of a program   This problem occurs only in the SAS windowing environment. In batch mode there is an implicit RUN statement at the end of every SAS program. The problem is that in the SAS windowing environement SAS has no way of knowing when it is time to execute your last step unless you tell it with a RUN statement. The solution is to submit the wayward statement:

```
RUN;
```

Not sure what the problem is?   If you are working in the SAS windowing environment, and you think you have an unmatched quotation mark, unmatched comment, or missing RUN statement, but you're not sure, you may want to submit the following set of statements:

```
*';
*";
*/;
RUN;
```

Together these statements form a sort of universal terminator for SAS programs. If the program has no problems, these statements do nothing since the first three would then be comments, and an extra RUN statement between steps does nothing. That means you can submit these without fear of causing any harm.

Out of time   Batch systems may have time limits, measured in CPU seconds, for computer jobs. These limits are set locally by your systems programmers. And these limits are helpful because they allow small jobs to be submitted to a special queue with a higher priority. That way your short job doesn't have to wait for some mega-job to finish processing. Time limits may also be set to stop jobs that accidentally get into an infinite loop. If your job stops in the middle, and you are running in batch mode, and you can find no unmatched quotation marks or comments, then you should consider whether your job might have stopped because it ran into a time limit. To find out how to fix this problem, talk to a systems programmer or to other SAS users at your site.

/* in the first column   Under z/OS there is a unique hazard. Recall that one style of SAS comment starts with a slash-asterisk (/*). Batch jobs under z/OS use Job Control Language (JCL). In JCL a /* starting in column one signals the end of your program file. So if SAS programmers start a comment with a /* in column one, they inadvertently instruct the computer to stop right then and there. SAS never even sees the remainder of the job. The solution, of course, is to move the comment out of column one or to change to a comment starting with an asterisk (*) and ending with a semicolon (;).

11.14 SAS Runs Out of Memory or Disk Space

What do you do when you finally get your program running, and you get a message that your computer is out of memory or disk space? Well, you could petition to buy a more powerful computer, which isn't really such a bad idea, but there are a few things you can try before resorting to spending money. Because this issue depends on your operating environment, it is not possible to cover everything you might be able to do in this section. However, this section describes a few universal actions you can take to remedy the situation.

It is helpful, in trying to solve the problem, to know why it happens. Usually when you run out of memory, it's when you are doing some pretty intensive computations or sorting data sets with lots of variables. The GLM procedure (General Linear Models), for example, can use lots of memory when your model is complicated and there are many levels for each classification variable. You run out of disk space because SAS uses disk space to store all its temporary working files, including temporary SAS data sets, and the SAS log and output. If you are creating many large temporary SAS data sets during the course of a SAS session, this can quickly fill up your disk space.

Memory and disk space One thing you can do to help decrease disk storage is decrease the number of bytes needed to store data. This can also help memory problems that arise when sorting data sets with character data. Since all numbers are expanded to the fullest precision while SAS is processing data, changing storage requirements for numeric data will not help memory problems. Both character (if you are using list input), and numeric variables have a default storage size of eight bytes. This works for most situations. But if memory or disk space is at a premium, you can usually find some variables which require fewer bytes.

For character data, each character requires one byte of storage. The length of a character variable is determined by one of the following: the INPUT statement, the LENGTH or ATTRIB statement, or, if it is created in an assignment statement, the length of the first value. If you are using list input, then variables are given a length of eight. If your data are only one character long, Y or N for example, then you are using eight times the storage space you actually need. You can use the LENGTH statement before the INPUT statement to change the default length. For example, the following gives the character variable Answer a length of one byte:

```
LENGTH Answer $1;
```

If you are using column input, then the length is equal to the number of columns you are reading; if you are using formatted input, then the length is equal to the width of the informat. You can change the lengths of variables in existing SAS data sets by using a LENGTH statement between a DATA statement and a SET, MERGE, or UPDATE statement.

Disk space If you are running out of disk space, in addition to shortening the lengths of character variables, you may also be able to decrease the lengths of numeric variables. Numeric data are a little trickier than character when it comes to length. All numbers can be safely stored in eight bytes, and that's why eight is the default. Some numbers can be safely stored in fewer bytes, but which numbers depends on your operating environment. Look in the SAS Help and Documentation for your operating environment to determine the length and precision of numeric variables. For example, under Windows and UNIX, you can safely store integers up to 8,192 in three bytes. In general, if your numbers contain decimal values, then you must use eight bytes. If you have small integer values, then you can use four bytes (in some operating environments two or three bytes). Use the LENGTH statement to change the lengths of data:

```
LENGTH Tigers 4;
```

This statement changes the length of the numeric variable Tigers to four bytes. If your numbers are categorical, like 1 for male and 2 for female, then you can read them as character data with a length of 1 and save even more space.

Another thing you can try is to decrease the number and size of SAS data sets created during a SAS session. If you are going to use only a fraction of your data for analysis, then subset your data as soon as possible using a subsetting IF statement. For example, if you needed observations only for females, then use the following statement in your DATA step:

```
IF Sex = 'female';
```

If you need to look at only a few of the variables in your data set, then use the KEEP= (or DROP=) data set option to decrease the number of variables. For example, if you had a data set containing information about all the zoo animals, but you wanted to look at only the lions and tigers, then you could use the following statements to create a data set with only those variables:

```
DATA partial;
   SET zooanimals (KEEP = Lions Tigers);
```

It is also possible to compress SAS data sets. Compressing may save space if your data have many repeated values. But beware, compressing can in some cases actually increase the size of your data set. Fortunately, SAS gives a message in your log window telling you the change in size of your data sets. You can turn on compression by using either the COMPRESS=YES system option, or the COMPRESS=YES data set option. Use the system option if you want all the SAS data sets you create to be compressed. Use the data set option when you want to control which SAS data sets to compress. For example:

```
DATA compressedzooanimals (COMPRESS = YES);
   SET zooanimals;
```

If you have more than one disk on your system, then you might be able to have SAS store its working files in a different location where there is more space. See the SAS Help and Documentation for your operating environment.

Memory If memory is your problem, then do what you can to eliminate other programs that are using your computer's memory. If you are using a windowing environment to run your SAS programs, try running in batch mode instead. The windows take quite a lot of memory, and it can be a significant fraction of the total available memory. Also, see the SAS Help and Documentation for your operating environment for potential ways to make more memory available on your system.

If you have tried all of the above, and you are still running out of memory or disk space, then you can always try finding a more powerful computer. One of the nice things about SAS is that the language is the same for all operating environments. To move your program to another operating environment, you would need to change only a few statements like INFILE, which deal directly with the operating environment.

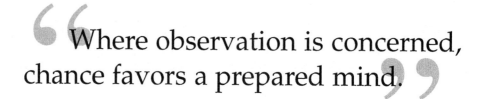

"Where observation is concerned,
chance favors a prepared mind."

LOUIS PASTEUR

Appendix Coming to SAS from SQL

If you already know Structured Query Language (SQL), then you will be pleased to know that you can use SQL statements in SAS programs to create, read, and modify SAS data sets. There are two basic ways to use SQL with SAS:

♦ You can embed complete SQL statements in the SQL procedure.

♦ You can use WHERE statements or WHERE= data set options to select rows in standard SAS DATA and PROC steps.

Both of these features are available with Base SAS, so you don't have to license any other SAS software to use SQL.

Terminology Terms such as table, row, and column that originated with relational databases are now standard SAS terms also. However, other terms can also be used with SAS. To help you understand SAS terminology, here is a brief dictionary of analogous terms:

SQL term	Analogous SAS term
column	column or variable
row	row or observation
table	table or data set
join	join, merge, set, update, or modify
NULL value	missing value
alias	alias
view	view
no analogous term	DATA step
no analogous term	PROC step

SQL does not contain structures like SAS DATA and PROC steps. Basically, DATA steps read and modify data while PROC (short for procedure) steps perform specific analyses or functions such as sorting, writing reports, or running statistical analyses. In SQL, reports are written automatically whenever you use a SELECT statement; sorting is performed by the ORDER BY clause; and the operations performed by most other SAS procedures don't exist in SQL.

SAS has fewer data types than standard SQL. The character data type is the same in both languages. All other SQL data types (numeric, decimal, integer, smallint, float, real, double precision, and date) map to the SAS numeric data type.

PROC SQL The SQL procedure in SAS follows all but a few of the guidelines set by the American National Standards Institute (ANSI) for implementations of SQL. One exception is that table names, column names, and aliases are limited to 32 characters in length. This complies with standard SAS naming conventions. The ANSI standard for SQL allows longer names. See the SAS Help and Documentation for more details on the implementation of ANSI standards in PROC SQL.

The basic form of the SQL procedure is

```
PROC SQL;
    sql-statement;
```

The possible values for the *sql-statement* in PROC SQL include ALTER, CREATE, DELETE, DESCRIBE, DROP, INSERT, SELECT, UPDATE, and VALIDATE statements—with a semicolon stuck on the end. You can have any number of SQL statements in a single PROC SQL step.

You can use PROC SQL interactively or in batch jobs. Unlike most other SAS procedures, PROC SQL will run interactively without a RUN statement. You just need to submit the program statements. Any results from SELECT statements are displayed automatically unless you specify the NOPRINT option on the PROC statement like this:

```
PROC SQL NOPRINT;
```

An SQL view is a stored SELECT statement that is executed at run time. PROC SQL can create views, and other procedures can read views created via PROC SQL.

Example The work performed by SQL, and therefore by PROC SQL, can also be done in SAS by DATA steps, PROC PRINT, PROC SORT, and PROC MEANS. To show how PROC SQL works and to provide a comparison to DATA and PROC steps, here are programs using PROC SQL and other SAS statements to perform the same actions.

Creating a table The first program uses PROC SQL to create and print a simple table with three columns. This program uses CREATE, INSERT, and SELECT statements in a single PROC SQL step:

```
LIBNAME sports 'c:\MySASLib';
PROC SQL;
   CREATE TABLE sports.customer
      (CustomerNumber num,
       Name            char(17),
       Address         char(20));

   INSERT INTO sports.customer
      VALUES (101, 'Murphy''s Sports ', '115 Main St.        ')
      VALUES (102, 'Sun N Ski        ', '2106 Newberry Ave.  ')
      VALUES (103, 'Sports Outfitters', '19 Cary Way         ')
      VALUES (104, 'Cramer & Johnson ', '4106 Arlington Blvd.')
      VALUES (105, 'Sports Savers    ', '2708 Broadway       ');

   TITLE 'Sports Customer Data';
   SELECT *
      FROM sports.customer;
```

Notice that the LIBNAME statement sets up a libref named SPORTS, pointing to a subdirectory named MySASLib on the C drive (Windows). The LIBNAME statement may be different for your operating environment. See section 2.19 for more information about LIBNAME statements. This program creates a permanent SAS table named CUSTOMER in the MySASLib subdirectory. No RUN statement is needed; to run this program you simply submit it to SAS. Here is the output:

Sports Customer Data

CustomerNumber	Name	Address
101	Murphy's Sports	115 Main St.
102	Sun N Ski	2106 Newberry Ave.
103	Sports Outfitters	19 Cary Way
104	Cramer & Johnson	4106 Arlington Blvd.
105	Sports Savers	2708 Broadway

The next program uses standard SAS statements to create the same table. Notice that the LIBNAME statement, the table name, and the TITLE statement are identical in both programs. LIBNAME statements stay in effect for the duration of a session or job. So, if you ran these programs in a single session or job, you would not have to repeat the LIBNAME statement. It is repeated here only for the sake of completeness.

```
LIBNAME sports 'c:\MySASLib';
DATA sports.customer;
    INPUT CustomerNumber Name $ 5-21 Address $ 23-42;
    DATALINES;
101 Murphy's Sports   115 Main St.
102 Sun N Ski         2106 Newberry Ave.
103 Sports Outfitters 19 Cary Way
104 Cramer & Johnson  4106 Arlington Blvd.
105 Sports Savers     2708 Broadway
  ;
PROC PRINT DATA = sports.customer;
TITLE 'Sports Customer Data';
RUN;
```

Here is the output from the standard SAS program. It looks a little different from the previous report, but it contains the same information.

Sports Customer Data

Obs	CustomerNumber	Name	Address
1	101	Murphy's Sports	115 Main St.
2	102	Sun N Ski	2106 Newberry Ave.
3	103	Sports Outfitters	19 Cary Way
4	104	Cramer & Johnson	4106 Arlington Blvd.
5	105	Sports Savers	2708 Broadway

Reading an existing table The next two programs read the CUSTOMER table and select one row. Here is the PROC SQL version of this program:

```
LIBNAME sports 'c:\MySASLib';
PROC SQL;
    TITLE 'Customer Number 102';
    SELECT *
        FROM sports.customer
        WHERE CustomerNumber = 102;
```

The PROC SQL output looks like this:

Customer Number 102

CustomerNumber	Name	Address
102	Sun N Ski	2106 Newberry Ave.

The following program uses SAS DATA and PROC steps to select and print the same row from the CUSTOMER table:

```
LIBNAME sports 'c:\MySASLib';
DATA sunnski;
   SET sports.customer;
   IF CustomerNumber = 102;
PROC PRINT DATA = sunnski;
   TITLE 'Customer Number 102';
RUN;
```

Here is the PROC PRINT output:

Customer Number 102

Obs	CustomerNumber	Name	Address
1	102	Sun N Ski	2106 Newberry Ave.

WHERE statement vs. IF statement The WHERE statement in SAS is modeled after the WHERE clause of SQL, and is similar to a subsetting IF statement. However, there are some differences in how a WHERE statement and a subsetting IF work. While subsetting IFs can appear only in DATA steps, WHERE statements can be used in DATA or PROC steps. WHERE statements are generally more efficient than subsetting IF statements, especially when they allow you to eliminate a DATA step by subsetting directly in a procedure. When WHERE statements are used in a DATA step, SAS applies WHERE statements earlier than IF statements. This has several repercussions:

◆ The WHERE statement is more efficient than a subsetting IF because it avoids reading unwanted rows.

◆ The WHERE statement can select rows only from existing SAS tables. The IF statement, however, can select rows from existing SAS tables or from raw data files being read with INPUT statements.

◆ With a WHERE statement, you can select rows based only on the values of columns being read. With a subsetting IF statement, you can also select rows based on the value of a column created in the current DATA step.

◆ The WHERE and IF statements may produce different results when two tables are combined in a MERGE, SET, or UPDATE statement. Operations that occur after SAS applies WHERE statements but before SAS applies IF statements may cause the statements to select different rows.

For more information about subsetting IF statements, see section 3.7; for more information about WHERE statements, see section 4.2.

WHERE= data set option vs. WHERE statement The WHERE= data set option is similar to the WHERE statement, but is even more flexible. Both can be used in DATA and PROC steps. But while the WHERE statement affects only SAS data tables being read, the WHERE= data set option can apply both to tables being read and to tables being written. In fact, you could use two WHERE= options in the same DATA or PROC step, one selecting the input rows, and another selecting the output rows. For more information on the WHERE= data set option, see section 6.13.

Examples To show how the WHERE statement and the WHERE= data set option work, and to provide a comparison with the IF statement, here are programs using these techniques to perform the same functions. All five of these programs read the CUSTOMER SAS data table created by the previous programs. The goal of these programs is to select and print one row from an existing SAS table. The output of these five programs is almost identical, but each method has advantages as discussed above.

Subsetting IF in a DATA step This program uses a subsetting IF statement to select one row:

```
LIBNAME sports 'c:\MySASLib';
DATA outfitters;
   SET sports.customer;
   IF Name = 'Sports Outfitters';
PROC PRINT DATA = outfitters;
   TITLE 'Sports Outfitters';
RUN;
```

Here is the output.

Sports Outfitters

Obs	CustomerNumber	Name	Address
1	103	Sports Outfitters	19 Cary Way

WHERE statement in a DATA step The next program uses a WHERE statement in the DATA step and then prints the results with PROC PRINT:

```
LIBNAME sports 'c:\MySASLib';
DATA outfitters;
   SET sports.customer;
   WHERE Name = 'Sports Outfitters';
PROC PRINT DATA = outfitters;
   TITLE 'Sports Outfitters';
RUN;
```

The output looks like this:

Sports Outfitters

Obs	CustomerNumber	Name	Address
1	103	Sports Outfitters	19 Cary Way

WHERE= data set option in a DATA step
The next program uses a WHERE= data set option in a DATA step and then prints the results with PROC PRINT:

```
LIBNAME sports 'c:\MySASLib';
DATA outfitters (WHERE = (Name = 'Sports Outfitters'));
   SET sports.customer;
PROC PRINT DATA = outfitters;
   TITLE 'Sports Outfitters';
RUN;
```

The output looks like this:

Sports Outfitters

Obs	CustomerNumber	Name	Address
1	103	Sports Outfitters	19 Cary Way

WHERE statement in a PROC step
The following program uses a WHERE statement directly in PROC PRINT:

```
LIBNAME sports 'c:\MySASLib';
PROC PRINT DATA = sports.customer;
   WHERE Name = 'Sports Outfitters';
   TITLE 'Sports Outfitters';
RUN;
```

Here is the output:

Sports Outfitters

Obs	CustomerNumber	Name	Address
3	103	Sports Outfitters	19 Cary Way

WHERE= data set option in a PROC step
This program uses a WHERE= data set option in PROC PRINT:

```
LIBNAME sports 'c:\MySASLib';
PROC PRINT DATA = sports.customer (WHERE = (Name = 'Sports Outfitters'));
   TITLE 'Sports Outfitters';
RUN;
```

Here is the output:

Sports Outfitters

Obs	CustomerNumber	Name	Address
3	103	Sports Outfitters	19 Cary Way

Notice that the row number (labeled Obs) for the first three reports is 1, while the row number for the last two reports is 3. This happens because the first three programs create a table with one row and then print it. In contrast, the last two programs never create a table; they simply read the existing table searching for the right row, which happens to be number 3.

Index

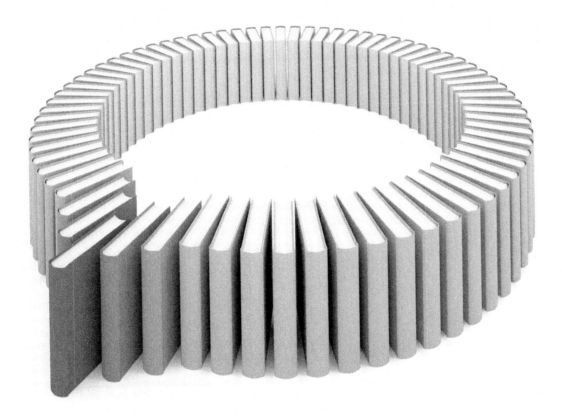

Gain Greater Insight into Your SAS® Software with SAS Books.

Discover all that you need on your journey to knowledge and empowerment.

support.sas.com/bookstore
for additional books and resources.

THE POWER TO KNOW®

CPSIA information can be obtained
at www.ICGtesting.com
Printed in the USA
LVOW02s0130200916

505274LV00003B/8/P